Satisfied *Do What You Are* readers respond:

•

"*Do What You Are* is the *best* career-help book that is on the market today! I have read quite a few books on choosing a career, but yours is the most helpful."

—Kathy Hance, Deaver, Wyoming

•

"*Do What You Are* is a marvelous book. I not only found appealing career suggestions but was able to put my finger on characteristics that would be necessary for a job to make me happy. Thank you. Thank you. Thank you."

—Serena Mitchell, Don Mills, Ontario

•

"*Do What You Are* is very useful and has provided me with some new insights into myself and what I should be doing. I would highly recommend your book to anyone wondering, 'What do I want to be when I grow up.'"

—Kathy Hence, Groveland, California

•

"This book has changed my life! *Do What You Are* helped me find a whole new career in the personnel and recruiting field. And not only did it help me make a great career change, but now I use it daily to help other people find work that lets them 'do what they are.' Thanks!"

—Gary Gardner, President,
M&M Personnel and Pro Placement, Cleveland, Ohio

•

"*Do What You Are* has unlocked a door to which I wasn't sure I would ever find the key. It is the last (and perhaps most important) piece of a puzzle that I need to complete to find career happiness."

—Don Ghostlaw, Windsor, Connecticut

•

"In reading *Do What You Are* I found tremendous satisfaction and insights."

—Susan Nickbarg, Madison, New Jersey

•

"Your book helps people use Type effectively in making career choices and conducting job searches. The information is presented in a very positive, empowering way so that people can be proud of their strengths and think of creative ways to deal with possible pitfalls. Thank you for this excellent book."

—Frieda Flint, The Private Industry Council, Portland, Oregon

•

"*Do What You Are* is an invaluable tool for anyone seriously interested in exploring career options. I have recommended it to many friends and co-workers. My copy is dog-eared from multiple readings."

—Paul Faulkner, Windsor Locks, Connecticut

Do What You Are

Other Books by Paul D. Tieger and Barbara Barron

Nurture by Nature
The Art of SpeedReading People
Just Your Type

Do What You Are

Sixth Edition

Discover the Perfect Career for You Through the Secrets of Personality Type

Paul D. Tieger, Barbara Barron, and Kelly Tieger

Little, Brown Spark
New York Boston London

Little, Brown Spark
Hachette Book Group
1290 Avenue of the Americas, New York, NY 10104
littlebrownspark.com

Sixth Edition: April 2021

Little Brown Spark is an imprint of Little, Brown and Company, a division of Hachette Book Group, Inc. The Little, Brown Spark name and logo are trademarks of Hachette Book Group, Inc.

The publisher is not responsible for websites (or their content) that are not owned by the publisher.

ISBN 978-0-316-49714-5 (6th ed.)
Library of Congress Control Number: 2020951214

Printing 4, 2024

LSC-C

Printed in the United States of America

Dedicated to Herb, Evelyn, Richard, and Helen

Contents

‖ Read This First

Why This Book?

Since its first publication in 1992, *Do What You Are* has helped over a million people find satisfying careers and conduct more successful job searches. We've heard from hundreds of people who report that by helping them discover the kind of work they were meant to do, *Do What You Are* forever changed their lives and made them feel more productive, more appreciated, and more satisfied.

Dozens of books have been written to help people make good career decisions. But *Do What You Are* is different from every other guide in a fundamental way. It does not offer generic, one-size-fits-all advice. For as certainly as people are different from each other, advice that's right for one person often is completely wrong for another. Our expertise in the well-respected, scientifically validated system called Personality Type enables us to truly *individualize* the career discovery process—to give you invaluable insights about yourself, and to enable you to find a career that makes the best use of your natural talents.

Why pick up a book to help when the internet is full of advice? Here's the truth: There are countless sites that can help you discover your personality type or give you other tools to categorize and understand yourself. But none of those sites provides the degree of depth that the book in your hands can offer. So, by all means, go online to verify your type and see what's out there (there's some great stuff!). But refer back here for a nuanced and individualized look at what career satisfaction could look like for you.

Let's Talk About You

We're assuming that you picked up this book because you're at a turning point in your work. Maybe you're a student just about to choose that first important job, or perhaps you're reentering the workplace after some time off and are considering all your options. Maybe you've been laid off and need to find another path. Maybe you're dissatisfied with your job and believe there must be a better alternative. Or perhaps you're finishing up one career and thinking about starting on another. Congratulations—you've come to the right book!

Some special encouragement is in order for career changers. If you're wondering about the wisdom of trying to change horses in midstream, you should know that millions of people change jobs every year. In fact, it is estimated that most people will hold twelve to fifteen different jobs in their lifetime. These statistics don't provide much solace, however, if you find yourself stuck in an unfulfilling job that you feel you can't quit.

There are some very practical reasons why people can't just impulsively leave their job and strike out in a new direction. You have bills to pay, maybe a family to support. It takes a lot of courage to give up a steady paycheck, even when it comes from an unsatisfying job. It's difficult to start a new job while you're still working the old one—anyone who has tried it can tell you it's like having a job on top of a job—and yet the idea of actually being out of work while you conduct a job search can be terrifying. Most of us don't have the financial resources to carry us over a period of unemployment, especially when there's no guarantee that we'll be successful in finding a new job quickly.

It can also be extremely difficult to go against what others expect of you. Even if you're unhappy in your job, you may feel pressure from others to stay right where you are. During a career change, support and encouragement from family and friends are important. If those close to you disapprove of your making a change, you're more likely to keep doing what you're doing.

It's also true that once you've established a particular lifestyle, it's difficult to imagine a different way of life. The longer you've been living a certain way, the more invested you become in keeping your life the way it is. If you've attained a certain level of success and are accustomed to being regarded as successful, starting all over can seem unimaginable.

To make matters worse, most of us don't really know what we need to satisfy us. We know what we *don't* like—that much we've learned from experience—but we don't know how to think up, much less find, a fulfilling alternative. On top of that, changing careers can be extremely stressful, and it's not uncommon for the process to take several months.

Here's the good news. By understanding your personality type, you can find a truly fulfilling career that enhances the quality of your life. Even though changing jobs is frightening, and even though it's easier to keep doing what you're doing, we hope you'll use this book to discover exactly what you need to be satisfied in your work and how to find the right work for you. It can be done, and it's well worth the effort—we promise!

How This Book Can Change Your Life

Do What You Are is designed to help you make better career choices, conduct a successful job search campaign, and be effective in any job. We're excited about what we've learned about the relationship between Personality Type and career satisfaction, and we want to share our most important discoveries with you. Please know, however, that we aren't going to rehash a lot of information you can get elsewhere, such as how to write a résumé or cover letter. Our main interest is in helping you figure out what career satisfaction is for you and in helping you go about finding work you'll love.

As you read *Do What You Are,* you'll start to enjoy many of the fringe benefits that come with an understanding of Personality Type. Recognizing and understanding your personality type can change the way you see yourself—which in turn affects everything you do and every aspect of your life. Personality Type is so well respected that the majority of *Fortune* 500 companies use it daily. Over the past thirty years, we've used Personality Type to help managers motivate and communicate with their employees; teachers to reach very different types of students; work teams to understand their strengths and blind spots and to communicate more productively; and, of course, we've used it to train thousands of career counselors and outplacement consultants to help their clients make the best career choices. If you are a parent, Type will give you a whole new perspective on your family dynamics and help you understand and communicate better with your children. If you are in a relationship, Type will help you understand, accept, and appreciate the similarities and differences between you and your partner. In short, we're confident that the knowledge you gain from this book will forever change the way you look at yourself and others.

How to Use This Book

Reading *Do What You Are* requires some active participation on your part. The fact is, we aren't interested in telling you what to do. Instead, we want to introduce you to a process that works and that will be useful to you all your life. So although we ask you all the right questions and provide you with as much information and as many examples as we can, ultimately the answers must come from you because you know yourself best. We see this as a collaborative effort: we supply the expertise and experience, and you supply the essential information about yourself. Together we'll be successful in finding the best possible career match for you.

We've divided *Do What You Are* into three parts. Part 1, "Unlocking the Secrets of Personality Type," will take you step by step through the discovery and understanding of your own personality type. Part 2, "The Formula for Career Satisfaction," will introduce you to the three ingredients you must have in your work if it is to be truly fulfilling. In Part 3, "Getting to Work," we'll show you how to put to good use all that you've learned about yourself. This part of the book is divided according to personality type. In your section you'll meet other people of your type and will learn what kinds of jobs they find fulfilling. Reading about their experiences, likes and dislikes, joys and frustrations, will help clarify what you need in a job for it to be really satisfying. To assist you further, we provide a type-specific list of key ingredients for career satisfaction, suggestions for your ideal work environment, a rundown of your work-related strengths, some exercises to highlight your basic values, and a list of potentially satisfying career options. Finally, we provide you with job search strategies that are designed specifically to be effective for you and people like you. We will show you how to make the most of your natural strengths and how to minimize your innate blind spots as you engage in information gathering, personal marketing, interviewing with prospective employers, following up, and decision making. And finally—should you choose to stay in your current job—we will outline specific things you can do to be happier and more successful.

The Story of *Do What You Are*

When we began studying Personality Type over forty years ago, we were extremely fortunate to be trained by some of the world's best-respected experts. We went on to discover how powerful this tool actually was by working with individual clients seeking career guidance. Then we designed and conducted the first workshops ever to provide specialized training for career professionals. Over the years we have trained thousands of career counselors, human resources specialists, and outplacement consultants. In 1986 we created the Personality Type Tool Kit, a resource that was highly regarded by career counselors. In writing *Do What You Are,* we have drawn not only on our experience with our clients and the counselors we have trained, but also on their experience with their clients.

As our expertise with Type grew and we had children, we began to appreciate how much Type could help parents truly understand and connect with their children. Using our own experience and extensive research with hundreds of parents, we wrote *Nurture by Nature: Understand Your Child's Personality Type—And Become a Better Parent,* which was published in 1997. In the book you can discover your child's type and learn the most effective strategies for nurturing them.

While we were researching and writing, we were also consulting—with organizations to train their managers and help them develop productive teams, and with trial lawyers to help them select jurors and present their cases most effectively. As a result of our work with attorneys, we developed a shorthand system for quickly identifying others' personality types and communicating with them in their language. The result was our third book, *The Art of SpeedReading People: How to Size People Up and Speak Their Language,* a tool for salespeople, managers, human resources professionals, and others, published in 1998. *The Art of SpeedReading People* has turned out to be a powerful tool for job seekers as well, as it enables them to quickly read job interviewers and present themselves in the way most likely to impress each individual interviewer.

As we traveled around the country talking about Personality Type, we found people were extremely interested in using Type to better understand their partners and to improve their personal relationships. And while we had plenty of anecdotal evidence that Type can provide rich insights into romantic relationships, there had been no serious scientific study to date on the subject. This prompted us to undertake extensive research—including an online survey filled out by more than twenty-five hundred people and interviews with hundreds of couples. Our findings became the basis for our fourth book, *Just Your Type: Create the Relationship You've Always Wanted Using the Secrets of Personality Type,* published in 2000.

In the following pages, you will begin—or continue—an incredible journey of self-discovery. While the goal of this book is to offer practical and prescriptive advice about your career, it will also provide you with some extraordinary insights into other aspects of your life. We wish you the greatest success!

Paul D. Tieger & Barbara Barron

The Story Continues

Being raised by Personality Type experts was an interesting way to grow up, to say the least! It was common in my childhood for my parents to Type everyone around us—from my friends in school to the server at a restaurant. Growing up with the framework of Personality Type has informed every part of my life. I believe it is an incredibly useful lens through which to examine the world—not the only lens, but certainly a helpful one.

In taking the helm for this edition of *Do What You Are,* I have endeavored to fully and critically revise this book. The world has changed a lot since it was first published in 1992, and while there have been five editions between then and now, it has been humbling and instructive to pore back over every word, making sure that each piece of information and advice is as applicable in the 2020s as it was in the 1990s.

To me, the greatest gifts of Personality Type are twofold: self-knowledge and empathy. Type allows me to look inward to understand my motivations, strengths, areas of growth. It often acts as a light shining on a behavior that helps to illuminate me to myself. It also acts as a light shining outward, helping me to obey the Platinum Rule: Treat others the way they want to be treated.

I hope you find the lens of Personality Type as useful as I have, and I wish you the very best on your journey to career satisfaction!

Kelly Tieger

Jobs and Careers: Trends and Forecasts

In the seven years since the last edition of *Do What You Are* was released, the world has changed in ways we could never have expected. A global pandemic has shifted the rhythms of daily life and work, and the impact of this moment down the line remains to be seen. As the parameters of career and home have adapted, we may not know exactly what the future of work will look like. From the economy, to health, to technology, to social interactions—it feels like the rules have changed. It may seem like a luxury to try to find a career that allows you to "do what you are" when so many people are struggling just to work at all.

Here's what we believe: It's not a luxury to do work that suits who you are. All jobs are not equal, and there's almost always another choice or another path. And if the rules are being rewritten, why not rewrite them to work better for you? Armed with the self-knowledge you will glean from this book, you can make choices and adjustments to find greater satisfaction at work. You hold in your hands a tool that can set you apart in an increasingly competitive market. This book can help you identify work that is satisfying and that you can excel at, even in a changing world. We can point you toward industries that remain resilient in the face of global changes and jobs that are evolving to become indispensable in the coming years.

Some people's choice of a career is dictated by their passions. They simply *must* create art, or make music, or seek the cure for cancer. And we are all better off for their efforts. Other people are more pragmatic and give more weight to practical concerns when making career decisions. Regardless of what camp you fall into, all career seekers can benefit from looking down the road at the careers the experts predict will be most in demand in the future. With this in mind, we share some new information about a few important trends.

According to the latest edition of the *Occupational Outlook Handbook* (published by the Bureau of Labor Statistics), employment growth from 2018 to 2028 is projected to be highly concentrated in the healthcare and social services industries. By 2028, the healthcare industry is expected to expand more than any other sector, growing 14 percent and adding about 1.9 million new jobs. In a moment when a robust corps of healthcare workers has never been more crucial, it's easy to see demand continuing to rise even beyond these estimates.

The technology industry is also on the rise, with smart technology evolving constantly and merging with other industries such as home design and transportation. Jobs in the gig economy offer more flexibility than the traditional nine-to-five, and many people are seeking opportunities to participate and build their own schedules and revenue streams. Alternative energy technologies and careers continue to explode and disrupt the fossil fuel industry, bringing with them many higher-paying jobs. And although automation will make many jobs obsolete, it will also create new opportunities and efficiencies for people.

THE TEN OCCUPATIONS PROJECTED TO GROW
THE FASTEST BETWEEN 2018-2028

Solar photovoltaic installers	63.3%
Wind turbine service technicians	56.9%
Home health aides	36.6%
Personal care aides	36.4%
Occupational therapy assistants	33.1%
Information security analysts	31.6%
Physician assistants	31.1%
Statisticians	30.7%
Nurse practitioners	28.2%
Speech-language pathologists	27.3%

Other occupations expected to grow at a rapid rate include physical therapist assistants (27.1%), genetic counselors (27.0%), mathematicians (26.0%), operations research analysts (25.6%), software developers for applications (25.6%), forest fire inspectors and prevention specialists (24.1%), postsecondary health specialties teachers (23.2%), and phlebotomists (23.0%).

Healthcare: Never More Essential

Healthcare has consistently been the most resilient industry in the past fifteen years. Despite ups and downs in the economy, healthcare jobs only continue to grow—almost three times faster than average. Increased demand for healthcare services is being driven by an upswing in both the volume and quality of medical technologies, paired with an aging population. As life expectancies continue to get longer, health services will continue to provide many of the job opportunities in this country.

Not only is healthcare the biggest and fastest-growing sector, it also tends to pay better than other industries. The median annual wage for healthcare practitioners and technicians is almost twice that of the national average. And in such a vast industry, there are many different types of positions and work environments. From technicians to social workers to administrators, many jobs outside the most well-known occupations of doctors and nurses abound. It's easy to see that the healthcare industry has something for everyone.

The Gig Economy

You've probably heard a great deal about the "gig economy"—a term for all the workers, products, and services that constitute the freelancer boom of the past decade. With the rapid rise of apps and services that outsource everything from food delivery to ride sharing to household chores, the gig economy creates many niche jobs that offer people flexibility above all else. Freelancers can opt in and out of jobs, creating schedules that work around childcare and eldercare needs, education, and other part-time employment.

Gig workers, unlike salaried employees, work project by project. They pick up each job, usually through some kind of technology-based platform like an app, and carry it out for the customer. The upside is greater autonomy and flexibility. The downside is less stability and fewer benefits.

From 2005 to 2015 alone, the number of people who counted themselves as self-employed grew by over 19 percent, in large part due to advances in tech over that decade and lower full-time employment opportunities during the 2009 recession. Upwork and Freelancers Union estimated that 36 percent of the American workforce was freelancing in 2017, and they expect that number to rise to 50 percent by 2027.

While the obvious jobs created by the gig economy are held by gig workers themselves, the gig economy also creates jobs in the companies that program and manage the platforms. App programmers, customer service reps, and marketing strategists are just some of the jobs that are needed.

The Future Is Green

Good news for the planet, and good news for jobs! The renewable energy sector is booming, with costs for implementing new technology decreasing every year. Forbes states that by 2025, the cost of operating coal plants in the U.S. will exceed the cost of building replacement wind and solar plants. With governments around the world setting goals to lower their carbon footprint, mandates for clean energy will only continue to drive demand for skilled workers. It's no wonder that the two fastest-growing jobs as predicted by the Bureau of Labor and Statistics are solar photovoltaic installers and wind turbine service technicians!

And this trend has already begun. In 2019 a report found that Americans working in clean energy outnumbered fossil fuel workers by three to one. That means 3.3 million Americans in the green energy sector! With wind farms in all fifty states and coal consumption falling to its lowest point in thirty-nine years, it looks like clean energy is poised to replace fossil fuels. And since clean energy jobs tend to pay higher wages than coal, the coal-to-clean economic transition is imminent, and good for workers—as well as good for all of us in the long term.

Automation: The Upside

Artificial intelligence, or AI, is a controversial topic to many Americans, conjuring images of humanoid robots and science fiction. At the heart of much of the fear surrounding automation is the idea that robots will take human jobs, leaving us unemployed. While increasing automation will surely change the nature of work, many people forget that technology has always changed the work that people do. (Think of the way that people who once sewed clothing by hand were made "obsolete" by the advances of the Industrial Revolution and factory-made clothes.) And with a pendulum swing toward mass-produced goods comes a swing back around toward new markets for handcrafted, artisan goods.

In a recent analysis from Oxford University, projections say that close to 50 percent of all jobs will be replaced with automation in the next twenty-five years, mostly in the fields of manufacturing and service. This will change the economic landscape considerably. But it's helpful to remember that we don't know what we don't know. When ATMs first appeared on the scene, many people worried that bank tellers would become obsolete. But with the cost savings from adding ATMs to their locations, many banks were able to open even more branches, ultimately increasing employment. Automation will create new kinds of jobs for humans, including a strong need for the development and enforcement of AI ethics, along with programming and design, managers to oversee the implementation of AI into workplaces, marketing, and others. And for people working in offices, automating "busy work" tasks frees people up to focus on the parts of their jobs that involve more creativity and critical thinking.

Education and Training: Finding the Right Fit

In an age of escalating costs for higher education, the degree and training requirements for a chosen occupation are no small consideration. Even people who pursue a degree full-time often need to earn an income simultaneously, making short or flexible programs a necessity. Add to the mix the increasing prevalence of career changers—those of us who have the need or desire to pursue a different field of interest—and you have a whole population balancing new schooling and professional transitions with responsibilities to partners and kids! Luckily, the way we pursue education is changing too. Options like accredited online universities can offer a cost-effective and flexible path to the degree of your choice.

The following table from the Bureau of Labor Statistics sheds some light on the education and training levels required for occupations that will grow the fastest over the next seven years. As you begin to identify the type of work that suits your personality type, this table may prove a helpful reference about how you might get there from here. In fact, if you find yourself interested in education and training itself, you can choose to pursue one of the 1.7 million projected job openings in the education, training, or library occupations!

Education or training level	Occupations with the most growth
Master's degree or higher	Physician assistants Statisticians Mathematicians Nurse practitioners Speech-language pathologists Genetic counselors
Bachelor's degree	Information security analysts Operations research analysts Software developers Registered nurses General and operations managers Market research analysts Management analysts
Associate's degree	Wind turbine technicians Occupational therapy assistants Medical assistants Physical therapist assistants
Short-term on-the-job training	Solar photovoltaic installers Home health aides Personal care aides Forest fire inspectors and prevention specialists Cooks Waiters and waitresses Construction laborers and helpers

As you proceed through the book and read your type-specific chapter, you'll notice that some trends apply more to you and people like you, while others are less applicable. If you'd like to find out more, visit the Bureau of Labor Statistics website—there are some great resources available there.

Part One | UNLOCKING THE SECRETS OF PERSONALITY TYPE

1 | SUIT YOURSELF

The Secret of Career Satisfaction

It's important to find the right job. Despite the universal fantasies of winning the lottery, buying expensive cars and homes, and doing fascinating work with interesting people in exotic places, the sober reality is that most of us have to work, hard, for a long time. If you spend forty to fifty years—not an unlikely scenario—working at jobs you'd rather not be doing, you are in truth throwing away a large part of your life. This is unnecessary and sad, especially since a career you can love is within your reach.

What Is the Ideal Job, Anyway?

The right job enhances your life. It is personally fulfilling because it nourishes the most important aspects of your personality. It suits the way you like to do things and reflects who you are. It lets you use your innate strengths in ways that come naturally to you, and it doesn't force you to do things you don't do well (at least, not often!).

How can you tell if you're in the right job? Here are some general guidelines. If you're not employed, keep them in mind as you search for your ideal job. If you are employed, see how your present job measures up.

If you're in the right job, you should

- look forward to going to work
- feel energized (most of the time) by what you do
- feel your contribution is respected and appreciated
- feel proud when describing your work to others
- enjoy and respect the people you work with
- feel optimistic about your future

3

We'd like to make something clear right away. It's important to recognize that there are as many different paths to career satisfaction as there are happily employed people. There is no one "ideal job" to which everyone should aspire. But there is an ideal job *for you.*

There are an infinite number of variables in the workplace. To achieve career satisfaction, you need to figure out what your preferences are and then find a job that accommodates them. Some jobs provide warmth and stability; some are risky and challenging. Some are structured, some aren't. One job may require a lot of socializing, while another may require quiet concentration. Do you know exactly what kind of job suits you best? Have you ever even stopped to think about it?

It's a good thing there are so many different kinds of jobs available, since people are so different in their abilities and priorities. Some people enjoy making high-level management decisions; others simply aren't suited to making these kinds of choices. For some people, money is a top priority. They want to make lots of it! Others, however, want most to make a contribution to society; the money is less important. Some people are perfectly comfortable with facts and details and statistics, while others get a headache just trying to read a profit-and-loss statement. And so on, and so on!

When we were hired to conduct a series of personal effectiveness training workshops for job placement professionals (also known as executive recruiters or headhunters), we came face-to-face with a dramatic example of how a job that is perfect for one person can be perfectly wrong for another.

We were training several headhunters who worked for the same recruiting firm. Their job was to find applicants to fill positions at a variety of companies by contacting people who were already employed and convincing them to apply for these positions. If an applicant successfully switched jobs and stayed with the new company for at least three months, the placement counselor received a generous commission. It was a highly competitive, results-oriented job that required excellent communication skills and the ability to fill as many positions as possible as quickly as possible.

One of the placement counselors we trained, Arthur, couldn't have been happier. He loved the fast pace of the job. Arthur was a high-energy person, a great talker who enjoyed meeting lots of people. He used his excellent reasoning skills to persuade other people to make a move to a new opportunity, and he got a lot of satisfaction out of meeting his goal and then some. Arthur knew and understood the formula: For every fifty attempts he made, he'd get ten people who were interested, and out of these ten, he might make two or three placements. Arthur's thick skin helped him in the job; he often heard "no" during the day but he never took the rejection personally. What Arthur found really energizing was closing the sale and moving on to the next challenge. He worked hard all day long and made a lot of money.

For Julie, it was a totally different story. Like Arthur, Julie enjoyed talking to lots of people all day and establishing relationships with them. However, unlike

Arthur, Julie wanted to help each person find the job that would be really right for them. She liked to look for opportunities that would enable her applicants to grow and experience personal success and satisfaction. Julie had been cautioned repeatedly by her supervisor about spending too much time with each individual rather than quickly determining whether or not someone was interested in a position and then moving on to the next prospect. Rather than filling jobs, Julie was counseling clients. The fact that she could make a great deal of money did not motivate her. She found little reward in simply filling a job opening with a person who probably wasn't right for the position but whom she had successfully pressured into giving it a try.

When we returned six weeks later for a follow-up training session, we weren't surprised to learn that Julie had quit.

People are different in their needs, desires, interests, skills, values, and personalities. Unless you and I have similar personality types, work that you find intrinsically enjoyable is likely to have a different, even opposite, effect on me. Different jobs and even different aspects of jobs satisfy different types of people, a fundamental truth which has, in our view, not been fully appreciated by career advisers or career manuals—until now.

To Suit Yourself, You Must Know Yourself

As we said earlier, the secret of career satisfaction lies in doing what you enjoy most. A few lucky people discover this secret early in life, but most of us are caught in a kind of psychological wrestling match, torn between what we think we *can* do, what we (or others) feel we *ought* to do, and what we think we *want* to do. Our advice? Concentrate instead on who you are, and the rest will fall into place.

Not long ago, our friend Ellen called us. This friend was mad. A co-worker of hers whom she regarded as "the most boring man on earth" had been given a prime assignment designing a complex computer system upgrade for a growing retail chain. Ellen, who had been hired just six months before to do exactly this kind of work, was stunned. Obviously something was wrong—but what?

Ellen had evaluated her new job with the utmost care before accepting it. She had both the analytical ability and the background experience the job required. She was well liked and found the technical aspects of the job challenging. She'd had a series of unsatisfying jobs before, but this one was going to be different. So what was going on here?

We thought we knew the answer. Ellen's co-worker, as she described him, was absolutely content to work long hours in relative isolation, quietly but steadily getting the job done. He wasn't a lot of fun around the office, but he was intelligent and dependable, and he never made waves. He was, in fact, the perfect person for the job—and he was happy doing it.

Ellen, on the other hand, loved the stimulation of rallying her staff for an urgent deadline and enjoyed talking to clients about their needs. She was terrific at explaining the intricacies of computer systems and could charm people into doing remarkable things. She liked going to industry conferences, and she didn't mind spending all day in meetings. Unfortunately, none of these activities were a significant part of her new position.

It was clear to us that even though Ellen could handle her responsibilities adequately, the job required more solitude, concentration, and what we call "task focus" than she liked. As she talked things through (and some people are like that—they like to think out loud), she began to recognize that in all her careful planning she had overlooked just one thing...her own personality!

At this point in our conversation, Ellen panicked. She was afraid she had spent eight years in the wrong career. No wonder she'd found her previous jobs less than thrilling! However, she wasn't actually in the wrong field—she was just working in the wrong end of it. Ellen moved over into the sales division of the same company, and today she is thriving in her new position.

Perhaps a little experiment will clarify what we're talking about. On a piece of paper, or even in the margin, write your signature. Done? OK. Now do the same thing, using your opposite hand. (If you just groaned, you are not alone; most people have a similar reaction.) How did it feel when you used your preferred hand? Most people use words like "natural," "easy," "quick," "effortless." How did it feel when you used the opposite hand? Some typical responses: "slow," "awkward," "hard," "draining," "tiring," "it took much longer," "it required more energy and concentration."

We think that handedness is a good way to think about using your natural strengths in your work. The use of your preferred hand is comfortable and assured. If you were forced to use your other hand, you could no doubt develop your abilities—but using that hand would never be as effortless as using your preferred hand, and the finished product would never be as skillfully executed.

The Traditional Approach—and Why It Doesn't Work

Career professionals have long been aware that certain kinds of people are better at certain types of jobs, and that it's important to find as good a match as possible between the person you are and the kind of job you choose. The problem is that the traditional approach doesn't take enough considerations into account. The conventional analysis looks at only the "big three": your abilities, interests, and values.

As career counselors ourselves, we recognize the importance of these factors. Certainly you need the right skills to perform a job well. It also helps if you're interested in your work. And it's important to feel good about what you do. But this is far from the whole picture! Your personality has additional dimensions that also need to be recognized. As a general rule, the more aspects of your personality you match to your work, the more satisfied you'll be on the job.

As we saw with Ellen, a vital consideration—often overlooked—is how much stimulation from other people you need in your work. Are you more energized by being around lots of people most of the time, or are you more comfortable in small groups, talking one on one, or maybe working alone? You can see what a profound impact this preference can have upon your choice of a job. Other important factors include the kind of information you naturally notice, the way you make decisions, and whether you prefer to live in a more structured or a more spontaneous way. These preferences reflect mental processes that are basic to every human being but that clearly differ from one personality type to another. Trying to find the best job for you without taking these preferences into account is like trying to find a tiny island in the vast ocean without a chart. With luck, you might get there—but you might not!

Joanne was a client of ours who came to us in a career crisis. At the age of thirty, she was at the end of her rope. After seven years of teaching math at the elementary school level, she was completely burned out and was wondering if she was in the right career.

Being a teacher had seemed the most natural thing in the world for Joanne. The eldest of four, she had grown up taking care of children. She had excelled in math throughout school and was interested in education. Joanne had received some career counseling early on, and all the signs had seemed to point in the same direction. In high school, and again in college, Joanne had taken the standard career aptitude tests and assessment instruments to determine her skills, her interests, and her values. Each time, career counselors had encouraged her to obtain a teaching degree and to teach math to young kids. Everything seemed perfect.

After her first challenging year, Joanne became increasingly frustrated with the rigid structure of the public elementary school setting. She disliked the endless rules both she and the students had to live by, as well as many of the rules she had to enforce. She hated having to prepare lesson plans six weeks in advance that left her unable to respond to the interests of the children and to her own creative inspirations. She found the standard workbooks inane, and the busywork that both she and her students were required to do left her drained and irritated. Joanne felt very isolated because her colleagues all seemed to have interests and values that were not like hers, and she began to discover that she missed the stimulation of working on challenging projects with others who shared her interests. She had tried switching grades and even changing schools, but nothing seemed to help.

After talking with us, Joanne was relieved to discover that she wasn't crazy; she was just in the wrong career. As her early counselors had determined, Joanne had many of the right qualifications for teaching. However, the things she found most stimulating—intellectual challenge, opportunities to raise her level of competence, and creative innovation—were lacking in her job. Moreover, the public school setting forced her to work in a highly structured and detailed way, which was not at all the way she liked to operate.

Luckily, the solution quickly became clear. We suggested that Joanne return to school and obtain a master's degree in order to teach math—still a thriving interest of hers—in higher education. In a college setting, she would be able to enjoy much more flexibility in her work schedule and obligations, teach more complicated courses, and be part of a culture of academia.

Joanne did get a master's degree, and shortly thereafter she accepted a position in the math department of a small college. Today she teaches graduate-level math courses while continuing her studies toward obtaining a Ph.D.

There's also another reason why the traditional approach to career counseling is inadequate. The "big three"—your abilities, interests, and values—all change with age. As you gain work experience, you gain new skills. As you live longer, you may pick up new interests and discard old ones. And often your goals are different later in life than they were earlier. You can keep changing your career according to where you find yourself at a particular point in time, or you can base your choice from the beginning on a deeper understanding of who you are (and who you'll always be!).

Alex is a thirty-nine-year-old internist with a successful practice in a Chicago suburb. While he was growing up it was always assumed that he would follow in the family tradition and become a doctor. Through twelve years of college, medical school, internship, and residency, he never allowed himself to question his decision. After practicing medicine for five years, he has come to a painful conclusion with far-reaching implications for himself and his family: He doesn't want to be a doctor anymore. What's more, he realizes he probably never did.

Alex's predicament is not unusual. If you doubt this, pick any ten people you know and ask them, "If you could have any job you wanted, what would it be?" Our experience as career counselors suggests that at least half would rather be doing something else.

Most of us make our most important career decisions when we are least prepared to do so. The decisions we make early in life set into motion a chain of events that will influence our entire lives. Yet when we're young we have little or no experience making job choices, and we tend to have an overabundance of idealistic enthusiasm, plus a reckless lack of concern for future consequences. We haven't lived long enough to see ourselves tested in a variety of situations, and we're highly susceptible to bad advice from well-intentioned parents, teachers, counselors, or friends. No wonder so many people get off to a poor start.

The solution? To achieve as great a degree of self-awareness as you can before making any decision with long-lasting career consequences. Happily, "finding yourself" does not require a guru, a lot of money, or any period of experimentation.

You Can't Help It—You Were Born That Way!

Since the right job flows directly out of all the elements of your personality type, you need to spend some time figuring out what makes you tick. By making a conscious effort to discover the "real you," you can learn how to focus your natural strengths and inclinations into a career you can love for as long as you choose to work. This is where Type is so helpful. It provides a systematic, effective way to evaluate both your strong points and your probable blind spots. Once you have these figured out, you'll know how to make sure you are always operating from a position of strength.

Each one of us has a distinct personality, like an innate blueprint that stays with us for life. We are born with a personality type, we go through life with that type, and when we are laid to rest (hopefully at the end of a long and fruitful life), it is with the same type.

Now you are probably wondering, "Wait a minute. I might be one way sometimes, but at other times I'm a very different person. Doesn't the situation influence my personality type?"

The answer is no, it doesn't. Do we change our behavior in certain situations? Certainly! Most human beings have a tremendous repertoire of behaviors available to them. We couldn't function very successfully if we didn't. Sure, we act differently at work than we do at home, and it makes a difference whether we're with strangers, close friends, at a ballpark, or at a funeral. But people don't change their basic personalities with every new door they walk through.

All this is not to say that environmental factors are not extremely important; they are. Parents, siblings, teachers, and economic, social, and political circumstances all can play a role in determining what directions our lives take. Some people are forced by circumstances to act in a certain way until they are literally "not themselves" (more about this later). But we all start off with a particular personality type that predisposes us to behave in certain ways for our entire lives.

If you are skeptical about the idea that personality type is inborn, take a look at different children from the same family. These could be your own children, your siblings, or even children from a family you know. Do they have different personalities? You bet they do, and often the differences are apparent from birth.

The concept of "personality type" is not new. People have always been aware of the similarities and differences between individuals, and over the centuries many systems and models for understanding or categorizing these differences have been developed. Today, our understanding of human behavior has been expanded to such a degree that we are now able to accurately identify sixteen distinctly different personality types.

Finding the right job for each of these distinct personalities may seem like an awesome task. However, all sixteen personality types do function in the world. As we will see, it is possible to identify your own personality type, and the types of others, to understand why certain types flourish in certain kinds of jobs, and to clarify why people find career satisfaction in different ways.

2 | JUST WHO DO YOU THINK YOU ARE?

Discovering Your Personality Type

In this chapter you'll learn how Type works, and, even better, you'll discover your own personality type. But before we assist you in identifying your type, we think it would be helpful for you to know something about how Type has come to be used by so many people in so many different ways.

A Brief History of Type

The concept of Personality Type owes its existence to the work of the Swiss psychologist Carl Jung and two American women, Katharine Briggs and her daughter, Isabel Briggs Myers. Jung, an eclectic psychoanalyst and disciple of Sigmund Freud, realized that behavior that seemed unpredictable could in fact be anticipated if one understood the underlying mental functions and attitudes people preferred.

While Jung was making his discoveries, Katharine Briggs, who had long been intrigued with similarities and differences between human personalities, began to develop her own system for "typing" people. In 1921, Jung's theory of personality was published in a book called *Psychological Types*. When Katharine read the English translation published in 1923, she realized that Jung had already discovered what she had been looking for, so she adopted his model and began a serious study of his work. Fortunately for us, she interested her young daughter Isabel in her pursuit.

The study of Personality Type, and the discussion of the subject in this book, owe a substantial debt to the pioneering research and writing of Katharine Briggs

10

and her daughter, Isabel Briggs Myers.* Myers and Briggs built upon the theoretical work related to type done by Carl Jung, and both expanded it and gave it a practical application. Jung posited that there existed three personality preference scales and eight personality types; Katharine Briggs and Isabel Briggs Myers determined, based on their many years of study, that there were four personality preference scales and sixteen distinct personality types. These are the sixteen personality types that we discuss in this book. Much of our discussion derives from the writings of Isabel Briggs Myers and other authors who, like her, are published by Consulting Psychologists Press. Certain material and quotations contained in this book are published with the permission of Consulting Psychologists Press, Inc.

Starting in the 1940s, Katharine Briggs and Isabel Briggs Myers began developing the MBTI® test instrument,† a detailed test to measure psychological type, which has been refined and improved over the years. Moreover, data from the MBTI® test has been collected and analyzed from the time the test was first given, providing scientific validation for the MBTI® test and the results it yields.

As Isabel Briggs Myers determined, and as our experience has verified over and over again, there are sixteen different personality types, and every person fits into one of them. This is not to say that people are not all unique, for they certainly are. One hundred people of the same personality type in a room would all be different because they have different parents, genes, experiences, interests, and so on. But they would also have a tremendous amount in common. Identifying your personality type helps you discover and learn how to take advantage of that commonality.

As you become more familiar with Type, you'll see that all personality types are equally valuable, with inherent strengths and blind spots. There are no better or worse, smarter or duller, or healthier or sicker types. Type does not determine intelligence or predict success, nor does it indicate how well adjusted anyone will be. It does, however, help us discover what best motivates and energizes each of us as individuals, and this in turn empowers us to seek these elements in the work we choose to do.

How to Determine Your Personality Type

As we discussed earlier, one way to determine your personality type is to complete the Myers-Briggs Type Indicator (MBTI®) instrument and have the results interpreted by a trained professional. However, since that is not practical for the purposes of this book, we offer another method that we have used to successfully help hundreds of clients discover their true types.

The first of this two-step process begins with reading the following section in which we describe each of the four dimensions of Personality Type.

---

*If you are interested in learning more about these remarkable women's lives, we suggest you read *Katharine and Isabel* by Frances W. Saunders.

†Myers-Briggs Type Indicator and MBTI are registered trademarks of Consulting Psychologists Press.

As you read about each type dimension, think about which preference sounds more like you. Most of what you read about your preference will ring true for you, but remember, the preferences are generalities and represent the extremes. Try to focus not on isolated examples of each preference, but rather on a pattern of behavior that is more consistently like you than its opposite. Even if one example sounds just like you, see how you feel about all the others before making up your mind.

At the end of the discussion of each dimension you'll find a continuum (or scale). Please place a check mark along the continuum at the point which you think most accurately reflects how strong your preference is. The closer your mark is to the center of the scale (on either side), the less clear your preference is; the farther away your mark is, the stronger your preference is. Even if you are not certain of your preference, try to indicate if you can which side of the midpoint you probably fall on, because what is most helpful in determining your type is which side of each scale you prefer, not how clear or unclear your preference is.

By "estimating" your type preference for each of the four type dimensions in this way, you will end up with a four-letter code. For most of you, that code will represent your personality type, or one that is very close to it. Toward the end of this chapter, we will provide a space for you to record the letters of your type code.

The second step in identifying your type comes after you've read the descriptions of the preferences and made your estimates. But that happens just a little later on. Now it's time to learn about Personality Type.

The Four Dimensions of Personality Type

The Type system of personality assessment is based on four basic aspects of human personality: how we interact with the world and where we direct our energy; the kind of information we naturally notice; how we make decisions; and whether we prefer to live in a more structured way (making decisions) or in a more spontaneous way (taking in information). We call these aspects of human personality **dimensions** because each one can be pictured as a continuum between opposite extremes, like this:

How we interact with the world and where we direct our energy	(E) Extraversion —+—	Introversion (I)
The kind of information we naturally notice	(S) Sensing —+—	Intuition (N)
How we make decisions	(T) Thinking —+—	Feeling (F)
Whether we prefer to live in a more structured way (making decisions) or in a more spontaneous way (taking in information)	(J) Judging —+—	Perceiving (P)

Everyone's personality falls onto one side of the midpoint or the other on each of these four scales. We call the opposite ends of the scales **preferences**. If you fall on the extraverted side, for example, then you are said to have a preference for Extraversion. If you fall on the introverted side, your preference is for Introversion.

In reality, you use both sides of each scale in daily life, but you also have an innate preference for one side or the other. Remember the exercise in which you used each hand to write your name? Your preference is generally more comfortable, automatic, and trustworthy; for these reasons, you are most successful while using it. If you don't have a particularly pronounced preference on one continuum, you may be just slightly to one side of the midpoint. If you have an extreme preference, you'll find yourself at one end or the other. People with strong preferences who find themselves at the opposite ends of a scale are very different from each other.

For the time being, don't worry too much about the terms used to describe the four dimensions (for example, "Sensing" versus "Intuition"). In some cases, these terms don't mean exactly what you think they do. Although they are words you know, they mean something different in this context. We'll explain them in detail shortly.

You'll notice that since each continuum has opposite preferences at either end, there are eight preferences in all, each represented by a particular letter. These letters are used in combination to designate the sixteen personality types. Your particular combination of preferences is more meaningful than any one preference by itself.

By now you may be wondering what is magical about sixteen. Why aren't there twelve personality types? Or twenty? Or two hundred? The answer lies in simple mathematics. If you calculate all the possible combinations of the eight letters (preferences), you end up with sixteen possible types. It's easier to visualize them when organized in a chart, like the one originally suggested by Isabel Briggs Myers.

ISTJ	ISFJ	INFJ	INTJ
ISTP	ISFP	INFP	INTP
ESTP	ESFP	ENFP	ENTP
ESTJ	ESFJ	ENFJ	ENTJ

Everyone fits into one of these sixteen categories. Although Type is systematic, it is also flexible; it is limited enough to be useful but accommodating enough to fit everyone.

(E) Extraversion / Introversion (I)

The first dimension of Personality Type concerns how we prefer to interact with the world and where we direct our energy. Carl Jung originated the concepts of "extraversion" and "introversion" to describe how we live in the world outside ourselves and the world inside ourselves. Each of us has a natural preference for either the outer or inner world, although by necessity we all function in both. Functioning in our preferred world energizes us; functioning in the opposite world is more difficult and can be tiring. We call those who prefer the outer world **Extraverts** and those who prefer the inner world **Introverts**.

Most people think that extraverted means "talkative" and introverted means "shy." This is a good example of how the terms used to describe the Type preferences can be somewhat misleading. There is far more to extraversion and introversion than talkativeness.

Because they focus their energy in opposite directions, there are clear, distinct, and profound differences between Extraverts and Introverts. Extraverts focus their attention and energy on the world outside of themselves. They seek out other people and enjoy lots of interaction, whether one-on-one or in groups. They are constantly (and naturally) pulled to the outer world of people and things. Because Extraverts need to experience the world to understand it, they tend to like a lot of activity. Extraverts get their "batteries charged up" by being with others and usually know a lot of people. Because they like to be at the center of the action and are approachable, they tend to meet new people frequently and with ease. Extraverts look at a situation and ask themselves, "How do I affect this?"

Introverts focus their attention and energy on the world inside of themselves. They enjoy spending time alone and need this time to "recharge their batteries." Introverts try to understand the world before they experience it, which means a lot of their activity is mental. They prefer social interaction on a smaller scale— one-on-one or in small groups. Introverts avoid being the center of attention and are generally more reserved than Extraverts. They prefer to get to know new people slowly. Introverts look at a situation and ask themselves, "How does this affect me?"

Peter, a true Extravert, puts it this way: "When I return from a trip to the supermarket, my wife always asks me, 'Well, was it a success?' You might assume that she's checking to see if I got everything I needed, but in fact, knowing how Extraverted I am, what she really means is, 'How many people did you see whom you know?' To me, interacting with people, especially friends, is fun and energizing. I love the fact that no matter where I go, I'll almost always run into someone I know."

Brent, who is quite Introverted, feels just the opposite. "I like people," he explains, "but I don't care for quick, superficial exchanges. My wife loves parties, but I just find them exhausting. To me, it's draining and unsatisfying to have to meet all those people whose names I can't remember and whom I'll probably never see again. What's the point?"

Someone's preference for Extraversion or Introversion can be seen in practically everything they do. For example, take the study habits of Jill, a college sophomore. As Jill explains it, "I always prefer to study with friends. In one class we have a study group which really works out well. If no one is around, I'll go to the library. I find it much less boring than sitting alone in my dorm room reading by myself. At the library I can always find somebody I know to take a break with."

We think it's safe to say that usually most Extraverts don't *really* go to the library to study. They go there to be with other people.

If you don't know what an Extravert is thinking...you haven't been listening, because they will tell you. If you don't know what an Introvert is thinking... you haven't asked, or, in some cases, you haven't waited long enough for an answer. Asked a question, an Extravert will usually start talking, because Extraverts are most comfortable doing their thinking out loud (in the outer world). In fact, Extraverts often need to talk to think. On the other hand, there will often be a pause before an Introvert answers a question, because Introverts are more comfortable thinking silently (in the inner world). Introverts "bake" their ideas inside, much as cake is cooked in the oven and presented to the outside world only after it is finished. Extraverts only partially "bake" their ideas inside, preferring to finish them out in the world (which, of course, occasionally results in "half-baked" ideas!). However, Extraverts *do* finish their ideas eventually.

Shawn, another Extravert, recalls, "When I was in elementary school, I used to get all excited when I wanted the teacher to call on me. I would wave my whole arm so vigorously I had to hold it up with my other hand to keep from getting tired! But when the teacher finally did call on me, I often didn't know the answer. Naturally she would say something very sensitive and understanding, like, 'If you don't know the answer, then why did you raise your hand?' I didn't know then, but I know now: I needed to talk the answer out. I just couldn't think it through quietly in my head."

Unlike Shawn, Introverted students need time to form their answers in their minds before they can respond to a teacher's question. Since many elementary school teachers are Extraverts, they tend to move quickly from one child to the next. In our workshops, we have trained teachers to wait just a few seconds after asking an Introverted child a question—and we hear from these teachers that their class participation rates have tripled!

Many Extraverts find that their preference helps them at work because they generally can think quickly on their feet. When asked a question, they just start talking. Eventually they come up with an answer, and usually they can persuade others that it makes sense.

Maja, like most Introverts, had a different experience. "I'll never forget how frustrating my first job was for me," she told us. "It seemed as if everybody in the company, including my boss, was a huge Extravert. For one thing, I was always being forced to do group activities, like attending brainstorming sessions and sales conferences—and we were always having meetings! But even worse, my boss wouldn't give me enough time to answer his questions. I guess he thought I was stupid, or else he figured I was taking so long because I didn't know the answer."

Extraverts tend to be much more public than Introverts and share personal information freely. Introverts are more private, as is demonstrated by a situation that Bailey, an Introvert, experienced. "A new co-worker in our department had heard that I was a good cook," reported Bailey, "so she kept badgering me to invite her over for dinner. Finally I did, and the meal went fine. But the next day, she began telling everyone at our weekly staff meeting about the great meal I'd made. Her effusive compliments were bad enough, but then she went on to describe, in great detail, the contents of my entire house! She talked all about the personal treasures I've been collecting for the past thirty years. I was furious. If I'd wanted all my co-workers to know that much about me, I'd have invited them over myself and conducted a tour!"

The Extraverted co-worker, incidentally, was mortified to learn that she had violated Bailey's privacy. She'd had the best of intentions and thought she'd only been sincerely complimenting Bailey's good taste.

It's important to recognize that the gift of Extraversion is breadth, and the gift of Introversion is depth. Usually Extraverts are interested in many things, but not necessarily at a very deep level. Introverts have fewer interests, but they pursue them in much greater depth. Once you get an Introvert talking about their interest, they may go on forever.

Despite their best efforts to get out of it, Sam and Miguel found themselves at the annual holiday party given by the company where both their wives worked. Since both men are Introverts, you can imagine the joy each felt as he anticipated spending the next four hours with 120 total strangers. Fortunately for both, they met early on while ordering drinks at the bar. After some uncomfortable small talk, they learned (by accident) that each was an avid sailor. They spent the entire party talking boats, equipment, and cruising spots, and telling near-disaster stories.

Bill, whose wife works for the same company, couldn't wait to get to the party. He'd met many of the employees' spouses last year and he was eager to rekindle these acquaintances. As soon as they arrived, Bill and his wife—who was also an Extravert—went their separate ways, and by the end of the evening Bill had talked with a dozen and a half people, covering about twice as many topics. He and his wife were so "charged up" by all the stimulation that they moved the party down to the hotel lounge with another group of Extraverts after everyone else left.

Although there is some controversy as to how many Extraverts and Introverts there are in the world, the latest research suggests that the American population is about equally divided between Extraverts and Introverts. However, because Extraverts tend to talk more and louder than Introverts, there seems to be a fairly strong bias toward Extraverts in our culture.

Extraverts	**Introverts**
Are energized by being with other people	Are energized by spending time alone
Like being the center of attention	Avoid being the center of attention
Act, then think	Think, then act
Tend to think out loud	Think things through inside their heads
Are easier to "read" and know; share personal information freely	Are more private; prefer to share personal information with a select few
Talk more than listen	Listen more than talk
Express enthusiasm readily	Reveal enthusiasm more slowly
Respond quickly; enjoy a fast pace	Respond after taking the time to think things through; enjoy a slower pace
Prefer breadth to depth	Prefer depth to breadth

Now that you've read about Extraverts and Introverts, can you guess which one you are? Sometimes it's hard to decide between these two preferences because of the way we change with age (for example, you may be more interested in your inner world now than you once were) or because of the demands made upon us by our jobs (for example, you may have learned how to function well in the outer world because that's what your job requires of you). If you are still undecided between Extraversion and Introversion, ask yourself this question: "If I had to be one way or the other for the rest of my life, which would I choose?" A thoughtful answer will often nudge the most ambivalent person in the direction of his or her true preference.

Please indicate your preference on the continuum below.

(E) Extraversion ————————————|—————————— Introversion (I)

(S) Sensing / Intuition (N)

The second dimension of Personality Type concerns the kind of information we naturally notice. Some people focus on "what is," while others focus on "what could be." These approaches—both valid—are fundamentally different.

Again, some definitions are in order. We use the term "Sensing" to describe the process of gathering data by means of the five senses. People who prefer Sensing—we call them **Sensors**—concentrate on what can be seen, heard, felt, smelled, or tasted. They trust whatever can be measured or documented and focus on what is real and concrete. Sensors trust their five senses to give them accurate information about the world, and they also trust their own personal experience. They are oriented to the present and concentrate on whatever is happening at the moment. A Sensor will look at a situation and want to contextualize it based on their past experiences.

While it's obvious that we all use our five senses to take in information, some people are more interested in meanings, relationships, and possibilities based on facts than in the facts themselves. You could say these people trust their "sixth sense" (Intuition) more than their other five. Those who prefer Intuition—we call them **Intuitives**—naturally read between the lines and seek context for all things. (Intuition is abbreviated by the letter *N*.) Intuitives focus on implications and inferences. They are oriented toward the future; they tend to anticipate events and generally try to make things different rather than maintaining them the way they are. An Intuitive will look at a situation and want to know what its implications might be.

Everyone uses both Sensing and Intuition in daily life. Intuitives are well aware of the data their five senses bring in, and Sensors can interpret the meaning of someone's words or figure out a new way to handle a problem. Even so, everyone has a preference for either Sensing or Intuition. We all use one process more naturally, more often, and with more success than the other.

Intuitives are especially good at connecting disparate ideas to come up with a working theory about something; Sensors are especially good at noticing and remembering facts to help a theory hold water. The following story shows this idea in action.

Elizabeth, a Sensor, and Monique, an Intuitive, work together at a cosmetics-manufacturing company. One day the president called all department heads together for a quarterly review. His tone was cheerful as he went through several slides related to the company's financial health, including the advertising budget, market share compared to their main competitor, and the business goals for the next period. The president ended the presentation abruptly.

Monique and Elizabeth immediately went behind closed doors to compare notes. Monique mentioned that she had felt something was wrong as soon as she'd walked into the meeting, despite the president's cheerful tone, and wondered if perhaps there was more going on than had been indicated. Monique had noticed several department heads exchange furtive looks, and now remarked to Elizabeth that relations seemed particularly strained between the president and the vice president for research and development. Although nothing had been said about it at the meeting, Monique wondered if the company's greatly anticipated new skincare line, still in development, was not performing as well in trials as they had hoped.

Elizabeth recollected a slide mentioning projected profits for the new line, and compared the numbers against the advertising budget she'd been working on. As she saw the discrepancy between the president's optimistic tone and the money allocated for advertising, she agreed with Monique's hunch.

As it turned out, both Monique and Elizabeth were correct. A few days later the president broke the bad news—and for completely different reasons, as we've seen, neither Elizabeth nor Monique was surprised. Although they had noticed different red flags at the meeting, they arrived together at the same conclusion.

Intuitives and Sensors also approach tasks differently, as you can see in the next story. While Sensors often take a pragmatic approach, collecting data and moving linearly through a process, Intuitives are outside-the-box thinkers and may take a more inventive or novel path toward a solution.

Lizzy and Maria are best friends, and they got engaged within months of each other. Naturally, they each were named maid of honor to the other. The two women started looking for wedding dresses. Lizzy tried on a dozen dresses, but she wasn't quite satisfied with any of them. The last dress she tried wasn't even a dress—it was a long, flowing skirt. Lizzy, an Intuitive, had an unconventional idea: She could buy the skirt and ask a family friend to construct a top to go with it out of the extra fabric on the bottom. While it took some twists and turns to get there, Lizzy ended up with a beautiful, one-of-a-kind gown that she loved. She'd had a vision of what could be, and it paid off.

Maria, a Sensor, was more traditional in her approach. She first created a Pinterest board with dozens of dresses to home in on the elements she was sure she loved. When it came time to try on dresses, she fell in love with the second dress, which fit her exact list of requirements. In fact, the dress Maria ended up with was almost identical to the one she had always imagined for herself. Every detail was exactly to her liking, and she couldn't have been happier.

Sensors have a great capacity for enjoying experiences in the here and now. Often they are content to let things be. Intuitives, on the other hand, anticipate the future and tend to agitate for change.

Abdul, a Sensor, and Jessie, an Intuitive, frequently take long walks near the town reservoir. Abdul enjoys these walks because they put him back in touch with nature. He loves the smell of the woods, and can identify most of the trees he passes. Best of all is watching the seasons change in real time. Often he'll notice something in bloom that two days before was just budding. Jessie likes being outdoors too. During their walks she spends much of her time thinking or talking about new ideas for her current project. The time outside talking with Abdul is invaluable to her as a place to brainstorm and bounce ideas. While she enjoys nature like he does, her pleasure comes more from what her surroundings inspire and remind her of than the trees and the flowers themselves.

Both Intuitives and Sensors have important roles to play in organizations. Intuitives naturally focus on possibilities; Sensors naturally focus on realities. Variations on the same scenario are played out thousands of times daily across the country whenever the two types meet. Sensors and Intuitives see the world in fundamentally different ways and sometimes can fail to appreciate the value of each other's perspective.

As Alex, an Intuitive, expresses it, "I'm an idea man. Nothing feels better to me than to take a troublesome situation and figure out a new approach that will make it work better. The problem with this company is that no one has any vision—especially my boss, Warren. I come to him with a terrific idea that can have a significant impact on the future of this company, and all he wants to know is 'What will it cost? How much time will it take? Who's going to do your job while you're out doing this new pet project?'"

Now, Warren, a Sensor, sees things differently, as you might expect. "Maybe it's because Alex is a more creative guy than I am, but frankly, I don't know where he comes up with half of his ideas. It's not that they're bad ideas—it's just that most of them are totally unrealistic. Alex doesn't understand what it takes to get things done around here. To recommend a plan to *my* boss, I have to present a well-thought-out cost–benefit analysis, which means I need to have realistic data concerning expenses, time frames, and the anticipated impact on the company. This all takes the kind of careful, methodical research that Alex doesn't seem to be interested in doing."

Like Extraverts, Sensors have something of an advantage in our society because there are more of them. About 65 percent of the American population are Sensors, which puts Intuitives in the minority.

Sensors	*Intuitives*
Trust what is certain and concrete	Trust inspiration and inference
Like new ideas when they have practical applications	Like new ideas and concepts for their own sake
Value realism and common sense	Value imagination and innovation
Like to use and hone established skills	Like to learn new skills; get bored easily after mastering skills
Tend to be specific and literal; give detailed descriptions	Tend to be general and figurative; use metaphors and analogies
Present information in a step-by-step manner	Present information through leaps, in a roundabout manner
Are oriented to the past and present	Are oriented toward the future

By now it should be clear that people really do take in information in two very different ways. Please indicate your preference on the continuum below.

(S) Sensing ——————————+—————————— Intuition (N)

(T) Thinking / Feeling (F)

The third dimension of Personality Type concerns the way in which we make decisions and come to conclusions. Just as there are two different ways of interacting with the world and two different ways of taking in information, so are there two different ways of making decisions: by means of Thinking or Feeling.

In the context of Type, Thinking refers to making decisions impersonally, and Feeling refers to making decisions based on personal values. Although emotions can play a part in decision making, Feeling here simply means making decisions based on what is important to you and others.

Thinkers prefer decisions that make sense logically. They pride themselves on their ability to be objective and analytical in the decision-making process. They make decisions by analyzing and weighing the evidence, even if that means coming to unpleasant conclusions. **Feelers** make decisions based on how much they care or what they feel is right. They pride themselves on their ability to be empathetic and compassionate. Obviously, Thinkers and Feelers have very different priorities.

Some people find it especially difficult to decide between Thinking and Feeling. Sometimes the terms carry certain connotations that may make one choice seem less desirable than the other. Also, in our culture there is a very strong gender bias regarding certain kinds of behavior. Different sex role expectations can cause some people to "falsify" their preference. A woman who is naturally a Thinker may be socialized to behave more like a Feeler (the life-giver, the mother, and the nurturer, ever sympathetic and supportive), and a man who is naturally a Feeler may be socialized to behave more like a Thinker (the hunter, the competitor, cool-headed, detached, and unemotional). When you read the following paragraphs, think about which preference suits the *real* you, not necessarily how you were raised or encouraged to be. For people who have been acting "out of type" for a long time, clarifying this preference can be an especially enlightening and liberating experience.

As we have said before (and will no doubt say again, because it is so important), everyone uses both preferences. Thinkers do have emotions and personal values, and Feelers can be perfectly logical. However, each of us uses one process more naturally, more often, and more successfully than the other.

Thinking is usually considered a rational way of making decisions, while a Feeling approach is considered irrational. This is not the case. Thinking and Feeling are both rational methods; they just use different criteria in the decision-making process.

Take the example of Robert, a Feeler, who is the assistant dean of students at a small liberal arts college. Robert is responsible for conducting disciplinary hearings for students accused of violating the college's rules. He also decides the appropriate punishments as needed. A student, Henry, was caught smoking marijuana in his dormitory, a violation that usually carries a penalty of suspension for one semester, followed by two semesters of probation. Looking into the case, Robert discovered that Henry, a freshman, had been assigned to a room with two upperclassmen who had both been in and out of trouble. Robert also learned that Henry had an excellent academic record, and he had never been in any trouble before. Henry appeared to be genuinely contrite, and he was terrified about how his parents might react if he were suspended, since they had made real sacrifices to send him to school. Taking all these things into consideration, Robert fixed Henry's punishment at mandatory attendance in a six-week campus drug awareness program, followed by one semester of probation.

The dean, a Thinker, thought this punishment was too lenient and made no sense. She thought that failing to hold all students to the same standard set a dangerous precedent, and she asked Robert to justify his decision.

As Robert put it, "I know I could have suspended Henry. But I looked at the situation this way: We never should have assigned him the roommates we did, especially knowing how eager freshmen are to be accepted. As far as I'm concerned, we created the problem. Henry is a good kid, a good student, and an asset to the school. And after all, we are first and foremost an educational institution. I feel Henry has learned a valuable lesson from this experience, and I see no need to punish him for a relatively minor offense in a way which could affect his whole life."

Although Robert's decision was based on his own personal values and interpretation of the situation, you can see that he certainly did not make his decision irrationally.

Lauren, a Feeler, and Jerome, a Thinker, are a good example of how people who are different on this preference can provide important balance for one another. They work together in the editorial department of a health and fitness magazine, and they have come to appreciate each other's values. "Lauren is very perceptive about people," explains Jerome. "When I have trouble with a particular writer, or when I can't understand why someone is acting a certain way, I'll discuss it with Lauren. She's always able to see why the person is feeling the way they are—and sometimes how I've been responsible. Lauren's insights and suggestions about how to handle specific situations have bailed me out on many occasions."

For her part, Lauren says, "Jerome is probably the most honest person I know. Not always the most tactful or diplomatic...but the most honest. I always go to him when I want to know what the logical thing to do is, instead of just going with what feels right to me. I don't always like what Jerome has to say, or the blunt way he says it, but I know I'll always get a truly objective view—something I need and appreciate!"

Thinkers can be analytical to the point of seeming cold, and Feelers can be personally involved to the point of seeming overemotional. When Thinkers and Feelers clash, more often than not the Feeler ends up hurt and angry, while the Thinker is confused about what went wrong.

Tony, a Feeler, is a salesman for a large office-furniture manufacturer. He booked a morning flight to Chicago to attend a lunch meeting with some representatives from a company that was refurbishing its offices. Tony's boss had flown in the night before in order to wine and dine these important prospective clients.

When Tony arrived an hour and a half late to the important ten o'clock meeting, his boss was clearly irritated. Tony explained that one of the engines on his first flight had burst into flames en route, necessitating an emergency landing—complete with waiting fire trucks—in Detroit. After he'd waited for two hours, the airline finally found Tony a seat in the first-class section of another flight so he could complete his trip.

When his boss's first question was how much the extra first-class accommodation had cost the firm, Tony stared at his boss with astonishment, hurt at his apparent lack of appreciation for what Tony had just been through.

Tony's boss was baffled and said, "I don't understand why you're upset with me. It's not that I don't care about your safety. But it's obvious that you're all right so now I'm simply curious about the added cost."

To help you decide which preference suits you, see which side you would take in the following disagreement.

Tara, a Feeler, has a tough decision to make. Because of a restructuring of her company, she is being forced to lay off one employee from the marketing department. The choice has come down to Ted, a fifty-seven-year-old with twenty-two years at the company, or Alan, thirty-six, who joined the firm two years ago. Both men have similar job descriptions and satisfactory performance.

At a meeting with her boss, Kate, Tara explained why she would like to keep Ted and let Alan go. "Ted has been a loyal employee, and I appreciate the fact that he is always willing to go the extra mile to get a job done right and to help others succeed. As far as his personal situation is concerned, Ted has one son in college and another starting next fall. His wife, Mary, is in poor health. I'm concerned that a man his age who has worked exclusively for one company this long would have a hard time finding a comparable job. Alan is young, ambitious, and mobile; he'll have no trouble finding a good job. Besides, I feel that by rewarding loyalty and hard work, we make all of our employees feel better about working here."

Kate, a Thinker, sees the situation differently. "No one's saying that Ted isn't a great guy and a good employee. Personally, I've always liked him. But this decision has to be based on what's best for the *company,* not what's best for one individual. Ted's best years are behind him, and it's unlikely that he will ever move up. Alan's best years are ahead of him. He is senior management material; with proper grooming, he could become a very important asset to the company. Also, because of his seniority, we pay Ted twenty thousand dollars more than we pay Alan, and there is a greater likelihood of significant healthcare costs down the road for Ted than there is for Alan. It's an unfortunate situation, but it just doesn't make sense to keep Ted and let Alan go."

If you vote to keep Ted, chances are you're a Feeler. If you vote to keep Alan, you're probably a Thinker.

The American population is evenly split between Thinkers and Feelers. However, this is the only type dimension in which clear gender differences show up. About two-thirds of men prefer Thinking, and about two-thirds of women prefer Feeling. We aren't sure to what extent these results are due to socialization.

Thinkers	*Feelers*
Step back; apply impersonal analysis to problems	Step forward; consider effect of actions on others
Value logic, justice, and fairness; one standard for all	Value empathy and harmony; see the exception to the rule
Naturally see flaws and tend to be critical	Naturally like to please others; show appreciation easily
May be seen as heartless, insensitive, and uncaring	May be seen as overemotional, illogical, and weak
Consider it more important to be truthful than tactful	Consider it important to be tactful as well as truthful
Believe feelings are valid only if they are logical	Believe any feeling is valid, whether it makes sense or not
Are motivated by a desire for achievement and accomplishment	Are motivated by a desire to be appreciated

Once again we'd like you to estimate where you think you belong on the continuum below.

(T) Thinking ————————————|———————— Feeling (F)

(J) Judging / Perceiving (P)

The fourth dimension of Personality Type concerns whether we prefer to live in a more structured way (making decisions) or in a more spontaneous way (taking in information). Again, there is a range between opposite extremes of behavior.

People with a preference for Judging—we call them **Judgers**—tend to live in an orderly way and are happiest when their lives are structured and matters are settled. They have a judging attitude and like to make decisions. Judgers seek to regulate and control life. People with a preference for Perceiving—we call them **Perceivers**—like to live in a spontaneous way and are happiest when their lives are flexible. They have a perceiving attitude and like to stay open to all kinds of possibilities. Perceivers seek to understand life rather than control it.

Judgers are *not* necessarily judgmental (opinionated); they just like to have issues resolved. Perceivers are *not* necessarily perceptive (astute about seeing things accurately); they simply like perceiving options.

An important distinction between Judgers and Perceivers is the issue of closure. Judgers experience tension until closure is reached and are constantly drawn toward making a decision. Perceivers, on the other hand, experience tension when they are forced to make a decision; they avoid closure and prefer to keep their options open.

Everyone uses both Judging and Perceiving in daily life. As with the other preferences, no one behaves strictly one way or the other. It's good to seek a balance of Judging and Perceiving, since Judgers run the risk of becoming rigid, dogmatic, and inflexible, and Perceivers run the risk of leaving things open-ended to the point that they procrastinate their lives away.

When Cynthia, a Perceiver, volunteered to put together a blog for a local bookstore, the other employees were enthusiastic. Cynthia seemed natural for the job: She was easygoing and well known in the community; she also was artistically talented and had created blogs before. Cynthia set about gathering important dates and ideas for posts, but weeks went by and no posts appeared. When pressed for an explanation, Cynthia was unperturbed. She explained that her mother had come to visit, one of her children had gotten sick, and she and her husband had gone skiing one weekend and she hadn't gotten as much done as she'd hoped. In addition, she was having trouble gathering some of the facts she needed and she hadn't yet been able to reach a few people. Eventually Cynthia posted something—and the process began all over again. In six months the bookstore published four entertaining, informal blog posts of which Cynthia was very proud.

This all drove Ashley, a manager at the bookstore, absolutely wild. Ashley, a Judger, expected a new post to appear each week, and she expected the main page to include a calendar of all the important dates for that month. Ashley was so irritated by Cynthia's performance that she eventually took over the blog herself. She had no trouble whatsoever gathering the information she needed, and if for some reason an article was missing, she simply posted without it. Ashley created a professional and succinct blog for the bookstore. Though the posts were sometimes dry, they were *always* on time.

Judgers prefer a planned and orderly world, living with structure that has a beginning, middle, and end. They like to be in control of what is happening and they like to make decisions. Judgers tend to see things in black-and-white and like to come down on one side or the other of an issue. They are more comfortable when issues are settled rather than being left up in the air—even if they aren't the ones making the decision! Judgers may not be particularly adaptable, and they generally don't like surprises.

Perceivers like their world to be flexible, allowing for lots of opportunities for spontaneity. They feel constrained by structure and prefer things to be free-flowing. Perceivers enjoy adapting to new and changing situations and tend to delay making decisions. They leave things open-ended whenever they can, wanting to suspend judgment as long as possible. Perceivers see issues in shades of gray and enjoy the unexpected in nearly all areas of their lives.

Jeff and Amy decided it was time to finally get in shape, so they went together to the sporting goods store to buy bicycles. Jeff, a Perceiver, found a salesman, and over the next half hour asked him about a hundred questions. He wasn't sure which bike was best for him, and he was troubled by the store's returns policy (you could return a bike, but only for store credit). Jeff finally left, saying he'd have to think over his decision. On the way home, he stopped at two other sporting goods stores to "get a little more information."

Amy, a Judger, looked over all the bikes on display for a few minutes, then found a salesman and asked, "Which bike do you recommend?" When the salesman showed her the store's top-selling bike, she said, "Fine. I'll take it."

In the work world, these two different styles can create conflicts, especially when Judgers and Perceivers are under pressure together. As is always the case, it helps to be aware of other people's preferences. Knowing that people naturally behave differently can make irritating behavior not only easier to tolerate but also easier to anticipate.

Irene and Suzanne, both employees of a corporate training department, were assigned to co-train a one-day management development program. Each of them had conducted this program individually many times before, but this was the first time they had worked together. They divided up the portions of the program each would be responsible for: Irene, a Perceiver, was to start the program at eight and conduct a thirty-minute introduction; then Suzanne, a Judger, would present the first section, which would last one and a half hours until the morning break at ten.

At eight, seven of the twenty-five participants had not arrived. Suzanne wanted to get started anyway, but Irene opted to wait until all were present, which took about fifteen minutes. During Irene's introduction, several people had questions about the program. Suzanne diplomatically tried to interject that many of the questions would be answered as the day progressed, but Irene decided it was important to address them at that moment. By the time Irene finished, it was nine, which meant that Suzanne had only one hour in which to make her ninety-minute presentation. She raced through her presentation, barely covering all the necessary information, and ended the segment feeling disorganized and very stressed.

At the ten o'clock break, Suzanne was furious and confronted Irene. They soon found themselves in a heated conflict. Suzanne accused Irene of having poor time-management skills and said she'd acted irresponsibly. She pointed out that Irene's mismanagement of the morning had put her in the position of having to scramble through her presentation. Suzanne felt that it had been ridiculous to make eighteen people who had come on time wait for seven who hadn't, and she said that rushing through her notes had made her look ridiculous. She felt that she had not had enough time to present her part of the program effectively, and she resented the fact that all of her careful planning had been ruined for no good reason.

Irene felt that Suzanne was overreacting and was being too rigid. She thought it was entirely appropriate to wait for the missing third of the participants. Moreover, she regarded interruptions as a typical and often necessary part of the program. She felt it was important to address questions early on in order to set the right tone for the day and knew they could make up the rest of the program later. Irene didn't appreciate the fact that Suzanne had tried to cut her answers short, and said she felt that Suzanne had undercut her authority in front of the group.

Since the two women still had a full day's program remaining, they ultimately realized that they had better figure out how to work together more smoothly. Irene promised to watch the clock more carefully, but was still committed to keeping the lines of communication open between herself and the program participants. Suzanne promised to try to be more flexible about what was discussed when, but she reserved the right to remind Irene of their schedule in front of the group. Fortunately the rest of the program went without incident.

One indication of your preference between Judging and Perceiving may be the condition of your desk. Typically (*but not always*), a Judger's desk is fairly neat. It is well organized. There are spots for pencils, pads, paperweights, and so forth, and these items can usually be found—at least at the beginning and end of the day—in their proper places. The IN basket contains information to be reviewed, and the OUT basket is reserved for completed work. Important information is filed away in a manner that allows for easy retrieval. It is not unusual to see on a Judger's desk a list of "things to do" with a line drawn through most, if not all, the items on the list at the end of the day.

A Perceiver's desk, on the other hand, is often (*but not always*) considerably less organized. It might contain several "works in progress," messages that need to be answered, toys, malfunctioning ballpoint pens, and perhaps the best indicator of all…the "just for now" pile (or piles). When put on the defensive, Perceivers will always claim that they can find anything they need in their office. (They just don't admit how much time it will take to do it!)

The condition of your desk (and possibly the inside of your closet, purse, or car) can reflect how your mind works. Let's say a Judger and a Perceiver both receive a brochure announcing an upcoming conference that is to take place in four months. The Judger is likely to do one of the following: 1) Throw the brochure away because he went last year or already has a prior commitment; 2) Fill out the application, write out the check to cover the registration fee, and send them in; or 3) Pass the brochure along to someone else who might be interested. The Judger makes a decision and gets the brochure off his desk.

The Perceiver in the same situation is likely to behave differently. First of all, four months into the future is a long time from now. Recognizing that a lot could happen between now and then (and that maybe something better will come along), the Perceiver believes it's too soon to make a decision. He realizes he should file the brochure someplace, but if he does, he'll probably forget all about it, so instead he adds it to his substantial "just for now" stack of papers and folders already occupying space on his desk. Unless it is truly important, the brochure is apt to get lost in the pile, only to be discovered after the deadline for registration (or even the conference itself) has come and gone. The Perceiver doesn't make a decision, so the brochure hangs around on his desk until the time for decision making has passed.

Everyone has a "to do" list or a "just for now" pile. That's not unusual. But Perceivers are likely to have all kinds of items in their "think about" pile, and they can probably recall several opportunities they missed because they procrastinated too long.

In the American population, about 60 percent are Judgers and 40 percent are Perceivers. There are no gender differences.

Judgers	*Perceivers*
Are happiest after decisions have been made	Are happiest leaving their options open
Have a "work ethic": work first, play later (if there's time)	Have a "play ethic": enjoy now, finish the job later (if there's time)
Set goals and work toward achieving them on time	Change goals as new information becomes available
Prefer knowing what they are getting into	Like adapting to new situations
Are product oriented (emphasis is on completing the task)	Are process oriented (emphasis is on how the task is completed)
Derive satisfaction from finishing projects	Derive satisfaction from starting projects
See time as a finite resource and take deadlines seriously	See time as a renewable resource and see deadlines as elastic

As you think about which preference suits you, keep in mind that circumstances often force us to behave in certain ways that don't necessarily reflect our true selves. Most of us have to behave like Judgers at least part of the time, particularly at work. If you have a demanding job, you have to get there on time, meet deadlines, and make lots of decisions. To complicate things further, as your personal and work lives get more and more intertwined, it may become increasingly difficult to tell which is the "real you." In this case, try to step back and see which preference would give you the most satisfaction if you could behave any way you wished.

It's time again to estimate your preference on the continuum below.

(J) Judging ———————————|——————————— Perceiving (P)

Now that you have estimated your preference for all four type dimensions, please write those letters in the spaces below.

E or I	S or N	T or F	J or P

```
                    KEY

        E  = Extraverted    I  = Introverted
        S  = Sensing        N  = Intuitive
        T  = Thinking       F  = Feeling
        J  = Judging        P  = Perceiving
```

Congratulations! By going through this exercise, you have more than likely identified your personality type. However, the process of making sure that you have identified your type correctly requires one more step, which we call "verification."

Verifying Your Type

Chapter 3 contains Verifying Type Profiles for each of the sixteen types. After reading the brief introduction to the chapter, we will ask you to find the profile for the type that you feel reflects the code you came up with in step one.

For example, suppose you estimated your type preferences to be: Extravert, Sensing, Thinking, and Judging (or ESTJ in Type language). You would first find and read the ESTJ profile.

If ESTJ is really your personality type, then you will probably think that it describes you very well. In fact, most people are taken aback at just how well their type profile describes them! If you feel this way, then you have very probably verified your type. We say "very probably" only to discourage those of you with the tendency to make quick decisions (and you know who you are!) from foreclosing any other possibilities which might be better fits. So until you have read several other chapters that describe Type more thoroughly, we suggest you think of the type you come up with by doing this exercise as a sort of working hypothesis.

On the other hand, if you read ESTJ and you think it sounds somewhat like you, but not very much like you, then you probably haven't yet identified your one true type.

If you find yourself in that situation, here's what to do. Go back to the continuums (scales) for each of the preferences. Note which ones you marked closer to the center line (in other words, the less clear preferences). Then see which ones you marked farther away from the center lines (the ones that seemed clearer to you).

Using the ESTJ again for an example, suppose that by going back you discover that you felt pretty clear about your preferences for Extraversion (E), Sensing (S), and Thinking (T), but less clear about your preference for Judging (J). Well, it's possible that you may really be an ESTP rather than an ESTJ. As you will learn shortly, these two types, while identical on three letters, are *very* different from each other in many ways. Therefore, you will want to read the ESTP profile as well.

If it turns out that your preference really is for Perceiving rather than Judging, then the ESTP profile should fit you much better. Thus you may have to go through this process of examining a few (and in rare instances, several) types to find your true type.

You may ask: "But shouldn't I be able to identify my type right away?" Not necessarily. Often circumstances just don't permit people to be themselves. For example, you may have had parents who encouraged only certain kinds of behavior, or you may have been obliged to do what was expected of you (say, run the family business) instead of what interested you (studying architecture). Some people who experienced very difficult childhoods were forced to adopt certain kinds of behavior as a form of self-defense. This, too, can affect how you see yourself and can place a barrier between the "you" who survived and the "you" you were meant to be. This is the time to try to determine who you really are deep down.

It is important to carefully pin down all four of your preferences, because your personality is in large part determined by the unique way in which your preferences interact with each other. Perhaps you're familiar with the concept of synergism. Basically, synergy occurs when the whole of something is greater than the sum of its individual parts. This is certainly true of Type. And as useful as it is for people to know that they prefer Sensing to Intuition, for example, no one is *just* a Sensor. People who prefer Sensing come in eight different varieties, depending upon their other preferences—and it is the *combination* of preferences (indicated by letters) that results in such useful information.

Although you don't *have* to know your personality type in order to benefit from the rest of this book, you'll certainly get more out of *Do What You Are* if you can successfully identify your personality type before going on to Part 2. As you review this chapter and read the next one, please keep in mind that there is *no time limit* for discovering your true type. The Type Police will not come crashing through your door if you haven't verified your type after finishing Part 1. Take your time and review this material as much as you need. Keep refining your working hypothesis until you have identified the personality type that most accurately reflects you. Then have a little celebration—you've found the real you!

Descriptions of the sixteen personality types in the next chapter draw substantially upon the following works: *Introduction to Type: A Description of the Theory and Application of the Myers-Briggs Type Indicator,* by Isabel Briggs

Myers (1987); *Introduction to Type in Organizations,* by Sandra Krebs Hirsh and Jean M. Kummerow (1990); *Manual: A Guide to the Development and Use of the Myers-Briggs Type Indicator,* by Isabel Briggs Myers and Mary McCaulley (1985); and *Gifts Differing,* by Isabel Briggs Myers (1980). All of these books are published by Consulting Psychologists Press, Inc., and certain material in the next chapter is reprinted with permission of Consulting Psychologists Press, Inc.

Note: For each profile, we provide an approximation of the percentage of this type found in the American population. These percentages were developed by Dr. Charles K. Martin of the Center for Applications of Psychological Type (CAPT), Gainesville, Florida.

3 | MIRROR, MIRROR

Verifying Your Personality Type

Included in this chapter are the sixteen Verifying Type Profiles. Your true type profile is among them.

Your type profile is not meant to be a totally comprehensive, all-encompassing description of your innermost thoughts and feelings. However, in a general way, it should ring true for you—perhaps not every word, but overall you ought to recognize a great deal of yourself in it.

The Verifying Type Profiles don't attempt to explain why different personality types behave the way they do. We'll get into these kinds of explanations in Part 2. For now, just concentrate on finding the type profile that best suits you.

In these profiles, we have deliberately avoided using descriptions from the workplace. This may strike you as a little odd, but remember, you are trying to pinpoint the "real you." How you are obliged to act at work may be very different from how you wish you were free to be. In Part 3 you'll find a list of the work-related strengths and blind spots that are commonly associated with your personality.

You may read through several of the Verifying Type Profiles and think, "Wait a minute. I can see something of myself in *all* of these descriptions." Actually, this isn't unusual, but the point is to find your true type profile, not bits and pieces that sound like you. Most people find that their type profile is very accurate and extremely insightful.

We hope that by now we've convinced you of the validity of Type. However, if you are a skeptical sort who suspects that the personality types are all interchangeable, we suggest that you read both a type profile *and its opposite* (for example, INTP and ESFJ). You'll see that the two profiles describe two very different kinds of people.

In the Verifying Type Profiles we've included not only descriptions of person-ality strengths but also information on possible blind spots. You'll find that sometimes the flip side of your greatest strength is your worst shortcoming. For example, excellent reasoning power can be coupled with a tendency to overlook the feelings of others. By being aware of the blind spots associated with your personality type, you can seek balance in your behavior—both on and off the job.

‖ ENFJ
Extraverted, Intuitive, Feeling, Judging
Approximately 3–5 percent of the American population

ENFJs are people-lovers. They place the highest importance on people and rela-tionships and are naturally concerned about others. They take a warm approach to life and feel personally connected to all things.

Because they are idealistic and live by their values, ENFJs are very loyal to the people, causes, or institutions they respect and admire. They are energetic and enthusiastic, as well as responsible, conscientious, and persevering.

ENFJs have a natural tendency to be self-critical. However, because they feel responsible for the feelings of others, ENFJs are seldom critical in public. They are acutely aware of what is (and isn't) appropriate behavior, and are gracious, charming, personable, and socially adept. Even-tempered and tolerant, ENFJs are diplomatic and are good at promoting harmony around them. They are natu-ral leaders, popular and charismatic. They tend to be good communicators, and usually use their expressive gift verbally.

ENFJs make decisions based on how they feel about a situation rather than how the situation actually stands. They are interested in possibilities beyond what is already obvious, and in the ways these possibilities might affect others.

Being naturally orderly, ENFJs prefer an organized world and expect others to be the same way. They like to have matters settled, even if someone else is mak-ing the decisions.

ENFJs radiate sympathy and understanding and are nurturing and supportive of others. They read people well and are responsible and caring. Since they are idealists, they generally look for the good in others.

Possible Blind Spots

ENFJs are so empathetic and caring that they can become overly involved with the problems or feelings of others. Sometimes they choose causes that aren't worthy of all the time and energy they pour into them. When things don't work out well, they can become overwhelmed, disappointed, or disillusioned. This can lead them to withdraw, feeling they weren't appreciated. ENFJs need to learn to accept their own limitations as well as those of the people they care about. They also need to learn how to pick their battles and how to maintain realistic expectations.

Because of their strong desire for harmony, ENFJs can overlook their own needs and ignore real problems. Because they avoid conflict, they sometimes maintain relationships that are less than honest and equal. ENFJs are so concerned about the feelings of others that they can be blind to important facts when the situation involves criticism or hurt feelings. It's important that ENFJs learn how to accept and deal with conflict as a necessary part of relationships.

Because they are enthusiastic and in a hurry to get on with their next challenge, ENFJs sometimes make incorrect assumptions or make decisions too quickly, without gathering all the important facts. They need to slow down and pay closer attention to the details of their projects. By waiting until enough information is known, they can avoid making mistakes.

ENFJs respond well to praise, but are easily hurt by criticism, which can make them appear touchy. They take even the most innocent or well-intentioned criticism personally, and they often respond by becoming flustered, hurt, or angry. ENFJs do well to stop, take a step back, and try to see a situation objectively before reacting.

ENFJs are so idealistic that they tend to see things the way they wish they were. They are vulnerable to idealizing relationships, and they tend to overlook facts that contradict what they believe. ENFJs who don't learn to face facts they find disagreeable end up ignoring their problems instead of finding solutions for them. In general, ENFJs need to try to keep their eyes open as well as their hearts.

‖ INFJ
Introverted, Intuitive, Feeling, Judging
Approximately 2–3 percent of the American population

INFJs inhabit a world of ideas. They are independent, original thinkers with strong feelings, firm principles, and personal integrity.

INFJs trust their own ideas and decisions even in the face of skepticism. They are motivated by an inner vision that they value above all else, including prevailing opinion or established authority. INFJs often see deeper meanings and have intuitive insights into situations. Their inspirations are important and valid to them even if others don't share their enthusiasm.

INFJs are loyal, committed, and idealistic. They are quietly forceful in having their ideas accepted and applied. They value integrity and can be determined to the point of being stubborn. Because of the strength of their conviction and their clear vision of what is best for the common good, INFJs can be great leaders. They are often honored or respected for their contributions.

Because they value harmony and agreement, INFJs like to persuade others of the validity of their viewpoint. They win the cooperation of others by using approval and praise rather than argument or intimidation. INFJs will go to great lengths to promote fellowship and avoid conflict.

Generally thoughtful decision makers, INFJs find problems stimulating and usually reflect carefully before they act. They prefer to focus in great depth on one thing at a time, which can result in periods of single-mindedness.

Empathetic and compassionate, INFJs have a strong desire to contribute to the welfare of others. They are aware of other people's emotions and interests, and often deal well with complicated people. INFJs themselves tend to have deep, complex personalities and can be both sensitive and intense. They can be reserved and hard to get to know, but are willing to share their inner selves with people they trust. They tend to have a small circle of deep, longstanding friendships, and can generate plenty of personal warmth and enthusiasm in the right circumstances.

Possible Blind Spots

Since they tend to be so absorbed with "the idea," INFJs can sometimes be impractical and are capable of neglecting routine details that need attention. Becoming more aware of what is around them and relying more on proven information helps INFJs anchor their creative ideas in the real world.

INFJs can be so committed to their own principles that they develop tunnel vision. They can be stubborn about change, and may resist changing a decision once it has been made. Sometimes they overlook important facts that don't support their position, or resist ideas that conflict with their values. They may not hear the objections of others because, to them, their position seems unquestionable. INFJs need to attempt to look at themselves and at their work more objectively, as others might.

Because they are so protective of their own vision, INFJs tend to overregulate. They are often perfectionists, and they can be hypersensitive to criticism. Although they are strong-willed, they also have difficulty dealing with conflicts in relationships and can become disappointed or disillusioned if conflicts develop. The more objective INFJs can be about themselves and their relationships, the less vulnerable they will be to these kinds of hurts.

‖ ENFP
Extraverted, Intuitive, Feeling, Perceiving
Approximately 6–7 percent of the American population

ENFPs are full of enthusiasm and new ideas. Optimistic, spontaneous, creative, and confident, they have original minds and a strong sense of the possible. For an ENFP, life is an exciting drama.

Because they are so interested in possibilities, ENFPs see significance in all things and prefer to keep lots of options open. They are perceptive and keen observers who notice anything out of the ordinary. ENFPs are curious; they prefer to understand rather than judge.

Imaginative, adaptable, and alert, ENFPs value inspiration above all else and are often ingenious inventors. They are sometimes nonconformists, and are good at seeing new ways of doing things. ENFPs open up new avenues for thought or action...and then keep them open!

In carrying out their innovative ideas, ENFPs rely on their impulsive energy. They have lots of initiative and find problems stimulating. They also get an infusion of energy from being around other people, and can successfully combine their talents with the strengths of others.

ENFPs are charming and full of vitality. They treat people with sympathy, gentleness, and warmth and are ready to help anyone with a problem. They can be remarkably insightful and perceptive, and they often care about the development of others. ENFPs avoid conflict and prefer harmony. They put more energy into maintaining personal relationships than into maintaining objects, and they like to keep a wide assortment of relationships alive.

Possible Blind Spots

Since they find it so easy to generate ideas, ENFPs have difficulty focusing on just one thing at a time and can have trouble making decisions. They see so many possibilities that they have difficulty selecting the best activity or interest to pursue. Sometimes they make poor choices or get involved with too many things at once. Carefully choosing where they will focus their energy helps ENFPs avoid wasting their time and squandering their considerable talents.

To an ENFP, the fun part of a project is the initial problem solving and creation of something new. They like to exercise their inspiration on the important and challenging parts of a problem. After this stage, they often lose interest and lack the self-discipline necessary to complete what they've started. They are likely to start many projects but finish few. ENFPs have more to show for their efforts when they follow through with the necessary but tedious parts of a project until it is completed. Often writing important facts or steps down on paper helps them keep from getting sidetracked.

Often ENFPs are not particularly well organized. They can benefit from learning and applying time management and personal organizational skills. They do well when they team up with other more realistic and practical people. This usually suits them fine anyway, since ENFPs don't like working alone, especially for extended periods of time. They find working with another person, even on a less interesting phase of a project, far preferable to working alone.

ENFPs are not much interested in details. Since they are more excited about using their imagination and creating something original, they may not bother to collect all the information they need in order to carry out a particular activity. Sometimes they just improvise on the spot instead of planning and preparing ahead. Because they find information gathering tedious, ENFPs run the risk of never getting past the "bright idea" stage or, once started, never finishing. Always restless, they'd rather put off dealing with troublesome details and move on to something else new or unusual. ENFPs are more effective when they consciously attend to the actual world around them and gather more realistic impressions to make their innovations workable.

‖ INFP
Introverted, Intuitive, Feeling, Perceiving
Approximately 3–4 percent of the American population

INFPs value inner harmony above all else. Sensitive, idealistic, and loyal, they have a strong sense of honor concerning their personal values and are often motivated by deep personal belief or by devotion to a cause they feel is worthy.

INFPs are interested in possibilities beyond what is already known and focus most of their energy on their dreams and visions. Open-minded, curious, and insightful, they often have excellent long-range vision. In day-to-day matters they are usually flexible, tolerant, and adaptable, but they are very firm about their inner loyalties and set very high—in fact, nearly impossible—standards for themselves.

INFPs have many ideals and loyalties that keep them occupied. They are deeply committed to whatever they choose to undertake—and they tend to undertake too much but somehow get everything done.

Although they demonstrate cool reserve on the outside, INFPs care deeply inside. They are compassionate, sympathetic, understanding, and very sensitive to the feelings of others. They avoid conflict and are not interested in impressing or dominating others unless their values are at stake. Often INFPs prefer to communicate their feelings in writing rather than orally. When they are persuading others of the importance of their ideals, INFPs can be most convincing.

INFPs seldom express the intensity of their feelings and often appear reticent and calm. However, once they know you, they are enthusiastic and warm. INFPs are friendly, but tend to avoid superficial socializing. They treasure people who take the time to understand their goals and values.

Possible Blind Spots

Since objectivity is not a priority for INFPs, they sometimes make errors of fact and can be unaware that they are being illogical. When their dreams become out of touch with reality, others may see them as flighty and mystical. INFPs do well to ask the advice of more practical people to find out if their ideas are workable and useful in the real world.

Because they are so committed to their own ideals, INFPs have a tendency to overlook other points of view and can sometimes be rigid. They are not particularly interested in physical surroundings, and often are so busy that they fail to notice what is happening around them.

INFPs may reflect on an idea much longer than is really necessary to begin a project. Their perfectionistic tendencies can lead them to refine and polish their ideas for so long that they never share them. This is dangerous, since it is important for INFPs to find ways of expressing their ideas. To keep from getting discouraged, they need to work toward becoming more action oriented.

INFPs are so emotionally entangled in their undertakings that they are very sensitive to criticism. To complicate things further, they tend to demand too much of themselves as they aspire to their own impossibly high standards. This can lead to feelings of inadequacy, even though they in fact are capable of accomplishing a great deal. When INFPs are disappointed, they tend to become negative about everything around them. Trying to develop more objectivity about their projects will help keep INFPs less vulnerable to both criticism and disappointment.

Because INFPs tend to try to please many people at the same time, it can be hard for them to stand up for an unpopular position. They hesitate to criticize others, and they have a hard time saying no. When INFPs don't express their negative opinions about ideas or plans, others can be misled into thinking they agree with them. INFPs need to develop more assertiveness and can benefit from learning how to offer honest criticism of others when needed.

∥ ENTJ
Extraverted, Intuitive, Thinking, Judging
Approximately 2–5 percent of the American population

ENTJs are great leaders and decision makers. They easily see possibilities in all things and are happy to direct others toward making their vision become a reality. They are ingenious thinkers and great long-range planners.

Because ENTJs are so logical and analytical, they are usually good at anything that requires reasoning and intelligence. Driven to achieve competence in all they do, they can naturally spot the flaws that may exist in a situation and see immediately how to improve them. They strive to perfect systems rather than simply accept them as they are. ENTJs enjoy working with complex problem solving and are undaunted in their pursuit of mastery of anything they find intriguing. ENTJs value truth above all else and are convinced only by logical reasoning.

Eager to continually add to their base of knowledge, ENTJs are systematic about planning and researching new things. They enjoy working with complex theoretical problems and work toward the pursuit of mastery of anything they find intriguing. They are much more interested in the future consequences of actions than the present condition of things.

Natural leaders with a hearty and frank style, ENTJs tend to take charge of any situation they find themselves in. They are good organizers of people because they have the ability to see ahead and then communicate their vision to others. They tend to live by a rather strict set of rules and expect others to do so as well. Therefore, they tend to be challenging and push others as hard as they push themselves.

Possible Blind Spots

Owing to their desire to move on to the next challenge or toward their larger goal, ENTJs sometimes make decisions too hastily. Slowing down occasionally will give them the chance to gather all relevant data and consider both the practical and personal ramifications of their actions. Their action orientation propels them to act on their decisions as soon as they are made rather than stopping to double check their facts and the realities of the situation.

Because ENTJs take a logical approach to life, they can be tough, blunt, impatient, and insensitive to the needs and feelings of others when they don't see the logic of those feelings. ENTJs can be argumentative and difficult to approach and don't often welcome the commonsense advice of others. Rather than automatically being critical, they need to listen to the input of those around them and express their appreciation for their contributions. ENTJs need to make a conscious effort—in fact to make it a rule—to stop and listen to others before charging ahead with their own ideas, and avoid acting domineering and dictatorial.

ENTJs' impersonal approach to life leaves little time, tolerance, or compassion for emotions, even their own. When they allow their feelings to go ignored or unexpressed, they can find themselves overreacting emotionally. They are particularly prone to this if they perceive someone to be questioning their competence, especially someone they respect. They can have explosive reactions to seemingly insignificant situations, and these outbursts can be hurtful to those close to them. ENTJs are more effective and happy when they give themselves time to consider and understand how they really feel. Giving their emotions a constructive outlet, rather than allowing them to take over their personalities, will actually allow them to stay more fully in control, a position they enjoy and strive for. Surprisingly, ENTJs may actually be less experienced and competent than their confident style indicates. They will increase their personal power and rate of success by allowing themselves to take some reasonable and valuable assistance from others.

‖ INTJ
Introverted, Intuitive, Thinking, Judging
Approximately 2–4 percent of the American population

INTJs are perfectionists. Their strong need for autonomy and personal competence, as well as their unshakable faith in their own original ideas, drives them to achieve their objectives.

Logical, critical, and ingenious, INTJs can see the consequences of the application of new ideas and live to see systems translated into real substance. They are demanding with themselves and others, and tend to drive others almost as hard as themselves. They are not particularly bothered by indifference or criticism. As the most independent of all types, INTJs prefer to do things their own way. They are usually skeptical, decisive, and determined in the face of opposition. INTJs are not impressed with authority per se, but can conform to rules only if they see them as useful to their greater purpose.

With original minds, great insight, and vision, INTJs are natural brainstormers. They are innately theoretical and work well with complex and global concepts. They are good strategic thinkers and can usually see with clarity the benefits and flaws of any situation. In subjects that interest them, they are fine organizers with insight and vision. If the idea or project is of their own making, they can invest incredible concentration, focus, energy, and drive. Their many accomplishments are achieved through determination and perseverance toward reaching or exceeding their high standards.

Possible Blind Spots

Being visionaries with sometimes unrealistically high standards, INTJs may expect too much from themselves and others. In fact, they tend not to care how they measure up to others' standards; it is their own that are important. They may lack an understanding of how their behavior affects others and can be critical and blunt in giving recommendations for improvement. They don't often encourage others to challenge their views or express any personal feelings. Because INTJs have a rather impersonal style, they may erroneously assume others wish to be treated in the same manner. They need to learn to understand the seemingly "illogical" feelings of others, and accept that they are rational and valid. This will help keep them from alienating and offending those around them.

Because INTJs place so much value on their own visions and ideas for the future, they are vulnerable to missing some important realities and facts of the present moment. They may also fail to recognize practical weaknesses in their ideas that may make their execution more difficult. Gathering all the relevant and factual data will help ensure that their ideas are workable. INTJs need to simplify their often theoretical and complicated ideas so they can communicate them to others.

Because INTJs often choose to be alone and are single-minded in their efforts, they can neglect to invite others to participate or assist in their activities. Soliciting the input and suggestions of others can help them recognize an impractical idea earlier in the process, or help them make the necessary changes and improvements before investing huge amounts of time.

Increased effectiveness for INTJs lies in making an effort to yield on less important points to win the more important ones. This will also decrease the likelihood of the INTJ becoming too stubborn and controlling. When they make an effort to adopt a more accepting approach to life and their dealings with others, INTJs will achieve more balance and competence, and will succeed at having more of their innovations accepted by the world.

‖ ENTP
‖ Extraverted, Intuitive, Thinking, Perceiving
‖ *Approximately 2–5 percent of the American population*

ENTPs love excitement and challenge. Enthusiastic and ingenious, they are talkative, clever, and good at many things, constantly striving to increase their competence and personal power.

ENTPs are born enterprising. They are fascinated with new ideas and are alert to all possibilities. They have strong initiative and operate on creative impulse.

ENTPs value their inspiration above all else and strive to turn their original ideas into reality. They are inquisitive, versatile, adaptable, and resourceful in solving challenging and theoretical problems.

Alert and outspoken, ENTPs can easily see the flaw in any position and often enjoy arguing for fun on either side of an issue. They have excellent analytical abilities and are great strategic thinkers. They can almost always find a logical reason for the things that they want.

Most ENTPs like to test the limits around them and consider that most rules and regulations are meant to be bent, if not broken. They are sometimes unconventional in their approach and enjoy helping others to push past what is accepted and expected. They like to live freely and look for fun and variety in everyday situations.

ENTPs deal imaginatively with social relationships and often have a great number and variety of friends and acquaintances. They can display great humor and optimism. ENTPs can be charming and stimulating company and often inspire others to become involved in their projects through their infectious enthusiasm. They prefer to try to understand and respond to people rather than judge them.

Possible Blind Spots

Because ENTPs value creativity and innovation above all else, they sometimes ignore the standard way of doing something simply because it is not original. Their intense dislike for the routine and predictable can make it difficult for them to notice the necessary details. They sometimes neglect the needed preparation when, in their zeal to take on something fresh, they dive in too quickly. And once major problems are solved, they are often off to the next exciting adventure rather than sticking around to see the original project through. They need to work toward making commitments to fewer projects so they will complete more of the ones they start.

Often, ENTPs talk so quickly, and so much, they don't allow others to contribute. They are honest and fair but can be blunt and tactless in their ready criticism of others. ENTPs need to consider the feelings of others as valid and important, even if they don't share them. While they can be charming, funny, and entertaining, they can also be insincere. ENTPs need to resist the urge to simply adapt and perform, and instead share their genuine emotions.

ENTPs' reluctance to commit to one thing stems from the fear that they may miss other, more appealing opportunities. Their desire to remain open and responsive to new challenges can make them undependable and inconsiderate of the plans and schedules of others. Thinking through how their actions affect others will help them be more dependable.

ENTPs' natural quickness and ability to anticipate what is coming means they occasionally assume erroneously that they knew what the person was going to say, and may jump in to finish their sentences. Taking the time to pay closer attention to what is actually going on in the real world around them and listening carefully to the input and reactions of others will help them avoid appearing arrogant and rude.

∥ INTP
Introverted, Intuitive, Thinking, Perceiving
Approximately 3–5 percent of the American population

INTPs are conceptual problem solvers. They are intensely intellectual and logical, with flashes of creative brilliance.

Outwardly quiet, reserved, and detached, INTPs are inwardly absorbed in analyzing problems. They are critical, precise, and skeptical. They try to find and use principles to understand their many ideas. They like conversation to be logical and purposeful and may argue to the point of hairsplitting just for fun. INTPs are convinced only by logical reasoning.

INTPs are usually ingenious and original thinkers. They prize intelligence in themselves, have a strong drive for personal competence, and are interested in challenging other people to become more competent as well. INTPs are primarily interested in seeing possibilities beyond what is currently known, accepted, or obvious. They like to develop models for improving the way things are or solving difficult problems. They think in extremely complex ways and are better able to organize concepts and ideas than they are able to organize people. Occasionally, their ideas are so complex they have difficulty communicating and making others understand them.

Highly independent, INTPs enjoy speculative and imaginative activities. They are flexible and open-minded and are more interested in finding creative yet sound solutions to problems than they are in seeing those solutions made into reality.

Possible Blind Spots

Because INTPs rely so heavily on their logical analysis, they can overlook what matters to others. If something is not logical, INTPs run the risk of dismissing it, even if it is important to them. Admitting to themselves what they really care about will help them stay in touch with their true feelings.

INTPs are excellent at detecting the flaws in an idea but are more reticent about expressing their appreciation. They can get bogged down on a minor flaw in one part of a plan and keep the entire project from moving toward completion because they refuse to let one illogical point remain within the whole. When they turn their highly honed critical thinking skills on the people around them, their naked honesty may translate into unintended hurtfulness. They need to be told, and need to learn to ask, what matters emotionally to others.

Because INTPs are fascinated with solving problems, they tend to be impatient with routine details and may lose interest in a project and never complete it if it requires too much follow-through or detail. Turning their energy outward will enable them to gain sufficient practical knowledge to make their ideas workable and acceptable to other people.

INTPs sometimes feel inadequate when they try to live up to their own high standards of perfection. Learning to share those feelings with someone else can help them get a more realistic and objective view of themselves.

ESTJ
Extraverted, Sensing, Thinking, Judging
Approximately 8–12 percent of the American population

ESTJs are great at getting things done. They like to run the show and make things happen. They are responsible, conscientious, and faithful to their commitments. They like structure and can remember and organize many details. They systematically set about achieving their goals on schedule and as efficiently as possible.

ESTJs are driven to make decisions. Often they base their decisions on their own past experience. They are logical, objective, and analytical and have great reasoning power. In fact, they are unlikely to be persuaded by anything but logic.

ESTJs are realistic, practical, and matter-of-fact. They are more interested in "real things" than in intangibles, such as abstract ideas and theories. They tend to not be interested in subjects for which they see no practical application. They know what's happening around them and are concerned primarily with the here and now.

Because they live by a certain set of rules, ESTJs are consistent and dependable. They tend to be traditional and interested in maintaining established institutions. They are consistent in their relationships, although their emotional and social life is not as important to them as other aspects of life. They are comfortable judging others, and can be crisp disciplinarians.

ESTJs are outgoing, sociable, direct, and friendly. They are usually easy to get to know, since what you see is what you get.

Possible Blind Spots

Because ESTJs adopt a strict code of ethics for both themselves and others, they can be seen as dictatorial when they attempt to impose their standards of behavior on others. Attempting to be more flexible and open-minded will prevent an ESTJ from becoming rigid.

Being logical and impersonal analysts, ESTJs don't naturally consider the impact their decisions have on others. They can be seen as cold and uncaring, and often need to become more aware of their own feelings as well as more respectful of the thoughts and feelings of others.

Since they are naturally critical, ESTJs usually don't demonstrate their appreciation of the positive attributes or contributions of those around them. They need to try to become more aware of the talents and efforts of others, and then offer compliments and praise.

Sometimes ESTJs are so intent on their own plans that they don't stop to listen to what others have to say. They don't naturally ask "what if," so they often miss possible meanings, implications, connections, and patterns. An easy way to protect against being close-minded is to wait a few seconds before speaking, giving others a chance to offer input.

ESTJs often jump to conclusions without gathering all the necessary information or taking the time to fully understand a situation. They need to learn to consciously delay making decisions until they have considered more information, especially alternatives they may have overlooked.

ESTJs who have been able to relinquish some of the control they seek and who have learned to see that there are gray areas in life (rather than seeing things only in black and white) become more adaptable and successful.

∥ ISTJ
Introverted, Sensing, Thinking, Judging
Approximately 11–14 percent of the American population

ISTJs are the serious, responsible, and sensible stalwarts of society. They are trustworthy and honor their commitments. Their word is their solemn vow.

Practical and realistic, ISTJs are matter-of-fact and thorough. They are painstakingly accurate and methodical, with great powers of concentration. Whatever they are doing they accomplish with orderliness and reliability. They have unshakable, well-thought-out ideas and are difficult to distract or discourage once they have embarked on what they believe to be the best course of action.

Characteristically quiet and hardworking, ISTJs have great practical judgment and memory for details. They can cite accurate evidence to support their views and apply their past experiences to their present decisions. They value and use logic and impersonal analysis, are organized and systematic in their approach to following things through and getting them done on time. They follow necessary systems and procedures and are impatient with those who do not.

ISTJs are cautious and traditional. They listen well and like things to be factual and clearly stated. ISTJ will tend to say what they mean and mean what they say. Private by nature, ISTJs appear calm even during times of crisis. They are duty bound and steadfast, but beneath their calm facade, they may have strong yet rarely expressed reactions.

Possible Blind Spots

A common problem for ISTJs is their tendency to lose themselves in the details and daily operations of a project. Once immersed, they can be rigid and unwilling to adapt or accept another point of view. They tend to be skeptical of new ideas if they don't see their immediate and practical application. They need to take time to look at their overall objectives and consider alternatives they may not have considered. Gathering a wider range of information and consciously trying to anticipate the future implications of their behavior will increase the ISTJ's effectiveness in all areas.

ISTJs sometimes have trouble understanding the needs of others, especially those that are different from their own. Because they keep their reactions private, they can be perceived as cold and unfeeling. They need to express their appreciation for others directly rather than keeping it to themselves.

Because they are logical, ISTJs tend to expect others to be so as well. They run the risk of imposing their judgments on others and overriding the opinions of less assertive people. They can demand conformity to their way of doing things and discourage more creative or innovative approaches. By staying open to untested or unconventional methods, they will develop more tolerance for differences in people, and also end up with more effective alternatives and options.

▌ ESFJ
Extraverted, Sensing, Feeling, Judging
Approximately 9–13 percent of the American population

ESFJs are motivated to help other people in real and practical ways through direct action and cooperation. They are responsible, friendly, and sympathetic.

Because ESFJs place such importance on their relationships with other people, they tend to be popular, gracious, eager to please, and talkative. They need harmonious relationships with others and work hard to achieve and maintain them. In fact, they often idealize whatever or whomever they admire. ESFJs need to be appreciated for themselves and their service, so they are highly sensitive to indifference or criticism. They usually express strong opinions and are decisive, and they like to have things settled.

Practical and realistic, ESFJs tend to be matter-of-fact and organized. They attend to and remember important facts and details and like others to be sure of their facts as well. They base their planning and opinions on their own personal experience or that of someone else they trust. They are aware of and involved with their physical environment and like to be active and productive.

Because ESFJs are conscientious and traditional, they are bound by their sense of duty and commitments. They nurture established institutions and tend to be active and cooperative members of committees and organizations. Their social ties are important and well maintained. They often go out of their way to do something helpful and nice for someone else and especially enjoy being responsive in times of trouble or great celebration.

Possible Blind Spots

Because ESFJs value harmony so highly, they tend to avoid conflicts rather than deal with problems head-on. They sometimes place too much importance and value on the opinions and feelings of those they care for. During tense or hurtful times, they can become blind to the facts of the situation. They need to learn to deal directly and honestly with conflict, trusting that their natural sensitivity to others' feelings will provide them with the necessary tact in even the most difficult situations.

ESFJs often overlook their own needs because of their desire to please or help other people. They have a difficult time saying no or asking for help because they don't want to risk offending or disappointing anyone. They usually have trouble giving or accepting constructive criticism because they take things so personally. They can become pessimistic and gloomy when they don't see ways to make changes in their lives. Taking a step back from their problems to get some objectivity usually helps them gain a fresh outlook.

In their efforts to help other people, ESFJs sometimes express their strong opinions in ways that are bossy and domineering. They do better to wait to find out if their help or suggestions are really wanted before offering them.

ESFJs often make decisions too quickly, before they've had adequate time to gather all the less obvious facts and consider the implications of their actions. They don't tend to look for new or different ways of doing things and can appear inflexible. Postponing judgments in favor of staying open to novel approaches to problems will give them a better base of information and help them make better decisions.

ISFJ
Introverted, Sensing, Feeling, Judging
Approximately 9–14 percent of the American population

ISFJs are loyal, devoted, compassionate, and perceptive about how other people feel. They are conscientious and responsible and enjoy being needed.

ISFJs are down-to-earth and realistic people and prefer others who are quiet and unassuming. They absorb and enjoy using a large number of facts. With great memories for details, they are patient with the follow-through phase of tasks. ISFJs like things to be clearly and explicitly stated.

Because they have a strong work ethic, they accept responsibility for things that need to be done, if they can see that their actions will actually help. They are painstakingly accurate and systematic in handling tasks. ISFJs tend to be conservative, with traditional values. They use practical judgment in making decisions and lend stability through their excellent commonsense perspective.

Quiet and modest, ISFJs are serious and hardworking. They are gentle, sympathetic, tactful, and supportive of friends and colleagues. They like to care for others and prefer to help in practical and tangible ways. They use personal warmth to communicate, and they relate well to people in need. ISFJs tend not to show their private feelings but have an intensely personal reaction to most situations and events. They are protective and devoted to their friends, service-minded, and committed to meeting their obligations.

Possible Blind Spots

Because ISFJs live so completely in the present, they have trouble seeing events in global terms or anticipating the possible outcomes of a situation, especially when it is unfamiliar. They need help looking beyond the moment and imagining what might or could be if things were done differently.

ISFJs can become mired in the daily grind and the unending work around them, both their own and others' for whom they feel responsible. They can easily become overworked, doing everything themselves to be sure that tasks are completed meticulously. Because they are not naturally assertive or tough-minded, they risk being taken advantage of. They need to express their frequently bottled-up feelings of resentment so they don't find themselves in the rescuing role. They also need to let other people know their needs and their accomplishments.

ISFJs often need extra time to master technical subjects. They tend to plan excessively and need to develop strategies that will help them refocus the energy they often expend worrying. ISFJs need to find ways of getting the much-needed enjoyment and relaxation they deserve.

‖ ESTP
Extraverted, Sensing, Thinking, Perceiving
Approximately 4–5 percent of the American population

ESTPs don't worry—they're happy! Active, easygoing, and spontaneous, ESTPs enjoy the present moment rather than planning for the future.

Extremely realistic, ESTPs rely on and trust what their senses tell them about their world. They are curious and keen observers. Because they accept things as they are, they tend to be open-minded and tolerant of others and themselves. ESTPs like real things that can be handled, taken apart, and put back together.

ESTPs prefer action to conversation and enjoy dealing with situations as they arise. They are good problem solvers because they can absorb necessary factual information and then find logical and sensible solutions quickly, without a lot of wasted effort or energy. They can be diplomatic negotiators, happy to try unconventional approaches and usually able to persuade other people to give their compromises a chance. They are able to grasp underlying principles and make decisions based on what is logical rather than on how they feel about things. Therefore they are pragmatic and can be tough when the situation warrants.

Friendly and charming, ESTPs are popular and at ease in most social situations. They are outgoing, versatile, and funny, and may have an endless supply of jokes and stories for whatever situation they find themselves in. They can be good at easing tense situations by lightening up the atmosphere and getting conflicting parties together.

Possible Blind Spots

ESTPs' preference for living in the moment and adopting an "emergency" style of responding to unexpected crises can result in a chaotic environment for those around them. They may miss opportunities through lack of planning. They sometimes take on too much at one time and find themselves overloaded and unable to keep their commitments. ESTPs need to look beyond the current moment and their interest in the material world to try to anticipate ways of finishing tasks on time.

ESTPs also tend to overlook other people's feelings and may be blunt and insensitive in their desire to be honest, especially when they are rushing from one experience to another. Their flamboyance can sometimes be perceived as crudeness and may alienate the people they are trying to entertain. ESTPs become more effective with others when they direct their keen powers of observation to be sensitive to the people around them. They are more effective when they rein in their boldness, energy, and love of a good time to a level where other people are more comfortable.

More interested in solving problems quickly and effortlessly, ESTPs tend to jump directly into the next crisis and not follow through on the less exciting portions of current projects. They do well to learn and apply time management and long-range planning techniques to help them prepare for and complete responsibilities. Slowing down to develop standards for their own behavior and considering the ramifications of their actions will make them more effective.

ISTP
Introverted, Sensing, Thinking, Perceiving
Approximately 4–6 percent of the American population

ISTPs are straightforward, honest, and pragmatic people who prefer action to conversation. They are unpretentious and often have a good understanding of the way things work.

Because they are analytical, ISTPs are most interested in the impersonal and underlying principles of things. ISTPs have an innate understanding of how mechanical things work and are usually skilled at using tools and working with their hands. They tend to make logical and private decisions, stating things clearly and directly, just as they see them.

Curious and observant, ISTPs tend to be convinced only by hard, reliable facts. They have a great respect for facts and can be veritable storehouses of information on the things they know well and understand. Because they are realists, they are able to capitalize well on available resources, which makes them practical, with a good sense of timing.

Quiet and reserved, ISTPs tend to appear cool and aloof and are inclined toward shyness, except when with good friends. They are self-leading, egalitarian, and fair. They tend to operate on impulse, so they are quite adaptable and responsive to immediate challenges and problems. Because they thrive on excitement and action, they usually like the outdoors and sports.

Possible Blind Spots

Because ISTPs make judgments privately, they often keep even the most important issues to themselves, which leaves the people in their lives in the dark about what is going on. They have difficulty sharing their reactions, feelings, and concerns with others because it seems unnecessary to them. They need to accept that other people want and need to know what is going on in their lives and realize they are the only ones who can provide an accurate explanation.

ISTPs are so realistic that they can usually see ways of minimizing effort on almost all projects. Because of their desire to have free time, they often don't prepare more than is absolutely necessary or may not stick with a project to its conclusion. This can lead them to cut corners. Mapping out a plan, complete with all the steps and details, will help them curb their potential lack of initiative and reduce their apparent indifference.

Because ISTPs are constantly on the alert for new sensory information and prefer to keep all their options open, they may be indecisive. Their need for excitement can make them reckless and also easily bored. Setting goals and making serious commitments to people and things will help them avoid the common disappointments and dangers of such a potentially haphazard lifestyle.

‖ ESFP
Extraverted, Sensing, Feeling, Perceiving
Approximately 4–9 percent of the American population

ESFPs enjoy people and have a real zest for living. They are playful and vivacious, and make things more fun for others by their pure and unabashed enjoyment.

Adaptable and easygoing, ESFPs are warm, friendly, and generous. They are extremely sociable and are often "on stage" with others. They enthusiastically and cooperatively join in activities and games and are usually juggling several activities at once.

ESFPs are realistic observers and see and accept things as they are. They tend to trust what they can hear, smell, taste, touch, and see instead of theoretical explanations. Because they like concrete facts and have good memories for details, they learn best from hands-on experience. Their common sense gives them practical abilities with people and things. They prefer to gather information and see what solutions naturally arise.

Tolerant and accepting of themselves and others, ESFPs don't tend to try to impose their will on other people. Tactful and sympathetic, ESFPs are generally and genuinely liked by many people. They are usually able to get people to adopt their suggestions, so they are good at helping conflicting factions get back together. They seek out the company of others and are good conversationalists. They enjoy helping other people, preferring to assist in real and tangible ways.

Spontaneous and charming, ESFPs are persuasive. They love surprises and finding ways of bringing delight and unexpected pleasure to others.

Possible Blind Spots

Because ESFPs place such a strong priority on experiencing and enjoying life, they sometimes allow their other responsibilities to suffer. Their constant socializing can interfere and get them into trouble, and because they are so easily tempted, they have difficulty disciplining themselves. ESFPs' tendency to become distracted from finishing the tasks they start can make them appear unmotivated. By working to prioritize their activities, and finding a balance between work and play, they will gain a broader perspective and longer-range vision for their lives. Using successful and accepted methods of organization and time management helps them overcome this natural predisposition.

Their active life keeps them so busy, they fail to plan ahead. This can leave them unprepared for life's changes that would be easier to cope with if clues of their approach had been noticed. ESFPs need to try to anticipate what might be coming down the road and develop an alternative plan in case things become unpleasant.

ESFPs also tend to make decisions without considering the logical consequences of their actions. Their own personal feelings are trusted and used to the exclusion of more objective data. Friends are so highly valued by ESFPs that they tend to look only at their positive sides. ESFPs need to take a step back to consider the cause and effect of actions and work toward becoming more tough-minded. Saying no will not be nearly as difficult if they do.

ISFP
Introverted, Sensing, Feeling, Perceiving
Approximately 5–9 percent of the American population

ISFPs are gentle, caring, and sensitive people, who keep much of their intensely personal ideals and values to themselves. They more often express their deeply felt passions through actions than through words.

Modest and reserved, ISFPs are really tremendously warm and enthusiastic people but tend not to show that side of themselves except with people they know well and trust fully. ISFPs tend to be misunderstood because of their tendency not to express themselves directly.

ISFPs are patient, flexible, and easy to get along with and have little need to dominate or control others. They are nonjudgmental and accepting of others' behavior in a rather matter-of-fact way. They are observant of people and things around them and do not seek to find motives or meanings.

Because ISFPs live in the present moment, they do not tend to prepare or plan more than is necessary. They are relaxed about getting things done because they are fully engaged in the here and now and like to enjoy the current experience without rushing on to the next.

Interested in what they learn and sense directly from their experiences and senses, they are often artistic and aesthetic, and seek to create beautiful and personal environments for themselves.

Without the need to lead, ISFPs are often loyal followers and good team members. Because they use their personal values to judge everything in life, they like other people who take the time to get to know them and understand their inner loyalties. Basically trusting and understanding, they need harmonious relationships in their lives and are sensitive to conflicts and disagreements.

Possible Blind Spots

The highly sensitive nature of ISFPs allows them to clearly see the needs of other people, and they sometimes work so excessively to fulfill those needs that they neglect themselves in the process. This can result in their becoming physically ill from exhaustion and overwork. They need to take time out from caring for others to take care of themselves.

Because they focus so completely on their experience in the moment, they tend not to look beyond the present, and miss the broader view. They sometimes have difficulty understanding things in a more complex context. Because they don't usually look for or see possibilities that don't exist at the present time, they don't tend to prepare in advance. They often have trouble organizing their time and resources. They may have to work hard to curb their impulse to go off and enjoy a quiet moment or participate in a favorite activity.

ISFPs are vulnerable to the criticism of others because they tend to take feedback personally and become offended and discouraged. They may be seen as gullible and too trusting because they accept people and things as they are and don't expect a malicious motive or read anything else into them. They need to become more assertive about their own needs and consider the implications of another's behavior. By applying some objectivity and skepticism to their analysis, they can become better judges of character.

Part Two | THE FORMULA FOR CAREER SATISFACTION

Now that you've discovered your true personality type, you may be wondering why we can't just point you to a career and send you on your way. Well, it isn't that simple. It is not true that certain personality types can find career satisfaction only in certain fields. People of your type, for example, don't "have" to be dentists, dog groomers, or designers. People of all types can find success in all fields. What matters most is finding the best job for you within each profession. As we've already seen, this depends on a solid understanding of yourself.

We've always known that Type is the key to career satisfaction, but it wasn't until recently that we realized exactly how to translate the intricacies of Personality Type into happiness and success in the workplace. We're now able to pinpoint the three aspects of Personality Type that are most important to people who are looking for career options that will be truly satisfying. Taken together, we call these three components the Formula for Career Satisfaction. The following three chapters examine each component in turn, as you will now see.

4 | WHAT A CHARACTER!
The Four Different Temperaments

You don't need us to tell you that people have different natures. But did you know that everybody can be divided into just four basic human temperaments?

Suppose your cousin is intense and excitable, but your neighbor is as steady as they come. This is in large part due to differences in their innate temperaments. If your cousin the thrill seeker takes a number-crunching job at an insurance company, chances are he'll be bored out of his head. Big mistake. If, however, he works for the same company doing field investigations of buildings that have burned to the ground, he has a better chance of being interested in his work—and therefore satisfied with it. And what about your dependable neighbor? He might be perfect for the number-crunching job!

Throughout history, philosophers, writers, psychologists, and other observers of humanity have noticed that there are four distinct "natures" into which all people fit. As far back as 450 B.C., Hippocrates described four different dispositions, or temperaments. In the Middle Ages, Paracelsus described four natures whose behavior was influenced by four kinds of spirits. The American Indian Medicine Wheel suggests four spirit keepers, similar to the temperaments, and Hindu wisdom postulates four central desires.

The psychologist David Keirsey was impressed that these four different temperaments, observed independently by people from diverse cultures and from different periods of history, all described remarkably similar characteristics. When he learned about Type through the work of Isabel Briggs Myers, he became intrigued with the relationship between Type and temperament. Many different labels have been used to identify the four temperaments. The names we use in this book, some borrowed and some original, were chosen because we feel they best describe each temperament's most central characteristic.

Keirsey determined that four combinations of type preferences correspond to the four temperaments people have posited throughout history. The four combinations are

"Traditionalists" (SJs) are people who prefer both **Sensing** and **Judging**.

"Experiencers" (SPs) are people who prefer both **Sensing** and **Perceiving**.

"Idealists" (NFs) are people who prefer both **Intuition** and **Feeling**.

"Conceptualizers" (NTs) are people who prefer both **Intuition** and **Thinking**.

Each of the sixteen personality types falls into one of these categories. In this book when we refer to temperament, sometimes we use the names, and other times the letter combinations (e.g., "Traditionalist" and "SJ"). We do this because some people find one easier to remember than the other. But *both* labels apply equally well. One way you can determine your temperament is to check the letters of your type. With SJs and SPs, they are the second and fourth letters. With NFs and NTs, they are the middle letters.

Traditionalists (SJs):	ESTJ	ISTJ	ESFJ	ISFJ
Experiencers (SPs):	ESTP	ISTP	ESFP	ISFP
Idealists (NFs):	ENFJ	INFJ	ENFP	INFP
Conceptualizers (NTs):	ENTJ	INTJ	ENTP	INTP

People with the same temperament have a great deal in common and tend to share certain core values. However, they are *not* all the same! People of each temperament come in four varieties. Their other preferences—Extraversion or Introversion, Thinking or Feeling, and Judging or Perceiving—give them very different personalities. Think of a particular temperament as a family of instruments. All stringed instruments, for example, have many important features in common, and yet there are obvious differences between a violin, a viola, a cello, and a double bass (not to mention a guitar and a piano). And they are *very* different from wind instruments.

Since it's important to find a job that suits your nature, we are now going to discuss the four human temperaments and how they best fit into the workplace. Within each discussion you'll find specific information regarding temperament-based strengths and blind spots. This will help you see how different personality types flourish in different settings, and it will help you begin to focus on the kind of work you would find personally satisfying. You may want to mark (or highlight or copy) your particular section once you've found it, for easy reference.

Even if you are already certain of your personality type, we suggest that you read about all four temperaments before deciding which one best describes you. For the time being, *do not* concern yourself with whether or not the letters of the temperament you choose match those of your personality type. There's a good chance they will—but there's also a possibility they won't.

Traditionalists (Sensing Judgers)
ESTJ ISTJ ESFJ ISFJ
Approximately 46 percent of the American population

You will recall that Sensors trust facts, proven data, previous experience, and the information their five senses bring them. Judgers prefer a structured, orderly world and are driven to make decisions. Taken together, these two preferences create a "Sensing Judger," a type of person who is down-to-earth and decisive, and whom we call a "Traditionalist."

The motto for Traditionalists might well be "If it ain't broke, don't fix it." Traditionalists, unsurprisingly, honor traditions and respect institutions. They value security, propriety, rules, and conformity. They are driven by a strong motivation to serve society's needs. Traditionalists respect authority, hierarchy, and the chain of command. They are bound by their sense of duty and always try to do the right thing, which makes them reliable, dependable, and, above all else, responsible.

Now because Traditionalists come in both Thinking (STJ) and Feeling (SFJ) varieties, there are clearly differences between them. Frequently, ESFJs and ISFJs won't identify as strongly with the Traditionalist description as their ESTJ and ISTJ friends do. For ESFJs and ISFJs the connection with others and the people-oriented criteria for decision making are critically important. So while most Traditionalists (regardless of their judgment preference) are happiest in occupations where the structure is clear and the expectations explicit, those with a Feeling preference will strive for harmonious affiliations with others and seek opportunities to do work that lets them help others in tangible ways.

Traditionalists at Work

Traditionalists need to belong, to serve, and to do the right thing. They value stability, orderliness, cooperation, consistency, and reliability, and they tend to be serious and hardworking. Traditionalists demand a great deal of themselves on the job and expect the same of others.

Strengths. Traditionalists are practical, organized, thorough, and systematic. They pay attention to regulations, policies, contracts, rituals, and timelines. They are excellent at guarding, monitoring, and regulating. Traditionalists prefer to deal with proven facts and use them to further the goals of the organization to which they belong. They take great pride in doing something right the first time and every time. They are good at seeing what needs attention and at getting the job done with the available resources as efficiently as possible. Once they've committed themselves, Traditionalists always follow through. At their best, Traditionalists are solid, trustworthy, and dependable.

Potential blind spots. Traditionalists are not particularly interested in theories or abstractions, and the future doesn't attract their attention as much as the present. Long-range vision usually is not one of their strengths. Traditionalists sometimes make decisions too quickly. They tend to see things in black and white rather than in shades of gray. They run the risk of being unable to change or to adapt quickly, and they tend to resist trying approaches that are new, different, or untested. They are likely to want to see proof that a solution will work before seriously considering it. At their worst, Traditionalists can be inflexible, dogmatic, and unimaginative.

A good job for a Traditionalist might be one that involves a relatively high level of responsibility within a stable institution that has a clear-cut chain of command. Since they like structure, they are generally comfortable in organizations that have a fair number of rules and standard ways of doing things. Traditionalists prefer working in an environment where both regulations and rewards are certain. (They *don't* like positions or organizations where everything is in a state of flux or confusion!) They prefer colleagues who share their dedication and respect for authority and who pull their own weight.

Traditionalists usually make good managers. They appreciate the need for structure and are often the mainstays of organizations, either in leadership or support positions. The role they most often play is that of the stabilizer—the maintainer of traditions and the status quo.

Remember how we said that people of all types can find satisfaction in all fields? For the purposes of this chapter, let's use the field of law enforcement as an example. Some temperaments are more likely to gravitate to law enforcement than others, but all can find satisfaction in this area if they find a way of meeting their individual needs.

It's not unusual for Traditionalists to become police officers. In fact, in some studies, more than 50 percent of police officers in a given area fit this temperament! This line of work appeals to them because a high priority of theirs is protecting and serving society. They find enforcing social rules, maintaining order, and aiding those in distress intrinsically satisfying.

Many police officers are also Experiencers—the next temperament we'll discuss—but they are attracted to law enforcement for different reasons, as you'll see.

|| Experiencers (Sensing Perceivers)
ESTP ISTP ESFP ISFP
Approximately 27 percent of the American population

Sensors, you'll remember, concentrate on what can be seen, heard, felt, smelled, or tasted, and trust whatever can be measured or documented. Perceivers like to stay open to all kinds of possibilities and prefer to live in a flexible way. Taken together, these two preferences create a "Sensing Perceiver," a type of person who is responsive and spontaneous, and whom we call an "Experiencer."

The motto for Experiencers might well be "Life is for living!" They are definitely the most adventurous of the four temperaments. They live for action, impulse, and the present moment. They focus on the immediate situation and have the ability to assess what needs to be done *now*. Since Experiencers value freedom and spontaneity, they seldom choose activities or situations that impose too much structure or too many rules. They are risk taking, adaptable, easygoing, and pragmatic. They admire skillful execution in any field or discipline. Many, but not all, are thrill seekers who like living on the edge.

Experiencers at Work

Experiencers need to be active and free to act on their impulses. In their work, they focus on what can be accomplished in the here and now. They value heroic deeds and masterful acts and like moving from one challenge to the next.

Like Traditionalists, Experiencers also come in two varieties, STPs and SFPs. Like their SFJ friends, some SFPs don't fully agree with the description of Experiencer temperament because it doesn't include their natural desire to help others or make decisions that are congruent with their values. So while all Experiencers are typically most satisfied in careers that are relatively free of excessive rules, planning, and structure, SFPs usually want to respond primarily to the needs of others and feel their work is making a difference to people in ways that are immediate.

Strengths. Experiencers can see clearly what is happening and are agile at seizing opportunities. They are excellent at recognizing practical problems and approach them with flexibility, courage, and resourcefulness. They are not afraid to take risks or improvise as needed. Because they are not invested in tradition the way Traditionalists are, Experiencers enjoy making changes in response to some immediate need or crisis. However, like Traditionalists, they prefer to deal with facts and real problems rather than theories or ideas. Experiencers are keen observers of human behavior and can be good negotiators. They are efficient, and use an economy of effort in achieving their goals. Many Experiencers (but not all) are especially skillful with tools and instruments, things they can physically manipulate and which require precision. At their best, they can be resourceful, exciting, and fun.

Potential blind spots. Experiencers often are not predictable to others, and they sometimes fail to think things through carefully before acting. They are not much interested in the theoretical, abstract, or conceptual, and they may fail to see important connections or patterns linking events. Experiencers tend to lose enthusiasm once the crisis phase of any given situation is over. Since they prefer to keep their options open, they don't always follow established rules and they sometimes avoid commitments and plans. At their worst, they can be irresponsible, unreliable, and impulsive.

A good job for an Experiencer might be one that provides autonomy, variety, and action. They prefer work that brings immediate results, and they enjoy being able to execute tasks skillfully and successfully. Since they like to have fun, whatever they do must give them a high degree of pleasure if it is to be satisfying.

Although they are not naturally drawn to structured organizations, Experiencers can find a niche in the role of corporate "firefighter"—the person who notices and responds to crises. And they are often involved in occupations that allow them to use acquired skills, often involving tools, independently and spontaneously.

Now that you're familiar with this temperament, can you guess why many Experiencers are drawn to law enforcement? According to some studies, as many as 25 percent of many U.S. police forces are Experiencers. Many become police officers because of the excitement, the unpredictability, and even the danger that can await them with every new door they knock on or car they pull over. For many Experiencers, the job of police officer satisfies their need for action, spontaneity, and fully experiencing the moment.

‖ Idealists (iNtuitive Feelers)
ENFJ INFJ ENFP INFP
Approximately 16 percent of the American population

Intuitives, you'll recollect, are interested in meanings, relationships, and possibilities. Feelers make decisions based on personal values. Taken together, these two preferences create an "Intuitive Feeler," a type of person who is concerned about personal growth and understanding for themselves and others, and whom we call an "Idealist."

The motto of Idealists might well be "To thine own self be true." They are the most spiritually philosophical of the four temperaments. It's as if they are on a perpetual search for the meaning of life. They place a very high value on authenticity and integrity in people and relationships and tend to idealize others. Idealists focus on human potential and are often gifted at helping others grow and develop, a task that gives them great satisfaction. They are often excellent communicators and can be thought of as catalysts for positive change.

Idealists at Work

Idealists enjoy using their natural ability to understand and connect with other people. They are naturally empathetic and focus on the needs of the people involved in their work—for example, employees, colleagues, patients, or clients.

Strengths. Idealists know how to bring out the best in others and understand how to motivate others to do their best work. They are excellent at resolving conflicts and at helping people work together more effectively, and have the ability to help people feel good about themselves and their jobs. Idealists are good at identifying creative solutions to problems. They bring vision, innovation, and often an artistic sensibility to their work. Idealists communicate well in speech and writing and can generate enthusiasm for their ideas and actions. At their best, they are charismatic, receptive, and accepting.

Potential blind spots. Idealists have a tendency to make decisions based exclusively on their own personal likes and dislikes. They have trouble staying detached. They tend to take other people's problems to heart and can become too involved and overwhelmed as a result. Sometimes they are too idealistic and not practical enough. Idealists are not particularly good at disciplining or criticizing others, although they have a great capacity for self-reproach. Sometimes they will sacrifice their own opinion for the sake of harmony. At their worst, they can be moody, unpredictable, and impractical.

A good job for an Idealist is one that is personally meaningful rather than simply routine or expedient. They value harmony and do not flourish in a competitive or divisive arena. And they prefer organizations that are democratic and that encourage a high degree of participation from people at all levels.

Idealists gravitate toward organizations that promote humanistic values or toward jobs that allow them to help others find fulfillment. They are often found in human resources or personnel positions, as well as in teaching, consulting, counseling, and the arts.

Where do you suppose Idealists fit into the field of law enforcement? Studies show that they make up well under 10 percent of most police forces, and they usually don't end up on the beat. Instead, they almost unfailingly find their way to the human resources department, community outreach programs, or training or development programs where they can use their natural gifts in reaching out to others.

Conceptualizers (iNtuitive Thinkers)
ENTJ INTJ ENTP INTP
Approximately 10 percent of the American population

By now you know that Intuitives look for meanings in all things and focus on implications, and you'll remember that Thinkers make decisions impersonally and logically. Taken together, these two preferences create an "Intuitive Thinker," a type of person who is intellectual and competent, and whom we call a "Conceptualizer."

The motto for Conceptualizers might well be "Be excellent in all things." They are the most independent of the four temperaments, driven to acquire knowledge and setting very high standards for themselves and others. Naturally curious, Conceptualizers usually can see many sides to the same argument or issue. Conceptualizers are excellent at seeing possibilities, understanding complexities, and designing solutions to real or hypothetical problems. Their role is often that of the architect of change.

Conceptualizers at Work

Conceptualizers enjoy using their abilities to see possibilities and analyze them logically to solve problems. They are interested in constantly acquiring knowledge, either for its own sake or for a strategic purpose.

Strengths. Conceptualizers have vision and can be great innovators. They can see possibilities as well as the big picture, and they can conceptualize and design necessary changes within an organization. They excel at (and enjoy) strategizing, planning, and building systems to accomplish their goals. Conceptualizers understand complex, theoretical ideas and are good at deducing principles or trends. They enjoy being challenged, are demanding of themselves and others, and can usually accept constructive criticism without taking it personally. At their best, they are confident, witty, and imaginative.

Potential blind spots. Sometimes Conceptualizers can be too complex for others to understand. They have a tendency to overlook necessary details. They can be deeply skeptical and often challenge rules, assumptions, or customs. They also sometimes have trouble with authority and can be seen as elitist. Conceptualizers often fail to see how they affect others, and they may not be interested in either harmony or the importance of feelings. They can be fiercely competitive and will sometimes not bother with a project or activity if they don't think they will excel at it. At their worst, Conceptualizers can be arrogant, remote, and in a world of their own.

A good job for a Conceptualizer might be one that provides autonomy, variety, plenty of intellectual stimulation, and the opportunity to generate ideas, and they must find their work challenging to be satisfying. Since they can be impatient with others whom they consider less competent than they, Conceptualizers need to be surrounded by very capable supervisors, colleagues, and employees. Many Conceptualizers value power and gravitate toward powerful positions or people.

Because their need for competence is so strong, Conceptualizers are often found in leadership positions. They show up in college-level teaching positions, in upper management, in the sciences or computer fields, and in medicine or law in great numbers.

You can probably guess where Conceptualizers end up on the police force. Although not found in law enforcement in large numbers, they can represent as much as 20 percent of upper management. High-level positions give them a chance to tackle complex problems, the opportunity to apply their vision and logic to long-range strategic plans, and the power they enjoy.

Temperaments in a Teapot

A peek into a staff meeting at a hospital will illustrate the strengths of each of the four temperaments. You can see that the department heads have very different concerns, but that each makes a vital contribution to the meeting.

Susan, the director of planning and marketing, is a Conceptualizer (Intuitive Thinker). She presents a proposal for a new Women's Health Services unit at the hospital. A potentially lucrative source of revenue, the unit would offer a wide range of medical services exclusively for women. It would provide both diagnostic and surgical services and would offer procedures and equipment on the cutting edge of technology. Susan's plan includes marketing the unit's expert, well-respected staff of physicians and technicians; she thinks it's very possible that the unit would create a competitive environment among hospitals, putting them in a position to choose the best personnel and to be seen as a leader in healthcare.

Ross, the director of finance, is a Traditionalist (Sensing Judger). He recommends a full investigation of comparable centers around the nation to determine their operating costs and to establish realistic start-up costs for the new unit. He cautions the group about starting too quickly before feasibility studies and certificate-of-need applications have been fully researched and documented. *If* the data supports the creation of the new unit, Ross recommends that they commit only to a three-year trial operation to reduce the overall risk to the hospital's fiscal stability. He cites the need for cost comparison studies to determine the best pricing strategies, and cost containment plans to keep overhead low while maintaining a realistic operating budget.

Raquel, the director of operations, is an Experiencer (Sensing Perceiver). She suggests that a task force be mobilized immediately to begin gathering information about the staff, materials, and equipment already on hand that could be appropriated for the new unit before any new purchases are made. She recommends that bids be solicited from construction and contracting firms, and she suggests that all negotiations be handled through her office. Raquel is concerned that if the hospital does not open the new unit relatively quickly, it will lose its opportunity to be an innovator as other hospitals try similar approaches. She encourages the group to work expediently and efficiently without an excessive number of meetings and without a lot of emails back and forth—in other words, to strike while the iron is hot.

Michael, the director of human resources, is an Idealist (Intuitive Feeler). He is enthusiastic about the new unit and recommends that it be designed to serve women of all social and economic backgrounds. Michael reminds the group that some employees and members of the community may see the new unit as a threat to their jobs. He points out the need for employee and community support for the project, and recommends that the hospital make continuous efforts to maintain enthusiasm for the unit through a variety of communication activities, including employee meetings, individual questionnaires, and a public information campaign aimed at residents and neighboring hospitals. He also recommends groundbreaking ceremonies, grand opening tours, and similar community-oriented events.

Which Temperament Are You?

By now you have probably identified which of the four temperaments you relate to most closely. Which one suits you best?

Traditionalist (SJ)   Experiencer (SP)

Idealist (NF)   Conceptualizer (NT)

What personality type did you think fit you in Part 1? _____

If your type is consistent with your choice of temperament, this is further verification that you have found your true type.

If your personality type is not consistent with your choice of temperament, there's a chance that you did not correctly identify your true personality type in Part 1. For example, let's say you thought you were an ENFP, but you relate strongly to the Conceptualizer temperament. It's possible that you really *are* an ENTP and not an ENFP. We suggest that you go back to Chapter 3 and read the Verifying Type Profiles for both ENFP and ENTP to see which one sounds most like you.

Suppose you reread the Profiles in Chapter 3 and still think you're an ENFP. Don't despair! There's another possible explanation for your conflicting results. As we grow older, we all naturally "round out" our personalities by developing our weaker preferences. This process is called **type development**, and we explain it in detail in Chapter 6. Briefly, in this situation it means that you really could be an ENFP but that you are busy developing your Thinking, which leads you to relate more strongly to the Conceptualizer temperament. By the time you've finished Chapter 6, you should have a good idea of how type development works, which will help you make your final decision about your true personality type.

Much of our own general knowledge about temperament has come from the excellent resource *Introduction to Temperament* by Louise Giovannoni, Ph.D., Linda Berens, Ph.D., and Sue Cooper, Ph.D.

5 | WHO'S ON FIRST?

Identifying Your Innate Strengths

The second ingredient in the Formula for Career Satisfaction is understanding which aspects of your personality are strongest and which are weakest. Although all of your preferences play important roles, certain preferences within each personality type are more powerful than others. Since you want to operate from a position of strength while you're at work, it makes sense for you to identify carefully which preferences you use most easily and most successfully.

The Type Functions

You will recall that Extraversion and Introversion are the two different ways we interact with the world, and that Judging and Perceiving are the two different ways we prefer to construct our lives. These four preferences are reflected in the first and last letters of your personality type. We refer to them as the **attitudes**.

You'll also remember that Sensing and Intuition are the two different ways we take in information, and that Thinking and Feeling are the two different ways we make decisions. These four preferences are reflected in the two middle letters of your personality type. We refer to them as the **functions**. The functions are the core of Type, and in this chapter we'll show you why.

	(E) Extraversion ———————+——————— Introversion (I)	
Functions	(S) Sensing ——————+—————— Intuition (N) (T) Thinking ——————+—————— Feeling (F)	
	(J) Judging ———————+——————— Perceiving (P)	

The Hierarchy of Functions

Each personality type has what is called a "hierarchy of functions." This hierarchy ranks your functions from strongest to weakest. Although you grow and change and develop your abilities over time, your hierarchy of functions stays the same throughout your life.

The hierarchy of functions does not rank all of your preferences (the letters of your personality type). It concerns only the functions (the middle two letters of your personality type). Since everyone uses all four functions to some extent, the hierarchy of functions includes both the functions you use most often (the preferences that are reflected in the letters of your personality type) and the functions you use less often (the letters that do not show up in your personality type).

For each personality type, there is one function that is the most important characteristic of that type—the captain of the ship, so to speak. We call this the **dominant function**. Any one of the four functions (Sensing, Intuition, Thinking, or Feeling) can be dominant, but for each personality type there is only one dominant function, and it always stays the same.

The next function in the hierarchy—the second-in-command—is called the **auxiliary function**. Again, there is only one auxiliary function for each personality type, and it never changes.

The dominant and auxiliary functions always refer to how you take in information (either Sensing or Intuition) and how you make decisions (either Thinking or Feeling). Since everyone needs to use both of these processes, the dominant and auxiliary functions never refer to the same process. If your dominant is an information-gathering function, then your auxiliary is a decision-making function, and vice versa.

The **third function** in the hierarchy of functions is always the opposite of your auxiliary function. The **fourth function** in your hierarchy of functions is always the opposite of your dominant function. In a way, it is a casualty of your dominant function. Since your dominant function is the most powerful preference in your personality, it figures that the opposite of this preference should be your weakest point. The fourth function is sometimes referred to as the inferior function—with good reason!

#1 Dominant Function
#2 Auxiliary Function
#3 Third Function (opposite of #2)
#4 Fourth Function (opposite of #1)

One way to understand the hierarchy of functions is to think of a family of four taking a car trip. There are two adults in the front seat: the dominant function is driving, and the auxiliary function is navigating. In the backseat are the two kids: the third function, who is about ten years old, and the fourth function, who is just a baby. Clearly, you want the dominant to be in charge (somebody has to drive!) and the auxiliary to help navigate. But you still have to pay attention to the other two (breaking up fights, stopping to go to the bathroom, etc.).

As long as your dominant and auxiliary are in command, you are functioning well. When your third and especially fourth functions take over, it's as if the kids climbed over the seat and started driving the car (with predictably disastrous results).

How do you know which functions are your dominant, auxiliary, third, and fourth? We'll tell you! Following is a table that shows the hierarchy of functions for each personality type. Take a moment to find yours.

The Hierarchy of Functions*†

ISTJ	ISFJ	INFJ	INTJ
1 Sensing	1 Sensing	1 Intuition	1 Intuition
2 Thinking	2 Feeling	2 Feeling	2 Thinking
3 Feeling	3 Thinking	3 Thinking	3 Feeling
4 Intuition	4 Intuition	4 Sensing	4 Sensing
ISTP	**ISFP**	**INFP**	**INTP**
1 Thinking	1 Feeling	1 Feeling	1 Thinking
2 Sensing	2 Sensing	2 Intuition	2 Intuition
3 Intuition	3 Intuition	3 Sensing	3 Sensing
4 Feeling	4 Thinking	4 Thinking	4 Feeling
ESTP	**ESFP**	**ENFP**	**ENTP**
1 Sensing	1 Sensing	1 Intuition	1 Intuition
2 Thinking	2 Feeling	2 Feeling	2 Thinking
3 Feeling	3 Thinking	3 Thinking	3 Feeling
4 Intuition	4 Intuition	4 Sensing	4 Sensing
ESTJ	**ESFJ**	**ENFJ**	**ENTJ**
1 Thinking	1 Feeling	1 Feeling	1 Thinking
2 Sensing	2 Sensing	2 Intuition	2 Intuition
3 Intuition	3 Intuition	3 Sensing	3 Sensing
4 Feeling	4 Thinking	4 Thinking	4 Feeling

*This chart is reproduced from *Introduction to Type in Organizations* by Sandra Krebs Hirsh and Jean M. Kummerow, page 9 (2nd edition, 1990), reprinted with permission of Consulting Psychologists Press, Inc.

†The formula for determining each type's hierarchy is complex and requires an in-depth explanation that we feel would be an unwelcome and unnecessary distraction to most readers. Therefore, we present the hierarchy and refer readers who wish to learn about the underlying theory to *Manual: A Guide to the Development and Use of the MBTI* by Isabel Briggs Myers and Mary McCaulley, published by Consulting Psychologists Press (Chapter 3, page 16).

Your Dominant Function

Your dominant function is the one in charge—the head honcho, the big enchilada, the top banana! It leads and directs your personality so that all of your functions are not constantly competing. Although everyone uses all four functions to some extent, the dominant function is the one you use most often and most naturally. People who have the same dominant function have a great deal in common, but they can also be very different, since their auxiliary functions and other preferences (don't forget the attitudes!) may vary.

If Sensing is the dominant function for your personality type, we call you a **Dominant Sensor**. You're not just a Sensor, you're a Super Sensor! Dominant Sensors usually pay extremely close attention to the facts and details of their experience. They trust and value above all else the data their five senses bring them, and their fundamental view of the world depends on exactly what they see, hear, touch, taste, and smell.

If Intuition is the dominant function for your personality type, we call you a **Dominant Intuitive**. You're not just an Intuitive, you're a Super Intuitive! Dominant Intuitives are much more interested in the meanings, possibilities, patterns, and relationships in what they perceive than they are in specifics or facts. Intuition dominates most—even all—of their perceptions. They look at a given situation and see implications and alternatives above all else.

If Thinking is the dominant function for your personality type, we call you a **Dominant Thinker**. You're not just a Thinker, you're a Super Thinker! Dominant Thinkers are driven to make decisions based on logic and impersonal analysis. Their immediate and strongest inclination is to come to a conclusion by looking at a given situation objectively, and it's hard for them to do otherwise.

If Feeling is the dominant function for your personality type, we call you a **Dominant Feeler**. You're not just a Feeler, you're a Super Feeler! Dominant Feelers are most comfortable making decisions based on their own personal values. They have a strong need to empathize, and they go through life constantly evaluating what is most important to themselves and to others.

Your Auxiliary Function

The auxiliary function balances the dominant function. It's the second-in-command, the counterweight, the Best Supporting Actor. It doesn't have a starring role, but it does play an essential one! As we've already mentioned, the auxiliary function is always a different process from the dominant function.

If your dominant function is either Sensing or Intuition (the information-gathering functions), your auxiliary function must be either Thinking or Feeling (the decision-making functions). Dominant Sensors and Dominant Intuitives naturally prefer to spend their time taking in information rather than making decisions. If you're a Dominant Sensor, there's a risk that you'll spend all your time collecting facts but never coming to any conclusions. If you're a Dominant

Intuitive, you may be so preoccupied with considering the possibilities that you may never take any action. This is where the auxiliary function kicks in. As second-in-command, it pushes you to make decisions based on the information you've gathered.

Most people have a reasonably strong auxiliary function, but occasionally you will meet a Dominant Sensor or a Dominant Intuitive who is unable to move from information gathering to decision making. Typically these people are either chronic procrastinators or are cripplingly indecisive. You can see why a strong auxiliary function is so important!

If your dominant function is either Thinking or Feeling (the decision-making functions), your auxiliary function must be either Sensing or Intuition (the information-gathering functions). Dominant Thinkers and Dominant Feelers naturally prefer to spend their time making decisions. If you're a Dominant Thinker, you are busy analyzing and critiquing everything. If you're a Dominant Feeler, you are eager to form opinions and determine how you feel about issues. Again, the auxiliary function helps balance your dominant function, in this case by pushing you to gather information before making judgments.

Occasionally you will meet a Dominant Thinker or a Dominant Feeler whose auxiliary function is extremely weak. These people are so driven to make decisions that they don't postpone making up their minds long enough to make sure they've collected all the information they need. They tend to be rigid, close-minded, and inflexible, whether their judgments are based on principles or personal values.

Of the sixteen personality types, four are Dominant Sensors, four are Dominant Intuitives, four are Dominant Thinkers, and four are Dominant Feelers. Let's take a look at each group.

Dominant Sensors
ISTJ ISFJ ESTP ESFP

Dominant Sensors—the Super Sensors!—trust facts and specifics above all else. However, Dominant Sensors come in four varieties, and they each do something a little different with data once they have gathered it.

ISTJs and ISFJs are both Dominant Sensors (they prefer facts), and they are both Introverted (they prefer to reflect on inner realities). Both types are traditional, practical, and organized. However, the auxiliary function for ISTJs is Thinking, which means that ISTJs focus on and gather impersonal facts, which they analyze. ISTJs tend to be matter-of-fact, sensible, and businesslike. The auxiliary function for ISFJs is Feeling, which means that ISFJs gather facts that relate to people and then base their decisions on their values, with a sensitivity to others. ISFJs tend to be loyal, patient, and service-minded.

ESTPs and ESFPs are both Dominant Sensors (they prefer facts), and they are both Extraverted (they focus on the specifics of the situation at hand). Both types are outgoing, adaptable, and energetic. Since the auxiliary function for

ESTPs is Thinking, they gather data and make decisions logically. ESTPs tend to be pragmatic, persuasive, and versatile. The auxiliary function for ESFPs is Feeling, which means that they make their decisions with more concern for others. ESFPs tend to be sociable, easygoing, and cooperative.

‖ Dominant Intuitives
‖ INTJ INFJ ENTP ENFP

Dominant Intuitives—the Super Intuitives!—see implications everywhere. Like Dominant Sensors, Dominant Intuitives come in four varieties, and they use the inferences they have gathered in different ways.

INTJs and INFJs are both Dominant Intuitives (they see implications), and they are both Introverted (they focus on inner meanings). Both types are original, visionary, and creative. However, the auxiliary function for INTJs is Thinking, which means that INTJs notice patterns and meanings and analyze them impersonally. INTJs tend to be logical, theoretical, and systems oriented. On the other hand, the auxiliary function for INFJs is Feeling, which means that INFJs see connections and associations and analyze them in humanistic terms. INFJs tend to be sensitive, compassionate, and holistic.

ENTPs and ENFPs are both Dominant Intuitives (they see implications), and they are both Extraverted (they naturally see all the possibilities around them). Both types are creative, perceptive, and imaginative. But the auxiliary function for ENTPs is Thinking, which means they are logical. ENTPs tend to be strategic, challenging, and theoretical. The auxiliary function for ENFPs is Feeling, which means they are people oriented. ENFPs tend to be curious, enthusiastic, and friendly.

‖ Dominant Thinkers
‖ INTP ISTP ENTJ ESTJ

Dominant Thinkers—the Super Thinkers!—have a strong drive to make logical decisions. However, the four varieties of Dominant Thinkers make their analyses in different ways.

INTPs and ISTPs are both Dominant Thinkers (they are very logical), and they are both Introverted (they use their own objective criteria to understand the world). Both types are independent and analytical. However, the auxiliary function for INTPs is Intuition, which means they are comfortable with the conceptual and abstract. INTPs tend to be original, speculative, and theoretical. The auxiliary function for ISTPs is Sensing, which means they are more application oriented. ISTPs tend to be practical, adventurous, and spontaneous.

ENTJs and ESTJs are both Dominant Thinkers (very logical), and they are both Extraverted (they seek to organize people and events). Both types are decisive and organized. But since the auxiliary function for ENTJs is Intuition, they are able to see the big picture and possibilities for the future. ENTJs tend to be theoretical, critical, and plan oriented. The auxiliary function for ESTJs is Sensing, which means they focus more on the specifics and concerns of the present moment. ESTJs tend to be efficient, practical, and conscientious.

∥ Dominant Feelers
ISFP INFP ESFJ ENFJ

Dominant Feelers—the Super Feelers!—have a strong drive to make decisions based on their personal values. Once again, this means something slightly different for each of the four types of Dominant Feelers.

ISFPs and INFPs are both Dominant Feelers (they care about what their decisions mean in human terms), and they are both Introverted (they focus on their inner personal values). Both types are sensitive, adaptable, and loyal. However, the auxiliary function for ISFPs is Sensing, which means they focus on the specific and concrete. ISFPs tend to be modest, observant, and trusting. The auxiliary function for INFPs is Intuition, which means they focus on possibilities, both for themselves and others. INFPs tend to be compassionate, empathetic, and creative.

ESFJs and ENFJs are both Dominant Feelers (they make decisions based on their own values), and they are both Extraverted (they focus on others). Both types are loyal, personable, and social. However, the auxiliary function for ESFJs is Sensing, which means they focus on the specifics about people. ESFJs tend to be thorough, systematic, and traditional. The auxiliary function for ENFJs is Intuition, which means they focus on the potential in other people. ENFJs tend to be idealistic, passionate, and persuasive.

Using Your Strengths (and Avoiding Your Blind Spots) at Work

Your greatest strengths are reflected in your dominant and auxiliary functions. Conversely, you are at your weakest when you use your fourth function and, to some extent, your third function as well. This is a vital little piece of self-awareness. It is exhilarating to be able to use your natural strengths, and it is very stressful to be made vulnerable by your innate blind spots.

There are obvious advantages to knowing your natural strengths. Once you're aware of your talents, you can seek out situations that allow you to use them to best advantage. You'll be confident of your own potential for success, and it will be easier for you to choose work that will be stimulating and satisfying.

Dominant Feelers are excellent at evaluating situations in human terms. For example, take Kelsey, a customer service representative. Kelsey's top priority is to establish a warm and friendly rapport with her customers and to be sure they have a positive and long-lasting experience with the company. She listens to their complaints, supports their feelings, and then assures them that she will help straighten out any problems they have. She, in effect, becomes their friend and advocate at the company.

Dominant Thinkers are without equal when it comes to making impersonal analyses. The legal maneuvering and tough decisions Ernesto makes as an attorney call his excellent Thinking skills into action repeatedly during a typical day in court. He looks at situations coolly, with clear and detached objectivity. He evaluates the logical effects of different strategic moves and then chooses his approach decisively and calmly.

Dominant Intuitives see connections and implications that no one else does. Abby works in an advertising agency as a copywriter. She writes headlines and radio and television ads for commonplace products and services. Using her natural creativity and ability to see connections between seemingly unrelated things, Abby comes up with clever phrases that evoke the kind of image her clients want to project and the kind of image consumers want to buy.

Dominant Sensors are unparalleled at remembering facts and putting them to good use. Herb is a biology researcher. His job requires that he use his superior attention to detail to observe and document minute changes in experiments. To test the validity of hypotheses, Herb runs experiments repeatedly with the same careful skill and accuracy.

There are also obvious and practical advantages to recognizing your blind spots—and we all have them. Acknowledging your innate weak points can help you avoid the types of circumstances or the kind of work that places you at the mercy of your lesser functions. Once you know where your own land mines are hidden, you know where to tread carefully! In unavoidably difficult situations, you can at least prepare an appropriate course of action while you are still relatively calm.

We are all stressed by having to use our fourth function too often or for too long. Dominant Feelers are at their weakest when they have to be impersonal and objective (use Thinking). Dominant Thinkers are at their weakest when they are called upon to deal with other people's emotions (use Feeling). Dominant Intuitives are driven crazy by having to attend to facts and details (use Sensing), and Dominant Sensors are at sea when they are obliged to find hidden meanings (use Intuition).

Let's use Jay, an ESFJ, as an example. Jay's dominant function is Feeling, which means he relies heavily on his values when he makes decisions. One of Jay's greatest natural gifts is his sensitivity to others. He is liked and appreciated for his caring, compassionate nature and his willingness to help others. As long as he makes decisions based on what he feels is the right thing to do, Jay feels good about himself and—not incidentally—receives reinforcement and support from others.

Jay's fourth function is Thinking. He finds it difficult to make decisions impersonally. When Jay is put in the position of having to think logically and disregard his feelings, he is operating out of his weakest function. This makes him nervous (it isn't the way his mind naturally works) and can also lead to poor decisions or behavior that seems irrational, overreactive, even childish.

Suppose Jay's boss criticizes one of his written proposals. In truth, this is not a reflection of how the boss feels about Jay. However, like many Dominant Feelers, Jay has great difficulty evaluating criticism objectively and impersonally, as it was intended. He just isn't wired for logical analysis. In this case, Jay misses all the constructive suggestions that his boss makes and responds with hurt feelings, as if his boss had made a personal attack.

Now, suppose Jay was aware of his dominant and auxiliary functions. He would recognize that he has a tendency to take things too much to heart, and he would know that being logical requires extra effort on his part. Instead of panicking and responding emotionally when confronted with criticism, he would remind himself to keep his feelings under control and his mind open, thereby getting the benefit of his boss's comments. Better yet, he would learn to write his next report as logically as possible so he wouldn't be placed in such a vulnerable position again.

6 | AGED TO PERFECTION

Developing Your Abilities
Over Time

The third and final ingredient in the Formula for Career Satisfaction is type development, the lifelong process during which we may gain access to *all* the type preferences—even our weakest or least comfortable. This process occurs naturally in everyone, but it can also be undertaken deliberately.

What we think of as "good type development" allows you to make the most of your natural abilities, enables you to make better decisions, and helps prevent you from being sabotaged by your innate blind spots.

We know someone who is fond of saying, "The trouble with getting old is that you get more like yourself!" Although we grow and change with age, we don't change our personality types, and our dominant and auxiliary functions remain the same. However, within each type it is possible—not just possible, but preferable!—to develop a well-rounded personality.

To some extent, people develop their personalities in predictable stages. Whether or not you've ever heard of Type, you are likely to have different interests at different times in your life. However, once you understand type development, you'll see that these changes don't just occur randomly. By recognizing where you are in your own type development, you'll be able to identify which functions you'll naturally find satisfaction using—and these might be very different for you at age forty-two than at age twenty-two. You'll also understand why certain activities that once satisfied you no longer do. Furthermore, you'll gain some insight into how you can expect to change as you grow older, and how your career choices may broaden.

The theory of type development was originated by an early user of Type, W. Harold Grant. Our experience confirms much of what Grant believed, although we've noticed a different timeline. We've found that the principles of type

74

development can be very useful in helping people determine their immediate and future career-related needs.

From Birth to Age Six

As we've already said, each individual is born with a personality blueprint that stays the same throughout life. However, it takes some time for definite preferences to become apparent. In children's early years, it is more difficult to conclusively identify their type preferences because they don't yet have the language skills to accurately describe their mental processes. While one's preference for extraversion or introversion may be the easiest to spot early on, the other preferences may be more elusive, especially with introverted children because, as with introverts of all ages, they are more difficult to get to know! And because the four functions do not develop simultaneously, before the age of six or so, it is usually difficult to determine most young children's full types with real accuracy. When we learn more about the cues and play behaviors of children of different types, the adults who care for them will be able to teach and parent according to the child's style rather than requiring that they adapt to ours. An excellent resource for understanding children's developmental patterns and how to individualize parenting and teaching strategies is our second book, *Nurture by Nature: Understand Your Child's Personality Type and Become a Better Parent.*

From Age Six to Age Twelve

Starting at about age six, a child's dominant function starts to pull ahead of the pack, and patterns of behavior become clearer. A Dominant Sensor may show an inclination for mastering skillful gymnastics routines; a Dominant Intuitive may create surprising musical instruments out of household odds and ends; a Dominant Thinker may construct impressive arguments against being punished; a Dominant Feeler may demonstrate concern and empathy for others, especially those in trouble or those suffering a tragedy. Without constraints, children will always naturally start to strengthen their dominant function during this period of their lives.

It is crucial to a child's healthy development that the use of his or her dominant function be encouraged by parents and teachers. The dominant function is the driving force behind our personalities and the source of our natural strengths. When encouraged, it will flourish and help produce a competent, confident adult. If a child is discouraged from using their dominant function, they may grow up not trusting the most central part of their personality. This obviously interferes with having a fulfilling life.

From Age Twelve to Age Twenty-Five

From about the age of twelve, we start to strengthen our auxiliary function. As you learned in the previous chapter, the auxiliary function balances the dominant function and ensures that we are proficient at both information gathering and decision making.

Once the dominant and auxiliary functions are firmly established, the third and fourth functions fall into line (although they are still quite undeveloped). By the age of about twenty-five, our personality types are distinct. Happily, this is not the end of personal growth!

From Age Twenty-Five to Age Fifty

At some point after the age of twenty-five, we start to develop our third function. We've found that most people don't start to do this in earnest or with great success until closer to the age of forty or even after. You'll notice that this timing coincides with another phenomenon that can occur at this age: the midlife crisis.

We believe that the connection between type development and midlife crisis—let's call it midlife reevaluation—is more than coincidental. For the first half of our lives, we use primarily our dominant and auxiliary functions. We rely on them, we trust them, and they work well for us. After many years, we are generally proficient at using both. At this point, having reached the top of the proverbial hill, we may also reach some disturbing conclusions: First, that there may not be that much time left ahead, and second, that there isn't much challenge in spending the remaining years exactly as we spent our earlier years. It is not uncommon for people to reassess their values at midlife and to change their priorities.

Based on our experience with our clients, we believe that midlife marks the beginning of a new phase of type development. Unconsciously, we seek to round out our personalities and to become more effective and capable. We start to develop our third and, later, fourth functions.

For example, take Mario, an ISFP. Mario is a Dominant Feeler. His auxiliary function is Sensing, his third function is Intuition, and his fourth function is Thinking. Up until now, Mario has been pretty much a "meat-and-potatoes" kind of guy, taking things as they are, not wondering about how they got to be that way and not looking for any deeper meanings. Now that he's thirty-eight, however, Mario has become more curious. He has become interested in *why* he acts the way he does and what influence his parents had on his upbringing. He has been talking more with his sister about their childhood, and he is even considering some personal counseling in order to learn more about himself and his patterns of behavior. Mario has become more interested in connections and in the reasons people behave the way they do—including himself. He is deepening his awareness of life's complexities, and he has a new appreciation for possibilities. These are all clear signs of developing Intuition.

Sometimes, developing your third function can be deeply unsettling. Naomi is a thirty-seven-year-old stockbroker. As an ENTP, she is a Dominant Intuitive. Her auxiliary function is Thinking, her third function is Feeling, and her fourth function is Sensing. Naomi is a brilliant wheeler-dealer. Her ability to analyze markets, anticipate trends, and persuade others that she is right have already made her very wealthy. Naomi finds the fast-paced, high-stakes, risk-taking financial arena exhilarating, and she has become very good at what she does. Lately, however, Naomi has been finding her work less satisfying. She has become somewhat less willing to work eighteen-hour days, especially now that she has a serious romantic partner who would actually like to see her once in a while. She still enjoys the challenges of her career, and being successful still means a lot to her, but she is realizing that being alone with her money and her collection of expensive possessions is not entirely satisfactory. Naomi's third function—Feeling—is making itself heard, and she is probably going to have to make some changes in her lifestyle to accommodate it.

Midlife doesn't always bring profound changes, as it did for Mario and Naomi. Many people quietly develop new interests or activities or simply start to live their lives a little differently. At midlife, we often become more open to other interests, other points of view, and other ways of doing things. We may become more flexible in our attitudes and may start to pay attention to things we once overlooked or considered unimportant.

Some people will simply develop hobbies associated with their third function (for example, a sign of developing Sensing may be a new interest in exercise). Other people will be drawn to the mental perspective associated with their third function (for example, a sign of developing Thinking can be a new emphasis on objectivity and fairness). Many people develop *both* the recreational activities *and* the mental awareness associated with their third function. This can occur simultaneously, or by starting with one and progressing to the other.

Once you understand type development, you can consciously work on strengthening your third function at midlife in order to add more depth, enjoyment, and capability to your life. How to go about doing this is unique to each individual.

Theo, an ENFP, is forty-one. He is a Dominant Intuitive. Theo's auxiliary function is Feeling, his third function is Thinking, and his fourth function is Sensing. Theo has always preferred harmony to conflict, and he has spent much of his life trying to make other people happy. Now, however, Theo is deliberately working on developing his Thinking.

Recently Theo purchased an expensive pair of sneakers that began to fall apart after only two weeks of use. When he brought them back to the store and explained the situation, the manager responded, "No problem! We'll just send these back to the factory, and if they can't be repaired, you'll be sent a new pair. It should only take a month or so."

Ten years ago Theo would have accepted this solution because he would have been so interested in having a positive, friendly interaction with the store manager that he wouldn't have been willing to risk a confrontation. At this stage of his life, however, Theo is more comfortable using his Thinking, and he is more willing to sacrifice harmony in order to be treated fairly. Instead, Theo answered, "That doesn't seem right to me. I don't want to stop exercising for a month because you sold me a pair of faulty sneakers. I didn't buy the sneakers from the factory, I bought them from you, and the extra markup I paid is for your service. I'd like you to replace the sneakers *now,* and I'd like you to deal with the factory."

The manager reluctantly complied. Without consciously planning to do so, Theo was drawn to use his emerging reasoning skills (his Thinking) and in the process, got better at doing so.

After Age Fifty

Later in life, we start to use our fourth function with more success. Some typologists believe that the fourth function is so underdeveloped that we are never really able to use it efficiently. However, we have found that many people are drawn to their fourth function at this stage in life, and that with conscious effort they can indeed make good use of it. Engaging your fourth function with some degree of success requires concentration—it is, after all, your weakest function—but it is worth the effort.

Aaron, fifty-seven, does consulting for the manufacturing industry, as he has for most of his working life. He has also always been extremely active in volunteer work. An ESFJ, Aaron is a Dominant Feeler. His auxiliary function is Sensing, his third function is Intuition, and his fourth function is Thinking. Aaron works hard as a community leader, helping to create affordable housing for homeless people in his city. Over the years, Aaron has become increasingly innovative at finding new funding sources and at thinking up alternative uses of space to create housing for the homeless (using his Intuition). While Aaron has always been passionate about the homeless, his developing Thinking abilities are now enabling him to be more objective and thick-skinned about the political process. He has started to work on implementing programs and systems that operate within the larger city structure (using his Thinking). This is a challenge for Aaron, but by using his head, he is more effective in solving the problems about which he cares deeply in his heart.

If you have experienced good type development throughout your life, you should be able to use all of your functions—Sensing, Intuition, Thinking, and Feeling—after the age of fifty or so, calling up the right one for the right situation. Your dominant and auxiliary functions are still the source of your greatest strengths, and your third and fourth functions require more supervision, but you'll have a wider range of skills at your command.

Remember the analogy comparing your functions to the family in the car? Well, with good type development, it's as if the third and fourth functions (the kids in the backseat) have grown up a little. The dominant and auxiliary are still in charge, but the third function is now a young adult, and the fourth function is an adolescent.

Interestingly enough, in the process of using all the functions, you'll find that you also gain access to all the type preferences, including the attitudes. (Remember them? The attitudes are Extraversion, Introversion, Judging, and Perceiving.) If you're an Introvert, you may find that you are more comfortable with Extraverted activities such as meeting new people or widening your area of interest. And if you're a Judger, you may find you are better able to use Perceiving—for example, to relax, play, and spend more time experiencing life instead of needing to control it.

Here's an example to show what we mean. Marian, an ENFJ, is a sixty-year-old woman serving on a jury for a medical malpractice case. As a Dominant Feeler, Marian might be expected to base all of her decisions on her personal beliefs and values, with special sympathy for the victim. Since Marian's auxiliary function is Intuition, she might also be expected to focus primarily on the implications of the evidence and the general patterns of the information she hears.

In fact, Marian is quite a different juror. Because she has gained better access to her Sensing, she pays close attention to the evidence, and during the jury's deliberations she remembers and recites specific relevant details. Perhaps surprisingly, she is able to stay impartial during the trial, using her fourth function, Thinking. She even cautions her fellow jurors not to base their decisions purely on empathy. Furthermore, although Marian is an Extravert, she has learned to listen closely before speaking (using Introversion) and to wait, reflecting carefully on all she has heard before rendering a final verdict (using Perceiving).

Has Marian changed from an ENFJ to an ISTP? No! But because she has good type development, she can call on all the preferences when she needs them. In this situation, it was clearly appropriate for Marian to work hard at gathering the facts and arrive at an impartial decision, something she would have had a very hard time doing twenty-five years earlier.

What Helps (and Hurts) Good Type Development

As we mentioned earlier in this chapter, it is essential that children be reinforced for using their dominant and auxiliary functions. We all know that how we were brought up has a profound effect on how well-adjusted we are today, but have you ever stopped to think of your life in terms of your own type development? Children who are encouraged to follow their natural abilities strengthen all of their functions over time and generally become fully functional adults. Children who are discouraged from using their innate strengths can grow up to be confused and ambivalent about their perceptions and inclinations—and this confusion can affect every aspect of adult life, including career issues.

Parents and teachers often readily value in children the qualities that they have themselves. Conversely, they can be mystified by—even disapproving of—behavior they don't easily understand. This isn't malicious or even intentional; it's just natural for people to enjoy and feel more comfortable with others who are like them because they understand them more easily.

We know a woman who spent much of her young life playing with imaginary friends. She lived on a farm in a remote area, and as far as we know, the day-to-day challenges of farming meant little to her. She spent her time inventing playmates who talked, interacted, and even misbehaved. Some parents (particularly Dominant Sensors) might, in this situation, fear that their child was hallucinating, but fortunately Rebecca's parents were just happy that their daughter was keeping herself harmlessly occupied. Today Rebecca is a very successful romance novelist, and she attributes much of her success to her early practice with characterization.

Of course, not all stories are success stories. We also know a young woman named Erica who is definitely a Dominant Thinker—cool, independent, and undemonstrative. As it turns out, both of Erica's parents are Dominant Feelers. They have never been comfortable with Erica's impersonal manner, and they've always wondered if maybe they did something wrong to produce such a remote child. Despite their best efforts to deny their own need for affection, Erica's parents unintentionally communicated to her from infancy that they wished she were different. Although Erica's parents never actively interfered with her inclinations, Erica was always plagued by self-doubt. Fortunately, identifying her true personality type has been a liberating experience for her.

If you're a parent, we know what you're thinking: Oh, great! Just what I need—another expert telling me how I'm screwing up my kid. We can appreciate your feelings. But our point is not that you're doing anything wrong; it's simply that it is easy to forget that our children may be very different from us, just as we may be very much unlike our parents.

At this point, it might be helpful for you to reflect on how you were brought up. We're not suggesting that you necessarily try to "Type" your parents and teachers, but do take a moment to think about your childhood. What natural talents did you exhibit when you were young? How were your efforts received by others? Do you think you were encouraged to develop your dominant function, or were you expected to behave in what was for you an unnatural way? Most people will be remarkably similar as adults to the way they were as children, but some people have a difficult time asserting their true personalities in the face of resistance or lack of understanding from others. Children are particularly vulnerable to others' expectations and often suppress their own natural preferences in order to fit in and be accepted.

Throughout life, circumstances can either work for or against your good type development. In addition to parents and teachers, we are also influenced by siblings, peers, and the culture in which we grow up. Consider this: More than 50 percent of the American population is made up of Extraverted Sensors. Only about 4 percent of the American population comprises Introverted Intuitives. Strong messages permeate our culture that it's better to be the former (action oriented, social, pragmatic, and practical) than the latter (thoughtful, introspective, complex, and creative).

Pressure to be what you aren't can cause lifelong confusion. If you are obliged to fit into a certain group mentality that really doesn't suit you (this could be a family dynamic, a school or community setting, or a professional environment), you may end up denying your true nature and not enjoying your required role. If you spend twenty years at a job you don't enjoy, you may end up not only out of touch with your natural interests but—even worse—with a distorted view of your own competence.

If you were never encouraged to "be yourself," or if you are confused about your true nature, take heart. We have found that Type can help lead people to a productive, fulfilling life based on a sound understanding of their true natures.

Where Are You in Your Type Development?

There are two ways to find out how you are coming along in your own type development. Before you do either of the following exercises, you will need to refer to your hierarchy of functions on the table on page 67. We suggest that you write it down and keep it close by for easy reference. This will be helpful in translating our general information about type development into information that applies to your specific personality type.

To get a rough idea of where you stand in your own type development, locate your age on the timetable below. If you're following the general trend, you are probably developing the function that appears above your age. Remember, this is only a rough estimate. Everyone progresses at his or her own rate.

TYPE DEVELOPMENT TIMETABLE

The Type Development Timetable is helpful really only in a general way. Nobody wakes up at age twenty-five and says, "Aha! Time to develop my third function!" People will focus on different dimensions of their personalities at different times in their lives. Even people who have the same personality type and who are the same age will not progress in exactly the same way. The age ranges given here are just approximate guidelines.

For another check on where you stand in your own type development, you'll need to examine your current interests and attitudes. It's usually best to focus on your behavior away from work, since during your free time you are more likely to pursue what you wish and be whoever you want to be.

Read through the following four descriptions of how people develop their Sensing, Intuition, Thinking, or Feeling and see which one sounds like you. Can you tell which function you are strengthening at this stage in your life? In making your decision, it might be helpful for you to write down a list of your latest interests, or to ask someone who knows you well if they have seen any evidence of a new perspective on your part.

After you've pinpointed the function you're currently developing, refer to your hierarchy of functions. Is it your auxiliary, third, or fourth function? If you want, you can check your results against the Type Development Timetable.

Evidence of Type Development

Developing Sensing

In general, people who are developing their Sensing start to focus more on the present moment, taking things day by day.

New attitudes may include:

- becoming more aware of how things look, sound, smell, taste, and feel
- a new appreciation of nature
- becoming more interested in facts and details; becoming more precise and accurate
- becoming more realistic; becoming more concerned with how long projects take and with the realities of getting them done

New interests may include:

- cooking
- building
- arts and crafts
- listening to music
- exercise
- hiking, camping
- gardening
- reading nonfiction
- careful attention to details
- greater interest in numbers

Developing Intuition

In general, people who are developing their Intuition become more open to change and to seeing things in new ways.

New attitudes may include:

- becoming more interested in underlying meanings and in what symbols represent
- developing or deepening an interest in spiritual matters and the meaning of life
- becoming more open to using imagination
- thinking about how people or things are related to each other; focusing on the big picture

New interests may include:

- art, design
- religion
- research, study, returning to school, advanced degree
- problem solving, brainstorming

- inventing
- creative writing
- reading fiction
- travel to learn about different cultures
- long-range planning/thinking

Developing Thinking

In general, people who are developing their Thinking become better able to stay objective when considering data.

New attitudes may include:

- a greater emphasis on fairness and equality, even at the expense of harmony
- a new awareness of cause and effect and the logical consequences of actions
- becoming more critical in evaluating people and things
- greater interest in efficiency and competency
- an increased ability to see both sides in an argument

New interests may include:

- the rights of others
- negotiating, arbitration
- strategy games (Scrabble, chess, etc.)
- debating
- consumer awareness
- political interests
- elevating one's standards
- being aware of others' standards
- striving to be consistent

Developing Feeling

In general, people who are developing their Feeling gain a new awareness of how their actions affect others. They often reassess their priorities in more human terms.

New attitudes may include:

- providing more emotional support for others; showing concern for other people's needs
- cultivating friendships; sharing personal experiences and feelings
- greater interest in communication and listening skills
- greater appreciation for the contributions of others

New interests may include:

- volunteer work
- mentoring

- rekindling past relationships
- initiating or attending reunions
- personal therapy
- open, thoughtful conversation
- writing
- keeping a journal
- expressing gratitude
- praising others

As an example, let's assume you are an INFJ and that you are fifty-two years old. Your hierarchy of functions is as follows:

#1	(Dominant)	Intuition
#2	(Auxiliary)	Feeling
#3	(Tertiary)	Thinking
#4	(Inferior)	Sensing

You've always been adept at seeing implications and meanings (Intuition), and you have learned how to use this information in making sound decisions based on your personal values and your understanding of others (Feeling). Over the years you've gotten better at anticipating the logical consequences of your decisions (Thinking). Recently, you've found yourself leafing through catalogues for gourmet cooks and you've signed up for a cooking course. You're also more determined to find that ten-cent discrepancy in your bank statement. These may both be signs of developing Sensing.

Sensing is your fourth function. According to the Type Development Timetable, you are likely to start developing your fourth function after age fifty.

Still Confused?

If you started this chapter with a very clear idea of your true personality type, and if you have been thoughtful about these exercises, chances are you found that you are pretty much "on schedule" in your own type development. You should have a sense of some of the ways you've changed over the years, as well as an understanding of why these changes occurred. However, if you're having trouble trying to figure out which function you are currently strengthening, don't despair.

If you're not certain about your personality type, try plotting the function hierarchies of the other personality type(s) you might be. (To do this, go back to the hierarchy of functions table on page 67.) This exercise can help you clarify your type as well as where you are developmentally.

Another possibility is that you've correctly identified your personality type but are developing in a unique way that has nothing to do with our Type Development Timetable. You're allowed! But don't throw this chapter out the window just because you're on your own private schedule. The concept of type development will still be useful to you; you'll just have to do a little more independent research to find out where you've been and where you're going.

Type Development and Problem Solving

You'll find that the more you develop your functions—Sensing, Intuition, Thinking, and Feeling—the better you'll be at making good decisions. This is a significant skill, especially when it comes time to make important, far-reaching decisions such as selecting a career. Luckily it is a skill you can consciously develop.

When you are faced with a decision, first use both information-gathering functions (Sensing and Intuition), and then use both decision-making functions (Thinking and Feeling). Don't automatically start with your dominant function (whichever it is). It will be easier for you to use your dominant and auxiliary functions, but make a special effort to use your third and fourth functions as well. Each function makes a valid and important contribution to the problem-solving process, and overlooking any one of the four can result in a seriously flawed decision.

The ideal approach to problem solving looks like this:

Problem-Solving Model

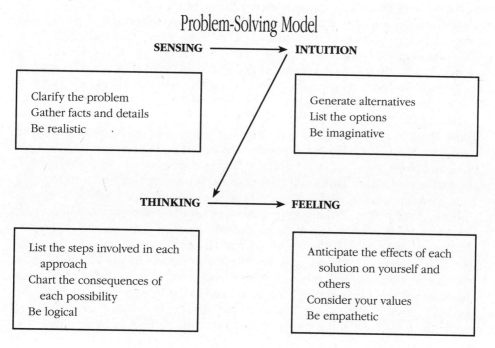

SENSING ⟶ INTUITION

Clarify the problem
Gather facts and details
Be realistic

Generate alternatives
List the options
Be imaginative

THINKING ⟶ FEELING

List the steps involved in each
approach
Chart the consequences of
each possibility
Be logical

Anticipate the effects of each
solution on yourself and
others
Consider your values
Be empathetic

Decide on a course of action!

Note: Even if you make a conscious effort to use all of these functions, you probably won't use them in this order in real life. The important thing is to consult them, even if you don't follow this pattern exactly.*

We all make a thousand decisions a day, so you should have plenty of opportunities to practice good problem-solving skills. If you are faced with a particularly important decision, it may be a good idea to consult someone you respect who has different strengths than you do. For example, if you're a Thinking type, ask a Feeler for their views. You might be amazed at how differently they see the situation. Seeking this kind of input from time to time will help you develop your weaker functions, resulting in more effective decision making. Strengthening your mental functions is just like building up muscles: The more you exercise them, the stronger they become.

Type Development and Career Satisfaction

Wherever you are in your career, whether you're starting out or starting over, keep in mind that type development is a natural process you can take advantage of. If you choose career options that fit into your own natural type development, you'll find your work more satisfying on many levels because it will provide you with opportunities for professional growth and enjoyment. Professionally, this translates into greater competency and, ultimately, greater success.

From the beginning, it's important to choose work that suits your dominant and auxiliary functions. This doesn't change with age. However, at some point you can also expect your third function to become more important. Sooner or later—preferably sooner!—you will want to exercise and express it in your work. Your fourth function, on the other hand, may never play a significant role in your professional life, except to the extent that you should avoid situations that require using it for too long.

Throughout your working life, you'll need to make constant career updates. These don't have to be dramatic changes (although for some personality types they probably will be). Expect to lose interest in certain professional activities you have mastered even as you become more interested in new challenges, approaches, or skills. This is all part of good type development. The stronger your third function becomes, the more viable career options you'll have at your disposal. Later in life, you may even gravitate toward work that would have been unsuitable for you ten or twenty years earlier.

Maureen, an ISTJ, is a Dominant Sensor. Her auxiliary function is Thinking, her third function is Feeling, and her fourth function is Intuition. Shortly after Maureen graduated from college, she accepted a job in medical research. Once she mastered the different procedures involved in the lab work, she grew to love her job and she excelled at it. Maureen was always precise and observant, her reports were detailed and accurate, and she enjoyed verifying data firsthand and

*Adapted by Elenor Corlett from *People Types and Tiger Stripes* by Gordon Lawrence.

recording it for later review. Maureen was glad that her work might someday result in a medical breakthrough, but mostly she was interested in the step-by-step progress on the different experiments going on in the lab. She was a steady, quiet, dependable worker, and for many years was quite content.

When Maureen's boss quit unexpectedly, Maureen was offered a supervisory position. She would be responsible for overseeing the work of all the lab technicians, making sure they did their jobs, helping them with difficult procedures, and training new technicians as needed. Maureen wasn't sure whether or not she should accept the job, and because she knew somebody who knew us, she came to us for advice.

We were certain that Maureen would do well with the new job. By means of exercises and discussion, we helped her see that she was developing her third function—Feeling—and that this professional opportunity would mesh nicely with her personal timetable. We urged her to try it.

To her own surprise, Maureen turned out to be an excellent supervisor. She developed a supportive managerial style and successfully kept her staff working together. She also continued with her own lab work, focusing in particular on cancer research.

Over the next several years, Maureen became more interested in the human consequences of her research. She formed many connections with doctors, hospitals, and organizations associated with finding and funding a cure for cancer. Eventually these relationships brought Maureen directly into contact with cancer patients, and she started volunteering some time on weekends to visit them. This would not have appealed to Maureen at all ten years earlier, but at this stage in her life she found that it added new meaning and urgency to her research.

Today, Maureen is exceedingly busy. She does far less hands-on lab work, and instead is concentrating on evaluating new developments in cancer research and treatment. In this latest phase of her career, Maureen is actively engaging her Intuition. She travels a great deal, learning new procedures and familiarizing herself with breakthroughs and advances occurring all over the world. Now an acknowledged expert in her field, she also lectures frequently—something she would never have felt comfortable doing when she was younger—and still finds time to visit the patients to whom her work means so much.

At this point, it would be difficult to separate Maureen's personal and professional lives, just as it would be impossible to separate her personal and professional growth. By choosing a career path that engaged her natural interests at different points in her life, Maureen has become not only an extremely capable professional but also an exceptional human being.

Recapping the Formula

Now you have it: The complete Formula for Career Satisfaction! Here, for your review, are the three things you must understand in order to find a career you can love:

1. Your innate temperament (Chapter 4)
2. Your hierarchy of functions (Chapter 5)
3. Where you are in your type development (Chapter 6)

In Part 3, you'll meet people of your same personality type who are a lot like you. After you've read their stories, we'll show you how they've found work that is consistent with their temperament, that makes good use of their dominant and auxiliary functions, and is in sync with their type development.

After you've finished reading this book, you'll be able to do the same!

Part Three | GETTING TO WORK

Profiles of Career-Satisfied People

It is said that the best way to learn is by one's own mistakes. If that's so, perhaps the next best way to learn is through the mistakes and successes of others, especially those who are a lot like us. The case studies that follow are the real-life career experiences of people from many different and varied professions, income levels, ages, and backgrounds. What they all have in common is that each one has found career satisfaction. For some it took many years and several different jobs; for others the path was carefully planned and more direct.

For each of the sixteen type chapters that follow, there are profiles of people who really enjoy their jobs—and have found the right match between their personality type and their career. Each profile provides an analysis to help you understand how their jobs let them use their natural strengths and therefore are satisfying. As you read these profiles, think about how you are similar to the people described. This will help you to identify what you require to find career satisfaction.

Following the case studies you will find a section called *Common Threads,* which lists specific and important criteria for career satisfaction for people like you. *Popular Occupations* contains a list of specific careers and the reasons why they offer the best potential for career satisfaction for people of your type.

After identifying a potentially satisfying career, you will need to conduct a successful job search campaign. Recognizing that people of different types will naturally approach this process differently, we provide specific and practical pointers to help you capitalize on *your strengths and minimize your possible blind spots to conduct the most effective job search possible.*

By the time you have finished reading your type chapter, you will be ready to *identify and evaluate one (or maybe more than one) career option that can give you real satisfaction—work that will finally let you Do What You Are!*

7 | ENFJ Extraverted, Intuitive, Feeling, Judging

"The Public Relations Specialists"

Profile 1: Emma, Director of Development

"Putting love and ability together."

The Job

Emma loves seeing an institution that she deeply believes in flourish as the result of her efforts. She is the director of development at an independent school and spends her days supervising a team of people, both volunteers and trained professionals, who raise money for the school. Emma's day typically consists of creating strategies for how best to ask people to make significant contributions, as well as figuring out how much to ask for. This involves research into potential donors' capabilities but also less factual investigations into their interests and tendencies. "It's the propensity, not just the capacity, for giving that I look into." In this way, Emma forms connections with donors and helps them find the perfect outlet for their largesse.

What Emma loves about development is the challenge of connecting the right person to the institution and seeing the joy that both parties derive from the interaction. Emma is energized by the positive change that occurs by putting love and ability together, a combination that typifies much of her work. She also admits to enjoying the "thrill of the hunt," the prospecting side that includes calling people and asking for gifts for the school, the sales mode. Emma's wholehearted enthusiasm for the institution makes her a persuasive salesperson, capable of sharing her passion with others and infecting them with the same insight for possibility that she has. Her attitude about what most people see as a terrifying aspect of the job—that is, asking for money—is this: "If I feel good about the institution, what's the worst that can happen? They can always say no, but I want to give them the opportunity to say yes and make a real impact with their generosity." Other features of the job that Emma likes are the collegial atmosphere, being part of a team, and the leadership role that her position affords. She loves helping people feel inspired and empowered about the future.

Backstory

Before taking this job, Emma worked as an independent consultant and a freelance special events coordinator. She often found herself involved in public relations work for causes that appealed to her values, such as planning functions for children's charities. An event that she is especially proud of is a black-tie dinner she arranged for the local chapter of Ronald McDonald House Charities, a fundraiser that included an auction of original artwork by children's picture book illustrators. Emma approached approximately forty big-name illustrators and asked them to donate their work, and the auction turned out to be an enormous success. She also worked in an advertising agency, as a management consultant, and as a workshop facilitator.

Emma explains that she never intended to become a director of development. "I fell into it—fell in love with the institution. My children were attending the school, and, like a lot of volunteers, I felt that I wanted to be a part of it. One nice thing about most nonprofits is that they allow people to get involved." So Emma began as a volunteer—a member of the school's board of trustees— and in that role she helped shape the bigger picture for the school. This led to her involvement in various special projects for students, parents, and faculty, until Emma proved her mettle. "I was supportive of the administration, a hard worker, and it was clear that our values were in sync." People close to Emma encouraged her, noticing that the work was making her happy. When a part-time development job opened up at the school, she decided to give it a try. Four

months in, it became clear that the job was a good match for Emma's skills. "I threw my hat into the ring for the director job."

A Good Fit

Emma's superpower lies in her ability to maintain her optimism and sense of what's possible. "If you believe in the mission and respect the people, then it's all good. I have to care deeply about what I'm doing and about the long-term possible results, because no matter how much they pay you, in the long run it won't work unless you really believe in the place."

Emma's mission of matching people with an institution that they feel good about supporting is right in line with her values. Her drive to help people find meaning and joy in giving, and her belief in nonprofits, reflect her Idealist temperament. Her skills as a communicator and her deep belief in her mission allow her to reach donors and appeal to their sense of purpose, resulting in satisfaction for all parties.

As a dominant Feeler, Emma is driven by making connections with people, and her career choices reflect her value system. Her people skills are highly developed, and she naturally enjoys meeting people and discovering what matters to them. Emma is articulate both in person and in writing, and she knows how to get the best out of people by making them feel good about themselves and their association with the cause.

Emma's auxiliary function, Intuition, is evidenced by her grasp of the big picture and her focus on what is possible in the future. Development requires a long-range mindset, and Emma spends a great deal of time envisioning and assessing the implications and potential results of her work five, ten, and fifteen years from the present. This allows her to create strategies and plans that incorporate both long- and short-term goals.

Looking Ahead

As Emma's children are getting older and are soon to graduate from the school, she is contemplating a new challenge. The impact that Emma is able to make in one institution may be limited, while a new adventure as an independent consultant could provide her with the ability to maximize her impact across many institutions. "I know I can help people to let go of the fear around fundraising and really see the opportunities to make independent schools work for everyone—the students, the faculty, families, and administration." With the combination of her expertise in the field, and her superlative skills as a communicator, it is easy to imagine Emma as a welcome addition to institutions in need of guidance.

Profile 2: Mitch, Human Resources

"Helping people achieve their fullest potential."

The Job

Helping other people has been a motivation and a theme for all of Mitch's career. As the manager of executive staffing and development in the human resources department of a large insurance company, he enjoys the opportunity he has every day to assist other people in the development of their own careers and their competency and leadership skills. Mitch's job entails three major areas: recruitment of executives, the "outplacement" or assistance offered when an individual's job is eliminated, and development of special programs to increase executives' effectiveness, usually through workshops and seminars.

With fluctuations of the economy, the amount of recruiting and outplacement he performs varies. But he enjoys all of the work, especially the competencies program he initiated, developed, and now is the spokesperson for. "The best part of my job, the part that I find energizing, is the counseling I do to help other people become more successful in their jobs. I enjoy the coaching I do with executives to help them develop their skills with their staffs. And I get a big charge out of the training sessions I conduct. I love to get up in front of people in a variety of audiences and give them some helpful information."

Backstory

Mitch came to his job in the corporate world as part of his overall career plan. His first job, however, was as a manager of a ceramic studio. He had worked there during his college years and upon graduation filled in as manager while the owner recuperated from a serious car accident. After a year, he returned to college to work toward a master's degree in guidance counseling and personnel. During the program, he participated in an internship in the career counseling department at a university, which helped him get his feet wet in the world of counseling.

Upon graduation, he accepted a position at another university as a career counselor. Within two years, Mitch was promoted to director of career development. "Here I was telling people how to prepare résumés for work in the big world, and I hadn't ever experienced the corporate world. So I took a job at a big insurance company in the human resources department. I fully intended to get a couple years' experience and return to university life. But I felt at home and stayed for seven years!" Since joining the insurance company, Mitch was promoted to the position of manager of staffing and then to the more autonomous position he holds now.

A Good Fit

Mitch is in the business of helping people develop their fullest potential. Whether working as a career counselor on a college campus or as a manager in human resources for a large corporation, he is naturally drawn to helping people see possibilities about themselves, figure out what is right for them, and develop the necessary skills to be their best. Like most Idealists, his genuine affection for and enjoyment of people helps him to be an excellent communicator.

A natural counselor, Mitch employs his dominant Feeling by establishing relationships with clients and colleagues. He demonstrates his empathy by reaching out to people who have lost their jobs and helping them understand and express their feelings. Whether he is coaching executives to be more effective or conducting general training workshops, he enjoys giving helpful information and receiving the positive reinforcement that often accompanies his presentations. Mitch is also a harmonizer. He puts people together who can benefit each other and in the process is himself rewarded for his efforts.

Since a large part of his work involves interviewing people and matching them to the right job, Mitch calls on his auxiliary Intuition to make connections and see possibilities. It also helps him to understand people's motivations. He expresses his creativity in many ways—one example is the mentoring program he developed for employees. Another way Mitch uses his Intuition is to take complex and sometimes dry technical information and figure out a way to make it understandable and even interesting to others.

Looking Ahead

For Mitch, the next steps are clear. His career goals are mapped out: assistant vice president within two years, vice president in five. Highly motivated to advance, Mitch most looks forward to expanding his reach and helping an even wider audience of people.

As Mitch has spent more time in this career, he's noticed some changes in himself. "I'm much more realistic about the world of work and about my own strengths and weaknesses. I'm more ambitious, and I realize now that money *does* matter. I also have a broader vision; I can see there are a lot of ways and a lot of places to help people. And I'm much thicker-skinned than I was ten years ago, because I can take criticism and be less defensive about it. I've even learned how to be tough when I need to be. Firing someone used to just be unbearable for me. Now, I still feel for the person and I present bad news in a gentle way, but I can also do the hard stuff." He hopes to continue to grow in these ways while moving up the corporate ladder and honing his craft.

Profile 3: Madeline, Special Education Teacher

"Making a difference every day."

The Job

Every day, Madeline works to unlock the potential that she sees within. She is a first grade teacher in an independent school focused entirely on special education. Each child that Madeline encounters, regardless of their needs, is an opportunity for her to reach inside and discover the unique ideas, perspectives, and talents that child can bring to this world. She works with students who have speech, language, and attention disabilities. Many of these children have found her school after struggling in a more traditional setting. Their families can be disillusioned, anxious, and even desperate to provide their child with the tools they need to be successful.

Madeline meets these families and children where they are, creating innovative lesson plans that scaffold learning and bring joy back into the equation. She differentiates her instruction to meet the needs of each individual student, in whole class, small group, and one-on-one settings. Madeline is tasked with creating a warm and collaborative classroom culture, tending to the social-emotional needs of her students alongside their academic needs. She also collaborates with other teachers and her administration, and is in constant communication with the families of her students as she guides them along the school year.

Backstory

Madeline always knew she wanted to be a teacher, like her mom. Throughout her childhood, even when she considered other possibilities such as marine biologist or actress, teacher never left the list. But in high school, as she watched her mother become burned out at the end of a thirty-five-year-long career in the classroom, Madeline shifted her career goals. She ended up going to school for film, then quickly changed her major to communications. After a series of internships that Madeline found "shallow and terrible," she realized she had drifted far from the mission that was important to her—being able to really help people.

Upon graduating, Madeline began to work at an urban nonprofit centered on nutrition education, and in her free time, she volunteered with her friend June at a program for homeless children. Once a week, as they drove the thirty minutes to the playgroup, June would tell Madeline about the courses she was taking in general and

special education. Suddenly, a light bulb went on for Madeline: "I was on the path for this all along, and somewhere I fell off. Of course I'm supposed to be working with kids!"

Madeline immediately applied for a national teaching corps and that fall was placed at an inner-city charter school while working toward her dual master's degree in general and special education. But the environment at Madeline's school was toxic: There was little trust between leadership and teachers, as well as a pervasive negativity that she found constantly draining. After struggling for two years in a school environment that felt all wrong, Madeline moved to her current position at a school devoted to meeting the needs of students with special needs.

A Good Fit

Madeline's new school is a huge shift in environment. Instead of being micromanaged, Madeline is trusted, and was given responsibilities right off the bat. Her dominant Feeling function is satisfied by the positive and harmonious working environment, as well as the belief that she is making a real difference—something that matters to most Idealists. Madeline is able to greet her students and their families with compassion and real understanding. Her ability to care deeply, and translate that caring into genuine empathy and connection, is a hallmark of her Feeling. Always concerned about the social and emotional learning that enables cognitive growth, Madeline sees each student as an individual, deserving of respect, love, and understanding.

With special education, innovation is the name of the game, and Madeline's auxiliary Intuition function leads her to find new and creative ways to reach her students. Whereas a general educator may have one lesson plan for a class of twenty-five, Madeline may have twelve students, and as many plans.

As both an Extravert and a Judger, Madeline is in control in the classroom, able to work the room and feed off of the energy of her students. She is both nurturing and firm, and her high expectations show her students that she has confidence in their capabilities.

Looking Ahead

While Madeline is much happier in her new school, she doesn't feel that her values are being completely fulfilled by her work just yet. "I would really like to find a school that serves a minority population, but with a progressive model of education. What I liked about the charter school was that I was serving a population that was underserved, and that felt really good. But I didn't think that they were doing it well. And at this school it's the opposite. The teaching is phenomenal, but everyone is rich and white. And I feel like it's so unfair that this great teaching is being given to kids who already enjoy so many advantages, and not to the other kids who need it, too." In the next five to ten years, Madeline would love to find a school that meets both of these criteria, and continue to reach all kinds of children with special needs, regardless of class or race.

Common Threads

Although Emma, Mitch, and Madeline have different backgrounds, experiences, and careers, there are certain common threads woven through their stories. Specific interests, abilities, and values may differ, but owing to their similar temperament values and the *same hierarchy* of their psychological functions, there are certain observations we can make about the needs of many ENFJs.

What follows is a list of the most important elements—the formula, if you will—for ENFJ satisfaction. Given the uniqueness of all individuals—even those

who share a type—this list will not describe each ENFJ equally well. The important thing is that these ten elements, with varying degrees of intensity and in different orders of importance, identify what ENFJs need to be satisfied.

After you have reviewed this list, we recommend that you go back and prioritize the elements in order of *their importance to you*. When doing this, think of past work experiences as well as your present job, and what you found particularly satisfying or unsatisfying. Try to look for *themes* that run through several experiences, not just *events* that might be true for one work situation but not for another.

As an ENFJ, I define career satisfaction as doing work that

1. lets me establish and maintain warm and supportive interpersonal relationships with co-workers, clients, customers, etc.
2. lets me develop creative solutions to problems on projects that I believe in and where I can see the positive results of my efforts for other people
3. is done in an environment where expectations are clear, contributions are appreciated, and personal and professional growth and development are encouraged
4. lets me be a part of a team of other creative people I trust
5. allows me time to develop creative solutions to problems and then share them with other supportive and caring people
6. is done in an active and challenging environment where I am able to juggle several projects at once and be highly productive
7. lets me use my organizational and decision-making skills and have

control and responsibility for my own projects

8. gives me a variety of activities but allows me to work in a relatively orderly and well-planned manner

9. is done in an environment that is free from interpersonal conflicts and ongoing tension

10. exposes me to new ideas and lets me explore new approaches, especially those that will improve the lives of other people

Popular Occupations for ENFJs

Because of their combination of preferences, ENFJs are naturally drawn to a wide variety of occupations.

In listing occupations that are popular among ENFJs, it is important to note that there are successful people of all types in all occupations. However, the following are careers ENFJs may find particularly satisfying, and some of the reasons why. This is by no means a comprehensive listing but is included to suggest possibilities you may not have previously considered. Although all of these occupations offer the potential for career satisfaction, the future demand for some careers is anticipated to be greater than for others.

COMMUNICATIONS
- Advertising account executive
- Public relations specialist
- Social media manager
- Communication director
- Writer/journalist
- Entertainer/artist
- Fundraiser
- Recruiter
- Recreational director
- TV producer
- Newscaster
- Politician
- Lobbyist
- Marketing manager
- Informational-graphics designer
- Magazine editor
- Graphic artist
- Web content editor
- Multimedia specialist
- Copywriter
- Reporter and correspondent
- Interpreter/translator
- Managing editor

ENFJs are masterful communicators. They are motivated to understand and please others, so they often possess great tact and diplomacy. They sometimes prefer the spoken word to the written word, but many ENFJs are good writers as well. They enjoy the process of gathering information by meeting and interviewing people and coming to understand the underlying and personal side of a story or issue. The world of advertising, public relations, and fundraising is often a satisfying one, especially when the ENFJ believes in the product, service, or cause involved and if the atmosphere does not become too competitive or conflict-ridden. ENFJs establish relationships quickly with clients, customers, and co-workers and can be persuasive and effective agents, producers, recruiters, and politicians. They are natural and charismatic leaders and enjoy facilitating large and small groups.

COUNSELING / HUMAN SERVICE
- Psychologist
- Social worker
- Career counselor
- Life coach
- Marriage and family therapist
- Mental health counselor
- Clergy/ministry
- Corporate outplacement counselor
- Substance abuse counselor
- Employee assistance counselor

- Rehabilitation counselor
- Vocational rehabilitation counselor
- School counselor
- Guidance counselor
- Eldercare specialist
- Director of assisted care living facility
- Social services coordinator
- Sociologist

Great numbers of ENFJs find career satisfaction helping others find happiness and contentment in their lives through self-understanding. They enjoy helping their clients become aware of personal issues and then overcome obstacles. ENFJs are usually warm, compassionate, and influential therapists. They often enjoy careers in the ministry, as they are able to share their own values with others and to help themselves and others reach their full potential. They easily see possible options or solutions and can help their clients see them as well.

Human service organizations are often appealing to ENFJs because they provide an opportunity to work toward improving the quality of life for themselves and others. They like to be leaders, in control of their projects as much as possible, and to see positive results from their efforts.

EDUCATION
- Teacher: health/art/drama/English
- College professor: humanities
- Dean of students
- Librarian
- Nonprofit organization director
- Special education teacher
- Early education teacher
- Bilingual education teacher
- Online educator
- Child welfare worker
- Director of childcare center
- Planned-giving officer
- Philanthropic consultant

- Educational program director
- Parent instructor, child development
- Music director
- College and university administrator
- Adult day care coordinator

ENFJs are often drawn to education because it gives them an opportunity to work directly with other people, helping them to grow and develop. They prefer teaching subjects where they can focus on the meaning of material and teach through interpretation and expression. They need a harmonious and cooperative work environment that is tolerant of all views and fosters the open sharing of opinions and feelings. While it is not uncommon for an ENFJ to become a teacher, they may also be called to other careers in the field, such as administrating, consulting, directing, and coordinating.

HEALTHCARE
- Occupational therapist
- Public health educator
- Holistic health practitioner (alternative medicine)
- Dietitian/nutritionist
- Speech-language pathologist/audiologist
- Chiropractor
- Genetic counselor
- Recreational therapist

Within the rapidly expanding field of healthcare, these occupations make the best use of an ENFJ's ability to view, diagnose, and treat the whole person. ENFJs are usually interested in the psychological, emotional, and spiritual causes of disease and are often intrigued with new and alternative methods of treatment. They frequently enjoy the creative problem-solving elements of occupational therapy and speech and language pathology.

BUSINESS / CONSULTING
- Human resource development trainer
- Customer service representative
- Employment specialist
- Sales trainer
- Personnel recruiter
- Executive: small business
- Program designer
- Sales manager
- Director of diversity, equity, and inclusion
- Corporate/team trainer
- Outplacement consultant
- Ecotourism specialist
- Labor relations specialist
- Meeting, convention, and event planner
- Industrial-organizational psychologist
- Hotel and restaurant manager
- Talent director
- Print designer

The many varied jobs within the consulting profession can provide satisfaction to ENFJs because they offer independence while maintaining a close affiliation with others. ENFJs are excellent presenters and trainers, especially when working with individuals or groups to help them improve their own effectiveness. They can be creative and energetic designers of new programs and services, but only if those programs benefit others. They tend to prefer executive positions in smaller companies or organizations where they can have a positive impact, enjoy variety and opportunities to explore new ways of doing things, and still maintain a certain amount of control.

TECHNOLOGY
- Customer relations manager
- Staff advocate (technology consultant)
- Project manager
- Engagement manager
- User experience designer

With the proliferation of technology, there is a rapidly growing need for people who understand technology but also have good people and communication skills. Being the liaison between the technology people and the end users appeals to many ENFJs, who find these jobs satisfy their need to help and be connected with their co-workers.

Remember, these are only some areas that provide satisfying expression for the unique natural talents of the ENFJ.

Customizing Your Job Search

Knowing the particular strengths and blind spots of your type can afford you a tremendous advantage in your job search campaign. In all aspects of the process, from conducting research into available positions, identifying and contacting prospective employers, developing personal marketing tools such as résumés, arranging and conducting job interviews, and negotiating salaries to finally accepting a position, people will act true to their type. Being able to capitalize on your assets and compensate for your liabilities can make the difference between a successful or an unsuccessful job search.

The differences between types are sometimes subtle and other times dramatic. It is the subtle variations in advice we offer that make the real difference between success and failure in a job search. The concept of networking serves as a good example. Extraverts will naturally enjoy networking and are advised to do so on a large scale, while Introverts find more limited and targeted networking, especially with people they already know, easier. Sensors tend to network with people in a defined scope, while Intuitives will go far and wide to find people often seemingly unrelated to their field of interest. Further, Feelers can often take networking personally and enjoy establishing warm rapport, while Thinkers will be more objective and detached in their style. Finally, Judgers tend to ask fewer and more structured questions during their networking, while Perceivers could ask questions of all sorts all day long! One valuable search technique, many ways to implement it.

Pathways to Success: Using Your Strengths

Because of the combined strengths and talents of an ENFJ, most find it fairly easy and often fun to conduct a job search. In fact, ENFJs are great job searchers! And because many career counselors are also ENFJs, it comes as no surprise that some of the classic recommendations offered to job searchers seem tailor-made for ENFJs.

As an ENFJ, you will find that your most effective strategies build on your abilities to do the following:

Plan and execute a creative and well-organized job search plan.

- Establish your criteria for a satisfying job ahead of time and adhere to the most important items on that list to be sure you stay true to what you originally determined was critical. Research potential options by talking with people and using other resources to learn as much as you can before an interview.
- Use your creativity to anticipate and then demonstrate the best way to sell yourself.

As a result of helping a good friend search for a new job, Michael decided to change from a career in secondary school administration to one in career counseling. Because he had no paid experience, he decided to use the help he had given his friend as a case study to demonstrate his

ability and skills in the process of looking for a new job. Before meeting with the director of a small counseling service, Michael sent an articulate cover letter and his résumé, along with the case study he had written about his friend. The study detailed the steps Michael had advised and assisted his friend with and the final result of his friend's finding a great new job. He finished by stating he was eager to offer the same energy and insightful direction and assistance to others.

Impress interviewers with your enthusiasm and self-confidence.

- Establish warm and friendly rapport quickly to demonstrate your ability to make others feel at ease with you.
- Express yourself articulately when discussing your skills, past work experiences, and reasons for interest in the position.

Benji was great at helping bolster other people's confidence. But when it came to preparing himself for an important job interview, he learned to seek out support and encouragement from his wife. Before the interview he would talk through his feelings of nervousness and then review his strengths and accomplishments. Then he would arrive for his interview early, park a distance from the building, and spend a couple of minutes reciting several self-confidence affirmations. He used this little routine to give his self-esteem a needed shot in the arm.

Develop and use a large and active network.

- Conduct the majority of your research in the form of informational interviews— meeting other people who have careers in fields of interest or who have jobs of specific interest to you.

- Call on friends, family, and past associates to let them know that you are looking for a job and ask them to refer you to anyone they know who might be able to help you.

When Evelyn wanted to change careers to training in human resource development, she called on everyone she knew. But most of her friends were connected to other industries and careers and weren't able to offer contacts in her newly chosen field. So Evelyn joined a professional organization for trainers and consultants. She knew no one at the first dinner meeting but set a goal for herself that she would leave the meeting with at least three contacts whom she would call to conduct an informational interview. She left with four.

See job possibilities that don't already exist.

- Brainstorm jobs that you might enjoy, and delay making quality judgments on any until you have a lengthy list. Ask friends who know you well to help you list jobs they think you would succeed at.
- During interviews, demonstrate your ability to see ways of matching your skills and experience to meet the needs of a potential employer.

Lindsey had been a volunteer for most of her life, even as a child. After her children started school, she decided it was time to get a job for which she would be paid for her hard work. But she wasn't sure what marketable skills she had, having never received a paycheck for her work before. When she came to us, we suggested she do some brainstorming with a friend. She and her sister decided to brainstorm over drinks one night. Lindsey returned to our office with a list of jobs that sounded appealing.

During our session, we developed another list of jobs that used the skills she had perfected during her volunteer assignments for various civic, church, and healthcare organizations. The most obvious was her love of the theater and organizing and promoting productions. After making contact with many of her old friends in the arts around town, she was hired to coordinate fundraising for the city's arts council on a part-time basis. It was a dream job and one she turned into a full-time success in a matter of months.

Follow through on all phases of the job search, especially the courtesies.

- Honor all commitments, be on time or a bit early for appointments, and send thank-you notes or other notes to follow up all appointments.
- Use your great memory for personal details to remember people's names and recall any personal information from your research or a common experience.

Debbie developed a foolproof system for tracking her prospects during her search for a job as a recruiter for a college or university. She used a series of index cards for each prospective employer and each person with whom she interviewed. Because in some cases she interviewed before a search committee, she kept a card for all members and then color-coded the whole batch to correspond with the college or university. She added notes when she learned something new or after a contact, so she was always up-to-date on where she stood with each prospect. Her system helped her avoid letting anyone or any detail of her search slip through the cracks. And when she ultimately found the position she wanted and was hired, she was able to write announcement emails to everyone she had met.

Possible Pitfalls

Although all people are unique, there are certain *potential* blind spots that many ENFJs share. We underscore "potential" because some of the following may clearly be true of you, while others may not apply. While considering them, you may notice that these tendencies do not relate just to the job search, but rather describe pitfalls that you may have experienced in other aspects of your life as well. It is therefore helpful to consider each one in terms of your past experiences by asking yourself, "Is this true for me?" And if so, "How did this tendency prevent me from getting something that I wanted?" You will probably notice that the key to overcoming your blind spots is the conscious and thoughtful development of your third and fourth functions (Sensing and Thinking). Many of the suggestions will be challenging to implement, but the more you use these functions, the fewer problems they will cause you in the future.

Try not to make decisions based only on your personal feelings.

- Use objective analysis to help you see the logical results of potential actions. Remember to focus on cause and effect, and seek perspective from a friend if needed.
- Don't dismiss an option because of your personal dislike for one person in the organization. Also resist the temptation to judge a whole job or organization on the basis of one positive interaction.

Don't take criticism and rejection personally.

- Take constructive criticism and feedback as they are intended. Relying on the support and encouragement of friends and family can help you avoid the tendency to become discouraged during the sometimes stressful career search time.
- When rejected for a job or interview you want, try to suspend the tendency to become self-critical. Make it a personal challenge to rise to the occasion and see it as an obstacle to be overcome.

Concentrate on collecting all the necessary facts.

- Pay attention to the details and realities as well as the people you meet. Don't ignore the less interesting tasks of your job search in favor of only making new contacts.
- Rather than simply accepting what you are told at face value, be prepared to ask plenty of questions to learn what the job or company is really like.

Try to be more realistic about potential careers and about other people.

- Try to look at people as they really are, and recognize their limitations. Consciously guard against idealizing people or expressing unquestioning loyalty to others.
- Confront conflict or misunderstandings quickly and directly rather than avoiding them and allowing them to become larger or more complicated.

Don't make decisions too quickly.

- Conducting plenty of research will help keep you from leaping before you have looked things over carefully. Ask for time to think things through before responding to any offer to be sure it is really right for you.
- If you don't resist your tendency to rush to closure, you may miss other

potentially good options still on the horizon, or accept a job that in reality isn't what you want.

The Final Piece: Changing or Keeping Your Job... the Key to Success for ENFJs

Now that you have a solid understanding of your type, you can see how your natural preferences make you better suited for certain kinds of jobs. You can also see how knowing your type-related strengths and blind spots can help you conduct a more successful job search. But as an ENFJ, you've already realized that you are not equally drawn to *every* career or field listed in the Popular Occupations section. The next and final step is to narrow down the field and find the work you were meant to do.

In addition to Type, several other factors—such as your values, interests, and skills—also contribute to your level of satisfaction on the job. The more compatible you are with your job, the happier you'll be. So prepare to use everything you've learned (in this book and in life) to create *your strategic career plan.* The exercises in Chapter 23, "Putting It All Together," are designed to help you do just that.

However, you may have decided it makes more sense (if perhaps only temporarily) to stay in your present job or with your current employer. There may be many valid reasons—financial pressures, family considerations, a tough job market for your specialty, or just bad timing. But take heart! What you've learned in this book can also help you be more content and successful *in your current job.* And should the time come when you're ready to make a major career move, you'll have a much better idea of where you want to go and how to get there.

"So, if you can't have the job you love (yet!)... love the one you've got."

The simple truth is, many jobs allow a good deal of flexibility in the way tasks are performed. Here are some ways you may be able to massage your current job into one that better fits your needs:

- Take and conduct communication workshops.
- Try not to get enmeshed in personality conflicts between co-workers.
- Volunteer to help draft your organization's/department's mission statement.
- Create a support group to help people with personal and/or work-related issues.
- Volunteer to do public relations for your department/organization.
- Limit your "informal counseling" of co-workers, especially when you begin to feel overwhelmed or before you feel caught in a no-win situation.
- Try (harder!) to leave your work at the office.
- Consider becoming a trainer or coach in your field of expertise.
- Email a friend with an inspirational message of support daily, weekly, or when the spirit moves you.
- Let your boss know that feeling appreciated is what really motivates you.
- Stay in the same occupation but switch employers.

One ENFJ turns lemons into lemonade:

Sarah worked as an administrative assistant for a nonprofit health agency. Although she loved the company and believed in its mission, she did not enjoy many of the detail-heavy aspects of the job.

Since she was always touting the agency's work and objectives everywhere she went, she thought it would be great to be paid for it. At the time, there were no openings in the public relations department, so in her spare time, Sarah visited schools as a volunteer to talk about the agency. She did a great job. Six months later a full-time position opened up, she applied, and she was hired.

Use what you've got to get what you need.

Simply put, the best advice on how to succeed is to *capitalize on your strengths and compensate for your blind spots.* Learning how to do this can make the difference between succeeding or failing and loving or hating your work. To help you, we include the following inventory of your potential strengths and blind spots. And while every individual is unique, many of the following should apply to you as an ENFJ.

Your work-related strengths may include

- excellent communication and presentation skills
- charismatic leadership and ability to build consensus
- enthusiasm and ability to enlist cooperation from others
- decisiveness and organizational skills
- eagerness to think outside the box and consider new possibilities
- empathy and ability to anticipate others' needs; a genuine concern for people
- varied interests and being a quick study
- ability to see the big picture and the implications of actions and ideas
- drive to be productive and reach your goals
- deep commitment to work you really believe in

Your work-related blind spots may include

- reluctance to work on projects that conflict with your values
- tendency to idealize people and relationships
- difficulty working in competitive or tension-filled environments
- impatience with structures or people who are inefficient or uncooperative
- avoidance of conflict and tendency to ignore unpleasantness
- tendency to make decisions too quickly, before gathering adequate information
- reluctance to discipline subordinates
- tendency to make errors due to haste
- tendency to micromanage and resist relinquishing control

Using your strengths is easy.
The secret to success for an
ENFJ
is learning to

slow down, relinquish some control, and take things less personally.

8 | INFJ
Introverted, Intuitive, Feeling, Judging
"Catalysts for Positive Change"

Profile 1: Violet, Audio Producer

"The people and the creative process."

The Job

Violet makes music—but not in the way you might imagine. Although she is a talented singer and songwriter, her day job involves producing the original music and audio that goes into commercials. Her official title is executive producer of the New York studio, which oversees all music and audio production projects—in other words, recording, arranging, mixing, mastering, and turning out the finished product that is used in a commercial.

Violet works with other producers, creative directors, composers, and engineers in her studio and the other studios in the company. On any given day, her job could involve asking a composer to write a thirty-second piece of percussion-driven hip-hop for a car commercial; overseeing the tire

squeal, basketball dribble, or birds chirping as part of sound design; or relieving an engineer of "ear fatigue" and giving them a fresh perspective on a piece of audio. Every once in a while, she'll even lend her own voice to a track, bang on a tambourine, or play a kazoo. All of this goes into creating the soundscape you hear when you listen to a commercial.

Backstory

Despite studying political science and French in college, Violet never really considered a career in politics, and was torn between her creative side and her pragmatic side. A gifted musician, she wondered if she could turn that passion into a career, while still realizing she needed a full-time job to pay for her student loans and her life. While working part-time for a voiceover artist after college, Violet was connected to an audio postproduction house that was looking to fill a client services position. "My main priority in finding a full-time job was to work with creative people in a creative environment, and there, I was able to learn about music supervision and audio post-production in advertising"—all the while having access to a studio on nights and weekends so she could pursue her music.

After a year or so, Violet was promoted to music supervisor, a sweet spot between the creative and logistic parts of her personality. Spending several years in this role, Violet moved over to the agency side, a stepping-stone that taught her that the corporate environment was not her ideal workplace. "I much prefer to work on smaller teams where I feel I have an authentic connection with everyone I work with." She left the agency and moved to her current company: a music and postproduction studio that specializes in original music, music supervision, and audio postproduction for commercials.

A Good Fit

Violet loves juggling lots of projects, budgets, and deadlines. Her dominant Intuition is activated constantly by the highly creative work she does, meeting the needs of her clients through inventive problem solving. Whether it's finding the missing sound needed to fulfill a client's wishes, or searching back through her extensive knowledge of music to pull something new together, Violet must think outside the box and trust her gut and her taste in all things.

Also in evidence is her auxiliary function, Feeling, as she works closely with her team of six: "I'm surrounded by insanely creative and smart people who deeply care about the work we do, and that motivates me to do the best I can for them and lead by example." Close and harmonious relationships are important to Violet's happiness at work. A natural leader, she sees her role as "synonymous with taking care of my team, making sure we're still having fun while

we're working, and not burning out." The key for Violet is balance: between sounds in a mix, between work and home, between her artistic and business sides.

Looking Ahead

"It's the people and the creative process that keep me here for now." Ultimately, Violet imagines working for herself or cultivating her own small team, working creatively in some capacity—although what exact capacity that is remains to be seen. "I'm always itching to try a million new things." And while she taps in to her music knowledge in some shape or form on a daily basis, she gets a sense that down the road she'll want to get back into her own music again in some way, even if just for herself.

In her current field of advertising, Violet keeps her eye on the trends and what they might foretell. "It's been interesting to see how sonic branding in particular has become in demand, with in-home devices and podcasts bringing audio-only branding back to the forefront again." Violet describes sonic branding as "a sound or mnemonic tied to a particular brand"—like a jingle you hear, or even a particular sound that is made when you make a purchase. While these sounds might filter into our experience subconsciously, there's always a person behind the design. One day that person might even be Violet!

Profile 2: Delia, Social Worker

"Solving problems in a compassionate way."

The Job

Delia moves at a pace that is thoughtfully slow and deliberate. In some professions, this tendency toward reflection might be deemed secondary to action. But in Delia's career, her natural qualities are just what the doctor ordered. Delia is a clinical social worker in a private geriatric psychiatric practice. About 80 percent of the patients Delia sees suffer some type of dementia. Her job is centered on working with patients and their families to educate them about the process, what to expect, and the available resources for treatment and coping. Delia also helps families deal with behavior problems that arise from dementia, and she supports families through the depression and other issues that sometimes accompany such conditions.

Backstory

Delia began her work in this field with a master of science degree in social work in adult psychology. She worked in hospitals and in community mental health offices, and as a therapist in private practice. After these various experiences, Delia spent eleven years as a therapist in a social service agency, where she commuted to her patients' homes, as most of the patients were aging adults with limited mobility. The strain of constant commuting and the atmosphere at the agency were not what Delia was looking for, however, and she left the practice.

Now, Delia visits with six to eight patients daily, usually seeing a patient together with a family member, and spends time in conversation assessing the current situation and then consulting with two staff psychiatrists to create strategies for managing the various implications of these tricky diagnoses. She talks the patients through the doctors' recommendations, medicine and treatment changes, and suggestions for how to manage behavior, and she helps break through the natural and inevitable denial that accompanies these diseases. Delia's ability to listen to patients and to let the natural process unfold make her extremely effective at what she does.

A Good Fit

Delia's Idealist temperament is well suited to the field of social work and therapy. Her instinctual drive to help and understand people coincides with her empathy and her grasp of larger connections. This makes her a born nurturer of people in pain, as well as an effective problem solver.

Delia is a dominant Intuitive, and she sees this as a huge element in her work. Much of her job is based on interpreting symptoms and behavior, a skill that relies on the connections she makes between pieces of information. Delia must be adept at paying attention to cues and tones of voice while building a story or pattern in her mind and then figuring how best to respond. Her intuitive grasp of the larger picture is instrumental in making sense of seemingly disparate or unrelated bits of information.

Delia's auxiliary function, extraverted Feeling, makes her extremely empathetic. "People feel comfortable with me—I've always been told that." Her nonjudgmental attitude and utter concentration while listening causes people to believe that she really hears them and cares about what they are saying. Delia's unconscious style of mirroring people allows all kinds of people to feel comfortable with her. Also important to her line of work is the fact that Delia doesn't treat elderly people as though they're invisible—something that tends to happen in our society. Instead, she is respectful and never talks down to them. Her mother had dementia, and Delia has struggled with depression, so she understands her patients and can relate to their circumstances.

Looking Ahead

Delia loves both the environment and the mission of her current place of work. Geriatrics is rapidly expanding, and it is an exciting field to be in. As dementia becomes much more widespread due to the general aging of the population, people in the field are constantly discovering new permutations of the disease, which keeps Delia interested. "Most people who work in this field had an older person in their life who was really important to them—for me, that was my uncle Frank." Aside from the patients, Delia feels supported and appreciated by her colleagues. She has two great bosses who recognize her strengths and play to them, and who also encourage her professional growth. Delia is gratified by the sense that she is part of a great, collegial team.

In addition to working with patients, Delia conducts research into the ever-expanding types of dementia and their particular manifestations in her patients. She loves the opportunity to delve deeply into fascinating research that could make a difference in people's lives. In the future, she hopes to do more of this type of work, perhaps even researching and writing a book someday.

Profile 3: Courtney, Book Editor

"Being a content creator—that's what's exciting to me."

The Job

Courtney is the boss of the book. As editor in a division of a major publishing house, she is responsible for shepherding each book in her care through numerous stages of development and production, working with people in each division—the production team, marketing, publicity, and sales. Unlike a traditional editor, who works with authors and guides the process of a book from inception to publication, Courtney works for a co-venture that discovers market trends and pitches ideas for

books, working with a packager to find writers to see the ideas through to completion in about half the time it takes a traditional book to be made. So in addition to being an editor, she also is a content creator, keeping an eye on what is selling in nonfiction and imagining books that could fit into market niches. This could be anything from a book to help children interview their grandparents to the *New York Times* crossword puzzle compilations—both projects she oversees. All in all, Courtney is in charge of about a hundred books a year.

Backstory

For a kid who loves books, the path to working as an editor at a publisher can seem like a straight shot. For Courtney, the journey was more meandering. At first she thought she would try her hand as a writer, so she got her undergraduate degree in creative writing. But she fell out of love with the constant criticism of the collegiate workshop model and moved toward the editorial side of things. She got her master's degree in English literature in London, and found her first couple jobs in the field—one as a proofreader at a small media company, another editing curricular content for an online university. "But it wasn't anywhere close to what I wanted to do. I wanted to edit books." While she had a vision of this job, Courtney wasn't exactly sure what it entailed. Finally, she decided to take the plunge and move to New York City, where she hustled and found an entry-level job at a major publishing house.

Courtney first worked as an assistant to the managing editor in production, the group that oversees proofreading, page layout, cover art, and that sort of thing. Still on her quest to move to editorial, where the content of the book is shaped, she became an assistant editor in the editorial department, working directly with agents and authors. When she saw that her company was starting a new co-venture for a different kind of publishing, Courtney saw an opportunity for advancement. In her pitch to her bosses, she made sure to outline the strengths she could bring to the undertaking. Her advocacy paid off, and Courtney was promoted to editor, fulfilling a dream years in the making.

A Good Fit

Courtney describes being the editor of a book as being the "captain of the ship": navigating a manuscript through the process of publication and directing all the people who work on it from beginning to end. Like many Idealists, she found herself in a creative field, being able to realize her vision for each book and pulling together resources to build a huge catalogue of books that she has helped publish.

Since Courtney's job involves coming up with the ideas for books based on current trends and then finding writers to write them, her dominant Intuition is always in play. "That's exciting to me, because it's almost like being a writer. It's being a content creator, as opposed to being hamstrung by what you're given." She must analyze the book market and look for the big picture in the industry, always staying one step ahead of the curve. This takes a great deal of imagination and insight.

Though an Introvert, Courtney likes that her work is collaborative and depends on fostering relationships with people in different departments. She has to be friendly and encouraging, constantly anticipating problems and solving them. A Feeling type, Courtney is buoyed by the camaraderie and teamwork she has built over her seven and a half years in the company. "I know how to interact with different people, because not everyone likes to be interacted with the same way."

Looking Ahead

Courtney hopes that by the time this interview goes to press, she will have moved on to senior editor. After all, the trajectory of her career has depended on making strategic moves and advocating for her next promotion. Eventually, she thinks she would prefer the role of publisher to editor—someone who oversees the business as a whole and is less weighed down in the nitty-gritty aspects of each particular manuscript. "I want to oversee a creative machine." A job like that requires someone with vision—something Courtney clearly has.

Indeed, vision is required more than ever in an industry that has survived technological advances despite some doomsday predictions. Going forward, Courtney predicts that the fields to watch in publishing are audiobooks, which have had a huge boost in popularity recently, as well as people moving more toward self-publishing. "There are more ways to publish a book, more ways than ever to get your ideas out there."

Common Threads

Although Courtney, Delia, and Violet have different backgrounds, experiences, and careers, there are certain common threads woven through their stories. Specific interests and abilities may differ, but owing to their similar temperament values and the *same hierarchy* of their psychological functions, there are certain observations we can make about the needs of many INFJs.

What follows is a list of the most important elements—the formula, if you will, for INFJ satisfaction. Given the uniqueness of all individuals—even those who share a type—this list will not describe each INFJ equally well. The important thing is that these ten elements, with varying degrees of intensity and in different orders of importance, identify what INFJs need to be satisfied.

After you have reviewed this list, you might find it useful to go back and try to prioritize the elements in order of *their importance to you.* When doing this, think of past work experiences as well as your present job, and what you found particularly satisfying or unsatisfying. Try to look for *themes* that run through several experiences, not just *events* that might be true for one work situation but not for another.

As an INFJ, I define career satisfaction as doing work that

1. lets me consider and create new ideas and/or approaches to a variety of problems, mostly those that help others to grow and develop
2. lets me produce a product or service that I believe in and am proud of
3. recognizes my authorship and ownership and my unique contributions
4. lets me express myself and see the results of my vision
5. lets me work with others on a one-to-one basis
6. is done in a friendly and tension-free environment where my ideas are seriously considered and where I am psychologically supported for my efforts
7. can be done independently but with the opportunity to share frequently with others in an environment that is friendly and free of interpersonal conflict
8. lets me organize my own time and work environment and exert significant control over both the process and product
9. gives me adequate time to formulate and process my ideas so they are thoroughly prepared

10. is in harmony with my personal values and beliefs and lets me maintain a high degree of personal and professional integrity

Popular Occupations for INFJs

In listing occupations that are popular among INFJs, it is important to note that there are successful people of all types in all occupations. However, the following are careers INFJs may find particularly satisfying, and some of the reasons why. This is by no means a comprehensive listing but is included to suggest possibilities you may not have previously considered. Although all of these occupations offer the potential for career satisfaction, the future demand for some careers is anticipated to be greater than for others.

COUNSELING
- Career counselor
- Clinical psychologist
- School counselor
- Employee assistance counselor
- Eldercare specialist
- Marriage and family therapist
- Child welfare counselor
- Substance abuse counselor
- Mental health counselor
- Developmental psychologist
- The counseling fields require close personal interaction, often on a one-to-one basis, allowing INFJs to make in-depth connections with others. INFJs are often deeply satisfied by helping others reach personal insights and growth in a 1:1 setting.

EDUCATION
- High school teacher: English/art/music/ social sciences/drama
- College professor: English/art/music/ social sciences/drama

- College professor: Education
- Educational consultant
- Curriculum designer
- Librarian
- Special education teacher
- Bilingual education teacher
- Early education teacher
- Online educator
- Sociologist
- Museum conservator
- Educational program director
- Parenting instructor, child development course
- Museum educator

Teaching occupations allow INFJs to use their ideas and knowledge to help others. Guiding students and watching them grow, designing inventive curriculum, and inspiring others are all aspects of education that INFJs tend to enjoy. INFJs also enjoy studying, learning, and the growth opportunities found in an educational context, so they are usually quite comfortable in an academic setting.

RELIGION
- Priest/rabbi/imam
- Religious worker
- Director of religious education

Religious work requires a deep and personal commitment and a work philosophy that can be characterized as a mission. INFJs frequently see their work that way and find deep satisfaction in sharing their philosophy and beliefs with others.

CREATIVE
- Artist
- Playwright
- Novelist
- Poet
- Interior designer
- Informational-graphics designer
- Universal design architect

- Freelance media planner
- Brand manager
- Editor/art director (online/print)
- Literary agent or editor
- Online publisher (e-books)
- Genealogist (family tree researcher)
- Print designer
- Interaction designer
- Creative producer
- Film editor
- Documentary filmmaker
- Educational software developer
- Curator
- Exhibit designer
- Costume designer
- Merchandise designer and displayer

The appeal of the arts to the INFJ is the ability to create unique works, using their own ideas and vision. The arts enable INFJs to express themselves in a personal way, and the result is often to have an impact on others. With these occupations, the work is generally done independently, allowing the INFJ to organize and control the environment, the process, and the product.

HEALTHCARE / SOCIAL SERVICES
- Director, social service agency
- Mediator/conflict resolver
- Social worker
- Social scientist
- Community health educator
- Dietitian/nutritionist
- Speech-language pathologist/audiologist
- Holistic health practitioner (alternative medicine)
- Massage therapist
- Occupational therapist
- Genetic counselor
- Chiropractor
- Grant coordinator
- Healthcare administrator
- Fundraising director
- Legal mediator

- Adult day care coordinator
- Crisis hotline operator

The social service occupations require a commitment to helping others, often within an organizational structure. Most INFJs enjoy working in such a setting, especially when it involves a small and close-knit staff. Social service enables the INFJ to consider and develop new approaches to the problems of individuals or society. Many times social workers work independently on a caseload, allowing them to have frequent and one-on-one interaction with clients and colleagues.

BUSINESS
- Human resources manager
- Marketing manager
- Organizational development consultant
- Employee assistance program coordinator/counselor
- Job analyst
- Director of diversity, equity, and inclusion
- Corporate/team trainer
- Preferred customer sales representative
- Merchandise planner
- Environmental lawyer
- Interpreter/translator
- Planned-giving officer
- Philanthropic consultant
- Outplacement consultant

Although INFJs do not tend to gravitate toward business careers in large numbers, there are areas of business in which INFJs may find satisfaction.

Human resources, or personnel, and organizational development consulting are the "people" parts of business, requiring an interest in and facility with many different types of people. These occupations enable the INFJ to help others find jobs, structure effective work environments, and engage in creative problem solving in which people are the focus.

The marketing occupations enable INFJs to use their creative problem-solving abilities, often working on a team. If INFJs have significant input into the process and are able to maintain a comfortable level of personal and professional integrity, they can find this type of work satisfying.

TECHNOLOGY
- Customer relations manager
- Staff advocate (technology consultant)
- Project manager
- Engagement manager
- Human resources recruiter

With the proliferation of technology, there is a rapidly growing need for people who understand technology but also have good people and communication skills. Being the liaison between the technology people and the end users appeals to many INFJs, who find these jobs satisfy their need to help and be connected with their co-workers.

Remember, these are only some of the areas that provide satisfying expression for the unique natural talents of the INFJ.

Customizing Your Job Search

Knowing the particular strengths and blind spots of your type can afford you a tremendous advantage in your job search campaign. In all aspects of the process, from conducting research into available positions, identifying and contacting prospective employers, developing personal marketing tools such as résumés, arranging and conducting job interviews, and negotiating salaries to finally accepting a position, people will act true to their type. Being able to capitalize on your assets and compensate for your liabilities can make the difference between a successful and an unsuccessful job search.

The differences between types are sometimes subtle and other times dramatic. It is the subtle variations in advice we offer that make the real difference between success and failure in a job search. The concept of networking serves as a good example. Extraverts will naturally enjoy networking and are advised to do so on a large scale, while Introverts find more limited and targeted networking, especially with people they already know, easier. Sensors tend to network with people in a defined scope, while Intuitives will go far and wide to find people often seemingly unrelated to their field of interest. Further, Feelers can often take networking personally and enjoy establishing warm rapport, while Thinkers will be more objective and detached in their style. Finally, Judgers tend to ask fewer and more structured questions during their networking, while Perceivers could ask questions of all sorts all day long! One valuable search technique, many ways to implement it.

Pathways to Success: Using Your Strengths

As we will detail in the following pages, your strength and talent for the job search lie in thoughtful planning, creative problem solving, and your ability to communicate your commitment to what you believe in. But beware your tendency to become single-minded in your research, and unrealistic in your objectives.

As an INFJ, you will find that your most effective strategies build on your abilities to do the following:

Think through and formulate an innovative, organized job search plan.

- Use your creativity to plot out a campaign in a new and different way—setting you apart from other candidates to potential employers.
- Use your organizational skills to stay on top of the project, make a plan, be on

time, remember to follow up with prospective employers.

While working with us to make a career switch from corporate law to the more specialized area of environmental law, Sue easily saw possibilities that could incorporate her legal skills and her interests. She brainstormed the names of organizations she might like to work for, then researched them thoroughly. Having attempted to determine their needs, she packaged herself in a way that made her attractive to prospective employers. An organized person by nature, Sue designed and conducted her search true to her type, by following up after interviews and keeping good records of her progress.

Network on a limited basis.

- Enlist the help of people with whom you have developed relationships over the years and who know you well to identify people to contact about career opportunities.
- During each interview, ask for additional recommendations of other people for you to see to more fully research the field or a particular job.

When Helen was looking for more fulfilling work—work that would serve her sense of mission—she began by speaking with friends and priests within the church. These informational interviews led her to discuss her job plans and interests with the then acting coordinator of the educational publishing project. In talking to him, she learned he was serving only temporarily and, therefore, the job was about to become available. For Helen, talking to friends and associates on a one-on-one basis helped her to find a satisfying position that (like many of the best jobs) was never advertised in the public job market.

Establish rapport with interviewers and potential employers.

- Use your extraordinary ability to read people's needs and motivations.
- Let employers sense your natural warmth and enthusiasm, and demonstrate your ability to listen and communicate articulately.

John was in the running for a personnel manager position at a small company. He learned that he was one of four applicants asked to return for a second interview and felt he needed to set himself apart from the other candidates. In preparation for this important interview, John spent some time rereading background information on the company with an eye for more personal details about the staff.

Being a father of two young children, John was interested to discover that two of the principals were parents of school-age children in his hometown. During the first moments of the interview, while everyone was getting seated, John asked how the children were enjoying the new playscape recently constructed on their playground. Thus, he was able to establish something they had in common while creating a friendly and relaxed atmosphere. The conversation also allowed John to demonstrate his knowledge of and interest in community activities and his ability to get along well with people.

Consider options thoughtfully, without rushing to judgment.

- Capitalize on your propensity for thinking things through in a careful way.
- Decide to give yourself a few minutes to keep open options you might have eliminated at first thought.

Upon relocating to New York City, Cynthia began interviewing for positions in art departments of advertising agencies. She found herself with a good problem: After completing interviews at four agencies, she was offered positions at two. Both would provide steady work at competitive salaries. Instead of making a hasty decision that would result in job security and an end to the search process, Cynthia asked both agencies for one week's time to consider her options. During that week she spent time carefully weighing the pros and cons of each opportunity until she came to a surprising decision: She declined both offers and instead began working on a freelance basis at all four agencies! Her decision gave her the flexibility, free time, and independence she would have given up had she accepted either of the staff positions.

Create a position that will meet your specific needs.

- Use your vision to anticipate trends, where people with your talents will be needed in the future, etc.
- Demonstrate that talent to prospective employers by letting them know how you will help them achieve goals or solve problems.

While working as a kitchen designer, Bob used his natural Intuition to see the need for a system that would allow his customers to actually see on paper what their redesigned kitchens would look like before spending the enormous amount of money it would take to have the work done. Imagining that the technology might be available to create such a system, or that it might already be in existence, he began his research. First he talked to a tech-savvy friend, which ultimately led him to the company he now represents.

His ability to see the possibilities and then demonstrate that vision to the potential employer won him the job he now loves.

Find creative solutions to obstacles that arise.

- Approach temporary setbacks as problems to be solved rather than rebuffs or insurmountable obstacles.
- Use your natural ability to look ahead, focus on the next opportunity, or recover from a disappointment.

Sandy tried unsuccessfully for six weeks to get an appointment with the director of human resources of a company he wanted to work for. In discussions with a neighbor who worked for the company, Sandy discovered that the director was an avid sailor. On a long shot, Sandy sent him an article listing new and innovative gadgets and supplies for outfitting sailboats. He mentioned in the email that he was trying to get an appointment to see the director and would like to talk with him further about the other creative ways Sandy might be able to make his life easier. When Sandy called to follow up three days later, the director not only remembered his name but interviewed him the following week.

Possible Pitfalls

Although all people are unique, there are certain *potential* blind spots that many INFJs share. We specify "potential" because some of the following *may* be true of you, while others may clearly not apply. While considering them, you may notice that these tendencies do not relate just to the job search, but rather describe pitfalls that you may have experienced in other aspects of your life as well. It is therefore helpful to consider each one in terms of your past experiences by asking yourself, "Is this true for me?" And if so, "How did this tendency

prevent me from getting something that I wanted?" You will probably notice that the key to overcoming your blind spots is the conscious and thoughtful development of your third and fourth functions (Thinking and Sensing). Many of the suggestions will be difficult to implement, but the more you use these functions, the fewer problems they will cause you in the future.

Concentrate on the facts and details of the situation, not just the more interesting big picture.

- This requires a conscious effort to tune in to what is actually before you—to read what is on the lines, not just what is between them.
- Make notes ahead of time to be sure you ask the practical questions about what a job is really like, including hours, duties, salary, benefits, reporting structure, etc.

Try to establish realistic expectations about the job search process and the potential outcome.

- Engage in "reality testing" to make sure you are being realistic about the market, your skills, and the amount of time a search will take. Ask a friend to help you by playing devil's advocate with your plan.
- Try to set more realistic goals to avoid the tendency to become overly perfectionistic and then experience the disappointment that comes from not accomplishing all you hoped.

Try to avoid making decisions based solely on your personal feelings rather than on more objective data.

- Remember that you naturally see things from a personal perspective and need to consciously engage your logical thinking skills.

- Don't confuse rapport established during an interview with personal friendship. Keep yourself a bit detached from the situation, deciding not to make a permanent connection until you know a lot more.

When discussing your skills and abilities, focus on how you can meet the prospective employer's needs rather than your own.

- Show the prospective employer you have done your research by incorporating information about the company's current challenges and then demonstrate how you might help meet them by recalling your past experiences and accomplishments.
- Express the willingness to take some necessary risks to handle a new challenge and prove yourself. Take an extra few seconds to consider another way, especially after you think you have made up your mind.

Avoid spending too much time considering possibilities and not enough time acting on them.

- Develop a reasonable list of options to pursue and a timetable in which to research them. Hold yourself accountable for meeting an established quota of emails written, applications submitted, or interviews completed within a particular time frame.
- Try to be flexible in setting job criteria and throughout the negotiation process, remembering that sometimes unexpected benefits appear when you stay open to another point of view.

The Final Piece: Changing or Keeping Your Job...the Key to Success for INFJs

Now that you have a solid understanding of your type, you can see how your natural preferences make you better suited for certain kinds of jobs. You can also see how knowledge of your type-related strengths and blind spots can help you conduct a more successful job search. But as an INFJ, you've already realized that you are not equally drawn to *every* career or field listed in the Popular Occupations section. The next and final step is to narrow down the field and find the work you were meant to do.

In addition to Type, several other factors—such as your values, interests, and skills—also contribute to your level of satisfaction on the job. The more compatible you are with your job, the happier you'll be. So prepare to use everything you've learned (in this book and in life) to create *your strategic career plan.* The exercises in Chapter 23, "Putting It All Together," are designed to help you do just that.

However, you may have decided it makes more sense (if perhaps only for the moment) to stay in your present job or with your current employer. There may be many valid reasons—financial pressures, family considerations, a tough job market for your specialty, or just bad timing. But take heart! What you've learned in this book can also help you be more content and successful *in your current job.* And should the time come when you're ready to make a major career move, you'll have a much better idea of where you want to go and how to get there.

"So, if you can't have the job you love (yet!)...love the one you've got."

The simple truth is, many jobs allow a good deal of flexibility in the way tasks are performed. Here are some ways you may be able to massage your current job into one that better fits your needs:

- Make sure you have plenty of uninterrupted time to think; close your office door and occasionally take a break from answering your phone or checking your email.
- Volunteer for planning committees where you can give your creative input.
- Try not to get enmeshed in personality conflicts between co-workers.
- Try to work on one major project at a time.
- Volunteer to help draft your organization's/department's mission statement.
- Seek out other creative people to hear your ideas.
- Try to put your ideas and thoughts on paper and get them published somewhere.
- Make sure to strike a balance between your work and personal life.
- Consider becoming a trainer or coach in your field of expertise.
- Email a friend with an inspirational message of support daily, weekly, or when the spirit moves you.

One INFJ turns lemons into lemonade:

Although Margo was a successful internist, she was extremely frustrated that the bureaucracy of managed care had severely limited the amount of time she could spend with each patient. While she had always valued having time to discuss with her patients their concerns, she realized what she missed most was the teaching aspect of these sessions. Margo ultimately decided to teach a course in family medicine at a nearby college, which she found extremely rewarding.

Use what you've got to get what you need.

Simply put, the best advice on how to succeed is to *capitalize on your strengths and compensate for your blind spots.* Learning how to do this can make the difference between succeeding or failing and loving or hating your work. To help you, we include the following inventory of your potential strengths and blind spots. And while every individual is unique, many of the following should apply to you as an INFJ.

Your work-related strengths may include

- integrity that inspires people to value your ideas
- focus and single-mindedness about projects that are important to you
- decisiveness and strong organizational skills
- creativity and ability to come up with original solutions
- empathy and ability to anticipate others' needs
- perspective to see the big picture and the future implications of actions and ideas
- ability to understand complex concepts
- genuine interest in others and talent for helping others grow and develop
- independent streak and strong personal convictions
- drive to be productive and reach your goals
- deep commitment to work you believe in

Your work-related blind spots may include

- single-mindedness that can result in inflexibility
- unrealistic sense of how long things take
- difficulty working on projects that conflict with your values

- tendency to be impractical about viability and/or feasibility of some ideas
- difficulty working in competitive or tension-filled environments
- reluctance to revisit or reverse decisions once they've been made
- difficulty dealing with conflict and tendency to ignore unpleasantness

- trouble disciplining subordinates with objectivity and directness
- difficulty changing plans or directions quickly
- difficulty communicating complex ideas simply
- tendency to be judgmental

Using your strengths is easy.
The secret to success for an
INFJ
is learning to

**pay attention to details,
be flexible, and be willing
to act spontaneously.**

9 | ENFP
Extraverted, Intuitive, Feeling, Perceiving

"Anything's Possible"

Profile 1: Joyce, Professor

"The energy magnet."

The Job

Joyce laughs a lot. And so do the hundreds of people who come in contact with her through her two occupations. She is a college professor of special education at a community college and a national lecturer on the subject of humor. Each year she gives approximately three hundred talks and workshops to corporations, schools, hospitals, and associations on the value of humor and laughter. Lots of people are laughing with Joyce.

"There's no question that what I love most about my work is the people I spend time with and the fact that it's so much fun!" She loves group interaction—all her classes are taught in the round. Joyce is like an energy magnet: People are drawn to her and she is energized by them. Teaching still excites her, and because every class is so different, it's as if she were teaching it for the first time. "I love being in front of and part of a group, doing very experiential things, not knowing exactly what will happen until it does."

Backstory

Joyce has an unusually linear work history for an ENFP. She received a bachelor's degree in education, then completed two master's degrees, the first in special education, the second in counseling. (Later on, she also picked up a sixth-year certificate.) Unable to find a job teaching the physically disabled when she began her career, she taught general special education for three years. She left the field to raise her two children and returned to teach special education part-time at the community college. Joyce has become a kind of local legend—she is so popular that her classes are always filled early, and students are delighted with what she delivers. She has been teaching at the college level for fifteen years.

Joyce has great many strengths and abilities. "I'm a terrific teacher; I have a high energy level and I put in a tremendous number of hours; I'm creative and perceptive, with good insight into people; I'm very friendly and I have a good sense of humor." Every class is an accomplishment because she is making a difference in what people understand about themselves and their students. Not surprisingly, the greatest satisfaction in her life comes from her work and her relationships with her students.

A Good Fit

Like most ENFPs, Joyce has a wonderful sense of humor. She is also very perceptive about people. She has found a unique way to combine these two qualities to carry out the mission of so many Idealists—to help people gain self-awareness and live happier lives. Joyce uses humor to entertain and educate—whether she is lecturing to her graduate school students or speaking before any one of the hundreds of audiences she is hired to address each year. Challenging people to open themselves up to new experiences, she makes people laugh and learn at the same time.

Everything is possible to Joyce. Her dominant Intuition is always tuned in to the new and different, which almost guarantees that something special will happen every day. She is clever and witty and has boundless energy; her enthusiasm quickly infects whomever she is interacting with. Because she is so tuned in to people, she can sense what will and won't work and is able to pick up subtle cues, adapting her style to connect with very different types of people.

The single most satisfying part of her job is the deep personal relationships that Joyce develops with her students. As a Feeling type, Joyce thrives on these close friendships. Once she has taken someone inside her circle, they become a friend for life.

Likewise, she values the relationships she has with her colleagues. Joyce's family is a central part of her life, and her college teaching schedule allows her lots of time to spend with them. Run by her values, Joyce believes that laughter is therapeutic and can make a serious impact on a person's physical and mental health.

Looking Ahead

"Teaching is really my favorite thing in the world. As a result, my only career goal is to do what I'm doing, only better." She admits that she would like to be famous on a national level, and one day hopes to write a book that she thinks might make her so. In the meantime, she has enrolled in a doctoral program in adult higher education. She anticipates how rigorous working on this degree will be for the next several years but feels the need to be challenged by learning something new, stretching her intellectual faculties.

She defines career satisfaction as "having fun, involving people, and making a difference." Consistent with her philosophy is the fact that her favorite course to teach is "How to Make Small Talk," which she particularly loves because her students (frequently many on the shy side) end up learning how to open themselves to new experiences. Joyce, like many ENFPs, enjoys being a catalyst—helping others grow and develop. In fact, she considers the secret of her success to be her ability to be open to different people and different opportunities that were not in her plans.

Profile 2: Eddie, Activist

"Making politics fun!"

The Job

Eddie is a twenty-first-century activist. Instead of picket lines, his platform is video content. As an activist video writer and producer, Eddie harnesses the power of comedy to enact real change on issues that matter to him. Because the vehicle is satire, Eddie can tackle serious problems without becoming pedantic or preachy, therefore winning more people over to his causes. His job involves conceiving an idea for a script, writing the script, and then working with a team to find talent, locations, and a crew, all within a budget. The most satisfying part is watching a video he has poured his heart and soul into take off like wildfire across the internet.

Backstory

All throughout college, Eddie loved to make people laugh. He studied improvisation and stand-up comedy, and after school moved to Los Angeles to try his hand in the big leagues. But the rat race started to get to Eddie, and something seemed to be missing. He'd always had his eye on a different goal—to do something important, effect political change, even become a senator.

Eddie had switched tracks and decided to go to law school, with the end goal of working for the American Civil Liberties Union, when a midterm election brought a slew of Republicans into Congress. He read an article about the new political climate posing a risk to internet neutrality, and made a post to Reddit suggesting a Reddit political action committee. The next morning he woke up to a huge response, and his life in activism began in earnest.

Eddie quickly realized he could use his background in comedy to garner a wider audience for the issues he cared about. Using parody and satire to make videos, Eddie caught the attention of a progressive Democratic lobby. He moved to New York City to work as a writer and producer of videos that brought awareness to meaningful political topics.

Having worked in New York for a couple of years, Eddie is now in the midst of an exciting change. His dream is to form a satiric organization that is centered on campaign finance reform. He has been in talks with another activist organization that is interested in helping to make his dream a reality. Eddie's goal is to reverse activism's stigma as serious and boring. He'd particularly love to create "a comedy show you actually want to come to, not because you feel like you should support this issue, but because it would just be fun."

A Good Fit

As a writer and producer, Eddie gets to use his natural creativity and originality on a daily basis. A dominant Intuitive type, Eddie is constantly absorbed with the big picture—the social and political issues that matter to him. He loves being the person in the room to pitch ten new ideas that no one else has thought of.

Eddie's values as an Idealist are front and center in his job, and he gets to tackle big problems through a medium that is actually fun. He enjoys seeing the various parts of producing and writing come together in service of his message. Beneath the satisfaction of using his creative and social skills are the personal values he is acting in service of. As a Feeler, Eddie sees the world through the lens of his beliefs, and cares deeply about the injustices he perceives in the world. An Extravert, Eddie's work has always been highly collaborative—from the days of being on an improv team through to the present—and he is able to work alongside other creative people to realize his vision. The charge he gets from meeting people and finding common ground with them propels him, and broadening his platform from dozens to thousands is invigorating.

Looking Ahead

Whatever Eddie accomplishes in the next five years, he hopes to do it through this comedy organization. "I'd love to be a politician if the system wasn't so god-awful." Eddie wants to effect real political change, but he is put off by how much of a politician's time must be spent raising money and kowtowing to special interests. The medium of comedy seems to be a way to wield cultural power and raise awareness about issues that matter, without experiencing firsthand the Washington meat grinder. While he enjoys producing, Eddie doesn't want to stay behind the scenes forever: "I do have a desire to be a leader. I have a desire to express my voice."

Profile 3: Sam, Director of Community Engagement

"Connecting the community."

The Job

Sam's job is all about people. He works in a small urban independent school as the director of auxiliary programs and community engagement. The first part of his title boils down to overseeing programming that happens outside of the classroom—including extracurriculars after school and summer camps run out of the school in June and July.

The second part of his title includes engaging with the school community, working with the communications team, and doing promotion and marketing for different programs that the school offers. Sam builds digital learning resources that highlight work happening in classrooms and creates systems for online registration for all extracurricular programs. He also communicates with and supervises all of the staff for the afterschool classes and liaises with a company that provides lunch for the school every day.

Sam gets his energy from all the relationships that make up his job. "I'm part of the team that makes decisions about the school and school policy. I'm part of a tight-knit community where I know all the kids, I know all the parents, and I get to work with our team of teachers, a hardworking and insightful group of people."

Backstory

As a kid, the community that mattered the most to Sam was his summer camp. Each year, Sam looked forward to the all-consuming fun and spirit of camp, and he idolized the counselors especially. "It was like Hogwarts. You're brought into this world where there's this community. You have your friends. And you have this history and mythology. Summer camp is like that, where you're brought into this lineage. The counselors were the bearers of that, bringing out the best in all that, making you feel special." When he was old enough, Sam became a counselor and worked summers at camp for many years. It felt natural, and he loved working with the kids.

When he graduated from college, Sam tried a job as the assistant director of the camp he went to. But the lifestyle of being on twenty-four hours a day for three months of the year, and spending the other nine months of the year so isolated, without the interactions with the community, wasn't for Sam. He also wanted to work with a more diverse population than the camp served. The transition to teaching seemed like a natural next step, and there were parts of it he really enjoyed. But much of what Sam loved about camp didn't necessarily translate to the classroom.

After a couple years of teaching, an opportunity arose on the administrative side of things. Sam's school had an afterschool program to serve children in the hours after the academic day had ended. Like many other independent schools, the afterschool programming was not up to the same standard as the programs during the school day. "It very adversely affected our students of color and those who receive financial aid to a greater degree." A position was created to reimagine the afterschool program and oversee the extracurricular aspects of the school overall, including summer camp programming. Sam's skill set was a perfect match, and he inaugurated the new role.

A Good Fit

As an Idealist, it's imperative to Sam to do work that serves his values. Part of why he left the camp world was that he felt he was serving a purely homogenous population. Now he gets to work every day to correct what he feels is an ethical problem in private schools—a barrier to quality programming after the school day is over. "I'm driven by the value of what I'm doing."

The creation of Sam's role itself is a testament to his creative problem-solving. Inaugurating any role is difficult without a road map to follow, but Sam was able to build the plane midflight. ENFPs are uniquely suited to tolerating that level of novelty; indeed, creating the role himself allowed Sam to customize it.

People are a huge part of Sam's job; collaborating, communicating, and managing. A Feeling type, Sam is thoughtful about this work and considers the feelings and needs of the people he works with and supervises. "I work really hard to make sure people feel supported. I think I put the right level of humanity into my decisions." The relationships Sam cultivates with the children

in his care are also deeply meaningful to him.

Looking Ahead

Sam is content in his current job for now, but allows that if certain criteria are met, his next job could look like many different things. "I want to work in a place with a clear mission that everybody subscribes to, and is led by a strong executive who subscribes to that mission very well, and is built around collaboration but also allows for a certain sense of creativity." He knows that he doesn't want to be the head of a private school, or perhaps even stay in the independent school world. As much as his current work allows him to address injustice in some small ways, Sam still chafes against the premise of private schools. "I need to be actively working to build an equitable society. We're in an unjust society, and I need to be a part of working against that."

Common Threads

Although Joyce, Sam, and Eddie have different backgrounds, experiences, and careers, there are certain common threads that weave through their stories. Their specific interests and abilities may differ, but owing to their similar temperament values and the *same hierarchy* of their psychological functions, there are certain observations we can make about the needs of many ENFPs.

What follows is a list of the most important elements—the formula, if you will, for ENFP satisfaction. Given the uniqueness of all individuals—even those who share a type—this list will not describe each ENFP equally well. The important thing is that these ten elements, with varying degrees of intensity and in different orders of importance, identify what ENFPs need to be satisfied.

After you have reviewed this list, we recommend that you go back and prioritize the elements in order of *their importance to you.* When doing this, think of past work experiences as well as your present job, and what you found particularly satisfying or unsatisfying. Try to look for *themes* that run through several experiences, not just *events* that might be true for one work situation but not for another.

As an ENFP, I define career satisfaction as doing work that

1. lets me work with a diverse group of people on a variety of projects, motivated by creative inspiration
2. lets me create new ideas, products, services, or solutions to problems that will help other people, and then see my projects become reality
3. is fun, challenging, and always varied
4. rarely requires me to handle the follow-through, routine details, or maintenance of a system or project
5. lets me work at my own pace and schedule, with a minimum of rules or structure and the freedom to act spontaneously
6. lets me meet new people, learn new skills, and continually satisfy my curiosity
7. is consistent with my personal beliefs and values and lets me create opportunities that benefit others
8. is done in a friendly and relaxed environment with humor, goodwill, and a minimum of interpersonal conflict
9. allows me the freedom to follow my inspirations and participate in exciting and intriguing adventures
10. is done in an environment that appreciates and rewards enthusiasm, ingenuity, and imagination

Popular Occupations for ENFPs

Because of their combination of preferences, ENFPs are naturally drawn to a wide variety of occupations.

In listing occupations that are popular among ENFPs, it is important to note that there are successful people of all types in all occupations. However, the following are careers ENFPs may find particularly satisfying, and some of the reasons why. This is by no means a comprehensive listing but is included to suggest possibilities you may not have previously considered.

Although all of these occupations offer the potential for career satisfaction, the future demand for some careers is anticipated to be greater than for others.

CREATIVE
- Journalist
- Screenwriter/playwright
- Columnist
- Blogger
- Actor
- Musician/composer
- Newscaster
- Interior decorator
- Artist
- Reporter/editor (print/online)
- Informational-graphics designer
- Interaction designer
- Editor/art director (website)
- Creative director
- Developer of educational software
- Producer
- Director of regional/community theater
- Documentary filmmaker
- Costume designer
- Television producer
- Radio/podcast producer
- Broadcast news analyst
- Cartoonist/animator
- Exhibit designer

The obvious appeal of these creative careers is the opportunity to continually develop new and original approaches. ENFPs enjoy the creative process, especially if it offers opportunity for collaboration and to be inspired by working with others. The more unconstrained and flexible the working environment, the better ENFPs like it. They work well independently but need frequent, spontaneous interaction with others to keep their creative juices flowing and to keep their work fun.

MARKETING / PLANNING
- Market research analyst
- Public relations specialist
- Marketing specialist
- Advertising account executive
- Copywriter/publicity writer
- Advertising creative director
- Strategic planner
- Social media manager
- Research assistant

ENFPs usually are excellent long-range thinkers and can easily see the possible effects of an idea, program, or service on others. They take the needs and concerns of other people into consideration in their planning and often devise innovative and humane solutions to problems. They enjoy creative problem solving, especially as part of a lively and energetic team. Often clever and funny, many ENFPs find satisfaction in writing advertising copy for print or online media. The fast pace and constantly changing face of advertising is also appealing. And they can be great spokespeople for organizations in the role of a public relations manager.

EDUCATION / COUNSELING
- Special education teacher
- Bilingual education teacher
- Early childhood education teacher

- Professor: art/drama/music/English
- Middle school or high school teacher
- Child welfare counselor
- Substance abuse counselor
- Marriage and family therapist
- Mental health counselor
- Development director
- Career counselor
- Residential housing director
- Ombudsperson
- Pastoral counselor
- Rehabilitation counselor
- Social scientist
- Educational psychologist
- School counselor
- Planned-giving officer
- Philanthropic consultant
- Social psychologist
- Anthropologist
- Parent instructor, child development course
- High school guidance counselor

Many ENFPs find work that has a positive impact on others to be intrinsically satisfying. They can be compassionate and supportive psychologists and creative and enthusiastic career counselors, helping their clients find new and original solutions to problems. Their focus is on possibilities, especially for others, and they have an infectious and energizing style that motivates their clients to try to make positive changes in their lives. They enjoy helping others develop their own spirituality and often are attracted to careers in some form of ministry. As ombudspersons, they are effective and innovative catalysts for change within organizations, helping individuals by serving as a guide to available resources.

HEALTHCARE / SOCIAL SERVICE
- Dietitian/nutritionist
- Speech and language pathologist/ audiologist

- Holistic health practitioner (alternative medicine)
- Massage therapist
- Employee assistance program counselor
- Social worker
- Physical therapist
- Legal mediator
- Chiropractor
- Urban and regional planner
- Public health educator
- Occupational therapist

These fields in healthcare and social service are generally appealing to ENFPs, in part because of their helping nature and opportunity to use creative approaches but also because these tend to be careers one can self-manage while remaining independent and flexible. ENFPs in these careers are most satisfied when they are able to work outside of a rigid traditional structure, perhaps as consultants serving a variety of clients.

ENTREPRENEURIAL / BUSINESS
- Consultant
- Inventor
- Sales: intangibles/ideas
- Human resources manager
- Human resources development trainer
- Meeting, conference, and event planner
- Employment development specialist
- Restaurateur
- Management consultant: change management/team building/diversity
- Merchandise planner
- Director of diversity, equity, and inclusion
- Corporate/team trainer
- Advertising account manager or account executive
- Public relations specialist
- Marketing specialist
- Outplacement consultant
- Environmental lawyer
- Personnel recruiter
- Labor relations specialist

ENFPs are born entrepreneurs! They enjoy working for themselves because it gives them the freedom and flexibility, and the opportunity, to choose the projects they wish to work on and the people they want to work with. They usually have an abundance of ideas they want to see turned into reality, particularly those that will affect other people. Many ENFPs enjoy consulting in the areas of team building, conflict resolution, or increasing effectiveness in the workplace. They also enjoy being independent salespeople, especially selling intangibles— ideas rather than products.

The conventional business world is usually not appealing to ENFPs because they dislike excessive rules, regulations, or standard operating procedures. However, within traditional organizations, ENFPs flock to the human resources departments in the role of trainers and counselors. They find that a career as an employment development adviser uses their abilities to plan ahead and devise creative ways for people to do their work while keeping the organization's goals in mind.

TECHNOLOGY
- Customer relations manager
- Staff advocate (technology consultant)
- Project manager
- Engagement manager
- Human resources recruiter

With the proliferation of technology, there is a rapidly growing need for people who understand technology but also have good people and communication skills. Being the liaison between the technology people and the end users appeals to many ENFPs, who find these jobs satisfy their need to help and be connected with their co-workers.

Remember, these are only some areas that provide satisfying expression for the unique natural talents of the ENFP.

Customizing Your Job Search

Knowing the particular strengths and blind spots of your type can afford you a tremendous advantage in your job search campaign. In all aspects of the process, from conducting research into available positions, identifying and contacting prospective employers, developing personal marketing tools such as résumés, arranging and conducting job interviews, and negotiating salaries to finally accepting a position, people will act true to their type. Being able to capitalize on your assets and compensate for your liabilities can make the difference between a successful and an unsuccessful job search.

The differences between types are sometimes subtle and other times dramatic. It is the subtle variations in advice we offer that make the real difference between success and failure in a job search. The concept of networking serves as a good example. Extraverts will naturally enjoy networking and are advised to do so on a large scale, while Introverts find more limited and targeted networking, especially with people they already know, easier. Sensors tend to network with people in a defined scope, while Intuitives will go far and wide to find people often seemingly unrelated to their field of interest. Further, Feelers can often take networking personally and enjoy establishing warm rapport, while Thinkers will be more objective and detached in their style. Finally, Judgers tend to ask fewer and more structured questions during their networking, while Perceivers could ask questions of all sorts all day long! One valuable search technique, many ways to implement it.

Pathways to Success: Using Your Strengths

As an ENFP, your strength and talent for the job search lies in your unlimited ability to see alternatives and creative approaches, and your endless energy for gathering information by talking with people. But while you will love the data collection phase, beware of your tendency to become overwhelmed by details and paralyzed by your lack of organization.

As an ENFP, you will find that your most effective strategies build on your abilities to do the following:

Create your own job opportunities.

- Use your ability to see opportunities that don't presently exist, and tailor your current job to meet your changing needs, or the changing needs of your employer.
- Invent an entirely new job for yourself that will fill a need you see or predict in the market.

Elizabeth began to feel restricted by the amount of red tape and rules being implemented in the rapidly growing advertising agency where she worked as a copywriter. She decided she needed a more relaxed environment in which to be creative. So she got together with a group of copywriter friends of hers and developed an idea for a small agency of copywriters. They realized that while the idea sounded great, they would need to hire at least a part-time person to help them schedule jobs, bill clients, and pay their own bills so each of the writers would be free to meet new clients and write.

They found someone who had some of the business strengths they lacked, and started their own firm.

Develop and use your active network of contacts.

- Conduct lots of helpful informational interviews. Constantly enlarge your circle of contacts each time you meet with someone by asking them to refer you on to someone else.
- Tell everyone you meet and all of your friends that you are looking for a new career or job. You'll spread the word quickly and learn helpful information along the way.

Gil was shopping in the supermarket with his family when he literally bumped into an old friend from graduate school. Joe told Gil that he was considering leaving the hospital where he worked for a position out of state. Gil replied that he was interested in Joe's marketing-and-planning-director job himself. Gil arranged to email Joe at the end of the week and was able to interview for the position the day after Joe offered his resignation.

Impress your interviewer with your natural enthusiasm and confidence.

- Establish instant rapport and demonstrate your ability to meet people and make them feel comfortable with you.
- Use your sense of humor to change the interview from a formal and basically stilted experience to one where you and the interviewer enjoy yourselves. It will be a welcome breath of fresh air for the interviewer.

Maggie credited her offbeat sense of humor for getting the job she loves as a trainer in the human resources department of a major insurance company. She went through the typical interview process and arrived at the final interview. It was a very stormy day and Maggie went directly into the ladies' room to try to dry off and do something with her hair. A woman entered, also soaked to the skin, hair dripping, makeup running down her cheeks. Maggie immediately struck up a conversation with the woman about their ridiculous situation. They got to laughing and talking as they pulled themselves together. A few minutes later, they started laughing all over again when Maggie discovered that the woman was the vice president of human resources and Maggie was her nine o'clock interview!

Consider and keep several options open.

- Adapt to changing situations and improvise when you find yourself against an unexpected obstacle.
- Use your natural curiosity to gather a great deal of information about potential careers, jobs, and organizations.

Pat was about at the end of his career search. But he went ahead and conducted yet one more informational interview at a university even though he thought he might accept a job offered to him at an in-house conference planning department for a major company. He learned during the interview that the university was creating a position for a new faculty ombudsman—a job he had always wanted but had not figured possible because the position is so rare. He realized if he had not kept his options open, he would already have accepted one of the other positions before this dream job came along.

Be resourceful in getting job interviews.

- Use creative approaches to get yourself noticed and remembered, especially if you are one of many candidates for a job you are sure you want.
- Use the same energy and ability to see options to help you get around barriers or resistance you encounter during your search.

Jenna had decided that she wanted the highly sought-after job of director of creative arts for a program for gifted and talented children. After several calls to inquire into getting an interview with the supervisor of special education, she was told the position was only being posted within the school system, and outside applicants would not be considered unless the position could not be filled internally. She did not let that obstacle deter her; in fact, she felt energized by the challenge. She created a series of emails to the supervisor of special education to be sent each day for a week. In each, she attached a different medium (PDFs of photography, paintings, music files, writing), and each detailed her experience, past work, and her interest in the position. She didn't have to call to follow up, because she received a call for an interview after the final piece was received.

Possible Pitfalls

Although all people are unique, there are certain *potential* blind spots that many ENFPs share. We specify "potential" because some of the following may clearly be true of you, while others may not apply. While considering them, you may notice that these tendencies do not just relate to the job search, but rather describe pitfalls you may have experienced in other aspects of your life as well. It is therefore helpful to consider each one in terms of your past experiences by asking yourself, "Is this true for me?" And if so, "How did this tendency prevent me from getting something that I wanted?" You will probably notice that the key to overcoming your blind spots is the conscious and thoughtful development of your third and fourth functions (Thinking and Sensing). We recognize that many of the suggestions will be difficult to implement, but the more you use these functions, the fewer problems they will cause you in the future.

Pay attention to the realistic facts of a career or job.

- Focus your energy and attention on seeing what is really in front of you rather than just what might be. Research online and by talking to other people to learn what a job is really like.
- Be realistic in planning your job search in terms of how long it will take, what will be required, how much it will cost, and how you will afford to live (and eat) while you are involved in it. Make contingency plans so you are ready if it takes longer than you hope.

Curb your tendency to leap before you look!

- Develop a job search plan in advance so you don't squander your inspiration and energy in areas that aren't right for you.
- Generate a list of criteria for the right job, including what you can't live without as well as what would be nice but not imperative. Continue to use that list as a guide, comparing potential opportunities to it before pursuing them fully.

Work on developing self-discipline.

- Use proven time management skills and systems to help you get and stay organized. Ask an organized friend to help you (and to make it more fun).
- Prioritize the most important tasks, issues, and activities so you can't become distracted as easily. Try not to let impromptu socializing take you away from the less exciting but nevertheless important parts of the search.

Don't put off making a decision.

- Procrastinating may mean that you lose out on potentially satisfying opportunities because you took too long to decide.

- Decide when you have enough information rather than go on indefinitely gathering more.

Follow through on all phases of the job search.

- Remember that some people use and respect established organizational procedures and expect others to as well. Consider it an opportunity to demonstrate your ability to adapt rather than viewing it as a repressive limitation.
- Develop and then *use* a system of your choosing to help you check your progress so that nothing slips through the cracks. Stick with whatever you decide rather than dropping it to try a more intriguing system before giving the first one a chance to help you.

The Final Piece: Changing or Keeping Your Job ... the Key to Success for ENFPs

Now that you have a solid understanding of your type, you can see how your natural preferences make you better suited for certain kinds of jobs. You can also see how knowledge of your type-related strengths and blind spots can help you conduct a more successful job search. But as an ENFP, you've already realized that you are not equally drawn to *every* career or field listed in the Popular Occupations section. The next and final step is to narrow down the field and find the work you were meant to do.

In addition to Type, several other factors—such as your values, interests, and skills—also contribute to your level of satisfaction on the job. The more compatible you are with your job, the happier you'll be. So prepare to use everything you've learned (in this book and in life) to create *your strategic career plan*. The exercises in

Chapter 23, "Putting It All Together," are designed to help you do just that.

However, you may have decided it makes more sense (if perhaps only for the moment) to stay in your present job or with your current employer. There may be many valid reasons—financial pressures, family considerations, a tough job market for your specialty, or just bad timing. But take heart! What you've learned in this book can also help you be more content and successful *in your current job*. And should the time come when you're ready to make a major career move, you'll have a much better idea of where you want to go and how to get there.

"So, if you can't have the job you love (yet!) ... love the one you've got."

The simple truth is, many jobs allow a good deal of flexibility in the way tasks are performed. Here are some ways you may be able to massage your current job into one that better fits your needs:

- If possible, delegate routine tasks to others.
- Team up with co-workers and/or work on teams.
- Find other creative people to brainstorm ideas with.
- Work different shifts, arrange more flexible hours, or job-share.
- Change your focus if you're not stimulated or challenged; work on something else.
- Make sure you have a variety of projects to work on.
- Talk through detailed projects with someone.
- Join or start organizations for people with similar expertise or interests.
- Attend conferences and get involved in professional organizations.

One ENFP turns lemons into lemonade:

A corporate trainer for a large service company, Alice longed for the autonomy and freedom of being a private consultant, but she knew she didn't want to work alone all day. Realizing it would take a long time to establish her own lucrative business and that her boss was under pressure to reduce costs, Alice convinced him he could save a substantial amount of money (a full-time salary plus benefits) if he hired Alice as an independent contractor. With this creative proposal, Alice managed to stay connected to her friends and colleagues and secured a well-paying, steady client. And most important, she bought the time she needed to develop her own business.

Use what you've got to get what you need.

Simply put, the best advice on how to succeed is to *capitalize on your strengths and compensate for your blind spots.* Learning how to do this can make the difference between succeeding or failing and loving or hating your work. To help you, we include the following inventory of your potential strengths and blind spots. And while every individual is unique, many of the following apply to you as an ENFP.

Your work-related strengths may include

- eagerness to think outside the box and consider new possibilities

- courage to take some risks, try new things, and overcome obstacles
- a broad range of interests and ability to quickly learn things that interest you
- natural curiosity and skill for getting the information you need
- ability to see the big picture and the implications of actions and ideas
- excellent communication skills and ability to rouse others' enthusiasm
- adaptability; you can shift gears and change directions quickly
- perceptiveness about people; you understand their needs and motivations

Your work-related blind spots may include

- difficulty setting priorities and making decisions
- impatience with uncreative people
- reluctance to do things in traditional or routine ways
- lack of discipline when attending to and following through on important details
- tendency to become bored or sidetracked, especially after the creative process is done
- dislike for doing repetitive tasks
- impatience working with systems or people who are too rigid
- propensity to always focus on what's possible rather than what's doable or probable
- tendency to be disorganized

Using your strengths is easy.
The secret to success for an
ENFP
is learning to

prioritize, focus, and follow through.

10 | INFP
Introverted, Intuitive, Feeling, Perceiving
"Still Waters Run Deep"

Profile 1: Darren, Video Game Designer

"The creator of fun."

The Job

Darren's work is to build worlds—literally. He is a video game designer responsible for creating the environments in which a game takes place. Imagine all that contributes to the scene: plants, grass, forest, sky. First Darren must imagine these settings and sketch out what a scene will need. Then he works with both engineers and artists to fulfill his vision and shape the player experience. Much of his time is spent directly interacting with the digital spaces he is orchestrating. It is absorbing and deeply creative work that supports a lifelong passion that Darren has had for video games and their potential to improve and enrich people's lives.

Backstory

Darren had been making video games in his spare time since elementary school, but it wasn't until a senior project in high school

that he first showcased his work to a large audience. The experience was life changing, and Darren began to realize that he could pursue a career in video game design, starting with a college degree. Savannah College of Art and Design fit the bill, and Darren began the BFA program in interactive design and game development.

During his junior year, Darren completed an internship working on a fantasy online role-playing game (RPG). Afterward, Darren was offered a permanent position, but he declined in order to finish his degree. It was a tough decision, but one that he doesn't regret, even though by the time he graduated, the position had already been filled. Darren spent a couple of months working on his portfolio and applying for jobs. In the fall he finally got his opportunity when he was offered his previous mentor's position.

The design team for an RPG often consists of content designers, who focus on story and narrative, and systems designers, who are in charge of the logistics, numbers, and strategy. Darren worked as an associate game systems designer for almost two years before being promoted to the mid-level position of game systems designer. By that time he was beginning to feel the need for change and new challenges. He transitioned to a new company, and his current position is that of game designer on a kid-oriented toys-plus-video-game experience.

A Good Fit

Like many Idealists, Darren has the soul of an artist. "What I've wanted to do since I was little is to craft these interactive experiences and to make things that people can get immersed in, like the way I did with games when I was young." Darren's job gives him the power to create and bring to life entire worlds that previously existed only inside his mind. His dominant function of Feeling is constantly rewarded by his opportunities to make art that has a direct impact on others and lets them enjoy his world. Working on a team with colleagues who respect his vision, Darren is upbeat and enthusiastic, inspiring them with his dedication.

Darren's auxiliary Intuition is constantly in play as he dreams up new worlds and explores the realm of possibility. As a designer, Darren has an eye on the greater whole and works to make the component pieces come together. Often he is confronted by problems that must be solved in brand-new and innovative ways. Being in an industry that resides on the cutting edge of technology means maintaining a growth mindset and always being open to learning more. As an INFP, the new and the novel is exciting to Darren, and he is enlivened by the constant change and evolution of his field.

Looking Ahead

When asked what his dream job is, Darren laughs, since in some ways he is already doing it. "But I think if you're ever in the position where you can't see yourself going

further, then you should rethink things." Like many designers, Darren can imagine opening his own studio five or ten years down the road and creating a work environment in which he would have greater control over all the projects. And this may be more possible now than ever: "The game industry has been undergoing a revolution, with crowd-sourcing allowing new start-up studios to get funded." Darren is excited by changes coming to the industry, pleased by the fact that about half of all gamers in the world are now female and that games are marketed toward increasingly broader audiences.

Profile 2: Deb, Therapeutic Counselor

"Each person is unique."

The Job

Deb has always been inspired by the Mother Teresa quote "Do small things with great love." After a dynamic thirty-year career as clinical director of a child crisis center working with abused and neglected children and their caregivers, she now lives a semi-retired lifestyle as a therapeutic counselor with a small practice as part of her local church. By quickly establishing positive rapport with clients and creating a foundation of trust and respect, Deb is able to inspire and encourage a sense of hope. "I enjoy teaching clients how to shift their thinking from irrational to more rational life perspectives."

Deb works part-time now and has a roster of clients who schedule their appointments through the church. One of two counselors in the practice, she primarily sees men and women who are coping with anxiety and depression and other stage-of-life issues. Her clients pay a fee for her services through the church, and she reports to the senior pastor, who is the administrator of the program. Deb enjoys balancing her autonomy with working closely with the other counselor in the program and supporting the staff and volunteers in any way she can. "I work best independently, but surrounded by interesting and supportive colleagues."

Backstory

The first in her family to go to college, Deb was first drawn to journalism, but dissuaded when a teacher advised her that "women journalists live in small towns and write obituaries." Luckily, Deb pursued her other passion—psychology—and earned a bachelor and then master's degree in counseling. Her early career involved counseling children first at an inpatient psychiatric hospital, and then at a crisis nursery for children ages newborn through eleven.

This expertise led her to eventually create a comprehensive counseling program at a child crisis center, where she served as clinical director, supervising counselors and interns. The center provided emotional and behavioral support for the children placed there, who often had severe behavioral and psychiatric needs.

The work was deeply fulfilling but also demanding. Deb was able to intervene in the lives of countless children and families, dedicating herself to a mission of meeting even the most extreme cases with love and care. At the same time, she was witness to the darkest impulses and realities of abuse and neglect. When the time came to shift to her current position, Deb was ready, because she knew she had given the better part of her working life to a cause she deeply believed in.

A Good Fit

Deb's natural compassion is the driving impulse behind her work. As a dominant Feeler, Deb displays an almost limitless ability to empathize and listen reflectively, creating spaces of trust and safety. This has been a theme throughout her career. Deb is guided by her values of generosity, kindness, and service to others. She enjoys the initial interviews with potential clients, and getting a deep sense of the context and narrative of their life. "Each person is unique with a complex history and life situation." Deb is hugely gratified by looking back on her career working in service of children and families. She feels harmony between her beliefs and her work—often the most important thing for an Idealist at work.

Deb's auxiliary function, Intuition, helps her to connect the dots with clients, gently guiding them toward realizations and healthier perspectives about their lives. She describes her approach as creative and innovative; each person is different, an individual, and she must tailor her method and practice to the needs of the client before her. And as an Introvert, she finds interacting one-on-one to be the most comfortable setting, creating warm and trusting relationships with both her clients and her colleagues.

Looking Ahead

At the end of a long and fulfilling career, Deb is looking forward to retiring soon, spending more time with her children and grandchildren and giving back in other ways, closer to home. When she looks at the future of the field of counseling, Deb notes several trends. "I see the counseling role as becoming more and more dependent on specialized training and on evidence-based practices. Much of this is being driven by contract providers that require progress reports for payment to be approved. Training programs will need to address specific populations and unique needs of those clients such as the LGBTQ community." She is hopeful that there will be a shift toward a preventive approach to care rather than just the intervention approaches now in place, as well as a greater emphasis on holistic wellness.

Profile 3: Emily, Illustrator

"No limits to my creative expression."

The Job

Emily has been an artist since the sixth grade and has earned her living through her art her whole adult life. Today she is a freelance illustrator specializing in editorial illustrations that accompany articles in magazines and newspapers. She works for a large number of different clients, exclusively from the studio in her home. Nearly all of Emily's assignments come directly to her from the art directors of publications. Emily is sent the text of an upcoming article to read, and given some parameters for size and color, and then she decides on the approach and style she wishes to use to communicate her message. "My favorite part of the job is the stimulation and challenge of solving a problem in a creative way. Working within the confines of the text I'm given, I can express my ideas and really say something that adds to the article."

Backstory

Emily came to a career in illustration after a series of less fulfilling jobs. She began work after college as a layout and paste-up artist, putting together advertisements for several large department stores. These jobs allowed her to do a lot of doodling, and since she didn't have to finish the ads, she was able to concentrate on design rather than production. Next she went to work for a publisher as an assistant to the art director. It was another learning experience where she

designed a book and did other freelance designs in her spare time. When she and her husband decided to move, she found a job in another department store, this time working on fashion ads. "That was great training. I learned how to make fast production decisions. But I was still free to experiment and doodle and didn't have to execute the finished drawings."

Eventually, Emily decided to try to make her living as a working artist. She began creating art and entering it in shows. She won several prizes and enjoyed the process of learning how to exhibit her work. She set up a studio in her home and for seven years made art, showed it in galleries, and sold it. "But the complete lack of outside stimulation began to bog me down. I wasn't productive because I wasn't trying anything really new. So I took a graduate painting course and started producing a different type of art. I wanted to try new techniques and styles, but unfortunately they turned out not to be very marketable." Finally, she realized she needed to change directions.

Emily was encouraged by an illustrator friend to put together a portfolio, which she took in to several magazines. She was hired immediately by a prestigious national magazine that continues today to be one of her favorite clients. "I realized that dealing with the agencies was much better for me. I could talk about my work because they were judging my work, not my soul. There aren't the same politics in agencies as there are in galleries. It felt pure—I was filling a need the art director had. I could be a little less personally involved."

A Good Fit

Like most Idealist artists, Emily's life's work is about creative expression, creative problem solving, and communicating through her art. It is important to her that both her clients and the readers of the books and articles she illustrates feel something special as a result of her work.

Because she is a dominant Feeler, Emily must, above all else, be true to herself. In her case, this means being able to exercise almost total creative control. By being in business for herself, she has few rules to follow other than those she lays out for herself. She is therefore free to do things her own way. She also enjoys the close relationships she has with some longstanding clients and the mutual respect and trust they have developed over the years.

Through her auxiliary function of Intuition, Emily constantly perceives things—especially the new and unusual. She then figures out ways to represent these ideas in interesting and different ways. Her Intuition also helps her interpret what she experiences and to characterize it so that it will have meaning for the reader. Most of her work is subtle and witty—suggestive rather than obvious.

Emily finds the most energizing projects to be the ones that involve text that is of excellent quality. "When I personally respond to the text, I especially love the job. But the very best is when an art director tells me to just have fun with the piece. That means I can use humor and there are virtually no limits to my creative expression."

Looking Ahead

"I've always been an artist and being an artist shapes everything about you. It's who you are, not just what you do." But the importance of her work has shifted in intensity over the last couple of years as she has become successful. "I feel like it's okay to let up on it a bit. I want to pursue some new interests, like piano, weight lifting, and taking Italian lessons. I can now justify time away from the studio, and I want to learn new things. I'm less focused on getting recognition for my work." In fact, Emily

believes she is much more objective and realistic about her work today. She is more self-confident and tolerant of other people in their interaction with her.

But she remains as uncompromising about her work as ever. "I have shaped my life to be the way I wanted it to be. Sometimes that has meant taking a risk or making what looked to others like a crazy mistake. But I always trusted myself and my convictions first. Even the boring jobs gave me a chance to build my skills, even if they didn't challenge me creatively. I'm better because of it. I tell young art students not to be discouraged if it takes a long time. Someday, maybe they'll find the satisfaction I've found—being able to do work that lets them express themselves and get recognition from their peers."

Common Threads

Although Emily, Darren, and Deb have different backgrounds, experiences, and careers, there are certain common threads that weave through their stories. Specific interests and abilities may differ, but owing to their similar temperament values and the *same hierarchy* of their psychological functions, there are certain observations we can make about the needs of many INFPs.

What follows is a list of the most important elements—the formula, if you will—for INFP satisfaction. Given the uniqueness of all individuals—even those who share a type—this list will not describe each INFP equally well. The important thing is that these ten elements, with varying degrees of intensity and in different orders of importance, identify what INFPs need to be satisfied.

After you have reviewed this list, we recommend that you go back and prioritize the elements in order of *their importance to you*. When doing this, think of past work experiences as well as your present job, and what you found particularly satisfying or unsatisfying. Try to look for *themes* that run through several experiences, not just *events* that might be true for one work situation but not for another.

As an INFP, I define career satisfaction as doing work that

1. is in harmony with my own personal values and beliefs and allows me to express my vision through my work
2. gives me time to develop substantial depth to my ideas and maintain control over the process and product
3. is done autonomously, with a private work space and plenty of uninterrupted time, but with periodic opportunities to bounce my ideas off people I feel respect me
4. is done within a flexible structure, with a minimum of rules or regulations, letting me work on projects when I feel inspired
5. is done with other creative and caring individuals in a cooperative environment free from tension and interpersonal strife
6. lets me express my originality and in which personal growth is encouraged and rewarded
7. does not require me to present my work frequently in front of groups of people or be called upon to share before it is completed to my satisfaction
8. allows me to help others grow and develop and realize their full potential
9. involves understanding people and discovering what makes them tick; allows me to develop deep one-to-one relationships with others
10. allows me to work toward fulfilling my ideals and not be limited by political, financial, or other obstacles

Popular Occupations for INFPs

In listing occupations that are popular among INFPs, it is important to note that there are successful people of all types in all occupations. However, the following are careers INFPs may find particularly satisfying, and some of the reasons why. This is by no means a comprehensive listing but is included to suggest possibilities you may not have previously considered. Although all of these occupations offer the potential for career satisfaction, the future demand for some careers is anticipated to be greater than for others.

CREATIVE / ARTS
- Artist
- Writer: poet/novelist
- Journalist
- Graphic designer
- Architect
- Actor
- Editor
- Musician
- Informational-graphics designer
- Editor/art director (print/online)
- Creative producer
- Video game designer
- Composer
- Film editor
- Set designer
- Interior designer
- Print designer
- Interaction designer

The appeal of the arts to INFPs is the ability to express themselves and their ideas in creative and personal ways. The personal freedom and flexibility of a working artist is a lifestyle often embraced by INFPs. Whether they work with the written word, a paintbrush or other medium, use their building designs or their own bodies as actors or musicians, INFPs strive to create original products that are authentic expressions of their inner voice. Many INFPs describe themselves as artists deep down, even if that is not how they earn their living.

EDUCATION
- College professor: humanities/arts
- Researcher
- Librarian
- Educational consultant
- Special education teacher
- Bilingual education teacher
- Early childhood education teacher
- Online educator
- Planned-giving officer
- Philanthropic consultant
- Grant coordinator
- Curator

Teaching enables the INFP to work with others to help them grow and develop their human potential. They often prefer the college atmosphere to elementary or even secondary education because the motivation of the students is higher. They enjoy the process of learning and enjoy exploring deeper and more meaningful levels of understanding as researchers or librarians.

COUNSELING
- Clinical psychologist
- Mental health counselor
- Marriage and family therapist
- Social worker
- Genetic counselor
- Employee assistance counselor
- Child welfare counselor
- Substance abuse counselor
- Social worker
- Legal mediator
- Career counselor/coach
- Genealogist

INFPs can be truly noble in their desire and efforts to improve the quality of life for others. They make compassionate and insightful counselors, psychologists, and social workers, and strive toward helping their clients gain self-understanding and harmony within their relationships and their lives. As counselors, they enjoy the process of understanding others as they come to understand themselves.

RELIGION
- Minister/priest/rabbi/imam
- Religious educator
- Church worker
- Pastoral counselor

For many INFPs the commitment of a religious career is rewarding. INFPs enjoy helping other people develop their spiritual side and receive pleasure from striving for and attaining their vision for themselves and others. They often prefer a one-on-one setting but with experience can come to enjoy preaching or lecturing. The bottom line for an INFP is to do work that is in harmony with their inner values and beliefs, and often careers within religion provide that.

HEALTHCARE
- Dietitian/nutritionist
- Community health educator
- Physical therapist
- Home health social worker
- Occupational therapist
- Speech-language pathologist/audiologist
- Massage therapist
- Holistic health practitioner (alternative medicine)
- Arts therapist
- Geneticist
- Ethicist

The appealing aspects of these healthcare fields for many INFPs is the ability to work closely and intimately with clients or patients. INFPs generally prefer the autonomy that most of these careers provide them, working in their own practice or as a consultant to a larger healthcare institution. The creative and often spiritual elements of diagnosis and treatment of physical therapy, holistic therapies, and massage are satisfying uses of an INFP's intuition and feeling preferences.

ORGANIZATIONAL DEVELOPMENT
- Employment development specialist
- Human resources development trainer
- Human resources recruiter
- Social scientist
- Director of diversity, equity, and inclusion
- Consultant: team building/conflict resolution
- Industrial-organizational psychologist
- Outplacement consultant
- Labor relations specialist
- Corporate/team trainer
- Interpreter/translator

Although INFPs are not usually satisfied in business careers, there are some selected fields that offer potential for success and satisfaction. Some INFPs enjoy a corporate setting when their work involves helping other people find jobs that are right for them. They often enjoy jobs in personnel, or human resources development, or designing and instituting jobs within a company. They need to work with other supportive people and feel that their contributions are valued and unique in order to find satisfaction in the tough and competitive world of business.

TECHNOLOGY
- Customer relations manager
- Staff advocate (technology consultant)
- Project manager
- Engagement manager
- Educational software developer

With the proliferation of technology, there is a rapidly growing need for people who understand technology but also have good people and communication skills. Being the liaison between the technology people and the end users appeals to many INFPs, who find that these jobs satisfy their need to help and be connected with their co-workers.

Remember, these are only some areas that provide satisfying expression for the unique natural talents of the INFP.

Customizing Your Job Search

Knowing the particular strengths and blind spots of your type can afford you a tremendous advantage in your job search campaign. In all aspects of the process, from conducting research into available positions, identifying and contacting prospective employers, developing personal marketing tools such as résumés, arranging and conducting job interviews, and negotiating salaries to finally accepting a position, people will act true to their type. Being able to capitalize on your assets and compensate for your liabilities can make the difference between a successful and an unsuccessful job search.

The differences between types are sometimes subtle and other times dramatic. It is the subtle variations in advice we offer that make the real difference between success and failure in a job search. The concept of networking serves as a good example. Extraverts will naturally enjoy networking and are advised to do so on a large scale, while Introverts find more limited and targeted networking, especially with people they already know, easier. Sensors tend to network with people in a defined scope, while Intuitives will go far and wide to find people often seemingly unrelated to their field of interest. Further, Feelers can often take networking personally and enjoy establishing warm rapport, while Thinkers will be more objective and detached in their style. Finally, Judgers tend to ask fewer and more structured questions during their networking, while Perceivers could ask questions of all sorts all day long! One valuable search technique, many ways to implement it.

Pathways to Success: Using Your Strengths

As we will detail in the following pages, your strength and talent for the job search lie in your ability to know what is important to you and to work tirelessly to find a career that will be an expression of your values. Beware of your tendency to be swept away by your idealism and in the process ignore practical realities.

As an INFP, you will find that your most effective strategies build on your abilities to do the following:

Readily see possibilities that don't presently exist.

- Use your creative energy to look beyond what is known, and imagine jobs that you might be satisfied with that meet the needs of the market or employer.
- Generate as long a list as possible of all the ways you can use your skills in fields that interest you. After you have created a lengthy list, research each option so you will be able to put together a more realistic plan of attack.

The staff at the magazine where Solange worked as a research assistant was being cut back. Instead of waiting to hear whether the ax would fall on her, Solange came up with an innovative staffing solution that would save her job and the job of another research assistant. Solange and her co-worker offered to job-share the research position, thus saving the magazine the cost of two full-time researchers. In exchange, Solange would write freelance articles for the magazine on an as-needed basis and be free to write for other publications as well. Her solution enabled her co-worker finally to have time to finish her master's degree. The magazine accepted the proposal and Solange saved her job.

Give thoughtful consideration to all potential career opportunities.

- Your patience with complex tasks will serve you well if you give time and thought to each possible career avenue, and you will be better prepared to talk about why you are the right person for the job.
- Time spent in reflection will give you the chance to clarify your true feelings and motivation before accepting or rejecting an option.

Greg was in the enviable position of having received job offers from three architecture firms. However, he felt overwhelmed by the decision he had to make. So he asked each for two weeks in which to consider the offers. One firm said they needed his answer immediately, so he declined, confident in the knowledge that a firm in that much of a hurry was not a place he wanted to work. He spent the next two weeks carefully thinking through the advantages and disadvantages of the remaining options and what was most important to him in a work environment. Because he took the time, he was able to recall some factors about each office that he had forgotten in the excitement of the interviews. When the two weeks were over, he was able to make a thoughtful and confident decision.

Express yourself well, especially after thinking things through ahead of time.

- Whenever possible, find ways to express yourself in writing.

- Use words to help you verbalize your vision for your career or for the ways in which you see yourself adding to the growth and development of an organization.

Timothy, a career counselor, found *himself* looking for work after cutbacks at the community college where he had worked left him unemployed. Though Timothy certainly knew the tricks of the trade, the tight job market made his job search difficult.

We suggested that he target a private career consulting firm and sell himself by what he could offer the company. Because he had many of the same skills as other candidates, he decided to set himself apart by expressing his personal motivation to help others find truly fulfilling work that would result in more referral business. The partners of the firm were impressed by his genuine concern and decided he would take the time to be sure their clients were well served, and increase the bottom line as well.

Demonstrate your motivation and commitment to causes you believe in.

- Allow prospective employers to see and hear your enthusiasm for a position you want. Most employers are impressed with a candidate who is direct and clear about his or her interest in a job.
- When discussing how a potential job fits with your ideals, use your natural persuasiveness to convince potential employers of the intensity of your desire for the position.

Each applicant was told to prepare a selection of music suitable for three church choirs for an audition for the position of choir director. Melissa chose to let her words and musical selections not only fill an assignment but also express her desire for the job. She spent hours going over her selections so they would reflect her love of music, her eagerness to work with singers of all ages, and her own personal faith. She wrote a statement that she read to the selection committee that explained her choices of music and how each was thematically connected to the other pieces so that the choir was essentially singing chapters of a book. She went a step further and left copies of her statement with her résumé and references. The committee was impressed with her diligence, care, and devotion, all the characteristics Melissa hoped they would associate with her.

Use limited, targeted networking.

- Start with close friends from your professional or personal life. Carefully select other people to help you, relying on people who know you well or are directly involved in the field you seek.
- Plot out your strategy, including a timetable for accomplishing objectives to keep you from becoming overwhelmed or discouraged.

Before she even got started on her job search, Lilly felt that she was in over her head. She knew she wasn't very organized and wasn't even sure how to begin finding out about available jobs. Her sister suggested she attend a time management seminar being offered through the continuing education department in their town. Lilly at first resisted the idea of a prepackaged program but finally succumbed to her sister's urging and went. She found that while parts of the seminar were too regimented, overall, it gave her an excellent framework. She modified and adapted the basic program to work for her. She also gained some added confidence because she now had a way of ensuring that she wouldn't let things slip through the cracks. Lilly was able to get started, and feel as if she was much more in control of the process.

Possible Pitfalls

Although all people are unique, there are certain *potential* blind spots that many INFPs share. We specify "potential" because some of the following *may* be true of you, while others may clearly not apply. While considering them, you may notice that these tendencies do not relate just to the job search, but rather describe pitfalls that you may have experienced in other aspects of your life as well. It is therefore helpful to consider each one in terms of your past experiences by asking yourself, "Is this true for me?" And if so, "How did this tendency prevent me from getting something that I wanted?" You will probably notice that the key to overcoming your blind spots is the conscious and thoughtful development of your third and fourth functions (Sensing and Thinking). We recognize that many of the suggestions will be difficult to implement, but the more you use these functions, the fewer problems they will cause you in the future.

Develop realistic expectations for yourself and your job search.

- Realize that finding the right job takes more time than you expect or wish. Paying attention to the facts of the situation and including them in your vision of the right career choice will make you more efficient during your search.
- You may have to decide to compromise some of your less central personal values from time to time. There may not

be the "perfect" job for you at the salary level or in the geographic area you live in—at least not at this time. Learning when to compromise on the less critical points is a valuable lesson.

Try not to take criticism or rejection personally.

- Bear in mind that many people offer criticism in a very objective fashion and expect that you will take it as it was intended. Try to look at it as *constructive* and use the knowledge to improve your approach.
- Draw some boundaries and don't try to please too many people at the same time. A career search is a time-consuming task. Being willing to say no to others when necessary will help you conserve needed energy and maintain your focus.

Look at the logical consequence of your actions.

- Try not to make important decisions relying exclusively on your personal feelings. Get input from trusted, more objective friends.
- Take a break from the situation to think more clearly about it. Imagine what might be the logical cause and effect of your choices so you will have a more balanced picture.

Resist the tendency to avoid eliminating options and to put off making decisions.

- Take charge of your job search by eliminating less desirable options rather than waiting so long that more attractive options are eliminated for you. You may find the whole process less overwhelming if you remove from consideration those possibilities that don't fit with your most important criteria for career satisfaction.

- Don't spend so much time in reflection that you leave no time for action! Develop a timetable and stick with it. Remember that getting started is often the hardest part, but once you do, you will gain momentum from your actions.

Concentrate on getting better organized.

- Use time-management techniques to be sure you get things done punctually. Employers will judge you on how well you follow through with commitments.
- Beware that you are naturally prone to perfectionism, which may delay you from completing tasks, hoping to find some way to improve them.

The Final Piece: Changing or Keeping Your Job . . . the Key to Success for INFPs

Now that you have a solid understanding of your type, you can see how your natural preferences make you better suited for certain kinds of jobs. You can also see how knowledge of your type-related strengths and blind spots can help you conduct a more successful job search. But as an INFP, you've already realized that you are not equally drawn to *every* career or field listed in the Popular Occupations section. The next and final step is to narrow down the field and find the work you were meant to do.

In addition to Type, several other factors—such as your values, interests, and skills—also contribute to your level of satisfaction on the job. The more compatible you are with your job, the happier you'll be. So prepare to use everything you've learned (in this book and in life) to create *your strategic career plan.* The exercises in

Chapter 23, "Putting It All Together," are designed to help you do just that.

However, you may have decided it makes more sense (if perhaps only for the moment) to stay in your present job or with your current employer. There may be many valid reasons—financial pressures, family considerations, a tough job market for your specialty, or just bad timing. But take heart! What you've learned in this book can also help you be more content and successful *in your current job.* And should the time come when you're ready to make a major career move, you'll have a much better idea of where you want to go and how to get there.

"So, if you can't have the job you love (yet!) . . . love the one you've got."

The simple truth is, many jobs allow a good deal of flexibility in the way tasks are performed. Here are some ways you may be able to massage your current job into one that better fits your needs:

- Volunteer to help draft your organization's/department's mission statement.
- Delegate certain details or routine tasks to others.
- Take a course in conflict resolution and become a mediator.
- Consider becoming a trainer or coach in your field of expertise.
- Work a different shift or arrange more flexible hours, or job-share.
- Do more of your work from your home.
- Email a friend with an inspirational message of support daily, weekly, or when the spirit moves you.
- Stay in the same occupation but switch employers.
- Go back to school for more or specialized training.

One INFP turns lemons into lemonade:

As a result of an unfortunate experience his sister had with her supervisor, Jason became aware of the pervasiveness of sexual harassment in the workplace. He felt so strongly that people should absolutely feel safe in their jobs that he began researching the workplace harassment problem and what was being done about it around the country. After conducting a lot of research and speaking closely with people who had been affected, Jason felt that he couldn't keep quiet, and recognized that he could use his relative power and status to be an ally. He offered to conduct a short workshop for his department. It was so well received that the director of the Employee Assistance Program offered Jason the chance to repeat the workshop, this time for the entire company.

Use what you've got to get what you need.

Simply put, the best advice on how to succeed is to *capitalize on your strengths and compensate for your blind spots.* Learning how to do this can make the difference between succeeding or failing and loving or hating your work. To help you, we include the following inventory of your potential strengths and blind spots. And while every individual is unique, many of the following should apply to you as an INFP.

Your work-related strengths may include

- thoughtfulness and the ability to focus on one issue or idea in depth
- eagerness to think outside the box and consider new possibilities

- deep commitment to work you believe in
- ability to work well alone if necessary
- natural curiosity and skill for getting the information you need
- ability to see the big picture and to see implications of actions and ideas
- perceptiveness about people's needs and motivations
- adaptability; you can shift gears and change directions quickly
- ability to work extremely well with people one-on-one

Your work-related blind spots may include

- need to control projects or you may lose interest
- tendency toward disorganization and difficulty setting priorities
- difficulty working on projects that conflict with your values
- reluctance to follow traditional ways of doing things
- natural idealism, which may prevent you from having realistic expectations
- dislike of doing things in traditional or routine ways
- difficulty working in competitive or tension-filled environments
- lack of discipline about attending to and following through on important details
- impatience working with structures or people who are too rigid
- tendency to be unrealistic about how long things take
- reluctance to discipline direct reports and criticize others

Using your strengths is easy.
The secret to success for an
INFP
is learning to

develop realistic expectations,
value compromise,
and not take things quite so personally.

11 | ENTJ
Extraverted, Intuitive, Thinking, Judging
"Everything's Fine—I'm in Charge"

Profile 1: Dan, Real Estate Developer

"A legacy that people can experience."

The Job

Dan is the managing director of a major real estate development project. It's a high-profile job. He is responsible for developing the most iconic square of land in Denver. "If the Broncos are on TV, they show you Larimer Square. My job is to lead the future of it." The whole project is one city block, with twenty-five buildings in all. Dan is leading the charge to shut down the square and restore the historical buildings, closing the streets to make it a big park, and building additional buildings. "It's as ridiculously complicated as a project can get. It's the most beloved area in the city: Colorado's first historical district." Dan has to balance the needs of residents, business owners, local and state government, and the public. "You have to think about fifty years in the future. You have to take the long view."

He equates being a real estate developer to being a movie producer. "I'm not the creative, but I'm picking the creatives and then telling them what our goals and outcomes look like. And I bring the money to the table, and if it's a success or a flop, it's on me." Dan manages laborers, public affairs consultants, media consultants, civil engineers, structural engineers, and analysts. He directs architects to build based on the framework and parameters that he designs. Most of all, he has to think about how people will interact with spaces, and what makes city spaces dynamic. "I love the fact that all of this process leads to something physical, a legacy that people can experience."

Backstory

When he was a kid, Dan wanted to be a businessman, and went to school expected to pursue a business major. While backpacking through Europe with a friend after sophomore year, however, Dan had a

146

turning point. "I was exposed to just amazing urban life and urban designing, planning, and architecture. It struck a nerve with me." Though Dan loved architecture, he couldn't draw. A professor and mentor told him about urban planning. "Architecture is the design of buildings and all the details of how the building works, structurally, mechanically, all that. Planning is more how cities function—thinking bigger and strategically. Where should a building go? Where might parks be? How do they relate to streets? Planning is systems oriented." He ended up graduating with two degrees: history and political economy, with a minor in city planning.

Dan got his master's in urban planning, and then his first job, which was a disappointment. He worked for the San Francisco Housing Authority, overseeing public housing. He found the department to be corrupt, and resigned in a public letter that went to the press. After that, Dan found his way to a consulting firm that was focused on environmental impact analysis, making sure that any building projects met the state law criteria. He was finally in the world he wanted to be in, advising on development projects. "But what I found out after doing that for six years was that I still wanted to be the guy with the Legos in his hands, versus telling someone where to put the Lego set when it was done."

Dan finally made the transition to real estate as the director of planning, and then did some other consulting work. He moved to Colorado and worked for one of the largest development companies in the state. Finally, six weeks ago, he started his dream job at Larimer Square.

A Good Fit

With his Conceptualizer temperament, Dan is a natural in the world of systems designing. He must synthesize an extraordinary amount of information and then make strategic decisions with a larger view in mind. "When there are twelve hundred steps and turns to get there, I can come up with a long-term vision."

Like many ENTJs, Dan is comfortable in a directorial role, calling the shots. "Most of what I do is managing teams both external and internal. I love working collaboratively with people on a team. I get a lot of satisfaction from working with really creative, smart people to figure out tough problems." A dominant Thinker, Dan is logical-minded and fair. "I can make strong, quick decisions."

And with his auxiliary Intuition, Dan can garner creative solutions that actually achieve practical effect. Part of that includes crafting an overarching narrative for a project to inspire others. "So much of what I do is tell the story so I can get the public and political support to get done what I want to do." An Extravert, Dan is comfortable with and effective in the public-facing side of his work. "I go to a lot of events, meet decision makers, planners, influential leaders in our community, and try to build a coalition of support."

Looking Ahead

When Dan thinks about the future, he reflects on goals he still has. "I'm in the later side of my career now, so my dream job is working with smart, progressive-minded people, people who care about making money but care about how they treat the world as well." He wants to work on projects that are focused on sustainability, environmental impact, community outreach, and ensuring diversity and inclusivity. In five years, he hopes to be welcoming others to the grand opening of Larimer Square, his biggest and best project so far.

Profile 2: Skip, Creative Producer, Social Networking Site

"Connecting the world."

The Job

Skip describes his job as crafting messages that matter to people. A creative producer in the communication design department of a social networking site, Skip works with an in-house creative team that conceives, produces, and designs all creative communication. Skip is responsible for producing projects that tie the website "to a cultural sphere, so that when people experience that cultural sphere, there's a personal resonance with the brand."

One project that exemplifies this is the real-time election map they produced for a presidential election that showed millions of users voting at the same time. "For the first time ever, we were able to visualize democracy in action. Through the simple act of clicking 'I Voted,' we helped present this website as a real-time network where people could express what they believe in." Skip's day-to-day involves wearing many hats, and communication between team members, as well as with the general public, is critical. Turning good ideas into action is the name of the game.

Backstory

Skip has been obsessed with telling stories for as long as he can remember. "I started writing little movies with my friends, and every class assignment that could remotely be related to film I made into a movie project." Despite some ambivalence from parents who weren't exactly sure how practical a film degree was, Skip went to college for film. Simultaneously, he was

becoming fascinated by a fledgling website for college students that in a matter of years would become the predominant social networking site in the world.

At the time, the site had been around for only a year and had less than one million users. "I just loved it—I thought it was the future." In the fall of his freshman year, Skip saw in an ad on the site that they were looking for a filmmaker in New York. At that point, the company had fewer than fifty employees and was trying to gauge public opinion of the website on college campuses. Skip was hired to produce a short holiday film capturing how students felt about the site, which was the beginning of his long relationship with the company. He continued making videos for the sales and marketing teams, and in the summer after his freshman year Skip moved out to their Palo Alto headquarters, where he worked to design and craft creative campaigns for companies looking for advertising opportunities.

That summer Skip watched the team in Palo Alto grow to more than 150 people, and when the summer ended, he struggled mightily with whether he should drop out of school and join the team full-time. "It was the hardest decision I've ever made." Ultimately, Skip decided to go back to school, a decision he doesn't regret. He continued to contract for the company almost full-time while attending school, and after graduation he pursued work with other clients—a start-up, script development—before returning to the website to work on directing product launch films for the company and then broadening his scope to branding.

A Good Fit

Skip's specialty is envisioning new ideas and then seeing them through to fruition. "It's about making sure that the team is working toward the overall vision and goals we had from the beginning and that we actually get the thing built." His dominant Thinking function gives him an architectural mindset and helps him make his ideas a reality. Like most Conceptualizers, Skip has a natural gift for problem solving. "I can't think of many other companies that are trying to solve a problem bigger than the one we are working to solve in the world: trying to connect humanity."

Skip's auxiliary function, Intuition, is very much in evidence in branding, as he works to make connections between his product and the cultural resonance he wishes to create. Skip's Extraversion explains both his initial draw to a social networking website as well as his belief in its mission to connect the world. Goal oriented, ambitious, and driven, Skip uses his Judging function to help him close the deal and focus on the end product.

Looking Ahead

While Skip loves the website and his role in the company, his end goal is to move into producing feature films, and more specifically, to run a production company that is vertically integrated. "I want to be on the ground floor of development and sourcing for material, conceiving and developing that material, producing it, and then distributing it in totally new ways that we haven't seen before."

Profile 3: Liam, Talent Agent

"Building people, building relationships."

The Job

There are three tenets to being a talent agent: signing, servicing, and selling. "Signing is getting the people, the clients, convincing them we can do a better job than any of our competitors." Servicing is the day-to-day maintenance of a client's career. "That can be handling deals, making sure our clients are compensated and credited. Or getting clients tickets to a Broadway show that are impossible to get." Selling is getting clients great jobs, or in some cases, "creating the jobs ourselves."

For Liam, this all boils down to relationship building. "I help people realize their dream job and that is so unbelievably validating for me. As someone who loves creative people and loves artists and art creation—I can actually help those people in real, concrete ways."

Backstory

Where do creative people meet in college? On the comedy improv team, of course. "It was the most exciting group of funny people I could find." After college, Liam wanted to find his way to New York City. He found a job as an advertising ops manager for an ad tech company, acting as a liaison between the clients and the programmers. While he didn't love the job, he learned a valuable lesson when a relationship with his mentor kept him employed through three acquisitions and reorganizations: People matter most.

While trying to figure out his next steps, Liam thought back to what had made him happy in the past, and remembered being around those creative, funny people. "I ended up taking a two-thirds pay cut and going to work in a mailroom at a talent agency. I saw the people at the top of the company, and I wanted their jobs. So I was able to motivate myself through this thankless job."

Liam quickly learned that turnover can happen in a split second when an agent's assistant quit one day at eleven a.m. By noon Liam was in training, and by one p.m. he was on the job full-time. As an assistant at a talent agency, Liam was "on the desk" of a senior agent, fielding somewhere between four hundred and two thousand emails a day. "It's sink or swim." With only 2 or 3 percent of assistants someday promoted to full agents, the job is truly an extreme sport. "The kind of people who succeed are the ones who want to be thoroughly exhausted by the end of the day and don't mind having breakfast, lunch, and dinner and then going to a comedy show or a play. They thrive on that."

To make the transition from a second-tier to top-tier agency, Liam started cold calling agents he wanted to work for. One shared an alma mater with him, and took his call. They had an informational meeting—"but any of those opportunities are interviews if you do a good job." When the call came two months later that she was moving agencies and needed an assistant that same day, Liam was ready.

A move to Los Angeles gave him another opportunity. Working for his next boss, a notoriously difficult person, Liam identified someone new who he thought could be a better boss and mentor. "I was already sending him ideas for his clients, sending him scripts. I was sort of doing the job already before I had the job." This paid off and he switched over to work in this new office, where he was later promoted.

A Good Fit

As a junior agent, Liam's job is to discover new talent. "My job is knowing everything about who's young and hot and cool and exciting in comedy." Liam sees what he does as building people and relationships, making introductions between comedians and bookers, and educating executives and decision makers in the company on up-and-coming talent. "We're matchmakers, essentially." Liam's canny sense of people

and his finely honed taste is essential to this work.

Liam's dominant Thinking side can be seen in his sharp negotiating skills, and his ability to make strategic moves for his clients and his career. "It's challenging and fun to set goals for my clients and reach them." Liam doesn't just set goals for his clients—he sets major ones for himself. Like many Conceptualizers, success is a major driver for Liam. In a ruthless industry, Liam can stay impartial and objective, and, as he says, "put my head down and do the work."

Trusting his gut about a new performer or a script is paramount in Liam's line of work, and evidence of his auxiliary function, Intuition. Liam has the vision to see a comedian in a small club and know that in five years that person could be huge.

Looking Ahead

Being one of the 2 or 3 percent to make it from assistant to agent is a huge deal in itself. But Liam will feel he's truly achieved his dream job when he wields enough power and influence to really make things happen. "A lot of my mentors will call someone and that gets things done. But you have to earn trust first." He will also need to see a roster of business that he's created where people are working consistently on exciting, quality work.

Liam sees that the entertainment world is in a moment of flux. "Streaming wars are in full effect. IP is king. You can churn out a lot of material but it has to be truly fantastic. People can watch anything now. So people who are specific and have something to say, something that feels different, that feels exciting."

Common Threads

Although Dan, Skip, and Liam have different backgrounds, experiences, and careers, there are certain common threads woven through their stories. Their specific interests, abilities, and values may differ, but owing to their similar temperament values and the *same hierarchy* of their psychological functions, there are certain observations we can make about the needs of many ENTJs.

What follows is a list of the most important elements—the formula, if you will—for ENTJ satisfaction. Given the uniqueness of all individuals—even those who share a type—this list will not describe each ENTJ equally well. The important thing is that these ten elements, with varying degrees of intensity and in different orders of importance, identify what ENTJs need to be satisfied.

After you have reviewed this list, we recommend that you go back and prioritize the elements in order of *their importance to you*. When doing this, think of past work experiences as well as your present job, and what you found particularly satisfying or unsatisfying. Try to look for *themes* that run through several experiences, not just *events* that might be true for one work situation but not for another.

As an ENTJ, I define career satisfaction as doing work that

1. lets me lead, be in control, organizing and perfecting the operating systems of an organization so that it runs efficiently and reaches its goals on schedule
2. lets me engage in long-range strategic planning, creative problem solving, and the generation of innovative and logical approaches to a variety of problems
3. is done in a well-organized environment where I, and others, work within a clear and definite set of guidelines
4. challenges and stimulates my intellectual curiosity and lets me work with complex and often difficult problems
5. gives me opportunities to meet and interact with a variety of other capable, interesting, and powerful people
6. gives me the opportunity to advance within the organization and to increase and demonstrate my competence
7. is exciting, challenging, and competitive; where I am in the public eye and where my accomplishments are seen, recognized, and fairly compensated
8. lets me work with other intelligent, creative, ambitious, and goal-oriented individuals whose competencies I respect
9. lets me set and meet goals and implement my organizational skills to keep myself and others focused on the larger goal while accomplishing all my objectives in a timely and efficient manner
10. lets me manage and supervise others, using logical and objective standards and policies that utilize each person's strengths but without having to deal daily with interpersonal squabbles

Popular Occupations for ENTJs

In listing occupations that are popular among ENTJs, it is important to note that there are successful people of all types in all occupations. However, the following are careers ENTJs may find particularly satisfying, and some of the reasons why. This is by no means a comprehensive listing but is included to suggest possibilities you may not have previously considered. Although all of these occupations offer the potential for career satisfaction, the future demand for some careers is anticipated to be greater than for others.

BUSINESS
- Executive
- Senior manager
- Office manager
- Administrative services manager
- Personnel manager
- Management analyst
- Business development director
- Market research analyst
- Network integration specialist
- Technical trainer
- Information services—new business developer
- Information security analyst
- Logistics consultant (manufacturing)
- Management analyst: computer/information services, marketing, reorganization
- Advertising account manager
- Marketing executive: online/radio/TV/cable broadcast industry
- Media planner/buyer
- International sales and marketing
- Franchise owner
- Sales manager
- Healthcare administrator
- College and university administrator
- Managing editor
- Theater producer
- Police and detective supervisor
- Human resources manager
- Association manager and adviser
- Program director
- Project manager
- Retail manager
- Real estate manager
- Real estate developer
- Restaurant and food service manager

The world of business is often enjoyed by ENTJs. They prefer to be in positions of authority, control, and leadership. As business executives, they are able to use their long-range thinking to develop

contingency plans and map out the best course to meet their goals. ENTJs use a style of direct management, able to make tough yet fair decisions and set policies for employees. They like to surround themselves with other independent, results-oriented people who can work without a lot of supervision or intervention. ENTJs usually rise to the top of organizations by using their ability to influence others and their ease at meeting and networking with people.

FINANCE
- Personal financial adviser
- Economic analyst
- Mortgage broker
- Credit investigator
- Stockbroker
- Investment banker
- Corporate finance attorney
- International banker
- Economist
- Treasurer, controller, chief financial officer
- Venture capitalist

ENTJs often excel in the field of finance. They enjoy making money and enjoy working with other people's money, too! They are energized by the competition of the field and take charge quickly and easily. These careers enable ENTJs to use their ability to forecast trends and design ingenious ways to take full advantage of opportunities for themselves and their clients. They do best when they have little work that involves details and follow-up, but instead can delegate to a competent support staff.

CONSULTING / TRAINING
- Business consultant
- Management consultant
- Educational consultant
- Program designer
- Management trainer
- Employment development specialist

- Labor relations manager
- Cybersecurity consultant
- Corporate/team trainer
- Technical trainer
- Legislative assistant
- Political consultant

The variety and independence offered in careers in consulting appeal to ENTJs. The wide field of options gives ENTJs the chance to satisfy their entrepreneurial spirit, work with a variety of people in a variety of business settings, and be compensated in proportion to the work they put in. ENTJs often excel in business or management consulting and can be excellent and stimulating trainers. They usually create a structured and challenging environment with creative designs and active sessions. They almost always prefer to take on new projects, and enjoy teaching other ambitious people ways to increase their competence.

PROFESSIONAL
- Attorney
- Judge
- Psychologist
- College professor: science/social science
- Chemical engineer
- Intellectual property attorney
- Biomedical engineer
- Psychiatrist
- Surgeon
- Medical scientist
- Environmental scientist
- Political scientist
- Pathologist
- Pilot

These professions offer the degree of status and level of influence ENTJs strive for in their careers. ENTJs often enjoy the field of law and have success as practicing and administrative attorneys and judges. The intellectual challenge of psychology and psychiatry appeals to many ENTJs, as do the complex field of chemical engineering and the growing fields of environmental and biomedical engineering. In education, ENTJs usually prefer teaching in the upper grades, especially secondary education, adult education, and at the college level. They enjoy applying their knowledge in the world around them and often have careers that let them expand their teaching responsibilities into other areas—such as politics or political consulting.

TECHNOLOGY
- Software developer: applications, systems
- Network and computer systems administrator
- Networking specialist
- Software and web development engineer
- Information and design architect
- Computer and information systems manager
- Computer and information research scientist
- Robotics network manager
- Artificial intelligence technologist
- Construction and development engineer
- Database administrator
- Project manager
- Engagement manager

Many ENTJs are ideally suited to careers in the ever-changing and expanding tech world. These jobs require several qualities that come naturally to most ENTJs: the ability to understand and process complex information, an extremely logical mind, the ability to grasp the big picture, and superior organizational skills.

Remember, these are only some areas that provide satisfying expression for the unique natural talents of the ENTJ.

Customizing Your Job Search

Knowing the particular strengths and blind spots of your type can afford you a tremendous advantage in your job search campaign. In all aspects of the process, from conducting research into available positions, identifying and contacting prospective employers, developing personal marketing tools such as résumés, arranging and conducting job interviews, and negotiating salaries to finally accepting a position, people will act true to their type. Being able to capitalize on your assets and compensate for your liabilities can make the difference between a successful and an unsuccessful job search.

The differences between types are sometimes subtle and other times dramatic. It is the subtle variations in advice we offer that make the real difference between success and failure in a job search. The concept of networking serves as a good example. Extraverts will naturally enjoy networking and are advised to do so on a large scale, while Introverts find more limited and targeted networking, especially with people they already know, easier. Sensors tend to network with people in a defined scope, while Intuitives will go far and wide to find people often seemingly unrelated to their field of interest. Further, Feelers can often take networking personally and enjoy establishing warm rapport, while Thinkers will be more objective and detached in their style. Finally, Judgers tend to ask fewer and more structured questions during their networking, while Perceivers could ask questions of all sorts all day long! One valuable search technique, many ways to implement it.

Pathways to Success: Using Your Strengths

As we will detail in the following pages, your strengths and talents in the job search lie in your ability to take command of the process, impressing others with your competence and inspiring them by your confidence. To avoid being perceived as overbearing, try to make a conscious effort to listen and ask questions as well as talk and give answers.

As an ENTJ, you will find that your most effective strategies build on your abilities to do the following:

Develop and follow an effective job search strategy.

- Establish your goals, including the criteria for the career or job you want, and map out your plan for obtaining it.
- Keep copies of your letters, log your appointments, and keep track of people you have followed up with or still need to contact to keep you organized and on time.

As Branson began his job search, he used the same time management and organization techniques that had served him well in his previous job as an administrator. He created a spreadsheet with a coding system to denote which people he had seen, was scheduled to see, or had yet to arrange a meeting with. After each interview, he made notes about the meeting and what his next step was to be. Then he sent an email thanking the individual for his or her time, and moved that name from the "pending" section to "next step" section. Using this system, Branson stayed on top of nearly twenty-five prospects and dozens of contacts without letting a single one slip.

Anticipate trends and forecast future needs.

- Use your ability to look at current situations and project how they will need to be different in order to meet the changing context.

- Demonstrate your ability to forecast future needs of potential employers by explaining how you see the market changing and how your input and involvement can help the employer meet those new demands.

During an interview at a small, newly formed market research company, Deonne noticed that the president seemed distracted and was, in fact, interrupted several times by frantic-looking members of her staff. When the president realized she was being rude, she explained to Deonne that her company was short-staffed and was in the middle of preparing a proposal for a major new client. Deonne suggested several vendors with whom she might subcontract to get her through the crunch. The president was impressed with Deonne's quick thinking, contacts, and understanding of the business. Then Deonne explained that she had experience troubleshooting similar projects and would be willing to freelance on the project as a way of demonstrating her abilities. The president was taken aback by the offer, but after taking a minute to consider it, realized she was looking at the solution to her immediate problem and perhaps long-term improvement in the operation of her business. Deonne was hired on the spot.

Solve problems creatively.

- Approach obstacles as challenges rather than roadblocks. Rise to the challenge of overcoming them by using your creativity.
- Demonstrate your ability to develop innovative strategies by preparing an assessment of the prospective employer's biggest problems and how you would help to solve them.

When Liam was hoping to switch from working as the assistant to one entertainment agent to another, he first made sure to know the field, and set his sights on someone he thought could be a mentor. He knew it wasn't enough to want the job; he had to make himself indispensable. So he vetted and sent over scripts and other opportunities that he thought would be a great fit for this person's clients. By the time Liam asked outright for the job, he had already proved his ability to do it.

Network extensively.

- Develop a list of everyone you know who knows you and your abilities, and make appointments to meet with them to discuss your career goals.
- Ask the people who know you to refer you to other people who might either be interested in your area of expertise or might have some knowledge that you will find helpful.

It's Jane's habit never to delete a contact, even if she doesn't have an immediate need or use for it. Ultimately, Jane used all those names to start her own business. She preferred to take people out for coffee, but because her time was at a premium, she also found that with a few minutes on the phone or even an email, she could usually reach several new contacts. Jane makes a point of returning the generosity shown her by agreeing to conduct informational interviews as often as possible, which results in an even greater network of contacts.

Become knowledgeable about the organization and the position of interest.

- Do some research at the library through industry trade publications or by talking to people already in the field or organization to find out as much as you can about what's happening at the company and in the field. Also find out what you can about your interviewer so you can find a common ground on which to establish rapport.

- Synthesize the information you have collected and distill it into a mini-report to review before a subsequent interview or to refer to during the interview to demonstrate your interest in and knowledge of the business.

After working unhappily in a bank for twelve years, Ezra decided that he wanted to make a career change to investment brokerage. He took a couple of training seminars offered through continuing education from a banking association of which he was a member. In one of the classes, he met an investment broker and queried him about the industry. Ezra's new friend introduced him to several other investment brokers and suggested Ezra check out a website that published helpful articles about the business and listed available jobs throughout the region. Later, in job interviews, Ezra was able to refer to interesting information he had learned about the industry and also to call on his new contacts to help make inroads at investment firms.

Possible Pitfalls

Although all people are unique, there are certain *potential* blind spots that many ENTJs share. We underscore "potential" because some of the following *may* be true of you, while others may clearly not apply. While considering them, you may notice that these tendencies do not just relate to the job search but rather describe pitfalls that you may have experienced in other aspects of your life as well. It is therefore helpful to consider each

one in terms of your past experiences by asking yourself, "Is this true for me?" And if so, "How did this tendency prevent me from getting something that I wanted?" You will probably notice that the key to overcoming your blind spots is the conscious and thoughtful development of your third and fourth functions (Sensing and Feeling). We recognize that many of the suggestions will be difficult to implement, but the more you use these functions, the fewer problems they will cause you in the future.

Avoid making decisions too quickly.

- Take time to gather all the relevant, albeit mundane, facts about a job or career before deciding whether you are interested in it. Refer to your list of criteria and be sure to ask all the necessary questions so that you have an accurate and realistic picture of the job and its opportunities.
- Be sure to reflect before acting. Ask yourself what you really want and how a potential job fits with the things you believe are important to you. Be honest with yourself and add those values and desires to your list of criteria.

Try not to appear aggressive and pushy.

- Be aware that other people may be put off by your energy and drive and consider you too aggressive. Take time to establish rapport, finding some common personal ground early on in an interview. Take time to recognize the contributions of those around you.
- Try to be understanding of the unpredictable delays and postponements that are a fact of life. These may slow down your journey toward your goal, but try not to let them frustrate or discourage you.

Don't discount opportunities you consider to be below your competency level.

- Realize that you may appear overconfident or arrogant, and unintentionally insult a potential employer by refusing to consider a position you see as beneath you.
- Think of everyone you meet as someone with whom you may have to work one day and do all that you can to establish good relations with them.

Be patient with all phases of the process, even the details.

- Don't overlook the practical considerations of a job search in favor of the more interesting aspects. Check out the time investment and costs associated with a quality job search and be sure they are budgeted into your overall plan.
- Delay starting your job search until you have fully researched your resources and are sure you will be able to complete it to your high standards before plowing ahead.

Work on developing active listening skills.

- Realize that you sometimes may interrupt others before they finish speaking because you have anticipated (correctly or incorrectly) what they are about to say. Instead, wait a few seconds after they have finished speaking and check with them to make sure you understood what they meant.
- Remember that, rather than appearing confident and competent, you may come across as impatient and domineering. Make a conscious effort to

curb that tendency by giving the other people plenty of time to gather their thoughts and finish their sentences.

The Final Piece: Changing or Keeping Your Job . . . the Key to Success for ENTJs

Now that you have a solid understanding of your type, you can see how your natural preferences make you better suited for certain kinds of jobs. You can also see how knowledge of your type-related strengths and blind spots can help you conduct a more successful job search. But as an ENTJ, you've already realized that you are not equally drawn to *every* career or field listed in the Popular Occupations section. The next and final step is to narrow down the field and find the work you were meant to do.

In addition to Type, several other factors—such as your values, interests, and skills—also contribute to your level of satisfaction on the job. The more compatible you are with your job, the happier you'll be. So prepare to use everything you've learned (in this book and in life) to create *your strategic career plan*. The exercises in Chapter 23, "Putting It All Together," are designed to help you do just that.

However, you may have decided it makes more sense (if perhaps only for the moment) to stay in your present job or with your current employer. There may be many valid reasons—financial pressures, family considerations, a tough job market for your specialty, or just bad timing. But take heart! What you've learned in this book can also help you be more content and successful *in your current job*. And should the time come when you're ready to make a major career move, you'll have a much better idea of where you want to go and how to get there.

"So, if you can't have the job you love (yet!)... love the one you've got."

The simple truth is, many jobs allow a good deal of flexibility in the way tasks are performed. Here are some ways you may be able to "massage" your current job into one that better fits your needs:

- Try to get appointed to strategic planning committees.
- Find a mentor (if you are new to the field or organization).
- Create opportunities to be a leader (volunteer to chair a committee, etc.).
- Develop a "critical friends group" (people that help critique each other's ideas).
- Seek professional development opportunities on a regular basis.
- Sign up for advanced training or a degree in your area of specialty.
- Join and/or become a leader in a professional association.
- Invite more input from direct reports.

One ENTJ turns lemons into lemonade:

Josh was the managing partner in a small law firm. Although he had reached the top of the ladder at his company and had even greater ambitions, he was not yet experienced enough to get the same position in a larger firm. He ran for office for his state bar association, worked hard, and within two years assumed its presidency. This added leadership experience and statewide exposure made him a great candidate for the kind of position he sought.

Use what you've got to get what you need.

Simply put, the best advice on how to succeed is to *capitalize on your strengths and compensate for your blind spots.*

Learning how to do this can make the difference between succeeding or failing and loving or hating your work. To help you, we include the following inventory of your potential strengths and blind spots. And while every individual is unique, many of the following should apply to you as an ENTJ.

Your work-related strengths may include

- ability to see possibilities and implications
- aptitude for creative problem solving; ability to examine issues objectively
- understanding of complex issues
- drive and ambition to succeed
- confidence and natural leadership ability
- strong motivation to be competent and to excel
- high standards and strong work ethic
- ability to create systems and models to achieve your objectives
- courage to take bold steps and the drive to reach goals
- logical and analytical decision-making skills
- decisiveness and strong organizational skills
- comfort with technology; you're a quick learner

Your work-related blind spots may include

- impatience with others who are not as quick as you are
- brusqueness and lack of tact and diplomacy
- tendency toward hasty decision making
- lack of interest in mundane details
- tendency to want to improve something that doesn't need improving

- potential to intimidate or overpower others
- tendency to not take the time to adequately appreciate and praise employees, colleagues, and others

- reluctance to reexamine issues already decided
- propensity to overemphasize work life to the detriment of home life

Using your strengths is easy.
The secret to success for an
ENTJ
is learning to

slow down, focus on the details, and tune in to others' needs.

12 | INTJ

Introverted, Intuitive, Thinking, Judging

"Competence + Independence = Perfection"

Profile 1: Kathleen, City Commission Coordinator

"Planning strategies and seeing them through."

The Job

Kathleen is a self-professed perfectionist and a juggler of many projects. She serves as coordinator and staff assistant to a city commission on women's issues and affairs. She also runs her own business providing training, education, and consulting in management planning and development. It's a full plate, and Kathleen works constantly. "Career satisfaction for me means I can do my work any day of the week and never say, 'Hey! Isn't this my day off?'"

Kathleen coordinates and manages the planning activities of a city human service and political commission. Her work involves research and analysis of proposals for potential programs, the writing of policy reports, and preparation and grooming of public officials to help identify and overcome potential obstacles to new policies. She facilitates internal task forces and handles negotiations among commissioners.

In her own business, which she runs after traditional work hours, Kathleen creates management planning and development programs for companies. Her consulting work is designed around helping teams work more effectively together. She works long hours keeping track of "the details nobody else thinks of. I'm the consummate planner, and I'm known for my prototypes."

Backstory

One of the things Kathleen values most about herself is her competency. Throughout her work history it seems that she has always worked toward that end. Her first job after college was as administrative account specialist at an international business corporation. She was naive about the norms of working in a large organization but was learning so much, she didn't mind all the detail work of administering the sales accounts. Soon she realized she wanted to be in a smaller work environment and accepted a job at a very small consulting firm where she developed the training programs they marketed. While she loved being "responsible for everything," the company couldn't offer her the salary she needed.

She next went to work for the U.S. government courts system as arbitration and deputy clerk. It was a highly technical position, and while it paid her a good salary, she was bored and hated it. She heard about a scholarship opportunity at a small university and entered the graduate program, where she obtained her MBA. "I loved being a student. The program let me explore and manipulate all kinds of information." It was in school that she decided to start her own business, which she has continued to run on a part-time and full-time basis for the past nine years. After completing the degree, she operated her business out of her home and also taught marketing management and human resources management at a community college. Typically taking on several challenges at once, she became director of communication for a local chapter of the United Way while still running her own business. After only a year at the United Way, Kathleen was offered the job she has now.

A Good Fit

Kathleen's career provides a rich example of the Conceptualizer temperament. She is driven to increase her competence, constantly acquiring new information and mastering new concepts. Hers is a quest for perfection, striving to be the best at everything she tries. She is motivated by any kind of challenge; working hard and single-mindedly to exceed even her own high standards.

Her Intuition demands that she see possibilities. The possibilities that receive the most attention are those that spring from her own mind and vision.. She loves planning strategies, considering theories, and anticipating the potential implications of her new ideas.

Kathleen uses her Thinking to analyze, coordinate, and manage her ideas into concrete and workable programs. She identifies problems in the systems and uses her logical thinking to analyze and organize solutions. She coordinates strategic planning sessions and facilitates the implementation of her projects. "I enjoy almost everything I do: Creating proposals and getting other people to accept them, especially when there is initial resistance, is challenging; and anything having to do with theories and the future implications of *anything* is exciting."

While Kathleen enjoys her work immensely, she is always looking forward to the next challenge. Her career goal is to start a liberal arts college for people of color. The school would have a strong economic and historical focus, and an emphasis on critical thinking. True to form, Kathleen has already begun the research to make her dream a reality.

"I've become more of a team player over the years. I'm more mature and have learned to tone down my sharp tongue." She hopes to continue developing her skills in facilitating group process, a skill she recognizes needs more work. She's able to express her feelings more freely now. "I still internalize most of it, but I'm learning to count on my friends to share that side of me with. I'm not there yet, but I hope someday people remember me as a person with spurts of genius in her; someone who was demanding of herself and others but was extremely loyal and compassionate to friends. Those are my goals."

Profile 2: Phil, Start-up Entrepreneur

"Creating something from nothing."

The Job

Phil had always wanted to create his own business. He has now created two. The first was a human resources tech start-up. The current one is a small company that helps HR teams to understand which tools they should buy for recruiting or ongoing human resources management. As the founder of his business, Phil does everything from marketing to sales and product research. "Most of my days are spent on figuring out how to get more people to our website, which means doing in-depth research into HRTech vendors and then creating video and written content to share that research."

Backstory

Phil bought his first stocks when he was ten years old. He and a younger brother began investing money from odd jobs in the stock market, even turning a profit. Ever since then, Phil knew he wanted to be in finance, and he went on to study business in college and spend several summers interning at different large investment banks. But it was Phil's experiences interning in the world of start-up companies that really inspired him: "It's the most direct way to change the world around me and see my work have an impact."

His first job out of college was in sell-side mergers and acquisitions. But when a recession hit hard and Phil was laid off a year later, it felt more liberating than disappointing. "Now I can go off and do something I'm more interested in," Phil remembers thinking. He launched a full-court press and landed his dream job working at one of the oldest and largest venture capital firms in the world. In the back of his mind, Phil always sensed that he wanted to be an entrepreneur, and what better way to confirm, he reasoned, than to talk to as many CEOs as possible and learn from them. Two years later, Phil had talked to over a thousand CEOs and started to strategize the next move toward his own start-up. He completed his MBA at Harvard Business School, and got ready to strike out on his own.

As a side project during business school—one of many for Phil—he developed a website to help others use self-reflection in the internship process. A self-described journal writer since fifth grade, Phil saved himself from a potential career misstep in college by going back to his journals and remembering what he hated about the work environment at the big investment firm that offered him a job. The website acted as a virtual time capsule to help interns remember at the end of the process what their goals were, what they thought of the work-life balance, and other critical factors.

This experience working on his website and especially guiding others through careful reflection set Phil up for his first real business venture: a human resources tech start-up. When it became profitable, Phil was able to hire someone else to run it as a general manager. "I still had the start-up itch, so I started a new business." Now his current company helps other HR teams to evaluate digital tools and choose the best ones to suit their needs.

A Good Fit

Many Conceptualizers are drawn to the competitive, intellectual world of entrepreneurship. Phil's work is idea driven, and innovation is essential in a field where a new idea can have big payoffs. Because Phil is a dominant Intuitive, his brain is wired to see the big picture, make connections, and seek creative solutions. In investing, this means having the vision to see opportunities and possibilities others might pass over. In the world of start-ups, everything comes down to Phil's vision and how to get it done.

As for many INTJs, independence is the name of the game with Phil, who trusts his own judgment and ideas more than institutions or traditions. He is a born problem solver, and his auxiliary Thinking function makes him logical, analytical, and objective. Phil's Judging function makes him solution oriented, driven to achieve his goals. An extremely hard worker, he's put in as many as 120 hours per week at some jobs—sometimes working 40 hours at a stretch. He excels in one-to-one interactions and exudes confidence and competence—one of the reasons he was able to make personal connections with so many CEOs. As he is the founder of his own company, the buck truly stops with Phil, and he gets to see the fruits of his labors on the macro level.

Looking Ahead

Ideally, in five years Phil will have enough money to retire if he wants to, allowing him to spend more time with family and friends, and continue to stretch beyond his comfort zone. Eventually, Phil would love to transition into a role as a board member, professor, or another mentorship role where he can share his experience and help others to realize their ambitions. Phil's focus and drive thus far make it easy to imagine him meeting, and exceeding, these goals.

Profile 3: Jim, Lawyer

"Winning a really tough case on the strength of my lawyering, not merely on the strength of the case."

The Job

Jim is a civil trial lawyer and partner in a plaintiff law firm, representing people who have been injured in a variety of ways. Medical malpractice and personal injury cases are his firm's specialty. "My clients come to me to help redress their injuries through the court system." His focus is entirely on the potential court case, yet he spends nearly 90 percent of his time preparing for the 10 percent of time he actually spends in court. This is due to the large number of cases that settle out of court and the relatively few that make it all the way to a jury trial.

Jim's duties include taking depositions (interviewing potential witnesses to find out their side of the story), preparing witnesses, finding and obtaining testimony from expert witnesses, negotiating cases with opposing counsel, and the myriad phone calls and emails surrounding each of these functions. "I spend what often seems like a great deal of my time on the phone with a client, helping solve problems that may seem mundane to me but are nevertheless very important to my client."

The court time, however, is what makes Jim enjoy his work as much as he does. "My goal is to do my job so well that I never make mistakes. That's obviously impossible, but I try to put the other side in a position to make errors and then I capitalize on those mistakes."

Backstory

Jim entered law school after first attempting divinity school. He thought he wanted to teach philosophy and theology but discovered he wasn't devoted to his subject area to the extent he ought to be in order to make it his life's work. He also realized that the market for theology or philosophy professors was a limited one, so he applied to law school. In school he clerked at several different law firms. At first he found the subject matter (real estate, or zoning and sewer work) too boring. At another firm he wasn't comfortable with the strong emphasis on socializing. Then he clerked at the firm of his trial practice teacher and liked the subject area, the people, and the attitude of the firm. He was hired upon graduation, and except for a few times over the years when he has considered offers from other firms, he has been happily and steadily increasing his position and interest in his firm for fifteen years.

The moments Jim considers great accomplishments are when he has won a case nobody considered winnable. "The really tough cases that I have won on the strengths of my lawyering rather than on the strengths of the case are most rewarding to me." He is also proud of the articles he has published in professional journals, and the status he has attained within important professional organizations.

A Good Fit

Jim's goal to be the best trial lawyer possible is consistent with his Conceptualizer temperament. His drive for competency pushes him hard to keep trying to improve his skills and to maintain extremely high standards. He is motivated to learn the tremendous amount of new material necessary to try cases often involving complex medical testimony. With practically every case, he is required to become an expert in some field. Like many Conceptualizers, he is drawn to being in positions of power that increase his stature, professional standing, and financial status.

Court time also gives Jim the control and autonomy he enjoys most, and that are so essential to an INTJ. "When you're on trial, everybody in the office knows and accepts that as your sole responsibility. There are no interruptions, no phone calls in the middle of a meeting. I can concentrate fully, and I am able to make independent decisions in

the best interest of the case. I am able to be my own boss."

As a dominant Intuitive, Jim is constantly strategizing in his head. Playing the ultimate chess match, he anticipates problems, forecasts his opponents' tactics, and tries to discover their weaknesses to figure out ways to overcome obstacles. His Intuition is particularly useful in helping him to look at an issue (or a case) as his opponent might see it, turning it over in his mind, enabling him to prepare more effectively.

Jim uses his Thinking function to help him deal coolly, objectively, and dispassionately with the many conflicts that occur during trials. He views the inevitable and necessary conflicts between opposing counsel as "just business, nothing personal," and as a result is able to maintain good working relationships with other lawyers. His Thinking also keeps him from getting so emotionally involved with the plight of his clients that he loses sight of the bigger picture—a verdict or settlement that is in their best interest.

Looking Ahead

Jim has returned to the classroom recently, teaching courses at the law school. "I think I've become more interested in incorporating positive reinforcement and mentoring some of the students. I feel as though I am making a contribution, and that's rewarding." He is finding more time to spend with his wife and children without the anxiety he used to experience when taking time off from work.

"I think I have developed an ability to get along with all kinds of people. I have increased my level of self-awareness and can appreciate my strengths and also take responsibility for my failures. Whatever I do, I want to do it well. My work affords me the chance to do something I really enjoy, providing a service that is recognized as important and I am rewarded for being the best."

Common Threads

Although Kathleen, Jim, and Phil all have different backgrounds, experiences, and careers, there are certain common threads woven through their stories. Their specific interests, abilities, and values may differ, but owing to their similar temperament values and the *same hierarchy* of their psychological functions, there are certain observations we can make about the needs of many INTJs.

What follows is a list of the most important elements—the formula, if you will—for INTJ satisfaction. Given the uniqueness of all individuals—even those who share a type—this list will not describe each INTJ equally well. The important thing is that these ten elements, with varying degrees of intensity and in different orders of importance, identify what INTJs need to be satisfied.

After you have reviewed this list, we recommend that you go back and try to prioritize the elements in order of *their importance to you*. When doing this, think of past work experiences as well as your present job, and what you found particularly satisfying or unsatisfying. Try to look for *themes* that run through several experiences, not just *events* that might be true for one work situation but not for another.

As an INTJ, I define career satisfaction as doing work that

1. lets me create and develop original and innovative solutions to problems to improve existing systems
2. lets me focus my energy on the implementation of my good ideas, working in a logical and orderly way and in a setting that rewards my perseverance
3. lets me work with other conscientious people whose expertise, intelligence, and competence I respect
4. gives me credit for my original ideas and lets me maintain authorship and control over their execution
5. allows me to work independently but with periodic interaction with a small group of intellectual people within a smooth-running environment free from interpersonal squabbles
6. exposes me to a steady stream of new information, providing me with new ways to increase my proficiency and competence
7. lets me produce a product that meets with my own high standards of quality rather than with the personal likes or dislikes of others
8. does not require the repetitive execution of factual and detail-oriented tasks
9. provides me with a high degree of autonomy and control, with the freedom to effect change and develop people and systems
10. is judged by uniform and fair standards for all, where performance evaluations are based on established criteria rather than on personality contests and that compensates me fairly for my contributions

Popular Occupations for INTJs

In listing occupations that are popular among INTJs, it is important to note that there are successful people of all types in all occupations. However, the following are careers INTJs may find particularly satisfying, and some of the reasons why. This is by no means a comprehensive listing but is included to suggest possibilities you may not have previously considered. Although all of these occupations offer the potential for career satisfaction, the future demand for some careers is anticipated to be greater than for others.

BUSINESS / FINANCE
- Management consultant: computer/ information services, marketing, reorganization
- Management analyst
- Start-up entrepreneur
- Economist
- Personal financial adviser
- Market research analyst
- Management analyst
- Investment banker
- International banker
- Credit analyst
- Financial analyst
- Strategic planner
- Budget analyst
- Treasurer or controller
- Private sector executive
- Real estate appraiser

The business and financial careers listed all require highly developed analytical abilities that many INTJs possess. The constantly changing worlds of investment and international banking, for instance, make good use of many INTJs' global perspective and ability to plan long range.

TECHNOLOGY
- Scientist/scientific researcher
- Information security analyst
- Network systems and data communications analyst
- Software developer: applications, systems
- Computer programmer
- Networking specialist
- Information and design architect
- Robotics and manufacturing engineer
- Artificial intelligence technologist
- Technician: electrical/electronic
- Astronomer
- Environmental planner
- Cybersecurity specialist
- Operations research analyst
- Information services developer
- Network integration specialist
- Database administrator
- Computer animator
- Network and computer systems administrator
- Print designer
- Interaction designer
- Computer programmer

The technical fields appeal to the INTJ's interest in logical systems. These fields offer an opportunity to work with rapidly developing high-tech equipment and products. Often INTJs are able to use their creativity to develop ingenious and inventive systems.

EDUCATION
- College professor: computer science/ math
- Academic curriculum designer
- Administrator
- Mathematician
- Anthropologist
- Curator
- Archivist

Higher education appeals to the INTJ much more than elementary or secondary education, because it usually involves teaching complex theories and systems with a more global perspective. Developing educational curricula or systems and making sure they are run efficiently allow the INTJ to make improvements. The world of higher education also exposes INTJs to an environment where they can gather and manipulate information and interact with other intellectual people with whom they can expand their own level of competence.

HEALTHCARE
- Psychiatrist
- Psychologist
- Medical scientist
- Neurologist
- Biomedical researcher/engineer
- Cardiologist
- Pharmacologist
- Pharmaceutical researcher
- Coroner
- Pathologist
- Microbiologist
- Geneticist
- Surgeon
- Cardiovascular technician

The more technical areas of medicine are fields in which many INTJs often find success and satisfaction. These fields include highly complex systems, and allow the INTJ to work independently, with minimal outside intervention or input.

PROFESSIONAL
- Attorney
- Strategic planner
- Judge
- News analyst/writer
- Engineer
- Metallurgical engineer
- Intellectual properties attorney
- Civil engineer
- Aerospace engineer
- Nuclear engineer
- Architect
- Universal design architect
- Environmental scientist
- Intelligence specialist
- Criminalist and ballistics expert
- Pilot

The professional occupations offer a variety of appealing aspects for the INTJ. All require independent research and planning. The development of strategies, systems, and long-range plans utilizes INTJs' future orientation (Intuition) and their ability to plan out how to reach their goals in a sequential and logical manner.

CREATIVE
- Writer
- Editor
- Artist
- Inventor
- Graphic designer
- Informational-graphics designer
- Freelance media planner
- Art director
- Columnist, critic, commentator
- Blogger
- Exhibit designer and builder

The appeal of the creative occupations is the ability to do original work. Writers and artists use their Intuition to create new expressions and statements. Inventors are able to create new systems or devices that improve current ways of living or solve vexing problems. All three of these jobs require that INTJs work independently, meeting their own goals and standards, with themselves as the ultimate critic.

Remember, these are only some areas that provide satisfying expression for the unique natural talents of the INTJ.

Customizing Your Job Search

Knowing the particular strengths and blind spots of your type can afford you a tremendous advantage in your job search campaign. In all aspects of the process, from conducting research into available positions, identifying and contacting prospective employers, developing personal marketing tools such as résumés, arranging and conducting job interviews, and negotiating salaries to finally accepting a position, people will act true to their type. Being able to capitalize on your assets and compensate for your liabilities can make the difference between a successful and an unsuccessful job search.

The differences between types are sometimes subtle and other times dramatic. It is the subtle variations in advice we offer that make the real difference between success and failure in a job search. The concept of networking serves as a good example. Extraverts will naturally enjoy networking and are advised to do so on a large scale, while Introverts find more limited and targeted networking, especially with people they already know, easier. Sensors tend to network with people in a defined scope, while Intuitives will go far and wide to find people often seemingly unrelated to their field of interest. Further, Feelers can often take networking personally and enjoy establishing warm rapport, while Thinkers will be more objective and detached in their style. Finally, Judgers tend to ask fewer and more structured questions during their networking, while Perceivers could ask questions of all sorts all day long! One valuable search technique, many ways to implement it.

Pathways to Success: Using Your Strengths

Because many of the tasks involved in the job search are not usually liked by INTJs, you may not find this process to be particularly enjoyable. Remaining focused on your larger goal of finding challenging and interesting work will prevent you from becoming too impatient with the necessary details and seemingly frivolous social niceties required.

As an INTJ, you will find that your most effective strategies build on your abilities to do the following:

Anticipate trends, forecast future needs.

- Use your ability to look at current situations and project how they will need to be different in order to meet the changing context.
- Demonstrate ability to forecast future needs by explaining how your involvement can help employers meet their new demands.

When James was debating a career as a college professor, he did a little research and learned there were very few colleges with large philosophy or theology departments. He realized that the trend would continue and the opportunities for good jobs would decline further, making the competition fierce. Recognizing his waning interest in his field of study, he looked instead to where he might find the challenge, intellectual stimulation, and opportunity to use his excellent analysis and strategizing skills and decided upon a career in law.

Synthesize information.

- Engage your ability to understand and assimilate complex information to become fully versed in the technology of the discipline.
- Demonstrate that ability by summarizing what you see as the strengths and weaknesses of the market or industry, explaining how your unique skills will help the employer by meeting his/her goals.

Monica's skills at understanding the big picture helped her get the job at the children's hospital. In fact, all of the jobs she has enjoyed are those where she had no predecessor and was hired because of her ability to sell her vision of a needed position. When she interviewed for the job as fundraising coordinator, she explained that she saw her role as one who would see what needed to be done, find the existing flaws in the system, and pull the people together who would create a successful event. She described her role and how she would manage those around her. She was able to see and then communicate her vision to others.

Create your own career options, design your own job.

- Use your natural ability to see opportunities before others do and put yourself in an advantageous position early on in the interviewing process.
- Use your creativity to develop a unique career opportunity, selling a potential employer on how that job will help meet goals and solve problems.

Frustrated with the way his original ideas were so altered during the production process, Jack left the world of advertising copywriting to become a news writer. Even though he lacked news-writing experience, Jack devised a plan to get himself where he wanted to go. He looked up an old friend in Arizona who was the editor of a small magazine. Jack wrote a couple of freelance articles that led to an offer as a staff writer. Instead of taking the job, he relocated to a larger city and took the experience and his portfolio with him. He was able to create a job as a reporter based on only a few articles and the letter of recommendation from his past employer.

Develop an innovative career plan.

- Use your creativity to plot out a campaign in a new and different way— setting you apart from other candidates with potential employers.
- Use your organizational skills to stay on top of the project, make a plan, be on time, remember to send a note after the interview, follow up with prospective employers, etc.

Margaret's situation was not unique. As a single working mother with two young children, she could not afford to quit her administrative job at a large hospital to go on an all-out job search. She decided what she lacked in free time, she would make up for in innovation. She determined that she wanted to use her skills and experience in finance to become an investment analyst. So in an effort to gain some real experience, and also to market herself, she developed a blog. She worked on her blog in the evenings, using a web template and designing it to be professional-looking, interesting, and valuable to potential employers. She focused each post on a particular industry and then on several new rising companies. She did analysis of their markets, looked into the major shareholders, and made predictions about their movement in the stock market.

She sent links to the blog to a very focused list of potential employers with cover letters that said she was interested in providing these kinds of insights for them should a position become available. She so enjoyed working on the blog that the next seven months flew by. When she was offered a job at one of the targeted companies, she persuaded them to let her continue to produce a blog, this time for their clients.

Make decisions.

- Organize your ideas into thoughtful and systematic work plans and stick with your agenda.
- Use your skills at critical analysis to eliminate unfavorable options along the way, reorganizing your plan when necessary.

When his husband accepted a job in a new city, it meant job search time for Carlos. He had been an assistant art director at a large advertising firm and decided he would look for an art director position. Carlos developed a list of criteria for the job, made an organized plan of attack, and began to call on agencies in the area.

After only a couple of days, he was offered an assistant art director job at another large agency. After thinking it over, he declined the offer because it would not give him the creative control or autonomy he had decided were critical to him. Finally, he received an offer from a small firm whose growth necessitated the creation of a new department devoted to consumer advertising, his area of expertise. While the position was still assistant art director, Carlos accepted, knowing he would have the autonomy and control he wanted as the head of the new division. He was willing to trade off the title because he was getting all that he had wanted in a director position.

Possible Pitfalls

Although all people are unique, there are certain *potential* blind spots that many INTJs share. We underscore "potential" because some of the following *may* be true of you, while others may clearly not apply. While considering them, you may notice that these tendencies do not relate just to the job search, but rather describe pitfalls that you may have experienced in other aspects of your life as well. It is therefore helpful to consider each one in terms of your past experience by asking yourself, "Is this true for me?" And if so, "How did this tendency prevent me from getting something that I wanted?" You will probably notice that the key to overcoming your blind spots is the conscious and thoughtful development of your third and fourth functions (Feeling and Sensing). We recognize that many of the suggestions will be difficult to implement, but the more you use these functions, the fewer problems they will cause you in the future.

Attend to all necessary and relevant facts, not just the new and novel ones.

- Spend time focusing on the realities and practical applications of your ideas rather than just on the innovative implications.
- Concentrate on not letting things fall through the cracks because you assume they are already taken care of.

Use tact and diplomacy in getting others to buy your ideas.

- Try to be persuasive in your approach rather than being unyielding in your style, allowing others to comment or challenge your viewpoint.
- Try to consider the ramifications and impact a decision or comment may have on another person, understanding that others often take criticism personally.

Avoid appearing unintentionally arrogant and condescending to potential employers.

- Remember you are in a selling position, attempting to portray yourself as part of a team of workers, someone who can and will contribute to the goals of the whole organization.
- Take time to listen fully and completely to other people and repeat back to them what they said to be sure you haven't made incorrect assumptions.

Try to remain flexible and open-minded when making decisions.

- Try to be willing to give in on less important points while still holding firm to the elements that are truly vital to you.
- Decide to give everything a second look, even after you discount it. Some opportunities may appear more attractive when you give yourself the extra time to get all the information.

The Final Piece: Changing or Keeping Your Job... the Key to Success for INTJs

Now that you have a solid understanding of your type, you can see how your natural preferences make you better suited for certain kinds of jobs. You can also see how knowledge of your type-related strengths and blind spots can help you conduct a more successful job search. But as an INTJ, you've already realized that you are not equally drawn to *every* career or field listed in the Popular Occupations section. The next and final step is to narrow down the field and find the work you were meant to do.

In addition to Type, several other factors—such as your values, interests, and skills—also contribute to your level of satisfaction on the job. The more compatible you are with your job, the happier you'll be. So prepare to use everything you've learned (in this book and in life) to create *your strategic career plan*. The exercises in Chapter 23, "Putting It All Together," are designed to help you do just that.

However, you may have decided it makes more sense (if perhaps only for the moment) to stay in your present job or with your current employer. There may be many valid reasons—financial pressures, family considerations, a tough job market for your specialty, or just bad timing. But take heart! What you've learned in this book can also help you be more content and successful *in your current job*. And should the time come when you're ready to make a major career move, you'll have a much better idea of where you want to go and how to get there.

"So, if you can't have the job you love (yet!)...love the one you've got."

The simple truth is, many jobs allow a good deal of flexibility in the way tasks are performed. Here are some ways you may be able to "massage" your current job into one that better fits your needs:

- Try to get appointed to strategic planning committees.
- Develop systems and work to get them implemented at your organization.
- Make sure you have enough uninterrupted time to think and work on projects that interest you.
- Develop a "critical friends" group to critique each other's ideas.
- Seek professional development opportunities.
- Sign up for advanced training (or a degree) in your area of specialty.
- Publish research and articles in your field.
- Invite more input from direct reports.

One INTJ turns lemons into lemonade:

Several months ago, Lucas—a design engineer—was promoted to manager of his department, and he soon designed several new systems to make the department more productive. The problem was, he was not especially skilled at managing *people*, and he was having a hard time getting certain staff on board. Recognizing this weakness, he asked three more experienced managers he knew to meet with him and critique his plans and approach. The initial meeting was so helpful to him, the group decided to meet monthly and take turns consulting with each other.

Use what you've got to get what you need.

Simply put, the best advice on how to succeed is to *capitalize on your strengths and compensate for your blind spots*. Learning how to do this can make the difference between succeeding or failing and loving or hating your work. To help you, we include the following inventory of your potential strengths and blind spots. And while every individual is unique, many of the following should apply to you as an INTJ.

Your work-related strengths may include

- ability to focus and concentrate deeply on issues
- ability to see possibilities and implications
- enjoyment of complex theoretical and intellectual challenges
- aptitude for creative problem solving; ability to examine issues objectively
- single-minded determination to reach your goals even in the face of opposition
- confidence and commitment to your vision
- strong motivation to be competent and excel
- ability to work well alone; independent and self-directed
- high standards and strong work ethic
- ability to create systems and models to achieve your objectives
- comfort with technology
- logical and analytical decision-making skills
- decisiveness and strong organizational skills

Your work-related blind spots may include

- loss of interest in projects after the creative process has been completed
- tendency to drive others as hard as you drive yourself
- impatience with others who are not as quick as you are
- difficulty working with or for others you consider less competent
- brusqueness and lack of tact and diplomacy, especially when you are rushed
- lack of interest in mundane details
- inflexibility about your ideas
- tendency to want to improve things that don't need improving
- tendency to be too theoretical and not consider practical realities
- tendency to not adequately appreciate and praise employees, colleagues, and others
- reluctance to reexamine issues already decided
- propensity to overemphasize work life to the detriment of home life
- impatience with "social niceties" required of some jobs

Using your strengths is easy.
The secret to success for an
INTJ
is learning to

consider practical realities,
recognize the value of input from others,
and balance your work and personal life.

13 | ENTP
Extraverted, Intuitive, Thinking, Perceiving

"Life's Entrepreneurs"

Profile 1: Brent, Design & Marketing

"What I love about this industry is that it can turn on a dime. "

The Job

Brent was born to be a marketer. A natural and persuasive communicator and creative thinker, Brent runs a design and marketing business with a partner. Brent's forte is working the creative side of the team, developing logos and websites. He is chief creative officer, as well as copresident of the company, so his role leads him to meet with clients and help them realize their vision of what their company could become if promoted with smart marketing. Brent says his mission is to "discover what that tiny nugget is that makes a company unique and to figure out how to tell a whole story around that. From there, the goal is to discover the voice of the organization and the visual vernacular to best describe their business."

One of Brent's favorite activities is walking around the office to see what people are doing. "The next thing I know, we have five people in the conference room with some crazy idea, and we'll run with it to build it." This organic and spontaneous method is right up Brent's alley. And his natural charisma, charm, and enthusiasm make other people feel valued and excited about their work.

Backstory

Brent has always had an artistic sensibility, coupled with an abstract, logical mind. He describes feeling torn between physics and illustration. He attended a highly creative arts school where he changed his major three times, vacillating between the two poles of his nature. From illustration, Brent moved to sculpture, but his pragmatic side forced him to acknowledge that he would struggle to find a use for that major. So he moved into graphic design.

Once out of college, Brent began working as a graphic designer and quickly found himself "hitting the ceiling," learning all he could and then constantly seeking new challenges. He worked as a freelance designer for online and print publications until one evening he simply decided to start his own business. Brent began his graphic web design firm the next day and expected to work alone for a year or two, but soon found himself with six full-time employees within three months.

A Good Fit

Brent is a creative strategist. His Conceptualizer temperament endows him with a thirst for inventive problem solving that makes this career a perfect match for him. The daily challenge of responding to clients with varied needs keeps him interested, and he enjoys flexing his creative muscles as he constantly adapts to new and exciting situations.

A dominant Intuitive, Brent sees possibilities everywhere, so he is constantly imagining new and better ways to do business. When meeting with clients, Brent quickly assesses where a business is and then leaps to where they want to go. His capacity for problem solving takes him and his clients from A to Z. Best in a brainstorming session where he can bounce ideas off his team, Brent is poised to explore an idea at any moment to see its possibilities and its limitations, with a fully open and curious attitude about the outcome. He has no advanced need for it to land one way or another, as long as it is a smart, creative, and ultimately workable landing.

Thinking is Brent's auxiliary function, and it is abundantly evident in his work. His grasp of logic and systems is reflected in his ability to plot strategy, and his cool understanding of the way things work enables him to remain impartial and objective about his own ideas. Brent follows his logic and abandons projects that are not coming together, and he never lets his own emotional attachment to one idea cloud his view of its place and necessity in the overall scheme of things. Technology is key to Brent's work, and he finds it both a challenge and a friend. He naturally understands the way most software and computer systems operate, and he enjoys untangling their mysteries.

Looking Ahead

Since Brent already runs his own company, he is satisfied for the moment and has no immediate career goals or plans to make a drastic change. But there is also a restlessness in Brent that means he really could land anywhere. "What I love about the marketing industry is that it can turn on a dime. We may be a hundred hours into a concept, prepared to pitch to a client in three days, and in the middle of the afternoon we decide to scrap it to come up with a brilliant new direction. That's the kind of business we're in. I'm not afraid to launch into something that's not completely polished yet. It's always a work in progress; it's the constant change." As the industry changes, and new technologies for marketing explode onto the scene, Brent wants to keep his eyes—and his options— open. He never knows where life might take him next, and that suits him just fine.

Profile 2: George, Online Video Producer

"What problems have I solved today?"

The Job

Content can refer to every single thing a person sees or interacts with on the internet. While "content creator" can become a dismissive term for anyone with a smartphone and a wifi connection, George makes the kind of content people watch, share, and share again. He's a producer who makes videos for an online sports hub. His job involves coming up with the ideas for a shoot, together with his team, and then guiding and overseeing all aspects of production. On set, he is setting up his team—director, crew, talent, craft services, etc.—for success. And he does it all with his eye on the larger questions of which videos have the best chance of going viral, what ideas are trending, and how the internet will interact with each piece of content he creates.

Backstory

Most cinematographers are at least thirty-five before they find success. George wasn't willing to wait that long. Although he had loved film throughout high school and his first year at film school, by his sophomore year George had begun to reconsider, changing his major first to neuroscience and then to casting. The problem was that George knew he was good at a lot of different things, but he didn't know how those interests and skills translated into a career, or even what a "career" might mean.

In his senior year he got an internship at a casting agency, which turned into a position after graduation as a casting assistant. With the economy tanking at the time, George felt lucky to have a job at all. "But it became boring." George thought he might want to work as a copywriter or as part of a creative team, in advertising, and also considered business school. Then, through a friend, he met Graham, who had moved to the East Coast to build a video department for a sports and pop culture website. George helped to cast the four shows Graham was developing, and a few months later he saw on Graham's blog that he was looking for an associate producer for the site's sports and pop culture show. George responded, interviewed, and had a job offer within the day. When the site was acquired by a larger sports conglomerate, George pitched an NBA show to his bosses. He now works as producer on the show, putting out ten to fourteen videos about basketball per week.

A Good Fit

As an ENTP, George is a dominant Intuitive type. As a producer, he is the big-picture person in the room. His overarching vision shapes the product, and he is always looking for the idea or thread that ties it all together. When producing a video, he combs through content with his eye on the end goal: "I want this hook out of it. I want people to get this feeling or think about this when they see it." Like most Conceptualizers, George is an ace strategist and problem solver. He describes looking back at the end of a day with great satisfaction at "all the different problems that had to be solved or handled." As an Extravert and a Perceiver, George is outgoing and flexible, and loves to think on his feet and roll with the punches. He gets along well with a variety of people and enjoys a good rapport with the many people who depend on him. George's job is fast paced and exciting, which is fulfilling to a person who considers boredom and downtime the ultimate drain on his energy.

Looking Ahead

George enjoys his current gig but describes his dream job as "something involving overarching strategy. I love the idea of reaching the level of senior vice president." He'd like to be with the thinkers and creators in a job that involves making large-scale problem-solving decisions, like how to brand a product or design a show. To be "the person who could integrate all those ideas" would be thrilling to George. Whether this job ends up being in the field of sports and entertainment, advertising, or entrepreneurship is just a matter of detail.

Profile 3: Alicia, Summer Camp Owner

"Making ideas come to fruition."

The Job

As co-owner of a successful sports camp in New England with her husband, Jackson, Alicia finds that her life changes with the season. While camp is in session, she's primarily responsible for supervising the staff and making sure everyone has an excellent, happy experience. "People describe me as the glue that keeps the staff together. I listen to them, and if they have an idea, they know they can talk to me and I'll make it happen. It's not about keeping just the campers happy—it's the staff as well."

In the off-season, everything changes again. It isn't quite as much fun, since Alicia is a people person and there just aren't that many people in the small, rural New England town where she and her family live. Still, there is much to do: helping Jackson hire staff, developing programs, creating marketing materials, writing staff manuals, and keeping the books. The off-season is also when she and Jackson have time to take a breath, think big thoughts, and come up with ways of improving how they do things at camp and how they market themselves.

Backstory

Although she was not born into the camping world like her husband, whose family has been involved in this camp for one hundred years, Alicia's personality type, education, and experiences converged to provide her with work that is intrinsically satisfying and at which she excels.

Alicia graduated college with a bachelor's degree that she designed herself, which combined art, philosophy, sociology, and literature. She spent a year volunteering as a childcare worker in a Kentucky shelter. After that, she managed small retail shops for a few years before going back into social work full-time to serve people with special needs. One facility served clients with profound disabilities who needed physical care 24/7. "I was the activity director—the 'fun girl.' When they saw me, they lit up because they knew they were going to do something fun." She loved making people feel better. "One girl had never seen the ocean, so I took her down to the water's edge, sat down, and held her in my arms as she experienced the feel of the waves for the first time."

Nine years after graduating, she met Jackson, who had recently purchased the camp and was in the process of turning it into a premier sports camp. "I was drawn to his enthusiasm and work ethic—it was so stimulating! I decided that if I was going to date this man, his camp was going to be a part of my life." While they worked on the transition, Alicia took a job at the writing center of a local college. Soon they married, and now with two small children, Alicia and Jackson made the decision to move up north and live at the camp permanently instead of just during the camp season, as they had been doing.

A Good Fit

ENTPs are particularly adept at finding or creating situations that make good use of their natural abilities, and Alicia is no exception. As is true of most Conceptualizers, Alicia is a lifelong learner who strives to be successful. Her self-designed quadruple college concentration—art, philosophy, sociology, and literature—speaks to her natural curiosity and desire to understand how things are related to each other. ENTPs are the kind of people who continually seek new challenges. When Alicia realized that she was going to be involved in the camp business, she jumped in with both feet, learning everything she could about what it takes to create the very best experience possible.

A dominant Intuitive, Alicia prides herself on her creativity. Not only is she a talented visual artist, but she is able to use her creativity to solve problems. She is simply wired to see alternative—and often better— ways of executing an idea or project. This comes in handy when creating marketing materials for the camp or finding innovative solutions to the daily problems that arise there.

Alicia's auxiliary function is Thinking. This provides her with important balance and the ability to analyze her ideas logically and objectively, ensuring that they really are as good as when they first come to her with a rush of extraverted energy. She also uses her Thinking to stay cool and calm when sorting through interpersonal conflicts between staff members.

Looking Ahead

The absolute best part of the camp season is the daily interactions with people. "With a key staff of twenty, it's a fun place to be— full of positive energy." Alicia counts among her top skills her empathy and her ability to connect with people. "I love that others think of me as a really good leader who people like to follow, and a get-it-done person." The best compliment she ever received was "Alicia is never satisfied with having an idea; she needs to see it come to fruition."

Her career goals align with this desire to spread her reach and broaden her community. Alicia can imagine stepping into a consultant role someday to help guide other camp owners and share her wisdom. She feels that she could find great satisfaction in seeing her impact extend out past just her camp, and her influence helping others to find the success she and Jackson have enjoyed.

Common Threads

Although Brent, Alicia, and George have different backgrounds, experiences, and careers, there are certain common threads woven through their stories. Their specific interests and abilities may differ, but owing to their similar temperament values and the *same hierarchy* of their psychological functions, there are certain observations we can make about the needs of many ENTPs.

What follows is a list of the most important elements—the formula, if you will—for ENTP satisfaction. Given the uniqueness of all individuals—even those who share a type—this list will not describe each ENTP equally well. The important thing is that these ten elements, with varying degrees of intensity and in different orders of importance, identify what ENTPs need to be satisfied.

After you have reviewed this list, we recommend that you go back and prioritize the elements in order of *their importance to you*. When doing this, think of past work experiences as well as your present job, and what you found particularly satisfying or unsatisfying. Try to look for *themes* that run through several experiences, not just *events* that might be true for one work situation but not for another.

As an ENTP, I define career satisfaction as doing work that

1. gives me opportunities to engage in creative problem solving and/or generating new and innovative approaches to problems

2. lets me implement my innovative solutions in the creation of more efficiently functioning systems
3. acknowledges and encourages my creativity, competency, and ability to improvise
4. lets me experience a variety of situations filled with fun, action, and excitement
5. follows a logical order and is based on objective and fair standards rather than the likes or dislikes of one individual
6. lets me increase my professional and personal power and interact frequently with other powerful people
7. lets me meet and have constant interaction with many different people, especially those I respect
8. can be done in a rapidly changing, high-energy environment with significant interaction with others
9. is done in an environment that is casual and unstructured; where I can experience a high degree of personal freedom, time off, and the opportunity to operate in a spontaneous way
10. allows me to design or start projects but does not require me to follow through with tedious details

Popular Occupations for ENTPs

In listing occupations that are popular among ENTPs, it is important to note that there are successful people of all types in all occupations. However, the following are careers ENTPs may find particularly satisfying, and some of the reasons why. This is by no means a comprehensive listing but is included to suggest possibilities you may not have previously considered. Although all of these occupations offer the potential for career satisfaction, the future demand for some careers is anticipated to be greater than for others.

ENTREPRENEURSHIP / BUSINESS
- Entrepreneur
- Management analyst
- Venture capitalist
- Literary / talent agent
- Owner: restaurant/bar
- Outplacement consultant
- Technical trainer
- Investment broker
- Trainer: diversity, equity, and inclusion
- University/college president
- Property manager: commercial/residential
- Attorney: litigator
- Sales agent: securities and commodities
- Agent and business manager
- Urban and regional planner
- Human resources recruiter
- Ombudsman
- Security analyst
- Manufacturer's service representative
- Hotel general manager
- Employee relations specialist

ENTPs are born entrepreneurs! The appeal of these careers to the ENTP is the ability to create a work environment that is new, flexible, and changing. These careers often involve the interaction and participation of many people, creating new concepts and approaches, thinking in innovative ways, and engaging in a certain amount of risk taking. The projects are often large scale, requiring the development of big budgets and the participation of powerful and influential people.

MARKETING / CREATIVE
- Advertising creative director
- Market research analyst
- Public relations specialist
- Social media manager
- Marketing manager
- Sports marketer
- Radio/TV talk show host

- Producer
- Art director
- International marketer
- Informational-graphics designer
- Creative director
- Print designer
- Interaction designer
- Digital marketing manager
- Blogger
- Actor
- Online content creator
- Creative writer
- Copywriter
- Photographer
- Journalist
- Director: stage, motion pictures
- Columnist, critic, commentator
- Reporter, correspondent
- Broadcast news analyst

The fields of marketing, advertising, and public relations allow the ENTP to be involved with other creative people, developing and implementing their ideas, often in creative and exciting ways. ENTPs enjoy the fast-paced, sometimes glamorous world of public relations and advertising and are able to use their charm and people skills selling their ideas and concepts. Market research requires ENTPs to use their abilities to spot trends. It also stimulates and satisfies their insatiable curiosity and active imagination.

PLANNING AND DEVELOPMENT
- Strategic planner
- Business development director
- Personnel systems developer
- Real estate agent/developer
- Special projects developer
- Industrial design manager
- Logistics consultant (manufacturing)
- Networking specialist
- Personal financial adviser
- Investment banker
- Urban planner

Careers in planning and development require the ability to use one's vision and anticipate trends and formulate creative plans. Developers work on speculative projects, often needing to convince others of their merit and potential for success, an activity ENTPs enjoy and often excel at. Developers also need to remain flexible, adapting to new opportunities, ready to put together new deals without much pre-planning or notice. ENTPs enjoy careers in strategic planning if they are allowed to focus on the development of innovative solutions to problems and then delegate the follow-through of the details to others.

POLITICS
- Politician
- Political manager
- Political analyst
- Social scientist
- Pundit
- Lobbyist
- Campaign manager

These occupations allow ENTPs to use their ideas, knowledge, and personal sophistication in a highly charged, fast-paced, and powerful arena. ENTPs are able to use their abilities to see trends, themes, and shifts of public opinion and adapt to those changes. ENTPs are drawn to the powerful and enjoy working with a variety of different people. The world of politics requires they meet and establish rapport quickly with those whom they wish to influence. ENTPs often enjoy public speaking and can be excellent orators, using figurative, expansive language, and expressing great vision.

MISCELLANEOUS
- Chiropractor
- Environmental scientist
- Educational psychologist
- Athletic coach and scout
- Criminalist and ballistics expert
- Detective

Remember, these are only some areas that provide satisfying expression for the unique natural talents of the ENTP.

Customizing Your Job Search

Knowing the particular strengths and blind spots of your type can afford you a tremendous advantage in your job search campaign. In all aspects of the process, from conducting research into available positions, identifying and contacting prospective employers, developing personal marketing tools such as résumés, arranging and conducting job interviews, and negotiating salaries to finally accepting a position, people will act true to their type. Being able to capitalize on your assets and compensate for your liabilities can make the difference between a successful and an unsuccessful job search.

The differences between types are sometimes subtle and other times dramatic. It is the subtle variations in advice we offer that make the real difference between success and failure in a job search. The concept of networking serves as a good example. Extraverts will naturally enjoy networking and are advised to do so on a large scale, while Introverts find more limited and targeted networking, especially with people they already know, easier. Sensors tend to network with people in a defined scope, while Intuitives will go far and wide to find people often seemingly unrelated to their field of interest. Further, Feelers can often take networking personally and enjoy establishing warm rapport, while Thinkers will be more objective and detached in their style. Finally, Judgers tend to ask fewer and more structured questions during their networking, while Perceivers could ask questions of all sorts all day long! One valuable search technique, many ways to implement it.

Pathways to Success: Using Your Strengths

As we will detail in the following pages, your strengths and talents will serve you well in the information-gathering stages of the job search. Your innovative approach and energetic and charming style will be great assets. Beware, however, of your tendency to underestimate the importance of following through on necessary details in your excitement to pursue yet another option.

As an ENTP, you will find that your most effective strategies build on your abilities to do the following:

Generate enthusiasm for yourself and your ideas.

- Use your natural enthusiasm for your ideas and inspirations when describing your abilities, success with past projects, and potential contributions.
- Express your confidence in yourself and your ability to master any project or challenge.

When Steven, an ENTP, faces the challenge of winning over a skeptical potential client, he lets his enthusiasm for the project and its potential for positive change lead the discussion. He speaks about past successes and also talks about what he will be able to accomplish for the client. Sometimes, those are goals the client didn't even imagine were attainable before Steven pointed them out.

See new and exciting possibilities.

- Develop ideas for ways you might benefit an organization or company using your ingenuity and imaginative use of systems.
- Discuss how those changes will solve present and future problems.

Jeff used his imagination and vision to see ways he could help make a developer friend's health club project a reality. During the first casual conversation about the project, Jeff began to brainstorm ways to improve and extend the original scope of the project. His enthusiasm was so infectious, he essentially sold himself to the developer as a vital element in the future success of the club. The fact that the job didn't formally exist yet did not deter Jeff from seeing its potential. Because he was able to communicate that energy to the developer, he secured an excellent career opportunity.

Create your own job opportunities.

- Use your "vision" to anticipate trends, where people with your talents will be needed in the future, and so on.
- Use your energy and ability to meet people and introduce yourself to those who might best connect you with other influential people.

When Ann's job was about to be phased out, she used her vision and personal charm to find out which areas of the firm would be expanding over the coming months. She developed a friendship with an upper-level manager and soon learned about a new, experimental project being designed. Ann made a proposal over lunch to her friend and was able to get in on the ground floor of the new venture before her current job ended.

Collect a great amount of information from talking to people.

- Network extensively, especially with those who know many people with whom you might talk in order to identify possible career opportunities.
- Ask others to brainstorm with you to develop a list of options you might research later.

When Maria relocated to Chicago, she developed a list of contacts through her old college friends in the Chicago area and the Chicago Advertising Federation. Maria called on everyone. She enjoyed the process of meeting new people and found that in four weeks she had a large roster of contacts. She ultimately met with a creative director of a large firm specializing in high-tech clients, which appealed to her because it was a new interest area to tackle. They hit it off, and she was offered a job. It was her twenty-second informational interview.

Understand what motivates others.

- Tune in to what others are saying and not saying about their needs as employers so you can discuss how your skills and abilities can assist them.
- Express your natural charm and sense of humor to create rapport and a positive working relationship.

Mike was applying for a high-paying job as special projects developer at a growing real estate development firm. He knew he was up against another candidate with more experience and a strong background in the financial market. He decided that he would use his natural charm to make friends with the interviewers. He immediately created a friendly, light atmosphere in which all members of the group were laughing and sharing war stories from past projects. Mike was offered the job, because, as he was later told, the group viewed him as a member of the team from the very start.

Improvise: Show others how you can think on your feet.

- Demonstrate your ability to deal imaginatively with unexpected situations.

- Discuss your abilities and experience with crisis management and other emergencies, generating confidence in your capacity for responsibility.

While Gigi was interviewing at a management consulting firm, the interviewer's assistant announced that proposals being prepared for a big presentation that afternoon were in a truck that had been disabled on the highway. Gigi offered to call a friend who operated a personal delivery service. She arranged for a driver to meet the disabled truck, load the proposals, and deliver them to the meeting. The interviewer and the firm's new client were impressed with Gigi's quick thinking and ability to avert a potential disaster.

Analyze long-range implications.

- Demonstrate your ability to anticipate consequences and to logically analyze products and processes.
- Demonstrate your ability to be objective by offering honest critiques of past work situations.

Possible Pitfalls

Although all people are unique, there are certain *potential* blind spots that many ENTPs share. We specify "potential" because some of the following may clearly be true of you, while others may not apply. While considering them, you may notice that these tendencies do not relate just to the job search but rather describe pitfalls you may have experienced in other aspects of your life as well. It is therefore helpful to consider each one in terms of your past experiences by asking yourself, "Is this true for me?" And if so, "How did this tendency prevent me from getting something that I wanted?" You will probably notice that the key to overcoming your blind spots is the conscious and thoughtful development of your third and

fourth functions (Feeling and Sensing). We recognize that many of the suggestions will be difficult to implement, but the more you use these functions, the fewer problems they will cause you in the future.

Avoid the tendency to generate so many options that it is impossible to make a decision and follow through on necessary details.

- Try to pay close attention to the facts, details, and timeliness of a project. Eliminate unrealistic options along the way and stick with your established list of priorities.

Try not to dismiss as illogical and unimportant the feelings of other people, therefore unintentionally appearing arrogant and/or rude.

- Try to focus on how a project or statement will affect others. Try to offer positive feedback before negative criticism, knowing that some people may take criticism very personally.

Discipline yourself and try not to procrastinate; don't put off decisions so long that options are eliminated for you.

- Establish and adhere to deadlines. Try to be conscious of the schedules and timetables of others and to notify people when you expect to be late.

Don't interrupt others before they have finished speaking because an idea has come to you.

- Engage your listening skills; wait until you are sure the person has finished speaking before offering your ideas and input.
- Try the trick of repeating back what the person has said so you are sure you understood what it was.

The Final Piece: Changing or Keeping Your Job...the Key to Success for ENTPs

Now that you have a solid understanding of your type, you can see how your natural preferences make you better suited for certain kinds of jobs. You can also see how knowledge of your type-related strengths and blind spots can help you conduct a more successful job search. But as an ENTP, you've already realized that you are not equally drawn to *every* career or field listed in the Popular Occupations section. The next and final step is to narrow down the field and find the work you were meant to do.

In addition to Type, several other factors—such as your values, interests, and skills—also contribute to your level of satisfaction on the job. The more compatible you are with your job, the happier you'll be. So prepare to use everything you've learned (in this book and in life) to create *your strategic career plan*. The exercises in Chapter 23, "Putting It All Together," are designed to help you do just that.

However, you may have decided it makes more sense (if perhaps only for the moment) to stay in your present job or with your current employer. There may be many valid reasons—financial pressures, family considerations, a tough job market for your specialty, or just bad timing. But take heart! What you've learned in this book can also help you be more content and successful *in your current job*. And should the time come when you're ready to make a major career move, you'll have a much better idea of where you want to go and how to get there.

"So, if you can't have the job you love (yet!)...love the one you've got."

The simple truth is, many jobs allow a good deal of flexibility in the way tasks are performed. Here are some ways you may be able to "massage" your current job into one that better fits your needs:

- If possible, delegate routine tasks to others.
- Take courses and seminars to continue to expand your expertise and credentials.
- Team up with co-workers and/or work on teams.
- Hire an assistant who is good with details and follow-through.
- Find other creative people with whom to brainstorm ideas.
- Join professional associations and attend conferences.
- Work a different shift, arrange more flexible hours, or job-share.
- Join or start organizations for people with similar expertise or interests.
- Change your focus if you're not stimulated or challenged; work on something else for a while.
- Make sure you have a variety of projects to work on.
- Develop a "critical friends" group to critique each other's ideas and plans.

One ENTP turns lemons into lemonade:

Danica realized her shortcomings. Although she was a great idea person, she frequently lost her enthusiasm and energy for projects once the creative stage was finished. So when she was promoted to a new position, she made sure that the person she hired to be her assistant was very organized and detail oriented, qualities she lacked but needed. With the right assistant, she was able to spend less time fixing her own mistakes and more time seeing her many creative ideas come to life.

Use what you've got to get what you need.

Simply put, the best advice on how to succeed is to *capitalize on your strengths and compensate for your blind spots.* Learning how to do this can make the difference between succeeding or failing and loving or hating your work. To help you, we include the following inventory of your potential strengths and blind spots. And while every individual is unique, many of the following should apply to you as an ENTP.

Your work-related strengths may include

- excellent communication skills and the ability to get others excited about your ideas
- eagerness to think outside the box and consider new possibilities
- great creative problem-solving skills
- courage to take some risks, try new things, and overcome obstacles
- broad range of interests and ability to learn new things quickly
- ability to withstand rejection and maintain optimism and enthusiasm
- great confidence and drive to continually increase your knowledge
- natural curiosity and skills for getting the information you need
- ability to see the big picture and the implications of actions and ideas
- ability to juggle several projects at once
- perceptiveness about people—their needs and motivations

- adaptability and ease in shifting gears and changing directions quickly
- great social ease and ability to fit comfortably into most social situations

Your work-related blind spots may include

- trouble keeping yourself organized
- difficulty setting priorities and making decisions
- overconfidence; you may misrepresent your abilities or experience
- propensity to always focus on what's possible rather than what's doable or probable
- tendency to promise more than you can deliver
- impatience with unimaginative or inflexible people
- tendency to lose interest in projects once problems are solved
- dislike of doing things in a traditional, established, or routine manner
- lack of discipline when it comes to attending to and following through on important details
- tendency to become bored or easily sidetracked
- dislike of repetitive tasks
- impatience with people whose competence you question

Using your strengths is easy. The secret to success for an
ENTP
is learning to

prioritize, focus, and follow through— especially with commitments made to others.

14 | INTP
Introverted, Intuitive, Thinking, Perceiving
"Ingenious Problem Solvers"

Profile 1: Mark, Software Engineer

"Seeing patterns and prescriptions for better healthcare."

The Job

When you work in a start-up, you have to bounce around. That's what Mark does as the senior software engineer of a healthcare technology start-up. The company collects patient-reported outcome data for orthopedic surgery. Hospitals and private practices contract with the company, which reaches out to patients before and after their surgery, using their assessment tools to gauge functionality after they have had surgery. Using this data, Mark's company can tell not just how well a patient is improving, but also track data such as the infection rates in various hospitals. Before them, "nobody was actually asking patients how they feel. They were just kind of telling patients."

Mark works on the software that maintains the web application where all this business takes place. This includes managing the survey-taking infrastructure as well as the patient enrollment system. "We went from manually enrolling maybe a dozen patients a week to creating a system that can enroll 10,000 a month." Because he works on such a small team, Mark's job involves wearing many hats. "Suddenly you're trying to solve a problem for a client you never thought of, and you go on to do some maintenance, and then something comes up and you have a great idea to make things more efficient."

Backstory

Mark grew up around computers. "We were one of the first families I knew to have a computer, which led to me teaching my teachers how to use a computer." Although his dad worked in the computer industry in various capacities, Mark never got any direct instruction from him. "They were just kind of there. So you could give me computer parts and that would keep me busy. I got to learn about the interworking of hard drives, computers, and game boards."

185

School was never exciting until Mark one day took a Java programming course and things clicked. "I went from dropping out and failing to getting all A-pluses. I realized I should have been doing this all along." He finished a computer science degree in half the usual time, and maintained an internship throughout school that became a full-time job once he graduated.

Next, Mark worked for the City of Phoenix. "I got to learn the full cycle of computer programming and software development. I had an office in three different departments." But Mark had always lived in Phoenix, and when a chance to move and try out another city came, he couldn't resist. The opportunity came in the form of a small healthcare start-up in Seattle.

Mark started out on the software team. The whole company was just three people, so much of Mark's work was just managing infrastructure and things like that. "I had to learn entirely new languages and roles, so it was pretty fascinating. It was really unique in the sense that I could develop something and it would be live and in production that day." Five years later, the company has weathered the inevitable start-up growing pains, and now things are leveling out.

A Good Fit

For a Conceptualizer like Mark, there is nothing more satisfying than solving challenging problems. "Hearing the problem someone is having and coming up with a solution that's both practical and exciting, solving the problem—I've always loved that back-and-forth." Mark prides himself on getting to the root of the issue rather than patching the initial problem. "I have to find the context of something I don't know anything about. Tell me more about how permits work. Tell me about the personality of a construction developer and how he uses this system or what he wants in the end. It's almost architectural in a sense."

A dominant Thinking type, Mark relies on his strong grasp of logic to follow these threads to their most efficient and effective conclusion. And since his work keeps him in the intellectual and technical sphere, he's usually spared the people management he enjoys far less. He can interact with people—which he enjoys—without needing to manage them.

Mark uses his auxiliary function, Intuition, in his work as well. His ability to see the larger picture separates him from other coders who keep their heads down and follow a protocol. Mark is always looking for ways to improve and innovate systems. "I think I'm overall a creative person and I have a lot of creative impulses. There's a lot of opportunities to be creative. There're opportunities to be efficient. It's about the harmony of the two things."

Looking Ahead

While Mark is capable and ambitious, he doesn't have an exact plan for the future or for where he sees himself in five to ten years. When he envisions his dream job, he thinks of a role that some companies have called a software architect. "It's the highest engineer without being a manager. In that sense you are aware of everything technological going on. You have a broad understanding but not necessarily a ton of depth. You're brought into conversations to make sure the solution implemented over here is well designed but also fits into the whole of all products in the ecosystem."

Mark can forecast certain trends for his field itself. When he started, a computer science degree was pretty much expected. "Now, there are probably eighteen-year-old programmers who are more talented than I am. You can learn to program on YouTube and you might learn more than in an actual class." In a future of autodidacts, Mark will likely find himself right at home.

Profile 2: Anna, Digital Marketing

"Marketing books in the digital age."

The Job

Have you ever wondered why it is that some books appear everywhere, reach a certain level of buzz, and just take off? And other books languish on the shelf or never make a splash at all? The landscape of which books make it and which don't depends on the marketing teams responsible for them. That's where Anna comes in.

Anna is the sales and digital marketing manager at an independent publishing house. Her job consists mainly of getting a strong sense of the books to be published and figuring out how best to sell them to audiences. Once she has a marketing strategy in place, she equips the sales team with the key points and facts they need to convince wholesale book buyers to purchase the books. This starts the process that ends with the book itself actually sitting on a shelf at a store or on a Kindle. Anna also manages the company's online presence, curating the website and running social media to promote their catalogue of books. She maintains a strong voice for the publisher, fostering online relationships with authors and culture writers whose opinions really matter in the life and success of a particular book.

Backstory

When she was a kid, Anna wanted to grow up to be an artist. In high school, she wanted to be a mathematician. And in college, she wanted to be a journalist. "After college, I realized that none of these is a job that is typically available for a twenty-two-year-old." Instead, Anna started doing editorial work for a food website, an experience that taught her a lot about the editorial process, publicity, marketing, and copywriting. She made a lot of connections with bloggers, writers, business owners, and book publicists, opening up a network of people who would later hire her for freelance work and recommend her for future jobs.

A year after college, Anna took a job as the marketing director for a craft beer start-up. The prospect of pioneering a start-up company's online platform was exciting to her, but she quickly found herself missing both the creative and intellectual aspects of editorial work. She left this job to pursue freelance copywriting and editing. While this work paid the bills and was often interesting, Anna wanted something with more stability, and relaunched her career search in earnest. After a few months, she was hired at an independent publishing house to do a combination of marketing and editorial work.

A Good Fit

As a Conceptualizer, Anna is an extremely strategic and architectural thinker. This is central to her role in marketing, as she calculates which moves will best ensure each project's success. "These days, any sort of editorial work has to be anchored with a sense of the business and marketing that sustains it. You have to understand how books are marketed and sold on a large scale." A dominant Thinking type, she is analytical and intellectual in her editorial duties, able to see both the flaws in a project as well as how best to fix them.

With Intuition as her auxiliary function, Anna is adept at seeing the big picture of a book, task, project, or company's mission, and then effectively communicating those ideas to others. One of the results of her well-developed Intuition is her skill at composing superior promotional materials for books: "It is easy for me to assess the style, aims, appeal, and target audience of a book and to articulate them." She has a keen and creative sense of aesthetics, which also makes her good at managing the company's online appearance.

Looking Ahead

Anna really appreciates the creative and intellectual sensibilities that go into editorial work. In five to ten years she sees herself in some sort of editorial leadership role either for a publication, like a magazine or website, or for a publishing company. She would like to take a larger role in the big-picture decision making and use her talents to envision and shape a long-range view of a book, publication, or season's content. As an editor or even editor in chief, Anna would have greater control and discretion over a product's outcome, a prospect she finds satisfying. Most of all, Anna would like to continue to work on publications she is proud of, and to see how the work takes on a life of its own.

Profile 3: Bert, Media Producer

"I value the process; it's the process that creates success."

The Job

At first glance it would seem that Bert is a producer of entertainment shows, audiovisual presentations, and custom marketing programs. But really, he's first and foremost an entrepreneur. "The day-to-day functions are totally incidental to what I do for a living. I'm always changing"—changing himself and helping create change for others around him, especially those people Bert respects and enjoys working with. "It doesn't feel like an occupation."

Each year Bert creates programs, entertainment shows, marketing presentations and corporate meetings, audiovisual presentations, and custom marketing programs for large corporate clients around the country. He runs a small office and supervises a full-time staff of four, as well as countless independent contractors on an as-needed basis. Sometimes he contracts with a major Broadway, film, or musical star, arranges for all the technical and musical equipment and support, and makes complete travel and accommodation arrangements. Other times he may develop a multiscreen audiovisual program to showcase a corporation's new marketing strategy during a national sales conference. The details are endless, the pressure intense. And as Bert says, "I'm only as good as my last show."

Backstory

None of this is what one might expect from a trained accountant. Bert received his college degree in accounting with the full, conscious knowledge that he would never be an accountant. It was a strategic decision, because he knew that he would someday run his own business and would need those skills. The practical skills he gained during his first job as business manager of his father's dental lab have been invaluable. But the lack of creativity of that position was too limiting, so he left to start a company that manufactured furniture kits.

After one and a half years, Bert accepted a job as business manager of a screen-printing company. He left that job because his boss was "running the company into the ground." He decided to start his own screen-printing company, which he ran successfully for six years until a recession hit and interest rates soared. Business dropped 85 percent in one month. His next venture was a special events company that created and marketed events and activities to colleges, universities, and corporations. He ran the business with two partners for five years and continues it on his own, in a different form, today. Now his market is exclusively corporations and businesses.

A Good Fit

Bert's Conceptualizer temperament drives him to constantly seek out new challenges. He has built his business around developing programs and services that continuously present him with new problems to solve. Being an entrepreneur satisfies his need for independence and his desire to surround himself with people whose competence and talents he respects. Bert thinks big, takes on huge and complex projects, and enjoys the status and power his success gives him. He also enjoys being highly respected for his creativity and integrity.

Bert's dominant Thinking allows him to see the logical consequences of actions, anticipate problems and identify solutions, and organize the competent execution of his concepts. He is run by his own principles and sets very high standards for himself.

It is Bert's auxiliary Intuition that helps him to see possibilities. He lives to provide exciting and original ways to meet clients' goals, generate enthusiasm for his vision, and get his clients excited about how positively the end result will be received. He naturally sees connections between the right people for the right job, and enjoys putting them together. Being innovative and shaking up the establishment are important to Bert.

Overall, Bert thrives on the freedom he has to work on the kinds of projects he enjoys and with the people he enjoys and respects. "The more competent people I work with, the easier it is to be successful at what I do." Bert enjoys the fact that the process of working with great people helps him and them fulfill their goals. He believes he helps others share and take risks they wouldn't ordinarily take on their own, work to their potential, and create an excellent product. "I get people to stretch, to understand the importance of 'going for it,' and to understand how great it will be to be successful at what they are reaching for."

Looking Ahead

Since the nature of Bert's work is constant change and challenge, he feels that he could continue to grow his business in new and surprising ways and never really get bored. As he gets older, Bert is learning to delegate more, and he's better able to trust others to get the job done, which makes his life easier and more fun. "I'm not there yet and may never really be there. But my goal is to increase my insight about others so I work less by myself and more with people I trust and know are competent."

Bert continues to work toward the optimum process: creating unique concepts, working with excellent people, achieving competent executions of his concepts and the satisfaction of those he works with to create them, and wowing his audience. For him, that is career satisfaction.

Common Threads

Although Mark, Bert, and Anna have different backgrounds, experiences, and careers, there are certain common threads woven through their stories. Their specific interests, abilities, and values may differ, but owing to their similar temperament values and the *same hierarchy* of their psychological functions, there are certain observations we can make about the needs of many INTPs.

What follows is a list of the most important elements—the formula, if you will—for INTP satisfaction. Given the uniqueness of all individuals—even those who share a type—this list will not describe each INTP equally well. The important thing is that these ten elements, with varying degrees of intensity and in different orders of importance, identify what INTPs need to be satisfied.

After you have reviewed this list, we recommend that you go back and prioritize the elements in order of *their importance to you*. When doing this, think of past work experiences as well as your present job, and what you found particularly satisfying or unsatisfying. Try to look for *themes* that run through several experiences, not just *events* that might be true for one work situation but not for another.

As an INTP, I define career satisfaction as doing work that

1. lets me develop, analyze, and critique new ideas
2. lets me focus my attention and energy on a creative, theoretical, and logical process rather than on an end product
3. is challenging and deals with complex problems, where I am able to try unconventional approaches, and take risks to find the best solution
4. lets me work independently with plenty of quiet, private time to concentrate and complete my thinking process
5. lets me set and maintain my own high standards for my work and determine how my performance will be evaluated and compensated
6. is done in a flexible environment, without useless rules, excessive limitations, or unnecessary meetings

7. lets me interact with a small group of highly regarded friends and associates, all of whom I respect
8. gives me opportunities to constantly increase my own personal competence and power and lets me meet and interact with other powerful and successful people
9. lets me develop ingenious ideas and plans and lets me delegate the implementation and follow-through to an efficient support staff
10. does not require me to spend time directly organizing other people or supervising or mediating interpersonal differences

Popular Occupations for INTPs

In listing occupations that are popular among INTPs, it is important to note that there are successful people of all types in all occupations. However, the following are careers INTPs may find particularly satisfying, and some of the reasons why.

This is by no means a comprehensive listing but is included to suggest possibilities you may not have previously considered. Although all of these occupations offer the potential for career satisfaction, the future demand for some careers is anticipated to be greater than for others.

TECHNOLOGY
- Software developer: applications, systems
- Computer programmer
- Mobile application developer
- Computer and information research scientist
- Computer systems analyst
- Strategic planner
- New market or product conceptualizer
- Networking specialist
- Change management consultant

- Management consultant: computer/ information services, marketing, reorganization
- Print designer
- Interaction designer
- Network and computer systems administrator
- Computer animator
- Information security analyst

Occupations falling into this category offer INTPs the opportunity to do what they do best—analyze problems and develop innovative solutions. Most INTPs enjoy working in technical areas, using their ability to understand complex systems and to find ways to eliminate errors or weaknesses. They easily see how the product, service, or system fits within the context of the whole company, industry, or technology and enjoy creating new, more efficient ways of doing things.

HEALTHCARE / SCIENCE
- Neurologist
- Surgeon
- Physician
- Pharmacist
- Medical scientist
- Scientist: chemistry/biology
- Pharmaceutical researcher
- Biomedical engineer/researcher
- Veterinarian
- Microbiologist
- Geneticist
- Physicist
- Biophysicist

These fields of medicine and other scientific technologies make good use of INTPs' excellent reasoning skills and facility with technical material. The rapidly growing areas of neurology, plastic surgery, and biomedical and pharmaceutical research are often interesting to INTPs because they are able to be on the cutting edge of innovative industries, some of which carry some amount of risk. Physics, chemistry, and biology offer opportunities to work with complex concepts, constantly learn new things, and repeatedly ask the question "What if?" These careers, especially when they involve a strong research component, allow the INTP to work independently. Because they are difficult and competitive fields, they tend to attract other intellectual and gifted people, whom INTPs find stimulating.

PROFESSIONAL / BUSINESS
- Lawyer
- Economist
- Personal financial adviser
- Psychologist
- Psychiatrist
- Market research analyst
- Financial analyst
- Architect
- Investment banker
- Investigator
- Intellectual property attorney
- Legal mediator
- Corporate finance attorney
- Entrepreneur
- Venture capitalist
- Business analyst
- Intelligence specialist

These professional careers also offer INTPs plenty of opportunities to analyze and solve complex problems. Often extremely challenging, these careers require clear, logical thinking and innovative approaches to problems and challenges. The creative process is central to the work of both the architect and the psychologist. Seeing how one element or event fits into an overall pattern or system is a particular strength of INTPs and is a frequent aspect of the work of an investigator and financial analyst. From developing flawless legal strategies to forecasting subtle yet powerful economic trends, these professions offer the excitement and personal challenge INTPs thrive on.

ACADEMIC
- Mathematician
- Archaeologist
- Anthropologist
- Historian
- Philosopher
- College professor
- Online educator
- Researcher
- Logician
- College faculty administrator
- Interpreter/translator
- Astronomer

The stimulating world of academia is one frequently enjoyed by INTPs. Because there is an emphasis on exploring and considering new and different approaches, INTPs often find career satisfaction in the role of college professor. They usually prefer teaching the more advanced and challenging students and courses. INTPs often enjoy the research element in any of the subject areas above and enjoy the opportunity to work alone and then share their insights and innovations with their intellectual peers. They work best when not restricted by excessive rules and bureaucracy, which many large universities and colleges are unable to avoid.

CREATIVE
- Photographer
- Creative writer
- Artist
- Graphic designer
- Entertainer/dancer
- Musician
- Agent
- Inventor
- Informational-graphics designer
- Columnist, critic, commentator
- Blogger
- Music arranger
- Producer
- Director: stage, motion pictures
- Film editor
- Art director

One of the strongest attractions of these careers for INTPs is the chance to create something entirely original. INTPs enjoy the creative process of working with different mediums and the variety of people and experiences they have access to. INTPs usually enjoy working alone or with small numbers of talented people who bring something different to the process. Depending on their area and their interest in expressing their art, INTPs can enjoy performance. But they don't necessarily need to perform their works to find satisfaction in them. Many INTPs are inspired by the world of creative people and enjoy working as an agent. And their ability to create innovative and clever products or services often gives them success as inventors.

Remember, these are only some of the areas that provide satisfying expression for the unique natural talents of INTPs.

Customizing Your Job Search

Knowing the particular strengths and blind spots of your type can afford you a tremendous advantage in your job search campaign. In all aspects of the process, from conducting research into available positions, identifying and contacting prospective employers, developing personal marketing tools such as résumés, arranging and conducting job interviews, and negotiating salaries to finally accepting a position, people will act true to their type. Being able to capitalize on your assets and compensate for your liabilities can make the difference between a successful and an unsuccessful job search.

The differences between types are sometimes subtle and other times dramatic. It is the subtle variations in advice we offer that make the real difference between success and failure in a job search. The concept of networking serves as a good example. Extraverts will naturally enjoy networking and are advised to do so on a large scale, while Introverts find more limited and targeted networking, especially with people they already know, easier. Sensors tend to network with people in a defined scope, while Intuitives will go far and wide to find people often seemingly unrelated to their field of interest. Further, Feelers can often take networking personally and enjoy establishing warm rapport, while Thinkers will be more objective and detached in their style. Finally, Judgers tend to ask fewer and more structured questions during their networking, while Perceivers could ask questions of all sorts all day long! One valuable search technique, many ways to implement it.

Pathways to Success: Using Your Strengths

As we will detail in the following pages, your strengths and talents for the job search—creative problem solving and critical analysis of potential options—will go a long way toward helping you endure the less interesting or challenging detail-chasing phases. You may also need to make a conscious effort to establish rapport and communicate your vision in simple enough language for others to understand.

As an INTP, you will find that your most effective strategies build on your abilities to do the following:

See possibilities that don't exist at the present time.

- Look past what is known or represented to you as "the way things are." Use your imagination to generate possibilities that may arise within the near future and plan how you can best capitalize on them.
- Consider less obvious means of getting an interviewer's attention or setting yourself apart from other candidates.

Brian was looking for a new job in publishing. Prior to an interview, he realized that he shared a contact via social media with a senior editor. When he came in to interview, he mentioned a mutual friend who ran a viral account. The interviewer remarked that she had just reached out to sign the manager of the account to write a nonfiction book. She was impressed that Brian's friend had his finger on the pulse, and the conversation naturally evolved from there.

Create your own job opportunities or an adaptation of existing but less attractive opportunities.

- Using your talents at anticipating future needs, develop a job description for a position that will solve current or future problems.
- Determine ways of altering and improving an existing opportunity into one that will use your strengths and still serve the needs of the employer.

Elena's upcoming promotion would mean good news and bad news. The good news was an increase in her salary, a support staff she could delegate follow-through details to, and more autonomy. The bad news was the job would require almost daily meetings, and

Elena would be reporting to an individual she had had the displeasure of serving with on a committee, someone she did not respect. After a great deal of reflection, she admitted to herself that all the perks of the promotion would not make up for the negative aspects of the job. So she created a proposal for a special pilot program that would analyze the costs and benefits of several of the company's less profitable products, something her current supervisor had long been interested in. She outlined how the position would require the support services of only one full-time person. Elena recommended that she conduct much of her work from her office at home and report, on a weekly basis, to her current supervisor. Because the position would be at a higher ranking, the salary and benefits package would rival those of the other job. Her supervisor was impressed with her initiative and trusted Elena enough to leave her alone to work on the pilot program for the following twelve months.

Anticipate the logical consequences of actions.

- Demonstrate your clear sense of cause and effect by offering examples of past experience when you were called on to contribute the skill, and recount what the positive outcomes were.
- Use your critical thinking skills when considering any job offer to anticipate both the positive and potentially negative outcomes of any decision.

For her second interview for a teaching position in the mathematics department of a small private university, Tanisha was glad to hear that she would be asked open-ended questions by the chairman of the department. The chairman presented several difficult challenges the department and

university currently faced and asked her how she might handle them if she were a member of the staff. Tanisha began by explaining how during her last job she had dealt with equally vexing problems. She spoke about the various possible outcomes of several solutions and what their future ramifications might be. Her interviewer was impressed with her long-range thinking skills and her ability to see many sides of an issue without becoming personally invested in any. It was obvious by the end of the interview that Tanisha had considerable skills and could make important contributions to the team.

Create and implement an innovative job search.

- View problems that arise as challenges to be met and use your creativity to come up with ways of overcoming them.
- Set yourself apart from your competition by marketing yourself as a creative, alternative thinker and let all your materials and correspondence reflect that.

Everything was going well for Eric in his job search. He had had several excellent interviews with one of the partners of a prestigious architectural firm and was preparing for his final meeting with the firm's senior partner. The morning of the interview, he arrived to discover that the partner who had been interviewing him had left the firm unexpectedly. The senior partner did not have the interview with Eric on his calendar, nor did he know anything about him. Eric had to start from scratch.

Fortunately, he was able to get another appointment and left the firm determined not to let the setback get him down. He spent the next three weeks finding out everything he could about the senior partner's past projects and the history of the firm. He prepared himself for the type of interview he might expect from the person he was learning about. At the interview, he used that experience as an example when he was asked how he dealt with unexpected stumbling blocks. The senior partner was amused and impressed by his creativity, persistence, and candor.

Keep all your career options open to gather all relevant and important information.

- Stay cool and detached; never be pressured into making a decision that you haven't had adequate time to reflect on.
- Ask lots of questions during all interviews to be sure you have an accurate picture of the job, its responsibilities, and limitations before deciding whether to consider it further.

Possible Pitfalls

Although all people are unique, there are certain *potential* blind spots that many INTPs share. We specify "potential" because some of the following *may* be true of you, while others may clearly not apply. While considering them, you may notice that these tendencies do not relate just to the job search, but rather describe pitfalls that you may have experienced in other aspects of your life as well. It is therefore helpful to consider each one in terms of your past experiences by asking yourself, "Is this true for me?" And if so, "How did this tendency prevent me from getting something that I wanted?" You will probably notice that the key to overcoming your blind spots is the conscious and thoughtful development of your third and fourth functions (Sensing and Feeling). We recognize that many of the

suggestions will be difficult to implement, but the more you use these functions, the fewer problems they will cause you in the future.

Make sure to eventually move your plans out of the conceptual stage and into practice.

- Once you have developed an innovative job search plan, ask yourself how realistic some of your ideas are. Is there time to get all you've imagined done? Is it possible to create what you have dreamed up? Decide on and hold yourself to a timetable to implement your ideas.
- Develop a step-by-step plan that includes all the facts (timetable, questions to ask, reminder to send follow-up notes, etc.) so you will be more likely to attend to them.

Establish realistic objectives and goals based on what is practical, not on what your confidence tells you is possible.

- Remember that, depending upon your level of experience and the field you are pursuing, a full career search can take from three to twelve months before you find the right job. Knowing that from the start and reminding yourself of it throughout the process will help keep you from becoming discouraged and disinterested.
- Ask for support from a close friend when you find your impatience mounting and/or confidence waning.

Make sure you don't appear unintentionally condescending or arrogant to potential employers.

- Pay close attention to how others perceive you. Ask someone you trust to role-play with you and give you an honest appraisal of your perceived attitude. In an interview, blunt honesty can be perceived as rudeness.

- Take the time to listen fully to the interviewer's questions or comments before forming an opinion about them. Make it a goal to try to establish rapport early in the interview.

Remember to follow through on important details involved in the process.

- Social niceties, such as thank-you emails to people who have conducted informational interviews with you, may seem superfluous, but they are an important part of the process.
- Stay on top of follow-up so you don't appear disinterested in a position you really do want.

Don't put off making a decision.

- After you have spent the necessary time considering your options and clarifying your needs and skills, take action! Discard less attractive options and decide to actively pursue good ones.
- Don't wait so long to decide that you inadvertently eliminate an opportunity by procrastinating.

The Final Piece: Changing or Keeping Your Job...the Key to Success for INTPs

Now that you have a solid understanding of your type, you can see how your natural preferences make you better suited for certain kinds of jobs. You can also see how knowledge of your type-related strengths and blind spots can help you conduct a more successful job search. But as an INTP, you've already realized that you are not equally drawn to *every* career or field listed in the

Popular Occupations section. The next and final step is to narrow down the field and find the work you were meant to do.

In addition to Type, several other factors—such as your values, interests, and skills—also contribute to your level of satisfaction on the job. The more compatible you are with your job, the happier you'll be. So prepare to use everything you've learned (in this book and in life) to create *your strategic career plan*. The exercises in Chapter 23, "Putting It All Together," are designed to help you do just that.

However, you may have decided it makes more sense (if perhaps only for the moment) to stay in your present job or with your current employer. There may be many valid reasons—financial pressures, family considerations, a tough job market for your specialty, or just bad timing. But take heart! What you've learned in this book can also help you be more content and successful *in your current job*. And should the time come when you're ready to make a major career move, you'll have a much better idea of where you want to go and how to get there.

"So, if you can't have the job you love (yet!)...love the one you've got."

The simple truth is, many jobs allow a good deal of flexibility in the way tasks are performed. Here are some ways you may be able to "massage" your current job into one that better fits your needs:

- If possible, delegate routine or mundane tasks to others.
- Make sure you have enough uninterrupted time to develop your ideas and think things through.
- Find other creative people to bounce your ideas off.

- Work a different shift or arrange more flexible hours.
- Make sure you have influence over the hiring of your direct reports.
- Try to find support people who are organized and good with details.
- Take courses and seminars to continue to expand your expertise and credentials.
- Change your focus if bored or not challenged.
- Develop a "critical friends" group to critique each other's ideas and plans.
- Try to surround yourself with others whose talent and competence you respect.

One INTP turns lemons into lemonade:

An internal computer consultant, Lila was candid about the most frustrating part of her job: "endless meetings with stupid people." Not only did she lack the patience to repeatedly explain basic concepts to novice end users, but the constant travel to meet with different groups ate up an enormous amount of her time. To solve her problem, she developed an interactive program that would address many of the common concerns of new users and placed it on the company website. By doing this, she was able to avoid answering the same questions over and over again and could spend more of her precious time dealing with the more complex, interesting problems of more experienced users.

Use what you've got to get what you need.

Simply put, the best advice on how to succeed is to *capitalize on your strengths and compensate for your blind spots.* Learning how to do this can make the difference between succeeding or failing and loving or hating your work. To help you, we include the following inventory of your potential strengths and blind spots. And while every individual is unique, many of the following should apply to you as an INTP.

Your work-related strengths may include

- eagerness to think outside the box and consider new possibilities
- ability to understand very complex and highly abstract ideas
- great creative problem-solving skills
- independence; courage to take risks, try new things, and overcome obstacles
- ability to synthesize lots of information
- intellectual curiosity and skills for getting information you need
- ability to analyze things logically even under stress
- great confidence and drive to continually increase your knowledge
- objectivity; ability to address issues without taking them personally
- confidence in your ideas and vision
- ability to see the big picture; to see implications of actions and ideas
- adaptability; you can shift gears and change directions quickly

Your work-related blind spots may include

- tendency toward disorganization
- overconfidence; you may misrepresent your abilities or experience
- impatience with unimaginative and/or incompetent people
- dislike of doing things in a traditional or established manner
- tendency to lose interest in projects once problems are solved
- difficulty communicating complex ideas simply

- tendency to be so theoretical that you ignore or miss the realities
- undisciplined about attending to and following through on important details

- dislike of doing repetitive tasks
- impatience with structures and people who are too rigid

> *Using your strengths is easy.*
> *The secret to success for an*
> **INTP**
> *is learning to*
>
> be better organized, be patient with less intelligent people, and work at improving your social skills.

15 ∥ ESTJ
Extraverted, Sensing, Thinking, Judging
"Taking Care of Business"

Profile 1: Anne, Education Nonprofit

"Honoring the human right to education."

The Job

Anne believes everyone deserves access to educational opportunities. She gets to live this mission every day as part of a community and partner solutions team for an education nonprofit. The company describes itself as a "search engine for learning"—a website similar to Google that performs free and open searches for teachers and students, but comprises only the best education resources on the web.

Anne works within the smaller subset of content partnerships. Her job is to communicate and coordinate with other organizations that have free and open educational resources and to curate their content into collections. The collections are basically streaming playlists of resources—videos, quizzes, articles—on a range of academic topics. Anne and her colleagues work to make this content available to teachers and students all over the world, and to ensure the resources are credited to their original creators. It's work that involves a lot of coordination, communication, and collaboration—and Anne loves it.

Backstory

Anne got her first lucky break in high school—a new charter school dedicated to theater arts opened in her town in New Hampshire, and she was one of a small batch of kids who got to attend. For Anne, an active participant in local theater productions since childhood, this was a dream come true. "It opened my eyes to the idea that there were other options for students besides the local public school. I became really passionate about other people being able to access those kinds of choices, even if they couldn't afford private school." Anne decided that she wanted to pursue education reform and give other kids the chance to experience the kinds of opportunities that she had.

In college, she worked at the New York State Education Department as a policy research intern, analyzing school and district data and preparing reports that dealt with proposed amendments to education law. Working in this sector was eye-opening for Anne. In her senior year, with graduation looming, Anne began looking for jobs on Idealist.org and found a job posting for an education nonprofit start-up that was hiring. Anne was hired, and upon graduation she made the move from New York to Palo Alto and began work immediately.

A Good Fit

As a Traditionalist, Anne is service oriented, motivated by her company's mission to contribute to the world of education. Her job entails a combination of interacting with partners and keeping track of the site's extensive content across the web. She describes herself as "obsessed with organization," a necessity in a job that involves coordinating eight million resources and counting.

Since her company is relatively new, the processes of organization are not as streamlined as those of other, more established companies. Anne has developed many of the systems used to keep track of the enormous amount of content the website oversees. Her Thinking and Judging functions are constantly in use, and she derives a great deal of satisfaction from implementing the systems she has created.

Anne is a detail-oriented Sensor, and a big part of her job involves quality assurance: double checking content, entering data into spreadsheets, and generally making sure nothing slips through the cracks. An

Extravert, Anne says that she loves her co-workers, who are motivated and good at multitasking, like her. "Everyone here is involved in too many projects, but that's how we thrive." The environment is fast-paced and interactive, requiring extensive collaboration among departments. Best of all, everyone is working in service of the same mission and toward the same objective.

Looking Ahead

Anne's company is unique in that it positions itself as a training ground for future nonprofit start-ups. "The culture they've created is to have people spend two to three years developing and honing their skills and then move on to continue the mission to honor the human right to education. So even if they're not working here, we're all working toward the same goal."

Anne can see herself spending a few years with her current employer before perhaps going back to school to study nonprofit management. "I'm so happy where I am now, and it's a new challenge every day. I'm learning new skills all the time." Someday she would love to start her own nonprofit focused on making arts education in schools accessible to all.

Profile 2: Steve, Insurance Sales

"Rejection affects me like rain on wax."

The Job

Steve is a perfectionist, and the challenge of his work as a self-employed salesman of insurance and investment products keeps him charged.

It's hard work. Steve admits that sometimes he's competing against others with less ethical motivations, so he needs to work harder. "Every day is like Game One of the World Series. Not the fifth game, when it's a total pressure cooker, or spring training, when it's not critical to win. But Game One—the real thing."

Steve spends a large part of his day prospecting for new clients, who are almost entirely referral-based at this point. The cycle begins with a fact-gathering interview with a new client. Then Steve prepares formal recommendations, including the most appropriate life insurance, disability insurance, or other investment, and presents his recommendations. He usually closes the sale.

He also services ongoing accounts, meeting with clients once or twice a year to update their portfolios. He has six hundred to six hundred fifty clients, but only about two hundred are truly active on an ongoing basis. Steve is constantly updating his knowledge of the products he sells, spending fifteen to twenty business days a year in training. He is also pursuing the professional status of Chartered Life Underwriter accreditation.

Backstory

Steve has always been a salesman. When he was seven he ordered hundreds of seed packets from a comic book and sold them all. He usually had a paper route, often several at one time. Interestingly, Steve went to college on a music scholarship to study trombone, with the aim of performing. Ever the pragmatist, he switched to the business school because he realized that while he was talented, he was unable to visualize himself performing at a professional level.

Steve got an internship during college with a life insurance company, and the job became permanent after graduation. The position required Steve to manage the internship program, teaching him that he "didn't want to baby-sit college students." He took a break from work for a couple of months to bike across the country with a friend and returned to the same company to sell insurance. He made a conscious decision not to get into management for five years, allowing him to build his own business. That was six years ago and he isn't interested in a switch yet.

A Good Fit

Steve has high ethical standards, as do many Traditionalists. Although he wants to be successful, it is important that he achieve his aim honestly, through hard work. He is comfortable working within an organization with many clear rules, goals, and requirements, and enjoys achieving the different status levels that indicate excellence.

The intellectual challenge is one of the aspects of the job that Steve likes best. Using his dominant Thinking function, Steve lays out logical, well-thought-out, and consequently convincing recommendations to his clients. He focuses on cause and effect: what benefits his clients will accrue if they follow his advice. His Thinking helps him persevere and not take rejection personally—an indispensable asset for a salesperson. "Rejection affects me like rain on wax." Finally, his ability to organize and prioritize his time well enables him to be efficient and productive.

Steve relies on his auxiliary Sensing function to pay particular attention to the many facts and details in his business. He likes gathering information about his clients and broadening his knowledge base about the various products he offers. His strong Sensing comes in handy in other ways, such as prospecting for new clients and reviewing his tickler files to know when to contact existing clients for possible updates.

Also in evidence is Steve's desire, as a Judger, to get the job done. "I enjoy the fact gathering. But closing the sale is the best part. I've earned the financial part by the end of the process. I've worked for a block of time, used my creative energy to come up with the best approach, given the correct financial advice, and built trust."

Looking Ahead

Steve is persistent, organized, and enthusiastic. He wants to be a big fish in a little pond. He also strives to be in the "top quartile, recognized nationally among professional people in the field." He marks his own success by his membership in the 100 Lives Club and the Million Dollar Round Table—national and international sales organizations. Achieving membership each year in both groups gives Steve the confidence to mingle with the top people in his industry. He competes in fierce sales competitions for trips and prizes, which sometimes is a source of stress as he becomes entirely focused on score sheets. But it motivates him, too. And the sheer amount of his activity helps him to eliminate the stress he experiences.

"The most rewarding part of this job is that I'm directly compensated for the work I do. And I choose to work with clients who are that type of person. I wish the world were more that way. I believe that if you work consistently and do a good job, the financials will take care of themselves."

Profile 3: Marilyn, Event Planner

"I'm a person of great energy, so I accomplish what I set out to do."

The Job

Creating and sustaining a stellar reputation for her corporate meeting planning and special events production company is the goal that drives Marilyn. After three years, it seems to be working. "Everyone doesn't know about us yet, but those that we introduce ourselves and our services to always hire us!" Once Marilyn sells the client on the event idea and the event is under way, "the client tells us it's better than they ever dreamed possible."

This is the fourth career for Marilyn. And aside from raising her two children, it's the one she has put the most of herself into. She and a partner plan and execute all aspects of a corporate meeting or special event, from developing schedules and arranging transportation and meals to creating themes, booking speakers or entertainers, and developing games. "We do everything ourselves but also hire the people necessary to carry our ideas off." They subcontract when necessary with vendors who do such specialty work as designing and producing invitations or props. Marilyn handles all phases of concept development, planning, budgeting, and setting up and taking down the event or meeting.

Marilyn and her partner also do all the sales for the company, one of the tasks she enjoys most. "Meeting new people, introducing ourselves, and getting hired. It's actually better than doing the event itself. We become friends with our client, become extensions of the client's company, and that's great."

Backstory

Marilyn's first career after college was as an elementary school special education teacher. She enjoyed the job for five years and stopped when she had her own children. After her kids were in school, Marilyn helped her husband, a doctor, set up his medical office and then managed the office for a couple of years.

But she was bored without a challenge, so she became a real estate agent. She was top salesperson in the company for two years and loved it. The sudden, tragic death of her husband forced her to quit her job in order to settle the estate, close his practice, and relocate. She took some time to help resettle her kids and help them adjust to their new life.

Then she began volunteer fundraising work for a national charity. She visited corporations and solicited funding. "I dreamed up events, and then ran them. It was great work, but after a while, 'thank you' wasn't enough anymore. I wanted to be compensated for my good work." Marilyn remarried and was encouraged by her businessman husband to find a job that would challenge and tap her many skills. Because she so enjoyed the volunteer fundraising work, she decided to look for a job in a special events company. She met her future partner, who was also considering a new venture, and they developed a business together.

A Good Fit

Like most Traditionalists, Marilyn takes her work very seriously (although she enjoys it tremendously). Her strong work ethic and philosophy of "Do whatever it takes to get the job done" has helped her develop a reputation as the best in her field. And with it have come recognition and financial success, both of which are strong motivators for Marilyn.

What Marilyn loves best is making sales. Her dominant function, Thinking, helps her present her ideas logically and allows her to persist where a less assertive person might give up. It also assists her in planning and executing organized events, skillful budgeting, and tough negotiating.

Marilyn's auxiliary Sensing helps her keep track of the hundreds of details that need attention in the planning and execution of an event. She also has a good sense of quality and a strong aesthetic, using her Sensing to determine if an invitation, prop, or decoration is just the way it should be. Many of her events involve hands-on participation in games and activities relating to the theme of the event, and each movement of the event is impeccably planned and carried out.

Looking Ahead

Marilyn is proud of her accomplishments in her company. She hopes to add staff so that she and her partner can "stop killing [themselves] doing everything." But the tenacity she demonstrates is one of her greatest skills. "Once I decide to do something, I'll do whatever it takes. I'm really devoted to my work, and the time just flies by until I realize it's seven o'clock at night!"

Over the past ten years, Marilyn has experienced major life changes with the death of her husband, her remarriage, and the maturity of her children. She is a more independent person and more goal oriented than she ever was. "I find that I rely on my own inner resources, including my inner strength. I recognize my abilities better now."

Career satisfaction for Marilyn is doing a good job and being recognized and rewarded for it. "We're becoming a real force in this city, developing a fine reputation. You know that you're doing well when your competitors stop talking to you because you've become a tremendous threat!"

Common Threads

Although Anne, Steve, and Marilyn have different backgrounds, experiences, and careers, there are certain common threads woven through their stories. Their specific interests, abilities, and values may differ, but owing to their similar temperament values and the *same hierarchy* of their psychological functions, there are certain observations we can make about the needs of many ESTJs.

What follows is a list of the most important elements—the formula, if you will—for ESTJ satisfaction. Given the uniqueness of all individuals—even those who share a type—this list will not describe each ESTJ equally well. The important thing is that these ten elements, with varying degrees of intensity and in different orders of importance, identify what ESTJs need to be satisfied.

After you have reviewed this list, we recommend that you go back and prioritize the elements in order of *their importance to you*. When doing this, think of past work experiences as well as your present job, and what you found particularly satisfying or unsatisfying. Try to look for *themes* that run through several experiences, not just *events* that might be true for one work situation but not for another.

As an ESTJ, I define career satisfaction as doing work that

1. lets me work systematically, organizing facts, policies, or people, and use time and resources efficiently toward a logical conclusion
2. lets me use mastered skills while working on concrete and straightforward assignments with clear specifications, using my strong reasoning powers
3. is measured and evaluated by fair, logical, explicit, and objective standards
4. is done in a friendly environment with other hardworking and conscientious people who do not bring their

personal problems to work or expect me to share my personal feelings on the job
5. is realistic and tangible in nature and has practical applications and concrete results
6. has clear expectations and reporting hierarchy
7. lets me be productive, organizing the necessary steps and resources, following established procedures, and setting and meeting deadlines
8. is done in a stable and predictable environment, but one that is also filled with action and a variety of people
9. can be done with other people, enabling me to be in charge of myself and others
10. lets me make decisions and have a great deal of control and responsibility; where my opinions, recommendations, and experience are considered important

Popular Occupations for ESTJs

In listing occupations that are popular among ESTJs, it is important to note that there are successful people of all types in all occupations. However, the following are careers ESTJs may find particularly satisfying, and some of the reasons why. This is by no means a comprehensive listing but is included to suggest possibilities you may not have previously considered. Although all of these occupations offer the potential for career satisfaction, the future demand for some careers is anticipated to be greater than for others.

SALES / SERVICE
- Insurance sales agent
- Salesperson (tangibles): computers, real estate, retail

- Sales representative: wholesale and manufacturing
- Pharmaceutical salesperson
- Police/probation/corrections officer
- Military officer
- Chef
- Government employee
- Funeral director
- Occupational health and safety specialist
- Sports merchandise/equipment sales
- Ship and boat captain
- Regulatory compliance officer
- Aviation inspector
- Personal trainer
- Athletic coach
- Athletic trainer
- Sales agent: securities and commodities
- Underwriter
- Credit analyst
- Cost estimator
- Budget analyst
- Police and detective supervisor
- Commercial airplane pilot
- Transportation coordinator
- Flight engineer
- Construction and building inspector
- Real estate appraiser
- Paralegal
- Legislative assistant
- Insurance adjuster
- Court clerk
- Hotel and motel manager
- Environmental compliance inspector
- Recreational therapist

These occupations allow the ESTJ to work in the real world, on realistic and tangible projects. Most of these careers demand adherence to standard operating procedures and require a great deal of interaction with the public or groups of people. ESTJs enjoy being in positions of authority and enjoy giving orders. Sales of real things offers the opportunity to engage in work that achieves immediate and tangible results.

TECHNOLOGY / PHYSICAL
- Engineer: mechanical/applied fields
- Auditor
- General contractor
- Construction worker
- Clinical technician
- Cybersecurity specialist
- Sound technician
- Security guard
- Accounting internal auditor
- Technical trainer
- EEG technologist/technician
- Diagnostic medical sonographer
- Paralegal
- Network and computer systems administrator
- Organic farmer
- Solar photovoltaic installer
- Wind turbine service technician
- Database administrator

These fields require the use of the ESTJ's technical and mechanical abilities. Each allows them to focus on gathering, organizing, and analyzing factual information, and engage in deductive reasoning. Each of these occupations requires a logical and organized work style, which is enjoyed by ESTJs who prefer a work environment that is orderly and neat. ESTJs are impatient with confusion and inefficiency.

MANAGEMENT
- Project manager
- Office manager
- Administrator
- Factory supervisor
- Database manager
- Purchasing agent
- Regulatory compliance officer
- Budget analyst

- Health services administrator
- Chief information officer
- Management consultant: business operations
- Logistics and supply manager
- Bank manager/loan officer
- Credit analyst/counselor
- Property manager: commercial/residential
- Bill and account collector
- Food service and lodging owner
- Network and computer systems administrator
- Nursing director
- Construction manager
- Association manager and adviser
- Treasurer, controller, and chief financial officer
- Private sector executive

The managerial fields are often satisfying for ESTJs because they like to be in positions of authority. They are good executives because they enjoy giving direction, making decisions, and supervising others. They are also very loyal to established institutions. Management requires constant interaction with other people and the ability to direct, monitor, and evaluate the work of others.

PROFESSIONAL
- Dentist
- Stockbroker
- Judge
- Executive
- Teacher: technical/trade
- Civil/mechanical/metallurgical engineer
- Corporate finance lawyer
- Electrical engineer
- Primary care physician
- Food and drug scientist/technician
- Industrial engineer
- Paralegal
- Pharmacist
- Statistician

- Lawyer
- School principal

The appeal of the professional fields is the ability to work in established, traditional institutions in positions of authority. Dentistry and medicine are technical occupations that generally include hands-on activities—helping people through practical and established routines. These occupations make use of the ESTJ's powers of deductive reasoning and ability to understand cause and effect. They prefer to do things following a detailed and clear procedure proven effective by their own experience and others whom they respect.

Remember, these are only some of the areas that provide satisfying expression for the unique natural talents of ESTJs.

Customizing Your Job Search

Knowing the particular strengths and blind spots of your type can afford you a tremendous advantage in your job search campaign. In all aspects of the process, from conducting research into available positions, identifying and contacting prospective employers, developing personal marketing tools such as résumés, arranging and conducting job interviews, and negotiating salaries to finally accepting a position, people will act true to their type. Being able to capitalize on your assets and compensate for your liabilities can make the difference between a successful and an unsuccessful job search.

The differences between types are sometimes subtle and other times dramatic. It is the subtle variations in advice we offer that make the real difference between success and failure in a job search. The concept of networking serves as a good example. Extraverts will naturally enjoy networking and are advised to do so on a large scale, while Introverts find more limited and targeted networking, especially with people they already know, easier. Sensors tend to network with people in a defined scope, while Intuitives will go far and wide to find people often seemingly unrelated to their field of interest. Further, Feelers can often take networking personally and enjoy establishing warm rapport, while Thinkers will be more objective and detached in their style. Finally, Judgers tend to ask fewer and more structured questions during their networking, while Perceivers could ask questions of all sorts all day long! One valuable search technique, many ways to implement it.

Pathways to Success: Using Your Strengths

Once you set your mind to finding the right job, no one will work harder searching for it than you. Your persistence and the seriousness with which you view the process will help you stay with the task until you find the work that is best for you. However, in your eagerness to accomplish your goal, you may be blinded to other possibilities, new information, or novel approaches.

As an ESTJ, you will find that your most effective strategies build on your abilities to do the following:

Organize and conduct an efficient job search.

- Use your organizational skills to stay on top of the project, make a plan, be on time, remember to follow up with prospective employers, and so forth.
- Use your practical skills to plot out a realistic campaign, beginning with the most obvious opportunities within your own company and other companies or organizations with which you are familiar.

Make realistic decisions based on known facts and objective data.

- Use your critical thinking skills to analyze the positive and negative aspects of each job option and eliminate those options in which you are not interested or qualified.
- Gather as much information about a potential employer's business and industry as possible.

The following example of the process one ESTJ client went through illustrates how both of these recommendations can be put into practical use.

The first thing Jackson did when he learned his company was downsizing and his job might be in jeopardy was to sit down and take stock of his situation. He prepared two spreadsheets; the first was financial, reflecting his assets, liabilities, and monthly expenses to determine how long he could live without an income. His second spreadsheet was his work-related strengths and weaknesses: what he had to sell in the marketplace.

Since Jackson knew he wanted to stay in the same line of work, he next developed an impressive marketing plan, complete with potential employers, strategies, and projected timetables for accomplishing various tasks. Jackson contacted potential employers, conducted informational interviews to learn more about particular jobs, and researched specific companies to determine if they interested him. The point is, Jackson approached this job search just as he had his job as a midlevel manager—with efficiency, skill, dispatch, and action.

Be direct and honest when giving a summary of how your skills and abilities will benefit the employer.

- Prepare before the interview by developing a list of questions the prospective employer might ask you. Practice answering these, focusing on your past experiences and accomplishments.
- Ask a friend to ask you potentially difficult questions so you can rehearse your answers.

When David was going through the grueling interview process for a CEO position, he was often asked difficult questions about what he might do in a hypothetical situation. Several times David wondered if the interviewer might be deliberately trying to make him angry, because he used a condescending tone. Instead of becoming insulted, David decided to be completely honest and told the interviewer exactly what he thought. He offered constructive criticism on how he thought the organization needed to be changed in order to succeed. Occasionally, during the five interviews, David wondered if he had done the right thing. He took a gamble because he wanted to demonstrate courage and the ability to make the necessary tough decisions. It paid off. Those were exactly the characteristics the company was looking for in a CEO.

Set and meet realistic job search goals.

- Develop a list of important characteristics in a new job, including salary, benefits, work schedule, location, room for advancement, and other important criteria. Use that checklist to evaluate each job opportunity.
- Realize that it can take as much as three to twelve months, and sometimes longer, to find the right job. Don't expect to find a job until you have gone through all the necessary steps.

After several years in the purchasing department of a small manufacturing company, Gina decided it was time to return to college to finish her business degree so she could get a job with more responsibility and a bigger salary. Because she couldn't afford to quit working completely and go to school full-time, she did a little homework and learned that a small private university offered the degree program she wanted, and something more. Because the school offered a tuition abatement program for employees, she applied for a job in the purchasing department, enabling her to take two courses a semester with no fee. She accepted the job with the full realization that it would take her two years to complete her degree, but she would be able to do so at no cost, while she was continuing to apply and sharpen her business skills in an area she was familiar with.

Present yourself as a capable, stable, and competent candidate.

- Express your skills in a clear and logical way on all written materials, including résumé and cover letter, and during all interviews. Be sure to include past experiences as examples to demonstrate your capabilities and accomplishments.
- Offer letters of recommendation from past employers attesting to your competency and quality of performance.
- Point out to prospective employers the ways in which you will be able to help the company accomplish its goals.

After working for one company for nearly twelve years, Tanya initiated a career change to find a more challenging position. Since she had always received excellent performance reviews from the three supervisors she had worked for during her tenure, she asked each of them to write a letter of recommendation for her. She gave them guidelines for what she wanted them to focus on. She asked that they refer to her consistently excellent performance reviews, her skills, and her measurable contributions to the goals of their departments. During interviews, she volunteered copies of the letters and encouraged her interviewers to keep them in her file.

Network extensively.

- Enlist the help of people with whom you have worked over the years and who know you well to identify people to contact about career opportunities.

When Devonte was looking for a new job, he contacted people on his softball team and in his church about opportunities within their own companies. After a series of informational interviews, one individual referred him to the director of the management training department at her company. Devonte learned that a position was about to become available owing to the relocation of an employee. He applied for and got the job before it was ever publicized.

Possible Pitfalls

Although all people are unique, there are certain *potential* blind spots that many ESTJs share. We underscore "potential" because some of the following *may* be true of you, while others may clearly not apply. While considering them, you may notice that these tendencies do not relate just to the job search, but rather describe pitfalls that you

may have experienced in other aspects of your life as well. It is therefore helpful to consider each one in terms of your past experiences by asking yourself: "Is this true for me?" And if so, "How did this tendency prevent me from getting something that I wanted?" You will probably notice that the key to overcoming your blind spots is the conscious and thoughtful development of your third and fourth functions (Intuition and Feeling). We recognize that many of the suggestions will be difficult to implement, but the more you use these functions, the fewer problems they will cause you in the future.

Avoid making decisions too quickly.

- Waiting even a few moments to ask yourself what you know and what you still do not know about a situation, and considering how you feel about the issue or choice at hand, will help you make a better decision.
- Try to ask more open-ended questions during all phases of the job search to get a better understanding of the possible implications of your choice.

Consider innovative or unconventional job search techniques as well as more customary practices.

- Enlist the help of friends or colleagues who may possess more Intuition to help you brainstorm alternative means of reaching a key decision maker within a company or a prospective employer.

Consider the long-range consequences in weighing job options.

- Attempt to look down the road and imagine how your goals or needs may change as you progress and age. Make a list of what your needs are now and try to predict how they may be different one year, five years, and ten years from today. Consider this information in making a decision with long-ranging implications.

- During the interview process, ask about growth potential within the company, relocation possibilities, and about the long-range goals of your prospective employer to be sure you are interested in going where the company may need to send you.

Try to establish rapport with interviewers and not be brusque and too businesslike.

- Try to relax before an interview and not allow the seriousness of the activity to affect your attitude negatively. Remember that you wish to be seen as someone with whom they could easily get along, one of the team.

Avoid being rigid and inflexible in job negotiations.

- Use your list of criteria as a guide in selecting a good job, rather than as rules cast in concrete. Be persistent about those elements without which you simply can't live, but be willing to be flexible about those that are less important.
- Try to give positive feedback before offering any negative criticism, knowing others can be offended and put off by a negative perspective.

The Final Piece: Changing or Keeping Your Job...the Key to Success for ESTJs

Now that you have a solid understanding of your type, you can see how your natural

preferences make you better suited for certain kinds of jobs. You can also see how knowledge of your type-related strengths and blind spots can help you conduct a more successful job search. But as an ESTJ, you've already realized that you are not equally drawn to *every* career or field listed in the Popular Occupations section. The next and final step is to narrow down the field and find the work you were meant to do.

In addition to Type, several other factors—such as your values, interests, and skills—contribute to your level of satisfaction on the job. The more compatible you are with your job, the happier you'll be. So prepare to use everything you've learned (in this book and in life) to create *your strategic career plan*. The exercises in Chapter 23, "Putting It All Together," are designed to help you do just that.

However, you may have decided it makes more sense (if perhaps only for the moment) to stay in your present job or with your current employer. There may be many valid reasons—financial pressures, family considerations, a tough job market for your specialty, or just bad timing. But take heart! What you've learned in this book can also help you be more content and successful *in your current job*. And should the time come when you're ready to make a major career move, you'll have a much better idea of where you want to go and how to get there.

"So, if you can't have the job you love (yet!)...love the one you've got."

The simple truth is, many jobs allow a good deal of flexibility in the way tasks are performed. Here are some ways you may be able to "massage" your current job into one that better fits your needs:

- Find an efficient assistant.
- Provide agendas to help people prepare for meetings.
- Seek advice and opinions of colleagues who are different from you.
- Join professional organizations and create opportunities to network.
- Implement efficiency systems and require direct reports to use them.
- Make sure to work around a lot of people to stay stimulated; delegate solitary tasks, if possible.
- If not in management, find a project that needs doing and volunteer to lead the effort.
- Ask your supervisors to be explicit about their expectations.
- Become part of a work team.

One ESTJ turns lemons into lemonade:

Jorge, a life insurance salesman, was looking to replace his administrative assistant. He knew he needed someone who would be both meticulous about the many details of his work and personable enough to handle considerable client contact. When traditional means of filling the position failed to attract the right person, he decided to try networking. He posted the position on LinkedIn and other social media networking sites, and mentioned the position to select clients after sales calls. It was this last tactic that paid off. A client recommended an able administrative assistant who was returning to the workforce after a few years at home raising his children.

Use what you've got to get what you need.

Simply put, the best advice on how to succeed is to *capitalize on your strengths and compensate for your blind spots.* Learning how to do this can make the difference between succeeding or failing and

loving or hating your work. To help you, we include the following inventory of your potential strengths and blind spots. And while every individual is unique, many of the following should apply to you as an ESTJ.

Your work-related strengths may include

- practicality and focus on results
- forcefulness in dealing with your commitments; you can be tough when necessary
- ability to stay focused on the organization's goals
- precision and accuracy and desire to get the job done right
- desire to follow established routines and procedures
- ability to recognize what is illogical, inconsistent, impractical, or inefficient
- organizational skills; you're good at making objective decisions
- belief in the value of a traditional structure and the ability to work within it
- sense of responsibility; you can be counted on to do what you say
- clear work ethic; need to be efficient and productive
- common sense and realistic perspective

Your work-related blind spots may include

- impatience with those who don't follow procedures or who ignore important details
- reluctance to embrace new, untested ideas
- discomfort with or resistance to change
- little patience with inefficiency or processes that take too long
- focus on present needs at the expense of future ones
- tendency to overrun people in an effort to meet your goals

- inability to see future possibilities
- potential lack of sensitivity about how other people will be affected by policies and decisions

- difficulty listening to opposing viewpoints; you may interrupt frequently

Using your strengths is easy.
The secret to success for an
ESTJ
is learning to

slow down, consider implications
for people, and be flexible.

16 ISTJ
Introverted, Sensing, Thinking, Judging
"Take Your Time and Do It Right"

Profile 1: Jackie, Executive Assistant

"Always behind the scenes, making sure everything runs smoothly."

The Job

Jackie is the glue that holds her boss—and his work—together. She is the special assistant to the executive director of an educational nonprofit. A highly organized and efficient person, Jackie functions as the grounding force for her boss, Tom, whom she describes as a visionary with "a lot of ideas; someone who wants to do everything, all the time. But because he moves so quickly from one project to another, he has a hard time getting anything done."

That's where Jackie comes in. She is in charge of scheduling, logistics, and routine "realism check-ins"—playing a stabilizing role and helping to maintain clear communications across all teams. Jackie describes "finding the blank spaces for meetings"—that is, balancing multiple schedules and job sites, and making sure there is adequate time to get done everything that needs to get done. Without her critical work, the good work the nonprofit is attempting would not be possible. Jackie finds this deeply satisfying.

Backstory

Jackie's career path has been, as she puts it, "a long and winding road." When she graduated from college with a degree in psychology and East Asian studies, Jackie thought she wanted to be a school counselor. She transitioned immediately to a master's program in education, a precursor year to a second year getting licensed in school counseling. After the first year, Jackie did a summer teaching fellowship at an inner-city charter school, an experience that confirmed her passion for education and her desire to go back for year two to get her license in school counseling.

Upon obtaining her degree, Jackie worked as a guidance counselor at an inner-city public middle school for several months, but she kept hitting roadblocks to transferring her license from out of state. Additionally, the school environment was less than ideal, and she considered the school principal inept and ineffectual. Jackie found that being a competent person in a disorganized and poorly run workplace meant that she had to do many people's jobs—without really getting to do her own.

After trying to improve the environment for several months, Jackie realized the problems were systemic, and so not within her power to fix. She found a job listing on Idealist.org and completed a rigorous set of six interviews before landing a position as special assistant to the executive director of an urban educational nonprofit. Now she is able to work toward the same goals she's been working toward in every job she's held so far—trying to make the education world a more equitable and functional place. Best of all, she's able to create those organized and efficient systems that were so lacking in her other work environments.

A Good Fit

Jackie is a logistical mastermind. A dominant Sensing type, she is queen of the details, practical and down to earth, with a realist's sense of the world around her. Whereas Tom is always focused on the long range, Jackie has a firm grasp on the present and helps fill in the gaps in his abilities. For instance, before Jackie, Tom was chronically late to meetings because he never accounted for travel time. Now he's five minutes early.

Jackie's auxiliary function of Thinking makes her a cool customer, rational and direct. As a Judger, she is prompt and planful: "I like being the person who organizes things, and I like following up

with people." Like many Traditionalists, Jackie has a deep pull toward community service and helping others. She sees a common thread between her role as a counselor and her new role supporting Tom.

"I just really enjoy being in the background and making sure that things are OK." In this job, Jackie the Introvert gets to play a supporting role to a cause that is important to her, serving the community in a real and meaningful way.

Looking Ahead

Since Jackie has been at her new job for only a couple of months, she's still focusing on learning the rhythm of the work. But she does see a future for herself within the organization and will soon be taking on more responsibilities, such as becoming the liaison for the school board, working with the director of finance, and playing a larger role in board governance.

Jackie could see herself eventually going back to business school and studying project management or possibly becoming a consultant. But for the time being, she thinks it will take a few more years to really get to know Tom and to understand how best to support him and the organization. It's clear they're lucky to have her!

Profile 2: Rashida, University Dean

"Getting things done right."

The Job

Rashida likes being in charge. And she is in charge of a great deal as dean of the school of allied health professions at a large state university. She is an academic administrator; her main priority is facilitating the activities of the faculty and making sure they have the resources they need to do their jobs. She enjoys being able to decide on a course of action and then make it happen, whether the action is a small detail or a broad decision about the governing of the school.

Much of what Rashida does falls under the heading of either planning or decision making. She is responsible for all personnel decisions, including hiring and evaluating faculty, and making promotional and tenure recommendations to her supervisor, the university provost. She generates the regular reports and documentation for the school, makes decisions about the dismissal of students due to either academic or disciplinary reasons, oversees the acceptance of entering students, helps make plans for recruitment of students, supervises the staff liaison to the admissions department, and prepares and monitors the budget for the school. She also teaches one course each semester. Finally, she develops long- and short-range plans for the school and then evaluates whether those goals have been met. Rashida represents the school on various committees and forums on and off campus. In her own words, she has "a large capacity for work."

Backstory

Rashida appears to have carefully planned and plotted her career path, although she never really had a grand scheme. She studied medical technology upon graduation and went to work in a major university hospital for eight years. "I loved it. And even today, I believe that if I wanted to leave academia, I could be happy to return to a hospital setting and be a full-time medical technologist." But she did leave to take on the added challenge of teaching students on a one-on-one basis.

She soon became a faculty member, then obtained her master's degree in education. Still on the teaching staff at the hospital,

Rashida received a Ph.D. in psychometrics. She was promoted to assistant dean of the allied health college at the university and continued in that job for another eight years. Rashida was really happy at the hospital university and honestly thought she would retire there. But while serving on the board of an allied health association, she met the current dean of another university who was stepping down. She persuaded Rashida to apply for her job. "I tell people it was an offer I couldn't refuse: more money, more responsibility, and more control."

A Good Fit

Rashida has a highly responsible position in a very traditional organization. Consistent with her Traditionalist values, Rashida works very hard in a structured environment and makes many important decisions during the course of her day. Like many Traditionalists, her career path has been a series of step-by-step progressions. One reason her work in both fields—medicine and education—has been so satisfying is that in both she has had the opportunity to serve others.

In her work, Rashida must keep track of lots of information. She is responsible for documenting all activities of the school, putting together reports, tracking personnel achievements, conducting performance appraisals, and so forth. She relies on her Sensing to assist her in all these tasks, as well as to engage in short-term planning, and in her own classroom teaching, which she does each semester.

A Judger, Rashida considers her goal-directed nature to be one of her greatest assets. "I'm good at setting priorities and being very clear about what needs to be accomplished." Her auxiliary function, Thinking, is how Rashida makes decisions—an activity she clearly enjoys. It also helps her to be honest with people, and has given her a reputation for being direct and no-nonsense in her dealings with others.

Looking Ahead

Rashida has been happy in her current position for the past five years. But she has ambitions to become a college president someday, expanding her reach and broadening the scope of what she's able to influence and shape. Having a real and documentable impact is something Rashida really enjoys about her career. With a seemingly infinite capacity for hard work and fortitude, there's no limit to what she can accomplish.

Profile 3: Dave, Property Management

"Being responsible and working hard to accomplish my objectives."

The Job

As vice president and director of property management for a commercial real estate firm, Dave oversees the operations and maintenance of six different office buildings around the city. He acts as on-site property manager at some and supervises the on-site property manager at others. "It's soup to nuts—I'm responsible for taking care of everything that goes on in the buildings so the actual owner doesn't have to." Dave is extremely detail oriented and thankfully so, because the job requires constant maintenance and inspection.

Dave deals with a variety of situations and people throughout the day, contracting with cleaning, security, and trash-removal services and supervising the many mechanical personnel who keep the buildings operating. At any given moment, he might be handling a tenant complaint about the office temperature, trying to get a new electrical plug installed or a light bulb replaced. He usually carries around a checklist of things he notices need fixing and then assigns the staff member, or hires the contractor, to get the job done. Occasionally he spends time renewing existing tenants' leases or answering operational questions during a tour for a prospective tenant. It's all part of his objective and duty to keep things running smoothly.

What he enjoys and finds the most energizing is being able to make physical alterations in the buildings that will have real and positive results. "I was bothered by how dark an elevator area was, so I got new lighting columns installed. It was great to see how much improved the area was!" He assesses and uses resources well, gathers plenty of important technical data, gets quotes from vendors, supervises the changes, and then sees the results of his labor and that of others. He gets a charge out of solving problems in effective and functional ways.

Backstory

Dave's career path started a bit off-track with a psychology degree he knew he would never use. But he discovered a graduate study program that would give him building operations and student activities experience while he worked toward a master's degree. He worked for two years in three different positions on a college campus—assisting in the operations of the campus center, developing student activities, and managing the campus pub. It was excellent hands-on experience that led to a full-time position as director of another university student center. He enjoyed the duties but found the more intellectual and politically active campus to be too serious an environment.

After two years, he interviewed for an assistant property manager position at the real estate firm he works for now. After the first interview, he later learned that the company executives weren't too impressed with him. But a second interview was held at his office at the campus center. "I think seeing me in my element, dealing effectively with everything I had to deal with (and still noticing to pick up a gum wrapper off the floor while I was walking with them) made them feel confident in my ability and impressed them with my conscientiousness."

He was hired and promoted to property manager within two years, and then to vice president and director of property management two years later. It's been a rapid rise, a bit too rapid for Dave. "I never said no to the offers. In fact, I always feel thankful for the opportunity to have more responsibility, but I do feel I have a long way to go in this position. I'm content to stay where I am and continue to expand my duties by taking on more properties."

A Good Fit

Dave's work as a property manager suits his Traditionalist temperament well. He is in the business of maintaining spaces, making sure operations run smoothly and equipment and facilities are kept up to standard and code. His job involves a good deal of responsibility—and both his tasks and the procedures required to accomplish them are clearly defined.

In his business, Dave must pay attention to everything. He is constantly "on alert" and uses his dominant Sensing function to notice how everything looks, sounds, feels, and even smells. As he inspects the properties he manages, he must pay attention to such things as lighting, temperature, and acoustics, down to the smallest details concerning the physical condition of the building. Additionally, he must keep track of the budget, making sure that maintenance

schedules are carried out on time, necessary reports are filed, and established procedures are followed.

Another of Dave's responsibilities involves contracting with vendors, tradespeople, and maintenance and security staff. Being a Thinker helps him to be fair and objective when evaluating the performance of the many people he supervises, and tough when negotiating the most favorable terms of their contracts. And taking on difficult challenges and seeing them through is something Dave finds rewarding, like many Judging types. He is motivated by closure and likes to get the job done.

Looking Ahead

For the time being, Dave is good where he is. "Someday it might be nice to be a partner in a project and share some of the risk, but I have no desire to become a developer, which is often the path people in this job want to take." Lately, Dave has also been spending his free time involved in local-level politics and serving on his condominium association board. "I can see myself running for an elected position someday—town selectman or city council. I care about what happens to my community, and I plan to become more active in the process."

Common Threads

Although Rashida, Dave, and Jackie have different backgrounds, experiences, and careers, there are certain common threads woven through their stories. Their specific interests, abilities, and values may differ, but owing to their similar temperament values and the *same hierarchy* of their psychological functions, there are certain observations we can make about the needs of many ISTJs.

What follows is a list of the most important elements—the formula, if you will, for ISTJ satisfaction. Given the uniqueness of all individuals—even those who share a type—this list will not describe each ISTJ equally well. The important thing is that these ten elements, with varying degrees of intensity and in different orders of importance, identify what ISTJs need to be satisfied.

After you have reviewed this list, we recommend that you go back and prioritize the elements in order of *their importance to you*. When doing this, think of past work experiences as well as your present job, and what you found particularly satisfying or unsatisfying. Try to look for *themes* that run through several experiences, not just *events* that might be true for one work situation but not for another.

As an ISTJ, I define career satisfaction as doing work that

1. is technical in nature and lets me depend on my ability to use and remember important facts and details
2. involves a real product or service done in a thoughtful, logical, and efficient way, preferably using standard operating procedures
3. lets me be independent, with plenty of time to work alone and use my excellent powers of concentration to complete projects and/or tasks
4. is done in a stable and traditional environment, where I will not be required to take unnecessary risks or use untested or experimental approaches
5. has results that are tangible and measurable, where precision and exacting standards are used and respected
6. has explicit objectives and a clearly defined organizational structure

7. gives me adequate time to prepare before presenting or turning in my work, preferably in a one-on-one or small group setting
8. gives me increasing levels of responsibility, with a minimum of social politics, whereby I am evaluated on how well I have achieved the requirements of the job description and am appreciated for my contributions
9. is done in an environment where my practical judgment and experience are valued and rewarded
10. allows me to set and reach stated goals by providing me with the necessary resources

Popular Occupations for ISTJs

In listing occupations that are popular among ISTJs, it is important to note that there are successful people of all types in all occupations. However, the following are careers ISTJs may find particularly satisfying, and some of the reasons why. This is by no means a comprehensive listing but is included to suggest possibilities you may not have previously considered. Although all of these occupations offer the potential for career satisfaction, the future demand for some careers is anticipated to be greater than for others.

BUSINESS
- Auditor
- Office manager
- Accountant
- Manager/supervisor
- Executive assistant
- Efficiency expert/analyst
- Insurance underwriter
- Bookkeeper
- Logistics and supply manager
- Regulatory compliance officer

- Chief information officer
- Actuary
- Property manager: commercial/residential
- Bill and account collector
- Construction and building inspector
- Construction manager
- Purchasing agent and contract specialist
- Insurance claims examiner
- Statistician
- Information and records clerk
- Billing and posting clerk
- Technical writer
- Association manager and adviser
- Project manager
- Real estate appraiser

ISTJs often enjoy careers in business and excel in the areas of managing systems and keeping things running smoothly. They usually prefer traditional, established organizations or businesses and by their presence provide a stabilizing effect on an operation. They are efficient and thorough in keeping track of costs and revenues and do not allow errors or omissions to go unchecked or uncorrected. As managers, they provide clear definition of roles and established ways of doing things for their employees.

SALES / SERVICE
- Police officer/detective
- IRS agent
- Government inspector
- Public servant
- Military officer
- Real estate agent
- Sports equipment/merchandise sales
- Corrections officer
- Industrial safety and health engineer
- Fire prevention and protection specialist
- Ship and boat captain
- Commercial airplane pilot
- Probation officer

- Landscaping manager
- Flight engineer
- Postmaster and mail superintendent
- Environmental compliance inspector
- Immigration and customs inspector
- Architectural drafter
- Organic farmer
- Musical instrument maker
- Flight navigator

Careers in civil service often appeal to ISTJs' desire to serve their community. They enjoy maintaining systems that serve or protect all people. They work well within a structured environment, and can take and give direction and supervision well. ISTJs apply their knowledge and past experience to efficiently and decisively handle current problems. They have good memories for facts and details and use practical judgment in all they do. They tend to enjoy sales of real products with which they have personal experience.

FINANCE
- Bank examiner
- Investment securities officer
- Tax preparer and examiner
- Stockbroker
- Estate planner
- Credit analyst
- Budget analyst
- Cost estimator
- Treasurer, controller, and chief financial officer

ISTJs often have a head for numbers. They use and remember facts and details and can cite evidence to support their views. They are not easily distracted and work painstakingly to complete tasks accurately and meticulously. Careers in finance often require the ability to work well alone, absorb great amounts of data, and follow through on the precise execution of the computation.

EDUCATION
- School principal
- Teacher: technical/industrial/math/ physical education
- Librarian
- Administrator
- Archivist

Careers in education are often satisfying for ISTJs, especially those involving administration and/or technical subjects. They do well when overseeing the operation of a school or curriculum. They look for practical possibilities and ways to maintain systems. Administrative and library careers enable the ISTJ to work independently, using objective analysis in keeping order or monitoring data such as test scores and budgets. Teaching can be enjoyable for ISTJs when working with technical and practical subjects, where there are plenty of opportunities for hands-on teaching and learning.

LEGAL
- Law researcher
- Paralegal
- Legal secretary
- Judge/magistrate
- Criminalist and ballistics expert
- Court clerk

ISTJs often find themselves at home in the world of law. Their ability to focus, retain detailed information, and maintain rigorous systems of organization makes them an asset to a law firm or practice. ISTJs enjoy the serious and critical work of law, and believe in knowing and adhering to precedent.

TECHNOLOGY / SCIENCE
- Electrician
- Engineer
- Mechanic
- Computer programmer
- Software developer: systems, applications
- Software and web development engineer
- Computer and information research scientist
- Construction and development engineer
- Technical writer
- Pharmaceutical salesperson/researcher
- Geologist
- Meteorologist
- Airline mechanic
- Solar photovoltaic installer
- Wind turbine service technician
- Mechanical/industrial/electrical engineer
- Agricultural scientist
- Reliability engineer
- Database administrator
- Network systems and data communications analyst
- Hardware engineer

These careers offer ISTJs the chance to use their technical skills and work with products that demand exacting accuracy. Because they take nothing for granted, they catch slips and oversights, and follow necessary procedures and systems faithfully. Many of these occupations give ISTJs the chance to work alone, employing their tremendous powers of concentration and applying their excellent factual recall and mastery of skills.

HEALTHCARE
- General surgeon
- Veterinarian
- Dentist
- Nursing administrator
- Healthcare administrator
- Pharmacist
- Lab technologist
- Medical researcher

- Primary care physician
- Biomedical technologist
- Exercise physiologist
- Veterinary technologist/technician
- Dental hygienist
- Pharmacist/pharmacy technician
- Surgical technologist
- Diagnostic medical sonographer
- Orthodontist
- Coroner
- Optometrist
- Public health officer
- Biology specimen technician
- Environmental science technician
- Medical records technician
- EEG technologist / technician

ISTJs are often drawn to medical careers, especially those that are within the traditional structure of a hospital. They pay close attention to the immediate and practical concerns of their patients. They listen carefully and offer thoughtful and conservative advice and treatment plans. ISTJs are also successful administrators within healthcare settings, working conscientiously and steadily to meet their responsibilities and honor their commitments. They enjoy an orderly environment and one that rewards task-orientation and jobs done on schedule. The more technical nature of dentistry and pharmacology is often enjoyable to ISTJs, who master factual information easily and retain it forever.

Remember, these are only some of the areas that provide satisfying expression for the unique natural talents of ISTJs.

Customizing Your Job Search

Knowing the particular strengths and blind spots of your type can afford you a tremendous advantage in your job search campaign. In all aspects of the process, from conducting research into available positions, identifying and contacting prospective employers, developing personal marketing tools such as résumés, arranging and conducting job interviews, and negotiating salaries to finally accepting a position, people will act true to their type. Being able to capitalize on your assets and compensate for your liabilities can make the difference between a successful and an unsuccessful job search.

The differences between types are sometimes subtle and other times dramatic. It is the subtle variations in advice we offer that make the real difference between success and failure in a job search. The concept of networking serves as a good example. Extraverts will naturally enjoy networking and are advised to do so on a large scale, while Introverts find more limited and targeted networking, especially with people they already know, easier. Sensors tend to network with people in a defined scope, while Intuitives will go far and wide to find people often seemingly unrelated to their field of interest. Further, Feelers can often take networking personally and enjoy establishing warm rapport, while Thinkers will be more objective and detached in their style. Finally, Judgers tend to ask fewer and more structured questions during their networking, while Perceivers could ask questions of all sorts all day long! One valuable search technique, many ways to implement it.

Pathways to Success: Using Your Strengths

As we will detail in the following pages, your strengths and talents for the job search include your conscientiousness, desire to work hard, and ability to keep careful track of details and commitments. Beware of your tendency to stick only to the tried-and-true traditional methods of job hunting and miss clever or less obvious approaches.

As an ISTJ, you will find that your most effective strategies build on your abilities to do the following:

Research career options completely and conduct thorough data collection.

- Be patient in collecting information during the gathering stage of your job search. Remember that it often takes several months to find the right job.
- Network on a limited basis with people who know you well, especially those you have worked with in the past who are in different jobs, or people they recommend.

When Francisco was looking for a position in the tax department of his state government, he asked a friend from the Rotary Club to refer him to someone he knew in the tax commissioner's office. Francisco talked at length with the person, who was able to show him the offices, give him a real sample of a typical week's workload, and even share some of the complaints people had about the job. As a result, Francisco had a more realistic view of the job's advantages and disadvantages before actually applying for the position.

Carefully prepare your marketing materials.

- Look at your résumé and cover letters with an objective eye. Ask yourself what kind of message they send about you. Are they an accurate reflection of you?
- Be sure to include work accomplishments from your recent and more distant past and have letters of recommendation ready if needed.

Juliana started work on her résumé by patterning it after a friend's in the same business. But she decided that what she needed was a finished product that would better sell her skills and experience. She focused her résumé on accomplishments and the skills that each one utilized. In the work history section of the résumé, Juliana showed how each position had given her increased levels of responsibility. When she sent the résumé with her personalized cover letters, she was confident that the person reviewing it would have a good picture of her experience and all she had to offer.

Patiently follow companies' recruitment and personnel procedures.

- Ask or read about company hiring procedures as part of your overall information gathering. Tailor your approach to the way the system works.
- Demonstrate the kind of employee you will be by going through appropriate channels, using the system, and respecting the chain of command.

When recruiters from a major manufacturing company came to Marta's university to interview graduate computer programming students, Marta decided to get some advance information before interviewing. She spoke to her career adviser and got the name of an alumnus who was currently employed by the company. She put what she learned into practice and was really prepared for the interview. Besides being ready for the standard questions, she was also ready to ask a few of her own to let the interviewer know that she had done her homework and knew something about the company. The interviewer was impressed with her initiative. More subtle, however, was a fact that Marta had learned from her contact—the company encouraged a conservative dress code. Marta even bought a traditional blue suit for the interview. It turned out the company representative conducting the interview was wearing an almost identical suit.

Follow through on all details.

- Focus your energy on completing large and small tasks relating to your job search. This includes mapping out a general plan, keeping track of your progress, and following up.
- Stay organized. Demonstrate your skills and don't be afraid to be persistent, showing your interest in a particular job.

Nyisha had narrowed down her first choice in her career switch. She had decided she wanted to be the director of nursing at a nearby hospital. The position was still being posted internally, so, for the short term, Nyisha would have to wait to find out if it would be opened to the public. She stayed in touch with each of her contacts at the facility and wrote regular emails to the vice president for personnel at the hospital to remind him of her interest. A couple of times during the wait, she had doubts about reaching out. But she decided that she should continue to show that as hard as she would work to get the job, she would work just as hard once she got it. Her persistence paid off. When the position was open for outside application, she was the first, and last, applicant.

Make thoughtful, practical decisions.

- Ask for the time you need to carefully consider a job offer. Let your prospective employer know that you take your commitments seriously and want to give the offer the same attention you give to all of your responsibilities.

- Take a realistic look at the current job market and your skills. Employ your logical reasoning to help you make logical decisions.

After Craig retired from the navy, he began the process of making a career change by seeking career counseling. One of the ways he developed a list of realistic options was to review his skills and also research the job market in his home state. He considered using his training in physical education to work with a professional or collegiate sports team but determined that there were too few opportunities. So he pursued a career in high school physical education at a school with a need for a new varsity football and baseball coach. He was able to structure a job where he would be able to do both.

Possible Pitfalls

Although all people are unique, there are certain *potential* blind spots that many ISTJs share. We specify "potential" because some of the following *may* be true of you, while others may clearly not apply. While considering them, you may notice that these tendencies do not relate just to the job search but rather describe pitfalls that you may have experienced in other aspects of your life as well. It is therefore helpful to consider each one in terms of your past experiences by asking yourself, "Is this true for me?" And if so, "How did this tendency prevent me from getting something that I wanted?" You will probably notice that the key to overcoming your blind spots is the conscious and thoughtful development of your third and fourth functions (Feeling and Intuition). We recognize that many of the suggestions will be difficult to implement, but the more you use these functions, the fewer problems they will cause you in the future.

Consider career possibilities that are less obvious.

- Look for career possibilities that don't currently exist. Get help generating a long list of potential careers in which you are interested. Also look for careers that require the same skills you have, even if your skills are in a different field.
- Resist the urge to rule options out as unrealistic simply because you lack direct experience in the field.

Don't overlook the implications of your decisions.

- Try imagining yourself in any job you are considering. Imagine yourself five, ten, or twenty years from now. Is there growth potential? Opportunities to change areas or add responsibility?
- Develop a set of long-term and short-range goals to use as a measuring stick during your search. Compare potential jobs against both sets of goals to discover if you might be selling out a future goal for a short-range objective.

Avoid the tendency to be overcautious and rigid in your thinking.

- Try to keep yourself open to the possibility of doing something very different than you have in the past. Consider taking some reasonable and necessary risks to find career satisfaction.
- Continue to get help or counsel from friends or professionals if you think you might be slipping back into a routine in your thinking.

Remember to consider the human element in your search.

- Take the time to think about your true feelings and motivation as well as what

makes logical sense, and what you are technically qualified for. Ask yourself what's really important to you in your life, as well as your work, and make sure you aren't compromising the former.
- Pay attention to the interpersonal subtleties during the interview process. Engage in what you may consider frivolous niceties simply because you now know that other people consider them important.

Express enthusiasm for the job and market yourself.

- Let people know if you really are interested in a particular job. Generate energy and enthusiasm for yourself and the position.
- Try not to underestimate your abilities and what you have to contribute to an organization. Demonstrate your confidence in yourself by talking about your accomplishments in the past and what you could offer the company.

The Final Piece: Changing or Keeping Your Job ... the Key to Success for ISTJs

Now that you have a solid understanding of your type, you can see how your natural preferences make you better suited for certain kinds of jobs. You can also see how knowledge of your type-related strengths and blind spots can help you conduct a more successful job search. But as an ISTJ, you've already realized that you are not equally drawn to *every* career or field listed in the Popular Occupations section. The next and final step is to narrow down the field and find the work you were meant to do.

In addition to Type, several other factors—such as your values, interests, and skills—also contribute to your level of satisfaction on the job. The more compatible you are with your job, the happier you'll be. So prepare to use everything you've learned (in this book and in life) to create *your strategic career plan*. The exercises in Chapter 23, "Putting It All Together," are designed to help you do just that.

However, you may have decided it makes more sense (if perhaps only for the moment) to stay in your present job or with your current employer. There may be many valid reasons—financial pressures, family considerations, a tough job market for your specialty, or just bad timing. But take heart! What you've learned in this book can also help you be more content and successful *in your current job*. And should the time come when you're ready to make a major career move, you'll have a much better idea of where you want to go and how to get there.

"So, if you can't have the job you love (yet!)...love the one you've got."

The simple truth is, many jobs allow a good deal of flexibility in the way tasks are performed. Here are some ways you may be able to "massage" your current job into one that better fits your needs:

- Find an efficient assistant.
- Try to schedule work on one project at a time.
- Implement efficiency systems and require direct reports to use them.
- Try to attend fewer meetings.
- Seek other points of view to balance your own.
- Ask people chairing meetings for a written agenda prior to meetings.
- Figure out how to avoid being interrupted (consider schedule changes, erecting physical barriers, forwarding your calls, moving your office, etc.).

- Ask your supervisors to be more explicit about their expectations.
- Set up short-term goals.

One ISTJ turns lemons into lemonade:

Though her boss knew she was a very hard worker, Jess could never finish her paperwork because of interruptions from people in her small, overcrowded office. Since there was no quiet office space available, Jess suggested she change her hours, so that by arriving one hour earlier than the other staff, she could do her work uninterrupted. As a bonus, Jess's leaving an hour early each day helped her avoid rush-hour traffic and made the trip to pick up her son at his daycare center a much less anxious affair.

Use what you've got to get what you need.

Simply put, the best advice on how to succeed is to *capitalize on your strengths and compensate for your blind spots.* Learning how to do this can make the difference between succeeding or failing and loving or hating your work. To help you, we include the following inventory of your potential strengths and blind spots. And while every individual is unique, many of the following should apply to you as an ISTJ.

Your work-related strengths may include

- precision and accuracy and desire to get the job done right the first time
- readiness to follow established routines and policies
- ability to focus and concentrate on one task at a time in great depth
- ability to work alone
- sharp organizational skills
- thoroughness and close attention to the specifics: facts and details

- belief in the value of a traditional structure and the ability to work within it
- strong sense of responsibility; you can be counted on to do what you say
- clear work ethic; you feel it is important to be efficient and productive
- perseverance and determination to accomplish your goals
- common sense and a realistic perspective

Your work-related blind spots may include

- reluctance to embrace new, untested ideas

- discomfort with or resistance to change
- impatience with processes that take too long
- unwillingness to focus on future needs at the same time as present ones
- inflexibility; inability or unwillingness to adapt when necessary
- inability to focus on the big picture and see the implications of actions
- lack of sensitivity as to how people will be affected by policies and decisions
- reluctance to change direction and shift gears when warranted
- unwillingness to instigate or support needed change and calculated risks

---

Using your strengths is easy.
The secret to success for an
ISTJ
is learning to

be open to possibilities, consider
implications for people,
and embrace change.

17 | ESFJ
Extraverted, Sensing, Feeling, Judging
"What Can I Do for You?"

Profile 1: Kristin, Sales

"Building rapport with just about everybody!"

The Job

Kristin makes a great first impression. It's an important part of her job as a sales representative for a company selling dental equipment and products to dentists' offices. Her official title is senior territory manager, and she covers a territory that averages $1.3 million in gross sales annually. Kristin's job consists mainly of traveling around her territory of five counties, including upper Manhattan and Westchester, and either upgrading equipment or introducing new products that will help the practice become more efficient. She grows a great first impression into lasting relationships with offices across her territory.

Kristin's day-to-day involves taking her show on the road, so to speak. Since she covers such a broad territory, she must travel to offices far and wide. And when she shows up to her clients' offices, it's like returning home. Kristin makes it her business to know everyone and slips instantly into the warm rapport she's known for. She looks to outfit the offices with what they need, from routine products to a brand-new machine. Kristin has to stay up-to-date, on the cutting edge, and know her products backward and forward, down to the smallest detail. Much of her job includes educating office staff on new products, but the lion's share of what she does is building relationships. "It's basically my job to befriend offices."

Backstory

Kristin has always been an outgoing and vivacious person. A musical theater major in college, Kristin worked throughout school as a bank teller, moving from senior teller to merchant teller, as well as performing customer service. "I liked it because I wasn't sitting behind a desk. I was talking to people all day long—it was fun!" After college, Kristin decided the stage wasn't for her, but she wasn't sure which path she was meant to take.

She spotted a posting online for a position in business-to-business outside sales with a competitive salary and benefits. The job was attractive to Kristin because it would entail selling business services to other businesses, and doing it face-to-face. "I presented well," remembers Kristin. "I didn't have a lot of experience, but I had a really nice résumé and cover letter, and was articulate and organized in the interview." She aced it and soon was selling an automated payroll service to small businesses looking for an alternative to hiring their own bookkeeper or accountant.

Kristin continued in this job for two years, cutting her teeth learning sales and becoming the top representative in the region. Kristin felt as at home in sales as she had once felt on the stage, learning the "script" for a product and giving her pitch. "Everything else is shooting the breeze with the person you're with—chatting them up." She moved from that position to a job working as a premier client manager at a bank, a job she felt ill-suited for, but which ultimately got her to New York City. After two and a half years, Kristin was laid off when the bank merged and eliminated her division. "I was devastated at the time, but it turned out to be the best thing for me. I got to clear my mind and think, 'What do I really want to do? What is a job I would be proud to say I had, that I would want to wake up every morning and go do?'" Kristin realized she wanted to be back in an elite sales job. She met with recruiters and was interviewed and placed at her current company.

A Good Fit

Kristin's charisma makes her a natural at sales. "It's easy for me to build rapport. I can pretty quickly assess the energy someone is giving off to me, and I will match it." An Extravert and a dominant Feeling type, Kristin is warm and friendly, a self-described "open book," and genuinely enjoys meeting and building relationships with the many people she interacts with daily. "You have to be the kind of person who's willing to expose yourself a little in this job, especially when you're going into the same offices repeatedly. My offices know me. I'm a real person and they're real people, and we're not just robots having this mechanical dental conversation."

With Sensing as her auxiliary function, Kristin is adept at memorizing and conveying detailed information about her wide assortment of dental products. Like many Judgers, she gets a competitive thrill from the hunt—seeking, and especially closing, a deal—and it is gratifying to see her efforts correspond with the bump in commission.

Looking Ahead

Kristin enjoys her job and definitely wants to stick around for a while. "I consider myself a loyal person. This company has been good to me, and in return I want to be good to them." Farther down the line, in five to ten years, Kristin could see herself branching out into the medical industry. "I've always really wanted to be in surgical sales, in operating rooms doing orthopedic. Those are the really coveted and hard jobs to get. But I'd like to get to that level." As motivated and competitive with herself as she is, it's easy to see Kristin leveraging her success to reach the next plateau in her career.

Profile 2: Dennis, Police Officer

"Helping other people to do their jobs better and more safely."

The Job

Dennis is a patrolman for a suburban police department. He's happy as a patrolman but has lately been enjoying a new assignment: as an instructor in the training department. He likes the interaction, the variety, and the opportunity to give tangible and helpful information to his fellow officers, who are faced with the same dangers and challenges he knows firsthand.

Each week, Dennis works with a different group of police officers from his own department and other departments around the region, teaching a variety of courses that are mandated by the state governing board. The courses include everything from human relations and law updates to ongoing recertification of firearms proficiency or defensive-driving courses. Dennis is given criteria for what is to be covered but can develop his own lessons for how he chooses to teach the material. He writes and submits lesson plans, researches his subject matter, presents the training sessions, and documents each class member's participation for their personnel records.

Dennis also works a patrol shift, but these days it's only on an overtime, occasional-need basis. While he enjoys those responsibilities, he enjoys the break from the constant "condition yellow" required of a police officer on duty, especially at night. "You're not on *full* alert, but you're never relaxed, either. It's a situation where you're constantly scanning, staying ready for that radio call that may come at any time, and the uncertainty of what you may face. It's the anticipation that can be crazy."

Backstory

Dennis began his career as a police officer nearly thirteen years ago. In college, Dennis studied business administration, but then enlisted in the army and served with an army medevac. He continued in the army reserves for eight years while working as a mechanic in his cousin's shop. He enjoyed it for several years, and raced cars on

weekends. But he began to tire of the work and didn't see any growth or security in it.

At the same time, he became friendly with several town police officers, and they encouraged him to study for and take the various eligibility tests required. He did and then applied to several departments, finally accepting a position with a governor's special security detail. Again he enjoyed it for about five years, but began to feel stagnant and eager for more responsibility and challenge. So Dennis began applying again to town police departments and was hired in the town where he still works. A patrol officer for ten years, he became an instructor two and a half years ago.

A Good Fit

As a police officer, Dennis is charged with protecting the public. As a Traditionalist, he is well suited philosophically to perform the responsibilities assigned to him, such as serving society's needs and enforcing its rules. Dennis works in a highly structured organization with a clear reporting hierarchy and well-defined objectives. Hard work and adherence to established policy and procedure are expected and rewarded. What is additionally satisfying to Dennis is the fact that he works for a small town with many people who have the same backgrounds and values, all of which add to the sense of community.

Dennis likes being respected and appreciated by his peers for doing a good job. A dominant Feeler, he clearly follows his own values and ethics. People contact is important to him; in addition to teaching, Dennis also volunteers as a counselor in the employee assistance program in the department. "I enjoy the interaction with other people in a more personal capacity. I like helping people with their problems, so I also help coordinate some of the training from that department. I guess it's the communication I find the most energizing. Listening to people, acting as a sounding board, giving information in a way that doesn't offend or hurt anyone, are what I do best."

Dennis's auxiliary Sensing is critical since he must be alert to everything when he is on patrol at night and on weekends. He also uses his Sensing in his teaching and training of hands-on skills such as use of firearms and defensive driving. These are real-life skills learned and practiced in the field, not classroom courses involving theories. He also enjoys conducting research, gathering facts about new equipment, testing them out to be sure they will work in the field or within the department.

Looking Ahead

While Dennis is enjoying his current position, he is realistic enough to know there will be changes. He has decided to concentrate on preparing for the sergeant's exam next year and hopes to "make rank." "I think I'm a more analytical thinker when it comes to looking at work. I can see the cause and effect of decisions. I know, for example, that I don't want to be a detective, even though some people would say that's the direction I should be headed in. I've looked into it and can see that the disadvantages outweigh the advantages, for me. I have clearer and more focused goals than I ever had. I won't let my work interfere with my home life and the time I spend with my kids, now that they are getting older and are more able to do things with me."

Profile 3: Robin, Real Estate Agent

"Getting families settled during a highly stressful time."

The Job

One of the greatest sources of satisfaction in Robin's work as a real estate agent is best demonstrated through the example of her very first client. "These poor people had been through the wringer. They'd had a contract on their house and put a deposit on another house out of state when their agent let some important details slip and both deals fell apart. The people lost their deposit money and their buyer, too. They interviewed me and another agent with ten years' experience. When they chose me, I couldn't believe it. They told me it was my honesty and enthusiasm that persuaded them. Anyway, I sold their house in three days and four days after that had found them another great house to buy. When they had their first baby a few months after the move, I went to visit them in the hospital. It was so great to be able to really help these people during what was a terribly stressful time in their lives. I just loved the connection I made with these people. It was really rewarding."

There are countless details involved in making a deal and closing a sale. Robin does it all herself, from developing strategies for selling the house, writing a sales description, staffing the open house, arranging work with appraisers, inspectors, and lawyers, writing ads, to communicating all the changes and progress to her clients. Robin manages all the details in service of her bigger mission—helping families in times of great stress.

Backstory

Family has been a theme throughout Robin's career. She began with a degree in family relations and child development. Robin went to work for a social service agency as a social worker in the adoption department, and quickly became part of a team of professionals who developed a program to better care for babies with diverse needs. The program became a model for the rest of the state, and Robin became coordinator of adoption. "It was amazing that

I got the job as coordinator because I don't have a master's degree in social work. My experience compensated for my lack of formal education. I really enjoyed the work and found it deeply rewarding to help people become a family."

Robin left the agency to have her first child, and she stayed home to raise both children until they were in school, at which point she decided to go back to work. "But I was demanding; the job had to leave me totally flexible to be there whenever my kids needed me to be." Robin enlisted the help of a professional career counselor to help her identify options, but followed the advice of her friends and her own real estate agent, who had all told her she would be great in real estate. She took the course and exam to obtain her license and was soon offered a job at an agency. Robin took the job on the condition that she would still have the flexibility and freedom she needed.

A Good Fit

Working with people and helping them find homes is the part of Robin's job she enjoys most. "Helping people solve their problems is great, especially when it involves a critical life decision. It feels good to find a home for someone, just like it felt good to find a permanent home for a baby!" Task oriented and well organized like most Traditionalists, Robin likes that her clients can rely on her to come through in a pinch. She enjoys working hard for her clients, just as hard as she works for her family.

Robin loves becoming a part of people's lives and establishing relationships with new people. When she is relying on her Feeling she is at her best, making connections and creating harmony between parties. She particularly enjoys negotiating to help each side win something and feel good about their interaction. Strongly Extraverted, Robin enjoys the collegiality she shares with her

associates and the many other people she interacts with on a daily basis.

Her Sensing helps Robin keep track in her head of an enormous amount of detail. On a typical day, she may be in contact with lawyers, mortgage brokers, appraisers, inspectors—not to mention buyers and sellers—all who have important information that requires her attention. And often, she must coordinate the schedules of many different people to get the job done. Her Sensing also comes in handy in assessing how a house will show to the public and in gauging the reactions of potential buyers to the properties they are looking at.

Looking Ahead

In this second career, Robin feels she has achieved a great balance between work and life. She has also recently become more involved in local politics, the children's elementary school Parent Teacher Organization, and environmental and world peace organizations. "I write to my congressional representatives and become informed about a whole range of world issues."

In fact, these days Robin thinks more globally. "I would like to do something someday that has a bigger impact. But I know that's what I'm doing with my children, and the way I treat other people will ultimately have a bigger effect. It's the ripple effect, touching one person who touches another."

Common Threads

Although Robin, Dennis, and Kristin have different backgrounds, experiences, and careers, there are certain common threads woven through their stories. Their specific interests, abilities, and values may differ, but owing to their similar temperament values and the *same hierarchy* of their psychological functions, there are certain observations we can make about the needs of many ESFJs.

What follows is a list of the most important elements—the formula, if you will—for ESFJ satisfaction. Given the uniqueness of all individuals—even those who share a type—this list will not describe each ESFJ equally well. The important thing is that these ten elements, with varying degrees of intensity and in different orders of importance, identify what ESFJs need to be satisfied.

After you have reviewed this list, we recommend that you go back and prioritize the elements in order of *their importance to you*. When doing this, think of past work experiences as well as your present job, and what you found particularly satisfying or unsatisfying. Try to look for *themes* that run through several experiences, not just *events* that might be true for one work situation but not for another.

As an ESFJ, I define career satisfaction as doing work that

1. lets me establish and maintain warm and genuine interpersonal relationships with other people, working in real and tangible ways to improve their quality of life
2. has practical benefits for people and gives me time to learn and master necessary skills before using them
3. lets me exercise control, as I work with many people and help them work harmoniously toward a common goal
4. has clear expectations, and where the evaluation of my performance is judged on established and explicitly stated criteria
5. is done in a cooperative environment, free from conflicts and tension between co-workers, supervisors, clients, patients, and others
6. lets me make decisions and use efficient procedures to see that all the details of my projects are carried out to my specifications
7. gives me plenty of opportunities to interact with other people throughout the day and to be an integral part of the decision-making process
8. lets me organize my own work and that of those around me to ensure that things are run as smoothly and efficiently as possible
9. is done within a friendly environment where people express their appreciation for my accomplishments, where I feel approval and support, and where I consider my co-workers to be my friends
10. is done in a setting with existing structure, where the chain of command is known and understood, and where authority is respected

Popular Occupations for ESFJs

In listing occupations that are popular among ESFJs, it is important to note that there are successful people of all types in all occupations. However, the following are careers ESFJs may find particularly satisfying, and some of the reasons why. This is by no means a comprehensive listing, but it is included to suggest possibilities you may not have previously considered. Although all of these occupations offer the potential for career satisfaction, the future for some careers is anticipated to be greater than for others over the next several years.

HEALTHCARE
- Registered nurse
- Medical/dental assistant
- Speech-language pathologist/audiologist
- Exercise physiologist
- Family physician

- Dentist
- Dietitian/nutritionist
- Massage therapist
- Optometrist/optician
- Pharmacist/pharmacy technician
- Respiratory therapist
- Veterinarian
- Veterinary technologist/
technician
- Home health aide
- Primary care physician
- Physical therapist
- Home health social worker
- Personal fitness trainer
- Fitness instructor
- Hospice worker
- Recreational therapist
- Radiation therapist
- Healthcare administrator
- Chiropractor
- Corrective therapist
- Dental hygienist
- Dialysis technician

The attraction of the healthcare field to ESFJs is the ability to work directly with other people in a helping capacity. Whether as a physician, nurse, or other practitioner, ESFJs enjoy using acquired skills to help make the lives of their patients easier, less painful, or less traumatic. They excel in careers that require hands-on application of practical skills and adherence to standard operating procedures. These careers in healthcare also enable ESFJs to establish and maintain strong personal relationships with their patients and co-workers.

EDUCATION
- Elementary school teacher
- Special education teacher
- Early childhood educator
- Childcare provider
- Athletic coach
- Bilingual education teacher
- Nursing instructor
- Director of religious education
- School principal
- Wilderness adventure leader

ESFJs teach by personal involvement and example. The younger student and those with special needs are especially appealing to ESFJs, who find rewards in helping others by teaching them foundational skills. Working directly with young children appeals to the ESFJ's natural energy and enthusiasm.

There is often a great deal of structure and order within a school setting, an environment that many ESFJs find comfortable. Many ESFJs also enjoy being physically active and teaching others physical skills and the importance of working on a team.

SOCIAL SERVICE / COUNSELING
- Social worker
- Community welfare worker
- Volunteer coordinator
- Religious educator
- Counselor
- Minister/priest/rabbi/imam
- Employee assistance counselor
- Child welfare counselor
- Substance abuse counselor
- Social worker (elderly and child day care issues)
- Law clerk
- Legislative assistant
- Court clerk
- Court reporter
- Paralegal and legal assistant

ESFJs are strong supporters of their community and often volunteer their time to establish and maintain civic organizations. Therefore, they often experience satisfaction in careers where they do the same type of work. The personal connection of social work—helping individuals and families overcome problems and become productive members of society—is rewarding for many ESFJs. Their ease and facility in meeting people and speaking to groups makes community action jobs satisfying for some ESFJs. Counseling, religious education, and the ministry attract ESFJs who enjoy the commitment of helping others in very specific and profound ways. ESFJs tend to be traditional by nature, and enjoy working within the context of existing and valuable organizations to make their contribution.

BUSINESS
- Public relations account executive
- Loan officer and counselor
- Market research/focus group facilitator
- Office manager
- Retail owner/operator
- Management consultant: human resources/training
- Credit counselor
- Merchandise planner
- Customer service manager
- Health club manager
- Lodging owner/innkeeper
- Property manager: commercial/ residential
- Childcare center director
- Customer relations manager (technology)
- Advocate (technology)
- Food service manager
- Nursery and greenhouse manager
- Hotel and motel manager
- Real estate appraiser

The world of business provides ESFJs the opportunity to meet a lot of people and to work hard to achieve their goals. They enjoy the active and busy pace of many businesses and enjoy the customer or client contact. When the business is of a personal nature, such as real estate or personal banking, many ESFJs find success because they are motivated to establish positive relationships with others and then work vigorously to maintain those relationships.

Public relations and marketing require the excellent interpersonal and communication skills most ESFJs possess. Both careers require careful attention to details and follow-through on all project coordination. The organizational skills of the ESFJ are used extensively in these careers.

SALES / SERVICE
- Sales representative
- Insurance sales agent
- Insurance and benefits representative
- Flight attendant
- Customer service representative
- Funeral home director
- Hairdresser/cosmetologist
- Host/hostess
- Personal care aide
- Caterer
- Fundraiser
- Travel consultant
- Ecotourism specialist
- Real estate agent/broker
- Marketing executive: radio/TV/cable broadcast industry
- Interpreter/translator
- Genealogist
- Home healthcare sales
- Dental and medical sales
- Sports equipment/merchandise salesperson
- Insurance special agent
- Land leasing and development specialist

ESFJs often gravitate to the service industries primarily because of the ability to work directly with other people and provide services that help make an experience more enjoyable or less stressful. The job of customer service representative provides them an opportunity to do this. ESFJs are steadfast and dependable during difficult times, and often rise to the occasion to help take care of all details during a crisis.

ESFJs often enjoy the variety, travel, and interpersonal contact of being a flight attendant. Most are warm and gracious and make excellent hosts/hostesses in the restaurant or catering business. ESFJs generally enjoy and often excel in sales, especially with real and tangible products and in instances where they can use their interpersonal skills, their resourcefulness, and their sensitivity to the needs of others to develop and cultivate long-term relationships with their customers. Retail is an area of interest because it involves public contact and the ability to become well versed in the features and benefits of special products.

Remember, these are only some of the areas that provide satisfying expression for the unique natural talents of ESFJs.

Customizing Your Job Search

Knowing the particular strengths and blind spots of your type can afford you a tremendous advantage in your job search campaign. In all aspects of the process, from conducting research into available positions, identifying and contacting prospective employers, developing personal marketing tools such as résumés, arranging and conducting job interviews, and negotiating salaries to finally accepting a position, people will act true to their type. Being able to capitalize on your assets and compensate for your liabilities can make the difference between a successful and an unsuccessful job search.

The differences between types are sometimes subtle and other times dramatic. It is the subtle variations in advice we offer that make the real difference between success and failure in a job search. The concept of networking serves as a good example. Extraverts will naturally enjoy

networking and are advised to do so on a large scale, while Introverts find more limited and targeted networking, especially with people they already know, easier. Sensors tend to network with people in a defined scope, while Intuitives will go far and wide to find people often seemingly unrelated to their field of interest. Further, Feelers can often take networking personally and enjoy establishing warm rapport, while Thinkers will be more objective and detached in their style. Finally, Judgers tend to ask fewer and more structured questions during their networking, while Perceivers could ask questions of all sorts all day long! One valuable search technique, many ways to implement it.

Pathways to Success: Using Your Strengths

As we will detail in the following pages, your many interpersonal strengths and talents, as well as your great organizational skills, will enable you to implement an efficient job search. Beware of your tendency to be overwhelmed by the uncertainty of the process and become discouraged by rejection, even when it is not personal.

As an ESFJ, you will find that your most effective strategies build on your abilities to do the following:

Establish rapport with interviewers.

- Demonstrate to interviewers your ease at meeting new people and your ability to make others feel comfortable with you.
- Find a common interest, using your keen powers of observation and your ability to create a friendly atmosphere with others.

Nate was interviewing for a sales position at a health food distributor whose client base was small independently owned and operated health food stores. Nate was primarily interested in the job because, being a vegetarian himself, he wanted to use his sales experience selling something he believed in. While driving into the parking lot, Nate saw a woman get out of her car and enter the building. He noticed her car because of its "I Love Labrador Retrievers" bumper sticker. When he was escorted into the interviewer's office, he recognized her as the woman who owned the car with the bumper sticker. He immediately asked if she owned a dog. She seemed surprised that he knew until he mentioned the bumper sticker and offered the information that he and his wife also owned a Lab. They talked for several minutes about the joys and chaos of owning that breed of dog. The interview went exceptionally well because Nate had made the effort to let his interviewer get to know him as a person.

Conduct informational interviews.

- Interview people in the careers that interest you to get a better understanding of what the job entails.
- Expand your existing network of friends and associates by asking people you meet to refer you to others who might know of positions you are qualified for.

During Ally's search for a career in social work, she called on everyone she knew. She started with her friends and family and expanded her list to include old college professors and even her childhood piano teacher. She rekindled relationships and obtained references from past employers and her minister to detail her involvement with community projects and to testify to her interpersonal skills. In all, she met, spoke to, or emailed nearly fifty people. All were eager to help her. When Ally was hired as a case

manager for a health and nutrition program for pregnant inner-city teens, she traced her path to that specific job through eight people and over sixteen years of contacts.

Conduct an organized, well-planned job search.

- Develop a timetable and budget for your job search, including any costs and how long you anticipate it will take. Set aside time each day, and keep a record of whom you have contacted and the status of each possibility.
- Demonstrate what type of employee you will be, using your job search as an example. Use your excellent organizational skills by creating an easy-to-read, well-designed résumé and cover letter. Be on time for interviews and follow up afterward.

Jessica took on her job search the same way she took on every job she had ever had. She was enthusiastic, thorough, and precise in preparing her marketing materials and stayed on top of every detail. She impressed interviewers with her organization and communication skills and always followed up informational interviews with thank-you emails. The only problem she faced was that she was offered two equally good opportunities on two successive days. She ultimately made her decision based on which job would let her utilize the same skills she used in her job search, this time on a daily basis.

Sell yourself as a team player who will work hard to reach the goals of the organization.

- Emphasize your experience working with a diverse group of individuals in one organization or during your career, providing examples of situations that challenged and utilized those skills and abilities.

- Learn as much as you can about the organization's or company's "personality" by reading about principals and recent events within the company. Read online and talk to people who know firsthand about the company before going into the interview.

Through Juan's career counseling, he had set his sights on working in property management. But he also learned from his research and informational interviews that some developers used approaches and tactics in business that went against his personal code of ethics. He was still sure that property management was what he wanted to do, so he set out to find a company he would feel comfortable being a part of. His search ultimately led him to a family-owned developer. He talked at length with the firm's president about the company's goals and philosophy until he felt sure that he would feel proud representing the firm. Interestingly, he was later told that it was his concern and refusal to sell out his principles that landed him the job, because he was seen as someone the president could easily trust and depend on.

Make decisions.

- Once you decide that you are interested in a position, act on it to minimize the risk of the opportunity slipping away.
- Eliminate unfeasible or less attractive options along the way so you can keep your focus on your goals. Remain realistic about your skills, interests, and needs so you aren't easily swayed by jobs that may tempt you with their excitement and glamour but won't provide the security or stability you seek.

While Dennis always enjoyed the excitement of racing competitively, he ruled it out as a realistic career because it would not provide the long-term job security or consistent income he needed once he married and had a family. He still keeps his interest in cars by working on them in his spare time and occasionally races on the weekends. Even though the opportunity to race professionally presented itself, his decision to become a police officer has proved to be in his long-term best interest.

Possible Pitfalls

Although all people are unique, there are certain *potential* blind spots that many ESFJs share. We underscore "potential" because some of the following *may* be true of you, while others may clearly not apply. While considering them, you may notice that these tendencies do not relate just to the job search but rather describe pitfalls that you may have experienced in other aspects of your life as well. It is therefore helpful to consider each one in terms of your past experiences by asking yourself, "Is this true for me?" And if so, "How did this tendency prevent me from getting something that I wanted?" You will probably notice that the key to overcoming your blind spots is the conscious and thoughtful development of your third and fourth functions (Intuition and Thinking). We recognize that many of the suggestions will be difficult to implement, but the more you use these functions, the fewer problems they will cause you in the future.

Avoid the tendency to burn your bridges once you think you've crossed them.

- Try not to view situations or job options as either all good or all bad. Look for the gray area that exists in most things. Sometimes trade-offs must be made.

- Take time to reflect on your options. Don't run the risk of making decisions too hastily before you have had a chance to gather all the information you can.

Try not to become easily discouraged.

- Accept constructive criticism in the spirit in which it is intended, and try not to take it personally.
- Seek out support and encouragement from friends during the sometimes trying job search process. Look for assistance from other people who are also going through or have recently gone through their own job search.

Gather more objective criteria for decisions rather than relying exclusively on your personal feelings.

- Take a step back from the situation to enable yourself to look at it more objectively. Resist the urge to base your opinions of a job on your like or dislike for the person conducting the interview.
- Ask yourself what the possible and logical consequences are of taking a job or embarking on a course of action.

Adjust your focus to more long-range career planning.

- Create a set of goals for one, five, and ten years from now. When considering potential careers or jobs, check them against this list to see if they will help move you toward your goals.
- Resist the tendency to take stopgap jobs because you are beginning to feel overwhelmed or uncertain about your security. Try not to compromise by taking jobs that will not provide satisfaction in the long run.

Look for career opportunities beyond what is already known.

- Ask yourself "What else?" when generating a list of possible jobs or careers. Consider less traditional approaches or settings if other important criteria exist. If needed, get help in brainstorming positions from friends (especially Intuitives) who know you well.
- Look for ways to demonstrate or explain how your skills are transferable from one work situation to another.

The Final Piece: Changing or Keeping Your Job . . . the Key to Success for ESFJs

Now that you have a solid understanding of your type, you can see how your natural preferences make you better suited for certain kinds of jobs. You can also see how knowledge of your type-related strengths and blind spots can help you conduct a more successful job search. But as an ESFJ, you've already realized that you are not equally drawn to *every* career or field listed in the Popular Occupations section. The next and final step is to narrow down the field and find the work you were meant to do.

In addition to Type, several other factors—such as your values, interests, and skills—contribute to your level of satisfaction on the job. The more compatible you are with your job, the happier you'll be. So prepare to use everything you've learned (in this book and in life) to create *your strategic career plan*. The exercises in Chapter 23, "Putting It All Together," are designed to help you do just that.

However, you may have decided it makes more sense (if perhaps only for the moment) to stay in your present job or with your current employer. There may be many valid reasons—financial pressures, family considerations, a tough job market for your specialty, or just bad timing. But take heart! What you've learned in this book can also help you be more content and successful *in your current job.* And should the time come when you're ready to make a major career move, you'll have a much better idea of where you want to go and how to get there.

"So, if you can't have the job you love (yet!) . . . love the one you've got."

The simple truth is, many jobs allow a good deal of flexibility in the way tasks are performed. Here are some ways you may be able to "massage" your current job into one that better fits your needs:

- Ask your boss to be clear about performance expectations.
- Work to resolve conflicts with co-workers, supervisors, direct reports.
- Leave environments where there is great interpersonal tension.
- Volunteer for a meaningful cause either inside or outside your organization.
- Make sure you have enough social stimulation during the day.
- Implement efficiency systems and require direct reports to use them.
- If not a manager, identify a project you think needs doing and volunteer to take it on.
- Find people with complementary strengths to give you input and balance.
- Set up short-term goals that you can meet.

One ESFJ turns lemons into lemonade:

Jacqueline liked her job and company but felt somewhat unfulfilled. So, at a friend's urging, she volunteered to head up the annual United Way campaign. Because she was so organized and genuine, her hard work paid off and her company exceeded its contributions goal by 20 percent. Jacqueline got a great deal of gratification from doing something practical for a charity that would ultimately help thousands of people.

Use what you've got to get what you need.

Simply put, the best advice on how to succeed is to *capitalize on your strengths and compensate for your blind spots.* Learning how to do this can make the difference between succeeding or failing and loving or hating your work. To help you, we include the following inventory of your potential strengths and blind spots. And while every individual is unique, many of the following should apply to you as an ESFJ.

Your work-related strengths may include

- great energy and drive to get things accomplished and be productive
- ability to cooperate and create harmonious relationships with others
- practical and realistic attitude and aptitude for working with facts and details
- nurturing and helpful nature; you praise and reinforce good behavior in others
- decisiveness and stabilizing factor
- ability to maintain an organization's traditions
- strong organizational skills and clear work ethic
- loyalty and belief in the value of working within a traditional structure
- sense of responsibility; you can be counted on to do what you say you will do
- ability to follow established routines and procedures
- common sense and realistic perspective

Your work-related blind spots may include

- reluctance to embrace new and untested ideas
- sensitivity to criticism; you feel stressed by tension-filled work situations
- desire to focus on the present rather than the future
- difficulty adapting to change and switching gears quickly
- tendency to be oversensitive and avoid unpleasant situations
- difficulty working alone for extended periods of time; strong need to socialize
- may sometimes show favoritism

- tendency to become drained by taking on others' emotional burdens
- inclination to make decisions prematurely before you have enough information
- focus on specific details rather than implications and the "big picture"
- can be opinionated and rigid
- difficulty hearing and accepting opposing viewpoints
- tendency to become discouraged without praise or expression of appreciation
- difficulty focusing on future needs as opposed to present ones

---

Using your strengths is easy.
The secret to success for an
ESFJ
is learning to

slow down, consider possibilities that don't already exist, and not take things quite so personally.

18 ‖ ISFJ Introverted, Sensing, Feeling, Judging

"On My Honor, to Do My Duty..."

Profile 1: Erin, Registered Nurse

"Helping women through a rite of passage."

The Job

Erin is an advocate, a guide, and a close and tireless monitor. She does all this and more in her job as a labor and delivery nurse, working with women to bring healthy babies into the world. Tasked with all the physical, social, and emotional parts of a woman's birth experience, Erin must be fully present to each moment, while also making sure absolutely nothing slips. The stakes couldn't be higher.

Erin's daily responsibilities fall to monitoring both the well-being of the women and the babies during labor, checking vital signs, administering medications, and helping women physically and emotionally cope during one of the most intense experiences of their lives. She also advocates for patients, serving as a resource and enabling women to actively take part in decisions about their care. "If a woman wants an epidural, I help her understand— what are the risks, what are the benefits, when will it happen—and help her through it. All these choices are happening all the time, and you're the emotional and physical guide through that process." Erin also must communicate with doctors and midwives, and make sure to chart and record absolutely every detail of a birth for legal posterity. "You can't miss a thing."

Backstory

If you had asked Erin in high school what she wanted to be, she would have told you without hesitation: an OB/GYN doctor. "I went to college thinking, 'This is it—I know what I want to do and I'm going to do it!'" But during a summer program in New York City, everything changed. Shadowing OB/ GYN doctors, Erin had "the first inkling that maybe it wasn't what I thought it was going to be. I had envisioned helping women through this rite of passage and being with them the whole time." But the doctors she

241

shadowed seemed to spend more time diagnosing and less time one-on-one with patients.

Back at school, Erin learned about nursing and found that it answered most of her concerns and desires to be in medicine but still serve the emotional and social needs of women. "What has drawn me to medicine in general is being there for and supporting people, and really what I've learned is, that's more the role of nursing. Doctors do a lot of diagnosing and problem solving and figuring things out. Nursing is definitely more holistic—you treat a person as a whole person and not just as the problem that's happening at the time." She changed her path to get an accelerated degree in nursing.

Unable to find a coveted labor and delivery position right after graduation, Erin found a position nursing on a post-surgical floor for gastrointestinal and transplant patients. Her years on the floor were not easy. She had many patients at once, and it felt like she never had enough time to really care for each individual one. "I could only do the tasks—I couldn't address what needed to be addressed emotionally and socially with patients and families."

After two years of watching religiously any openings posted for the labor and delivery floor, Erin finally had her chance. She made sure to personally email the manager as well as apply online, and was thrilled to move to the L&D floor. Erin worked for two and a half years at that hospital, and then a personal move brought her to the same role at a new hospital, where she's worked for the past several years. "I really like being able to focus on one patient, one family, through their experience, rather than being torn in many directions."

A Good Fit

Like many Traditionalists, Erin is service oriented and driven to contribute

meaningfully to society. Her dominant function is Sensing—a function that, in nursing, is constantly in use. In fact, noticing details can be a matter of life and death. "A delivery can go very quickly from being normal to being an emergency situation, and you have to be alert at all times and pay attention to so many details." Erin is adept at picking up and learning routines, and the set number of tasks is comforting to her. She is able to face a new situation by visualizing a series of steps she needs to know, and once she learns them, she feels confident and capable. An organized Judger, Erin is well suited to the procedure-driven world of a hospital.

Erin's auxiliary function of Feeling is very important in her job as a nurse, since she spends so much of her time in the "super emotionally charged situation" of labor and delivery. She is compassionate and empathetic, qualities that the best nurses utilize to put patients at ease. Erin's Feeling function also helps her to anticipate her patients' needs and allows her to be able to support them emotionally as well as physically.

Looking Ahead

For Erin, a dream job looks like finding herself working as a labor and delivery nurse in a hospital that better centers women's experiences, where she feels more closely aligned with the values of the institution. This could mean more midwives and birthing options, including less conventional setups such as birthing tubs, and more people like doulas, or birth coaches, involved in the process. She is also happiest when the nurse-to-patient ratio is as close to 1:1 as possible. In her current hospital, the ratio can be higher depending on the day, staffing, and budgetary concerns.

Overall, the health of the institution, the support for the staff and employees, and the atmosphere of respect and choice have the highest bearing on Erin's happiness at work. The more of these elements she has in place, the better.

Profile 2: Benjamin, Accountant

"Assisting organizations in meeting their missions."

The Job

Since college, Benjamin knew he would become an accountant, but until recently, that career left him dangerously stressed, guilty about the lack of family time he had at the end of a crazy day, and completely overworked during the tax season. He decided to change all that and now has found a truly satisfying career as a sole practitioner CPA, working exclusively for nonprofit organizations.

Today, Benjamin conducts audits of nonprofit organizations. His clients include a private school, a battered women's shelter, a family planning center, an adoption agency, a library system, and a host of other social service organizations. He reviews their financial statements before attaching his authorization that the statement is fairly presented. Once an audit is completed, Benjamin presents the final financial statement to the organization's executive director or to its board of directors.

Being a part of human service organizations is one of the things Benjamin likes best about his career. "These are really good people, doing really good work trying to improve the community. Their goal isn't making a huge profit but satisfying their mission, which is helping others. I enjoy being associated with them."

Backstory

After serving in the army reserves, Benjamin began his accounting career in a series of firms, always moving from larger to smaller in size. His first job was as one of one hundred staff accountants at a large firm. After one year, he moved to a midsize firm with fifteen other accountants. Next he became one of four CPAs at a small firm. Each move allowed him to attain increased client contact and responsibility. But all of the jobs required primarily the "ticking and tracing" process and limited contact with the client.

"Finally I decided to go out on my own. I wanted the control and freedom and the opportunity to deal directly with the clients. So I started out alone and built my practice over ten years to where I had two other CPAs working with me and a support staff. I'm really very proud of the fact I did it all on my own."

But over those ten years, Benjamin was experiencing too much of the stress and strain of the tax business. "The change came to me slowly. I was going nuts with the traditional individual and corporate tax practice. I searched my mind for a way to get out of the stressful hole I was in. I was making lots of money but the rest of my life suffered. My health was in jeopardy, and I never stopped thinking about work. I brought work home, and it interfered with my family and my personal interests. I had to make a change, so I sold the part of the practice that I didn't like and held on to and expanded the part I did like." He located another person who was interested in buying an established accounting practice. "I was really lucky to find the right person who wanted to take over the tax end of my business. This person moved in to share the office space, took over responsibility for the employees, bought the furniture, and handled the clients. I kept the part of the practice I enjoyed and built it up to where I have the volume I can handle and not have it run my life."

A Good Fit

These days Benjamin is focused on contributing to society on a daily basis by helping organizations meet their missions. Career satisfaction for Benjamin is working with decent people, attempting to give something back to society while keeping his priorities in order.

In many ways, Benjamin is becoming less ambitious than he used to be. He used to think it was important to own a big practice with a lot of people working for him. "Now I understand that all equals stress for me. Instead I'm more concerned with maintaining my business so I can keep my family in focus. I used to never be able to say no, even to people who walked in my door on March fifteenth looking for preparation of their tax returns. I used to say yes to people I now will not. I won't deal with unscrupulous people. I'm just more selective."

Profile 3: Charlotte, Special Education Supervisor

"Making a dent in the world in a positive way."

The Job

Charlotte may have a slightly unusual job for an ISFJ. She is the supervisor of special education for a small suburban town, a position she really enjoys. What's unusual is that Charlotte spends huge amounts of time working with many other people, traveling around the town to attend meetings with some of the thirty-five professionals she supervises, and visiting the off-school sites where forty students are placed. It's a job that demands volumes of communication and perpetual meetings with parents,

teachers, other educational professionals, and school administrators—none of which is usually enjoyed by ISFJs. But it's work that matters, and Charlotte has loved special education all her adult life.

Charlotte spends about 70 percent of her time in the field, meeting with teachers and special education professionals, including school psychologists, speech pathologists, teachers of English Language Learners, and—the bulk of her work—teachers of special education. Besides handling budgeting, hiring, and the other more routine administrative functions required of a supervisor, Charlotte has the responsibility of ensuring that the school district complies with all state and federal mandates requiring that free and appropriate education be provided to children of all abilities. She appraises students by observing them in the classroom, meets with parents to help them understand their child's differences, and participates in formal diagnostic and placement conferences with teachers, parents, and other necessary professionals. She stays visible and accessible. Even when she's back in her office, she is barraged by calls and emails from parents and teachers looking for advice, direction, or resources.

What Charlotte enjoys most about her work is helping people. She likes being supportive and gets great satisfaction from "watching things happen—positive things, changes for the better." She is energized by the relationships she develops with parents, teachers, and administrators. "I just love seeing things through, making something that we knew would be a change for the better into a reality. For example, when one school really needed a staff psychologist, I did what it took to get the position filled. Today, it's so rewarding to see that person in place and really helping make the school work better."

Backstory

Charlotte is currently celebrating twenty-two years in the field of education. She's proud that she's not burned out, like so many of the educators she has known over the years. She attributes that to the fact that special education is something of a calling for her.

Charlotte started out teaching special education in elementary schools for nine years, all ages and exceptionalities. She moved to a self-contained classroom after running a resource room, because it provided more control and independence. Looking for added responsibility, she started a diagnostic center within the school system. "It was a unique approach because we did testing and diagnostics and still taught in the same setting. I enjoyed it more because it was professionally challenging, and I was part of a small team of really good people."

After five years, she sought a more demanding job and became an administrator within the system. "One of the best parts of the job was training student teachers. That's where I realized I could have greater impact if I was helping teachers, because they would each be touching so many lives." After nine years, she began to hear from colleagues in smaller school districts that they had more responsibility and control in their jobs than she did in hers working for a large city. "I wanted more involvement in the big decisions affecting the children, so I began to apply for openings in the suburbs. It took four tries before I got this job. I had the practical experience but lacked the Ph.D. other candidates had. Then this opportunity came along in a small, very closely knit community. Parental support and involvement are tremendous here." Now, instead of having a positive impact on a class of twelve or fifteen, she's able to have a greater impact on teachers, student teachers, parents, and the students themselves.

A Good Fit

Charlotte has spent her life working in education—an environment that many Traditionalists find satisfying. She works in a highly structured, traditional organization with a clear mission—to oversee special education for a school system. Charlotte's in the business of helping both students and teachers get their needs met. Much of what she does involves complying with federal mandates and state regulations, and making sure that certain procedures are followed. Practically all the tasks she engages with are ones to which Traditionalists are particularly well suited.

Charlotte's dominant Sensing function helps her store the tremendous amount of information required to help match students with the most appropriate services. Collecting and disseminating information is an important part of her job, and she draws on her own personal, real-life teaching experience to guide her. Attention to details such as budgeting, hiring, and completing administrative tasks makes good use of her Sensing, as do observing and evaluating students in the classroom setting.

Another satisfying aspect of Charlotte's job is the opportunity it affords her to relate to many different people. She uses her Feeling with the students, parents, teachers, and administrators with whom she interacts frequently. She's sensitive, able to read people, and able to tell them how to become more effective. She's tactful and likes to help others become part of decisions. Charlotte also shows her Feeling when promoting her strong values concerning how to improve the school, make it work better, and make people happier. And she enjoys the frequent collaboration she creates between parents, teachers, and herself in an effort to help a really challenging child.

Looking Ahead

At this point Charlotte doesn't imagine changing jobs for some time. "I need to master all the skills I can before I feel ready to go after another challenge. Perhaps someday I'll apply for a principal's position in an elementary school. But for now, my goal is to be the best special education director in the whole state. When I do that to my satisfaction, I may go on to something else. And I may not."

Common Threads

Although Charlotte, Benjamin, and Erin have different backgrounds, experiences, and careers, there are certain common threads woven through their stories. Their specific interests and abilities may differ, but owing to their similar temperament values and the *same hierarchy* of their psychological functions, there are certain observations we can make about the needs of many ISFJs.

What follows is a list of the most important elements—the formula, if you will, for ISFJ satisfaction. Given the uniqueness of all individuals—even those who share a type—this list will not describe each ISFJ equally well. The important thing is that these ten elements, with varying degrees of intensity and in different orders of importance, identify what ISFJs need to be satisfied.

After you have reviewed this list, we recommend that you go back and prioritize the elements in order of *their importance to you*. When doing this, think of past work experiences as well as your present job, and what you found particularly satisfying or unsatisfying. Try to look for *themes* that run

through several experiences, not just *events* that might be true for one work situation but not for another.

As an ISFJ, I define career satisfaction as doing work that

1. requires careful observation and meticulous accuracy, where I can use my ability to remember facts and routines
2. lets me work on tangible projects that help other people, often requiring great attention to detail
3. lets me express my compassion and devotion by working hard behind the scenes, but where my contributions are recognized and appreciated
4. is done in a traditional, stable, orderly, and structured environment, where the results are practical and service oriented
5. requires that I adhere to standard procedures, use practical judgment, and follow through in a careful, organized way
6. lets me focus all my energy on one project or one person at a time, working on products or services that have observable end results
7. gives me a private work space so I can concentrate fully for extended periods of time and with a minimum of interruptions
8. lets me work primarily one-on-one, helping others, or with other people who share my personal values and beliefs
9. requires me to be organized and efficient in completing my assignments
10. does not require too frequently that I present my work in front of groups of people without having adequate time to prepare well in advance

Popular Occupations for ISFJs

In listing occupations that are popular among ISFJs, it is important to note that there are successful people of all types in all occupations. However, the following are careers ISFJs may find particularly satisfying, and some of the reasons why. This is by no means a comprehensive listing but is included to suggest possibilities you may not have previously considered. Although all of these occupations offer the potential for career satisfaction, the future demand for some careers is anticipated to be greater than for others.

HEALTHCARE
- Registered nurse
- Dental hygienist
- Family physician
- Medical technologist
- Physical therapist
- Medical equipment sales representative
- Healthcare administrator
- Dietitian/nutritionist
- Speech and language pathologist/audiologist
- Optician
- Medical records technician
- Pharmacist/pharmacy technician
- Radiological technician
- Respiratory therapist
- Veterinarian
- Veterinary technologist/technician
- Primary care physician
- Home health aide
- Medical/dental assistant
- Pharmaceuticals salesperson
- Hospice worker
- Medical researcher
- Biologist
- Botanist
- Dentist
- Orthodontist
- Occupational therapist
- Biochemist
- Massage therapist
- Surgical technologist/technician
- Dental laboratory technician
- Corrective therapist
- Dialysis technician

These occupations allow ISFJs to work in a field in which their contributions have a personal and direct impact on others. Many of these occupations require hands-on and one-on-one interaction with clients and patients. ISFJs like to be able to help others in real and practical ways. Many of these positions allow the ISFJ to work relatively independently within a traditional and organized culture. The field of medicine makes good use of ISFJs' ability to learn and practice technical skills, and gives them the chance to establish personal connections with other people.

SOCIAL SERVICE / EDUCATION
- Preschool teacher
- Librarian/archivist
- Social worker
- Personal counselor
- Probation officer
- Home health social worker
- Child welfare counselor
- Substance abuse counselor
- Social worker
- Personal care aide
- Elementary school teacher
- Special education teacher
- Curator
- Educational administrator
- Guidance counselor
- Religious educator
- Eldercare specialist
- Vocational rehabilitation counselor
- Historian
- Athletic trainer
- Residence counselor

Education is a field frequently of interest to ISFJs because it allows them to help other people and make a contribution to society. ISFJs often enjoy teaching elementary school because of the personal interaction with students and the ability to teach foundational skills. Many ISFJs enjoy careers in educational administration, especially when they are responsible for a specific area of specialty (for example, special education) or a relatively small service area (one town rather than a large city school system). ISFJs enjoy working independently but within an organization where they are appreciated for their contribution and know what is expected of them.

The field of research offers satisfaction for ISFJs because it allows them to work independently and follow through on specific tasks of investigation. Curators are required to create and maintain complete and accurate records, which lets them use their organizational and factual recall skills.

While often personally challenging, the field of social work often provides great satisfaction for ISFJs. ISFJs find the contribution they make rewarding because they are able to help clients make practical and tangible improvements in their lives. These occupations offer the same opportunities for one-on-one interaction and independent working environments, all of interest to an ISFJ.

BUSINESS / SERVICE
- Administrative assistant
- Clerical supervisor
- Customer service representative
- Personnel administrator
- Real estate agent/broker
- Bookkeeper
- Credit counselor
- Paralegal
- Home healthcare salesperson

- Lawn service manager
- Organic farmer
- Tech support agent
- Fish and game warden
- Horticultural specialty grower
- Franchise owner
- Retail owner
- Merchandise planner
- Police identification and records specialist
- Museum research worker
- Funeral director
- Grant coordinator
- Preferred customer sales representative
- Bed and breakfast proprietor
- Title examiner and abstractor

These careers require a great deal of interaction with people on a one-on-one basis and are often enjoyed by ISFJs. Many are support positions, which enable ISFJs to use skills in organization and follow-through of important details, especially when working in support of someone they respect and admire. These positions also require knowledge and use of both technical and communication skills to help others get the information or assistance they need.

Retail sales and merchandising are careers often enjoyed by ISFJs, especially when they are able to work in either a small specialty shop or one department of a larger store. ISFJs often make good owners of boutiques. Their attention to the details of how their shop looks and feels to customers often wins them longstanding repeat business. They enjoy spending time with one customer at a time, finding just the right item or accessory to work with what the customer already has. ISFJs are also good at following through and maintaining relationships with customers, and treat staff with kindness and loyalty.

CREATIVE / TECHNICAL
- Interior decorator
- Electrician

- Artist
- Musician
- Jeweler
- Stringed instrument repairer

These careers are not necessarily related to one another, but have some common characteristics and requirements. Each requires the person to work with real things that have to do with daily living. As an interior decorator, the ISFJ uses his or her aesthetic sense to find the right decor for the client. The job requires attention to detail and a strong ability to work with another toward satisfying that client's needs and wishes in his or her home. ISFJs usually place great importance on the way their own home is decorated and can easily understand and relate to the desires of their clients to create homes that are comfortable for them.

An electrician is responsible for technical accuracy and adherence to standard procedures and codes. ISFJs enjoy focusing their attention on tasks that require hands-on work and enjoy using skills they have mastered. If the ISFJ feels their contributions are valued and appreciated and if they have quality interaction with either the customer, partner, or co-workers, the job of an electrician can be satisfying.

Remember, these are only some of the areas that provide satisfying expression for the unique natural talents of ISFJs.

Customizing Your Job Search

Knowing the particular strengths and blind spots of your type can afford you a tremendous advantage in your job search campaign. In all aspects of the process, from conducting research into available positions, identifying and contacting prospective employers, developing personal marketing tools such as résumés, arranging and conducting job interviews, and negotiating salaries to finally accepting a position, people will act true to their type. Being able to capitalize on your assets and compensate for your liabilities can make the difference between a successful and an unsuccessful job search.

The differences between types are sometimes subtle and other times dramatic. It is the subtle variations in advice we offer that make the real difference between success and failure in a job search. The concept of networking serves as a good example. Extraverts will naturally enjoy networking and are advised to do so on a large scale, while Introverts find more limited and targeted networking, especially with people they already know, easier. Sensors tend to network with people in a defined scope, while Intuitives will go far and wide to find people often seemingly unrelated to their field of interest. Further, Feelers can often take networking personally and enjoy establishing warm rapport, while Thinkers will be more objective and detached in their style. Finally, Judgers tend to ask fewer and more structured questions during their networking, while Perceivers could ask questions of all sorts all day long! One valuable search technique, many ways to implement it.

Pathways to Success: Using Your Strengths

As we will detail in the following pages, your strengths and talents for the job search lie in your ability to demonstrate your efficiency, sincerity, and desire to work hard. However, your job search might become stalled if you fail to see workable alternatives, or derailed when you take rejection too personally.

As an ISFJ, you will find that your most effective strategies build on your abilities to do the following:

Research opportunities thoroughly, collecting all relevant facts.

- Use all resources available to you to find out as much as you can about the company, industry, or position you are considering.
- Spend the amount of time necessary until you are comfortable with your knowledge base before proceeding to the interview stage.

When Charlotte was beginning to consider a career change, she was counseled by several colleagues in other school districts to look at a smaller school system to get the added responsibility she was looking for. She fully researched the town she works in now to find out about the level of parental and town support for the special education program before even applying for the position. Because she knew those elements were critical to her satisfaction in the job and her ability to do her job well, she talked with parents, teachers, and other administrators to get a feeling for the emotional climate of the town.

Make thoughtful decisions based on practical considerations.

- Establish a list of criteria and refer to it frequently during the job search process, comparing potential job opportunities against it.
- Try to be objective during the decision-making process so as to remain pragmatic and realistic about what a possible job will really be like, not just how you wish it might be.

Benjamin made a major career change to working with not-for-profits after determining that his personal and professional life were equally important to him. He wanted more time to spend with his family and with his hobbies outside of work. He weighed the pros and cons of the change

and decided, after careful consideration, that the change would afford him the more relaxed and peaceful lifestyle he wanted, while still using his skills and experience in accounting.

Conduct an organized, well-planned job search.

- Prepare résumés with individualized cover letters to address your specific interests and qualifications for the job in question. Follow up to secure an appointment rather than waiting for a potential employer to contact you.
- Stay in touch with people who have given you time or an interview. Write them thank-you emails and send them a notification when you find the right job.

While researching the personnel department of a large department store, Layla decided she would apply for a customer service representative position. She found out the manager's name and title and sent an email highlighting her experience and her interest in the company. After several email exchanges, she secured an appointment and interviewed with the manager. There was no position available at the time, so Layla continued to search while staying in contact with the manager. One day Layla read an article online about a new preferred-customer tracking system being developed for use in retail. She emailed the article with a brief note to the manager. A few days later, she was called in for a second interview, and later offered a job. The manager told her that her perseverance had won the job for her over candidates with more experience.

Capitalize on your solid, stable, dependable work experience.

- Provide prospective employers with several examples of past successes,

including any citations, awards, or letters of recommendation.
- Demonstrate your consistency in meeting job requirements and reaching organizational goals.

Jeremy was a biology teacher at a college and an active faculty adviser to students. He had always been particularly interested in the problem of student attrition (students leaving the college before graduation). Over the many years of his tenure, he kept his own careful records of student attrition, which he collected from interviews with his own students, the college counseling center, and other faculty advisers.

When the associate dean of students position became available, Jeremy was interested. He might not ordinarily have been considered a likely candidate, but he took all the information he had collected over the years and compiled it into a report. He met with the dean of students and shared his observations. His self-acquired (but acknowledged as such) expertise in the area of student trends, combined with his reputation as a caring and popular student adviser, helped move him into the front-runner's position for the job.

Possible Pitfalls

Although all people are unique, there are certain *potential* blind spots that many ISFJs share. We underscore "potential" because some of the following *may* be true of you, while others may clearly not apply. While considering them, you may notice that these tendencies do not relate just to the job search but rather describe pitfalls that you may have experienced in other aspects of your life as well. It is therefore helpful to consider each one in terms of your past experiences by asking yourself, "Is this true for me?" And if so, "How did this tendency prevent me from

getting something that I wanted?" You will probably notice that the key to overcoming your blind spots is the conscious and thoughtful development of your third and fourth functions (Thinking and Intuition). We recognize that many of the suggestions will be difficult to implement, but the more you use these functions, the fewer problems they will cause you in the future.

Look for and stay open to considering possibilities that do not currently exist.

- Engage in the sometimes difficult exercise of brainstorming: generating lists of possibilities while resisting the urge to eliminate the seemingly impossible ones. Keep all ideas until you have generated a lengthy list. Consider each and ask yourself "Why not?" several times before discarding it as a viable option. You may want to call on the help of friends for whom brainstorming comes more naturally.
- Ask other people currently enjoying jobs you may wish to consider how they went about getting trained for the job or obtaining an interview. Consider less traditional or unconventional approaches.

Be aggressive, or at least assertive, when planning and implementing your job search.

- Realize that the adage "the squeaky wheel gets the grease" is often true, especially in the competitive world of employment.
- Use all your excellent organizational and follow-through skills to stay on top of all opportunities. Follow up appointments with communication to remind the prospective employer of your continued interest in the position. Contact old friends and business associates and ask them to help you

develop a list of potential people to add to your network. And most important, ask for interviews and tell interviewers of positions that you want!

Don't underrepresent your enthusiasm and interpersonal skills.

- Save the humility for another time and place. Speak up and tell prospective employers about your past accomplishments. Demonstrate your abilities by offering past reviews and letters of recommendation from supervisors.
- Work from the assumption that you are exactly what the prospective employer is looking for and that you have a lot to offer. You will project the confidence and energy most employers want in employees.

Try to be objective and do not allow your personal feelings to be the sole criterion of important decisions.

- Suspend making any decisions about a person or a position until you have left the interview and had some time to think back on it. Try to stay clear on the fact that it is easy to confuse rapport with friendship.
- Consider the cause and effect of your decisions. Make a list of possible outcomes and results of your choices, using your original list of criteria as a benchmark against which to measure potential jobs, rather than your personal feelings about the interviewer or the worksite.

Avoid being rigid and inflexible, seeing options as either all good or all bad.

- Again, refer to your list of criteria. Adhere to those elements that you

simply can't live without, and be willing to be flexible about those that are less important.
- Try to imagine yourself in each job opportunity you consider. Ask a friend to help you generate a list of the pros and cons of each opportunity and look at both sides fairly before making any decisions.

Try not to take rejection personally and get discouraged.

- Remember that just because you look at the world from a personal perspective, that is not true for everyone else. Most rejections are not directed at you personally but at your qualifications for a job. It sometimes takes several weeks or months to find the right job. Patience will pay off if you keep going.
- Get support from friends or family members when you are starting to lose your energy and confidence. Ask for the encouragement you need. Let friends help *you* for a change.

The Final Piece: Changing or Keeping Your Job ... the Key to Success for ISFJs

Now that you have a solid understanding of your type, you can see how your natural preferences make you better suited for certain kinds of jobs. You can also see how knowledge of your type-related strengths and blind spots can help you conduct a more successful job search. But as an ISFJ, you've already realized that you are not equally drawn to *every* career or field listed in the Popular Occupations section. The next and final step is to narrow down the field and find the work you were meant to do.

In addition to Type, several other factors—such as your values, interests, and skills—contribute to your level of satisfaction on the job. The more compatible you are with your job, the happier you'll be. So prepare to use everything you've learned (in this book and in life) to create *your strategic career plan*. The exercises in Chapter 23, "Putting It All Together," are designed to help you do just that.

However, you may have decided it makes more sense (if perhaps only for the moment) to stay in your present job or with your current employer. There may be many valid reasons—financial pressures, family considerations, a tough job market for your specialty, or just bad timing. But take heart! What you've learned in this book can also help you be more content and successful *in your current job*. And should the time come when you're ready to make a major career move, you'll have a much better idea of where you want to go and how to get there.

"So, if you can't have the job you love (yet!)...love the one you've got."

The simple truth is, many jobs allow a good deal of flexibility in the way tasks are performed. Here are some ways you may be able to "massage" your current job into one that better fits your needs:

- Find people with complementary strengths to give you input and balance.
- Ask your boss to be clear about performance expectations.
- Work to resolve conflicts with co-workers, supervisors, and direct reports.
- Leave environments where there is great interpersonal tension.
- Implement efficiency systems and require direct reports to use them.
- Volunteer for research projects in which you have a personal interest.
- Make sure you have plenty of uninterrupted time to do your work.

- Ask for meeting agendas in advance.
- Set goals that you can meet.

One ISFJ turns lemons into lemonade:

Laura worked in the bookstore of a small college, but she had always been interested in research and was considered good with numbers. Knowing the college was experiencing some trouble retaining students, she volunteered to conduct a study that would interview students who were transferring to other schools. Not only did she enjoy the process immensely, but the information she collected helped administrators develop new programs that would reverse the trend. Helping her school in such a tangible way was very gratifying to Laura.

Use what you've got to get what you need.

Simply put, the best advice on how to succeed is to *capitalize on your strengths and compensate for your blind spots*. Learning how to do this can make the difference between succeeding or failing and loving or hating your work. To help you, we include the following inventory of your potential strengths and blind spots. And while every individual is unique, many of the following should apply to you as an ISFJ.

Your work-related strengths may include

- great depth of focus and concentration
- strong work ethic; you're responsible and hardworking
- good cooperation skills; you create harmonious relationships with others
- very practical and realistic attitude
- accuracy with facts and attention to details

- love of being in service to others; you are supportive of co-workers and subordinates
- strength at maintaining the organization's traditions and keeping track of its history
- strong organizational skills
- loyalty and comfort working within a traditional structure
- excellence at managing sequential, repeated procedures or tasks
- strong sense of responsibility; you can be counted on to do what you say
- enjoyment using established ways of doing things; respect for status given by titles
- common sense and realistic perspective

Your work-related blind spots may include

- tendency to underestimate own value; you may not be assertive about your own needs

- reluctance to embrace new and untested ideas
- sensitivity to criticism; you feel stressed by tension-filled work situations
- desire to focus on details and the present rather than implications and the future
- tendency to take on too much
- difficulty adapting or switching gears quickly
- tendency to be overwhelmed by too many projects or tasks at the same time
- propensity to become discouraged if you no longer feel needed or appreciated
- difficulty changing your mind or position once a decision has been made

Using your strengths is easy.
The secret to success for an
ISFJ
is learning to

speak up, consider possibilities that don't already exist, and try to be more flexible and spontaneous.

19 ⎮⎮ ESTP
Extraverted, Sensing, Thinking, Perceiving

"In on the Action"

Profile 1: Lou, Private Investigator

"I'm a naturally curious guy, and I can think on my feet."

The Job

Lou's work can be described in one word: gumshoe. In fact, he remembers telling a high school girlfriend that he would someday be a private investigator. And he has been one, and more, for thirty-five years. The chief investigator for a state public defender's office, Lou has worked his way up through a variety of jobs to the one he enjoys now, each time taking what was to be learned and moving on when he became bored. Now, he finds the challenge and intrigue in the cases he handles very satisfying.

Lou supervises more than fifty investigators located around the state in more than thirty court sites, and works on all phases of criminal defense investigation—searching for important, and often previously unknown, information to assist in the defense. His responsibility covers juvenile court through and including felony and capital felony court, which handles death penalty cases. Lou's job often involves traveling around the state to assist other investigators with complex cases by helping to gain access to special services such as forensic analysis. Lou also hires staff, conducts background checks of applicants, does training, and conducts any in-house personnel investigations of a sensitive nature.

"The job is really a problem-solving job with lots of personal contact. I find the most energizing parts to be the challenge to search for and solve problems. When I can get good defense material that an attorney might not even be aware of, that's the best!"

Backstory

Having set his sights on investigation at an early age, Lou completed two years in college and two years' service in the Marine

Corps before becoming an insurance investigator. For ten years he investigated casualty claims and managed an office of investigators. He decided he wanted to work for himself, so he led private investigations and insurance investigations for fifteen years. "I always enjoyed the private investigations most because I found them more challenging."

His next job was as deputy sheriff and then investigator for the state's attorney. This gave him the opportunity to learn the prosecution side of investigation. But he was limited to the lower courts and didn't find the cases to be "intense enough." So after three years, he applied for an opening in a higher court in the public defender's division. He got the job and continued with it until an opportunity presented itself on a new unit devoted exclusively to death penalty cases. "I really enjoyed that job until the position here became available one year ago. Each job has offered me more freedom and autonomy, and the intensity and seriousness of the crimes increased with each job as well."

A Good Fit

Among the strongest of Experiencer needs is the freedom to act spontaneously. Lou has designed his job so he is often out in the field, where he can experience the more exciting aspects of his job and satisfy his Experiencer curiosity. He also has a variety of tasks to perform, which ensures that he is seldom bored. Sometimes, with a major case, Lou might be told to go to another state to find and return with a surprise witness to appear in court the next morning.

The job of investigator requires the heavy use of Sensing, which is Lou's dominant function. In looking for clues, he has to be extremely observant—paying attention to the most minute and subtle details, seeking out and following up on tips, and carefully scrutinizing information provided by sources to determine if it is credible or accurate.

Once Lou has taken in all this information, he relies on his Thinking to make some sense of it, drawing logical conclusions and using deduction to solve problems. His Thinking also helps him to stay objective and not get personally involved in even the grisliest murder cases.

Looking Ahead

Lou feels he has achieved his career goal in his present position. "I guess if there was a chief investigator job for the whole nation, I'd go for it. But there isn't. I've gone as far as I can go, so I'm satisfied. My job is really my life, but that doesn't mean my wife of twenty-seven years and my three kids aren't very important to me." Currently, Lou is looking ahead to retirement in the next three or four years and plans to remain near his children and aging parents, who need him more and more.

Lou starts each day with enthusiasm. "I never look at work as drudgery." His secret is that he never takes setbacks personally. "I just stack 'em up behind me and keep going. I've applied for several jobs I didn't get. But if you keep trying, they'll remember you. Just put your neck out and people will remember you. Sometimes they'll give you a bone. Eventually, even if you were a loser for one job, you'll be the winner of another."

Profile 2: Nikki, Rock Climbing Instructor

"Bringing people to amazing experiences."

The Job

Nikki spends her days doing something many people would balk at. She's a rock climbing instructor, and most days will find her scaling a hundred-foot cliff using anchors and ropes. Bringing clients with her and introducing them to this high-intensity activity, Nikki sees her job as helping people have amazing experiences and getting the most out of people. "Everyone leaves more confident and happy than before they came. Whether it's testing their fear or testing their skills, or just taking them somewhere remote. It's different for everyone. But no matter what, it's a good time."

Her main clientele are women in their twenties through fifties who started climbing indoors. "They were climbing in the gym and feeling like they always had to be with someone who knew more than them. So I try to help them see, 'You can be the expert, you don't need to wait for your boyfriend or your husband to go out. You can learn to build the anchors. You don't need to be afraid.'" Nikki gives people a "play-by-play in digestible increments" about what they're about to do, guiding them along each step. And she gets to do it all in her favorite place—outside, in nature.

Backstory

Nikki found this career without a plan. "Making plans and trying to commit to a major or a plan in college, even choosing things like signing up for summer programs, always felt like a lot of commitment." When she tried climbing as a hobby, Nikki was pulled in instantly. "It was my first time trying it and it just clicked." Since she'd never really had a passion for anything, she felt she needed to pay attention. She quit her marketing job and went to Thailand to climb for herself. Soon Nikki was able to get a job as a climbing guide, taking tourists climbing on a small island in Thailand.

When she returned to the states, Nikki planned on getting a desk job, but something just didn't feel right. She considered other paths, such as becoming a teacher. "But why

would I go into a classroom when the outdoors is the classroom I like best?" She did her due diligence and took all the classes she needed to at the American Mountain Guide Association in order to get her certifications as a climbing instructor. "I didn't really know what was going to happen. I just loved it so much—so why not try?"

Nikki moved to Las Vegas, Nevada, an epicenter for climbing. She started waitressing to pay for her dream, climbing recreationally and making connections with people in the climbing scene. "It was haphazard—know the right people, get involved with the crowd, know the scene, know the key players. It just kind of all fell into place." Nikki started building her clientele: five or six women who would come back to the area two or three times a year, along with tourists signing up for a day. She worked for a service that provided the necessary gear and insurance, taking care of the administrative end, which allowed her to focus on what she liked best: getting outside and making connections with people.

A Good Fit

Nikki's job is a dream for most Experiencers. She spends her time setting up thrilling circumstances and coaching people through their fears. The combination of adrenaline and skill is a perfect mix. Because she brings people out to a natural conservation park with lots of visitors, often she'll be climbing with an audience. "All these people are always looking at you like 'What are you doing? How can you do that?' Doing an activity that boggles people's minds makes it exciting."

A dominant Sensing type, Nikki is completely present to the moment—the client before her, the risks and safety precautions. She has mastered the skills that are required, and she is confident managing each of the detailed safety procedures that allow her clients to feel safe taking risks. The stakes are literally high—hundreds of feet in the air—and every knot, every anchor, must be perfectly executed.

Nikki's auxiliary function, Thinking, helps her stay cool and calm in the face of high-stress moments. She is encouraging, clear, and concise as she explains step by step what her clients will be doing. While the experience can unlock many intense emotions for her clients, Nikki keeps the tone positive and the successes front and center.

Looking Ahead

As for the sport, Nikki is seeing an explosion of popularity in rock climbing, mostly due to the gym climbing scene. Many climbers have developed a following on Instagram and Facebook—beautiful people in beautiful places. "A lot of it is the image that draws people to it, not necessarily the raw *I just want to connect with the mountain*." The upside of this is that more people are becoming curious and venturing out to learn more. The inclusion of climbing in the summer Olympics will also likely cause a big bump in business. "It may be the tipping point."

Nikki and her partner have thought a lot about starting their own guide service, and what that would look like. "From a purely financial point of view, the best way to pay the bills are big corporate groups, because there's a lot of team building you can do with that, and there's money there. But what I actually enjoy a lot more is taking underserved youth out who don't normally have those kinds of opportunities." She's also drawn to the idea of working with kids who do mostly competitive, in-gym climbing. "I think we need young people as advocates

for the true ethics of the sport and not just the competition. They're just so focused on the benchmarks rather than the experience."

Profile 3: Kristine, Biomedical Equipment Craftsman

"Getting in on the action."

The Job

In a medical emergency, there's no time to waste. A life support monitor running smoothly could be the difference between life and death. That's where Kristine comes in. A biomedical equipment craftsman for the U.S. Air Force, Kristine is on hand to diagnose and repair life-saving machinery at a moment's notice. The high stakes of being in the military adds another element to her job. When Kristine is deployed, she never knows what she might be working with or what access to materials she may or may not have. Adrenaline and the ability to think clearly under pressure—it's all in a day's work for Kristine.

The details of her job depend on the circumstances she finds herself in. "I have the most fun in deployed environments. I've built tents, fixed plumbing, worked with generators, and many other things that require you to go outside and get dirty." She thrives on adrenaline and thrill, and can use this energy to go to extraordinary lengths: "If a piece of lifesaving equipment is down, I work twenty-five hours straight until the unit is up and running, and sit next to the patient for another six hours to ensure it doesn't fail again."

Backstory

Kristine has always been fascinated by how things work. "My dad is a computer-networking engineer, and I used to hover over his shoulder as he dismantled and rebuilt computers." By the age of ten, Kristine was reverse-engineering household appliances—taking apart VCRs, radios, and anything else her parents would let her get her hands on—just to figure out how they worked. A good student throughout middle and high school, Kristine hit a wall in college when the general education prerequisites failed to interest and engage her. She began to skip class and ended up becoming academically disqualified. Kristine attended summer school, improved her grades, and was readmitted to the university. But her parents, upset with her deviation from the path, cut her off financially, and she had no means to pay for tuition.

For the next three years, Kristine reports, she "had no direction." She attended community college, waited tables, and worked in a saddlery shop. Eventually, she started bartending, which marked an important turning point. "My customers would talk to me about their different family members joining the military and how much this had improved their lives. The military paid for their education and armed them with invaluable skill sets, which they were able to turn into lucrative civilian careers. With their stories of success rattling around in my head, I visited recruiters from every branch to decide which service was best for me."

Kristine settled on the air force. She earned high scores on the Armed Services Vocational Aptitude Battery, and her recruiter pushed her toward biomedical equipment repair, assuring her she would love the job. "He was absolutely correct!" After completing basic training in the top 7 percent of her class, Kristine started technical school. For the next year, she learned how to troubleshoot, maintain, and repair a wide variety of medical equipment. Upon graduation, she was stationed and has been an active-duty military member for the last six and a half years, winning an impressive array of honors, such as Outstanding Biomedical Equipment Repair Airman of the Year.

A Good Fit

Kristine's job is a perfect fit for her skills and personality. As an Experiencer, Kristine loves the aspects of her job that are hands-on. "The most energizing tasks are ones that require me to build and/or dismantle things." Like many Experiencers, she is able to respond to whatever arises spontaneously with quick reflexes and a cool head. This is essential when she is deployed and working in often dangerous environments.

A dominant Sensor, Kristine is extremely practical and has a great eye for the details and mechanisms that make things work. She has acquired a vast amount of specific knowledge and technical skills, and puts these to good use daily, repairing the equipment she is responsible for.

Kristine's auxiliary Thinking function makes her logical and objective, able to stay cool and calm in high-pressure situations. She is a natural and pragmatic problem solver and enjoys troubleshooting. The aspects of schooling that bored Kristine—all the theoretical, academic, and indoor activities—don't exist in this job. Instead, every day is an adventure.

Looking Ahead

When asked what her dream job might be, Kristine answers without hesitation that she already has it. The ever-changing nature of the military makes it impossible to know where she might be in five to ten years. The career path for people in her position typically leads to running one's own maintenance shop. And although this would be an honor, Kristine feels it would take her away from the hands-on experiences she enjoys most. Luckily, her skills maintaining and repairing equipment translate easily to the civilian sector, where she could continue the same kind of work post-service if she wished.

Common Threads

Although Lou, Nikki, and Kristine have different backgrounds, experiences, and careers, there are certain common threads woven through their stories. Their specific interests and abilities may differ, but owing to their similar temperament values and the *same hierarchy* of their psychological functions, there are certain observations we can make about the needs of many ESTPs.

What follows is a list of the most important elements—the formula, if you will—for ESTP satisfaction. Given the uniqueness of all individuals—even those who share a type—this list will not describe each ESTP equally well. The important thing is that these ten elements, with varying degrees of intensity and in different orders of importance, identify what ESTPs need to be satisfied.

After you have reviewed this list, we recommend that you go back and prioritize the elements in order of *their importance to you*. When doing this, think of past work experiences as well as your present job, and what you found particularly satisfying or unsatisfying. Try to look for *themes* that run through several experiences, not just *events* that might be true for one work situation but not for another.

As an ESTP, I define career satisfaction as doing work that

1. lets me meet and interact spontaneously with many people; offers something different every day, and is fun

2. lets me use my keen powers of observation and my capacity for absorbing and remembering facts

3. lets me use my ability to search for solutions to problems, using firsthand experience and then critically analyzing these solutions to find the best ones

4. is active and full of adventure and fun, where things happen quickly, and where I am allowed to take risks and be alert to new opportunities

5. lets me respond to unplanned situations, using unconventional approaches, where I can skillfully negotiate satisfactory solutions

6. is done in an environment without a lot of rules or restrictions, where I work with other practical and lively people and am able to enjoy free time after completing my assignments

7. lets me organize myself as I go along and as I deem necessary rather than according to someone else's standards

8. is practical and logical, where I can use my reasoning abilities to find discrepancies or flaws in the logic of a system and fix it on the spot

9. leaves me free to respond to a crisis and work in an expedient manner dealing with pressing issues

10. Involves real people and things, not theories or ideas; where my efforts are directed to producing a tangible product or service

Popular Occupations for ESTPs

In listing occupations that are popular among ESTPs, it is important to note that there are successful people of all types in all occupations. However, the following are careers ESTPs may find particularly satisfying, and some of the reasons why. This is by no means a comprehensive listing but is included to suggest possibilities you may not have previously considered. Although all of these occupations offer the potential for career satisfaction, the future demand for some careers is anticipated to be greater than for others.

SERVICE / "ACTION"
- Police officer
- Firefighter
- Paramedic
- Detective
- Investigator
- Corrections officer
- Emergency medical technician (EMT)
- Exercise physiologist/sports medicine practitioner
- Respiratory therapist
- Flight attendant
- Ambulance driver and attendant
- Insurance fraud investigator
- Private investigator/detective
- Personal fitness trainer
- Flight instructor
- Flight engineer
- Commercial helicopter pilot
- Ship and boat captain
- Military officer
- Intelligence specialist
- Probation officer
- Pest control expert
- Criminologist and ballistics expert

Many ESTPs find careers in the area of civil service to be satisfying because they offer a high degree of action, variety, and the opportunity to interact with many people from diverse backgrounds. Many of these positions require the ability to think and react quickly to rapidly changing situations and keep cool under stress. Naturally curious and observant, ESTPs often make excellent detectives and investigators.

SALES / FINANCE
- Real estate agent
- Sports merchandise salesperson
- Insurance adjuster/examiner
- Personal financial adviser
- Auditor
- Stockbroker
- Banker
- Investor
- Insurance salesperson
- Budget analyst
- Insurance agent/broker
- Retail salesperson
- Car salesperson

The world of finance is often interesting to ESTPs, especially when it involves rapidly changing situations and contains a certain amount of risk. A love of excitement and risk taking means they often do well gambling or "playing" the stock market. ESTPs are realistic and pragmatic people, enjoying careers that require problem solving, even if it means using unconventional approaches. Many ESTPs, with their charm and charisma, are naturals at sales. They enjoy lots of interaction with the public, and their friendly and easygoing style helps them meet people, acquire new clients, and close deals. ESTPs like the competitive nature of insurance or car sales and do well within systems that offer incentives and prizes for sales goals.

ENTERTAINMENT / SPORTS
- Sportscaster
- News reporter
- Promoter
- Tour guide and agent
- Dancer
- Bartender
- Auctioneer
- Gaming facility manager
- Professional athlete/coach/umpire
- Fitness instructor/trainer
- Rock climbing instructor

- Talent agent
- Radio and television talk show host
- Television camera operator
- Musician
- Studio, stage, and special effects technician
- Actor and performer

These entertainment careers offer plenty of opportunity to have fun, a critical element in career satisfaction for ESTPs. ESTPs live for the here and now and enjoy work that lets them be active and lively. They are natural promoters yet also enjoy the adventure and thrill of performance. Many ESTPs are sports fans and excel in jobs where sports are central, including competing with and training others. They prefer to work around other people as much as possible and can be charming and persuasive bartenders and auctioneers.

TRADE / TECHNOLOGY
- Carpenter
- Craftsperson/artisan
- Organic farmer
- General contractor
- Construction worker
- Brickmason, blockmason, stonemason, tile and marble setter
- Robotics and manufacturing engineer
- Construction and development engineer
- Vehicle and mobile equipment mechanic
- Mechanic, installer, repairer: electrical and electronic equipment
- Team assembler
- Chef/cook
- Electrical engineer
- Technical trainer (classroom setting)
- Logistics and supply manager (manufacturing)
- Network integration specialist
- Civil engineer (repairs of transportation infrastructure)
- Biomedical engineering technician

- Industrial/mechanical engineer
- EEG technologist/technician
- Radiological technician
- Aircraft mechanic
- Marine biologist
- Data processing equipment repairer
- Property manager: commercial/ residential
- Systems support operator and installer
- Video game developer
- Lawn service manager
- Transportation coordinator
- Park naturalist
- Audiovisual specialist
- Landscape architect
- Forester
- Exercise physiologist
- Chiropractor
- Teacher: trade/industrial/technical
- Aviation inspector
- Soil conservationist
- Professional photographer
- Wilderness adventure leader
- Airplane dispatcher and air traffic controller
- Flight attendant
- Travel consultant
- Construction and building inspector
- Blacksmith
- Ecotourism specialist
- Ship carpenter and joiner

The appeal of the trades to ESTPs is the opportunity to work with real things and use tools in efficient, economical, and skillful ways. They usually have good mechanical understanding and work well with their hands. ESTPs like working for themselves as long as they have the chance to be around other people. They enjoy the physical and active nature of these careers, including the sometimes high pressure of working within tight time frames (for example, in farming or cooking).

BUSINESS
- Entrepreneur
- Land developer
- Wholesaler
- Management consultant (business operations)
- Franchise owner
- Internet marketer
- Insurance claims examiner (property and casualty)
- Product safety engineer

In general, many ESTPs find the world of business too restrictive and slow-paced to be satisfying. However, these careers offer more flexibility in schedule, personal freedom, and variety, which may capture the ESTP's attention. ESTPs are excellent entrepreneurs, enjoying the element of risk found in starting a new business enterprise or being a developer. They enjoy negotiation processes and are fair arbitrators.

Remember, these are only some of the areas that provide satisfying expression for the unique natural talents of ESTPs.

Customizing Your Job Search

Knowing the particular strengths and blind spots of your type can afford you a tremendous advantage in your job search campaign. In all aspects of the process, from conducting research into available positions, identifying and contacting prospective employers, developing personal marketing tools such as résumés, arranging and conducting job interviews, and negotiating salaries to finally accepting a position, people will act true to their type. Being able to capitalize on your assets and compensate for your liabilities can make the difference between a successful and an unsuccessful job search.

The differences between types are sometimes subtle and other times dramatic.

It is the subtle variations in advice we offer that make the real difference between success and failure in a job search. The concept of networking serves as a good example. Extraverts will naturally enjoy networking and are advised to do so on a large scale, while Introverts find more limited and targeted networking, especially with people they already know, easier. Sensors tend to network with people in a defined scope, while Intuitives will go far and wide to find people often seemingly unrelated to their field of interest. Further, Feelers can often take networking personally and enjoy establishing warm rapport, while Thinkers will be more objective and detached in their style. Finally, Judgers tend to ask fewer and more structured questions during their networking, while Perceivers could ask questions of all sorts all day long! One valuable search technique, many ways to implement it.

Pathways to Success: Using Your Strengths

As we will detail in the following pages, your strengths and talents for the job search include your energy, curiosity, realism, and ability to roll with the punches. Beware, however, of your tendency to be casual about the process, missing opportunities or communicating a lack of serious commitment.

As an ESTP, you will find that your most effective strategies build on your abilities to do the following:

Conduct an active, high-energy job search campaign.

- Use your large network of friends and associates to spread the word that you are looking for a job and to explore career options.

- Put all your focus on your job search campaign. Harness your tremendous energy; look at the process of finding the right career as an adventure.

Riley tackled his job search the way he tackled everything else in his life—with full force. While he was a bit nervous about approaching some of the decision makers, he decided to turn it into a game. He made a little bet with himself each day—how many people he could meet and how many jobs he could find out about in a day. He treated himself to a game of basketball at the gym when he reached or exceeded his bet. Riley found he looked forward to each day, and by the time he started his new job, he was in the best shape of his life!

Sell yourself.

- Establish rapport with interviewers quickly, demonstrating your ease and facility meeting new people and making them feel comfortable with you.
- Generate excitement about your abilities, talents, and energy that employers will find attractive and a valuable addition to their workforce.

Lulu was a bit intimidated when she arrived for her interview with the vice president of news at a local television station. She had the experience and good references from a station in her hometown. But this was a big step up. She took a deep breath and told herself she could do it and then walked into his office. After answering some standard questions, Lulu was asked why she wanted to work at that station. She began to talk about her love of investigative journalism and some stories done by reporters that she had admired. She found herself relaxing and becoming excited rather than nervous. The vice president was impressed with her ability

to talk and her energy and enthusiasm for her work. She left his office a bit stunned because she was offered the job.

Use your powers of observation to discover important environmental factors.

- Tune in and pick up on subtle cues from other people to learn whether they really like working where they do—the amount of interaction, privacy, personal time, and flexibility they have on the job.
- Compare what you learn with what you realistically know about yourself and the things that are important to you. Find the flaws in the situation before making a commitment to invest a lot of your time there.

Cal was sure he wanted to sell real estate. He took the course, passed the exam, and got his real estate license. Now he just needed to find the right agency. He asked everyone he met for references to good agencies. He narrowed it down to several and finally got an appointment for an interview at his first choice. When he arrived at the office, however, he had second thoughts. Everyone seemed so serious and glum. He was ready for a competitive and active office, and he was disappointed to see that nobody seemed to be enjoying the work. He also noticed that everyone in the office was at least twenty years older than he—he had hoped to meet some new friends through work. Cal reconsidered his first choice and, following the interview, decided he needed to continue looking for a firm in which he would feel more comfortable and challenged.

Negotiate effectively and diplomatically.

- Decide ahead of time what is of critical importance to you and what you are willing to give in on. Then negotiate in a flexible and reasonable manner.

After retirement from professional football, Mac was recruited by a local television station to be the sports director. While several elements of the job appealed to him—the salary, celebrity status, and variety of sports he would report on—the job sounded a bit too restrictive to him. He wasn't looking forward to being responsible for supervising several other sports reporters, scheduling assignments, and being tied down to the studio for two on-air reports each day. So Mac made a deal.

Mac agreed to take the job and fulfill most of the requirements of the job, giving the station the benefit of having a high-profile, well-known sports figure with experience and contacts in the sports world. But for a slightly reduced salary, he negotiated a guarantee to cover ten special "on the road" assignments each year, which got him out of the studio and into the world of sports in a more active capacity. The weekend sports reporter filled in for him while he was on assignment, and everybody was happy with the arrangement.

Assess and then capitalize on available resources.

- Begin to view your friends and associates (past and present) as resources to help you meet influential people within the organization you are pursuing. Use unconventional approaches if necessary to meet someone who may be difficult to reach through traditional methods.
- Use your natural spontaneity to take advantage of opportunities as soon as they present themselves by moving quickly, expressing your interest immediately, and responding to sudden deadlines.

Minutes after Jodie, a physical fitness specialist, learned about a corporate fitness center that was being built, she called the company to find out when they would begin to accept applications. She was one of the first to apply and the first to be hired. In fact, she was hired before the facility was even completed, which gave her the opportunity to be around when important decisions were being made about staffing, layout of staff offices, and the purchase of key exercise equipment.

Possible Pitfalls

Although all people are unique, there are certain *potential* blind spots that many ESTPs share. We specify "potential" because some of the following *may* be true of you, while others may clearly not apply. While considering them, you may notice that these tendencies do not relate just to the job search but rather describe pitfalls that you may have experienced in other aspects of your life as well. It is therefore helpful to consider each one in terms of your past experiences by asking yourself, "Is this true for me?" And if so, "How did this tendency prevent me from getting something that I wanted?" You will probably notice that the key to overcoming your blind spots is the conscious and thoughtful development of your third and fourth functions (Feeling and Intuition). We recognize that many of the suggestions will be difficult to implement, but the more you use these functions, the fewer problems they will cause you in the future.

Don't be limited to considering only career opportunities that are evident at the present time.

- Look beyond what you have already done to what you might like to do. Generate a list of ideas, even including

266 Part Three: Getting to Work

those you think are impractical. Find out more about all of them before eliminating any.

- Focus on the future and try to imagine the possible implications of your actions down the road. Once you look past the material pleasures you may be aiming for, you may see how a job that looks good on the surface (or at the moment) may ultimately be unsatisfying in the long run.

Invest the time developing a long-range career plan.

- Curb your impulse to dive right in to what may turn out to be the wrong direction for you. Spending the time carefully thinking about what is important to you and what your real motivations and wishes are will help you focus your energy and avoid dead-end jobs.
- Develop a list of criteria for career satisfaction (or use the one we have provided on page 313) and then set some long- and short-term goals. This will provide you with a yardstick against which to measure career options realistically.

Work on developing stick-to-itiveness and follow-through.

- Resist the urge to deal only with immediate problems instead of with the less exciting but still important follow-through necessary to conduct a thorough campaign.
- Prepare yourself for interviews by learning as much as you can about the job, its requirements, and the company so you can address questions asked about yourself and your past experience well. This step will give you the added

advantage of knowing what you need to ask to get a clear picture of what the job will actually be like.

Avoid being perceived as unreliable or unpredictable.

- Go the extra mile in all cases, even if you don't think you'll pursue a particular option. Demonstrate your dependability by keeping all appointments, arriving on time or early, and calling back when you say you will.
- Remember that many people respect the standard way of doing things within organizations. Don't run the risk of offending someone because of your natural distaste for following rules.

Concentrate on communicating serious interest.

- Your easygoing and relaxed attitude can be charming and infectious. It can, however, also communicate a lack of seriousness to potential employers.
- Be careful not to be blunt or insensitive to the feelings of others. Tune in to the reactions of others and perhaps tone down your assertiveness so you won't offend others.

The Final Piece: Changing or Keeping Your Job . . . the Key to Success for ESTPs

Now that you have a solid understanding of your type, you can see how your natural preferences make you better suited for certain kinds of jobs. You can also see how knowledge of your type-related strengths and blind spots can help you conduct a more successful job search. But as an ESTP, you've already realized that you are not equally drawn to *every* career or field listed in the

Popular Occupations section. The next and final step is to narrow down the field and find the work you were meant to do.

In addition to Type, several other factors—such as your values, interests, and skills—contribute to your level of satisfaction on the job. The more compatible you are with your job, the happier you'll be. So prepare to use everything you've learned (in this book and in life) to create *your strategic career plan.* The exercises in Chapter 23, "Putting It All Together," are designed to help you do just that.

However, you may have decided it makes more sense (if perhaps only for the moment) to stay in your present job or with your current employer. There may be many valid reasons—financial pressures, family considerations, a tough job market for your specialty, or just bad timing. But take heart! What you've learned in this book can also help you be more content and successful *in your current job.* And should the time come when you're ready to make a major career move, you'll have a much better idea of where you want to go and how to get there.

"So, if you can't have the job you love (yet!)...love the one you've got."

The simple truth is, many jobs allow a good deal of flexibility in the way tasks are performed. Here are some ways you may be able to "massage" your current job into one that better fits your needs:

- Look around and find projects you would like working on; volunteer for them.
- Consider taking a time-management course.
- Ask supervisors to be clear about their expectations.
- Find time during the day to get outside and do something physical.

- Join the company's/organization's or outside recreational activity.
- Think about where you want to be five years from now.
- Get out from behind your desk or out of the office on a regular basis.
- Find others with complementary strengths to give your ideas balance.
- Suggest ways of making your work more enjoyable.
- Recruit and hire an efficient and organized assistant or support person.
- Delegate some of the follow-through of projects to others if possible.

One ESTP turns lemons into lemonade:

Charlie enjoyed her job but wished her company wasn't quite so stuffy. When she learned her friend's firm had a policy of letting people dress more casually on Fridays, she immediately began lobbying her boss to implement the same practice. And after a few months the plan was adopted. Although this didn't drastically change the corporate culture, it created a little shift in thinking that allows Charlie—and other employees like her—to feel a little less restrained and freer to be themselves at work.

Use what you've got to get what you need.

Simply put, the best advice on how to succeed is to *capitalize on your strengths and compensate for your blind spots.* Learning how to do this can make the difference between succeeding or failing and loving or hating your work. To help you, we include the following inventory of your potential strengths and blind spots. And while every individual is unique, many of the following should apply to you as an ESTP.

Your work-related strengths may include

- keen powers of observation, with excellent memory for factual information
- ability to see what needs doing and be realistic about what's necessary to complete a job
- being charming and making friends easily
- lots of energy; you enjoy being active on the job
- ability to adapt well to change and shift gears quickly
- ability to make work fun and exciting
- enjoyment in being part of a team
- practicality, realistic perceptions, and good common sense
- process-oriented approach; you create a lively and fun atmosphere at work
- flexibility and willingness to take risks and try new approaches
- willingness to accept differences and ability to "go with the flow"

Your work-related blind spots may include

- difficulty working alone, especially for long periods of time
- dislike of preparing in advance; you have trouble organizing your time
- tendency to be too casual with people's feelings and blunt and insensitive at times
- inability to see opportunities and options that don't exist at the moment
- impatience and/or intolerance with administrative details and procedures
- difficulty making some decisions and/or prioritizing projects
- tendency to be impulsive and easily tempted or distracted
- difficulty seeing the long-term consequences of actions
- dislike of excessive rules and structured bureaucracy
- resistance to setting long-term goals and difficulty meeting deadlines

---

Using your strengths is easy.
The secret to success for an

ESTP

is learning to

think before you act, consider people's feelings, and follow through on your commitments.

20 | ISTP
Introverted, Sensing, Thinking, Perceiving
"Making It Work"

Profile 1: Simon, Tattoo Artist

"Getting into a flow state."

The Job

For Simon, the art of tattoo is serious business. "Tattooing has been around in every indigenous culture since humanity and it's still practiced today. It clicked that this was a way to work one on one with people to make something people would live with for the rest of their life. This was a way that I felt my art could have a life of its own and people could appreciate it the most." Whereas many people think of tattoo as permanent, for Simon, it's really about transience. "It's about transformation, letting go, embracing change, and moving forward. Looking at art museums filled with pieces of art from thousands of years ago, we only have a handful of tattoos, preserved on mummies, essentially. They don't last. They go back to the earth and where we came from."

Each day, Simon meets with clients who mostly find his work through Instagram and other social media platforms—"the lifeblood of tattoo artists." A client will make an appointment, and then come into the shop. Sometimes the drawing happens beforehand, and sometimes it happens on the person's body. "It's really a collaboration where they can make active choices as I'm applying them." The process of getting a tattoo can take several hours, depending on the scale of the piece. "I like the ritual of setting up the machines. I have my order of operations, my system that I enjoy doing. And once you start, there's no stopping until the piece is done. I find myself in a flow state."

Backstory

Give Simon a pencil and a piece of paper, and he's happy. "I always knew I was going to go to art school. To what end I didn't really know." Simon went to school for fine arts drawing, an experience that dissuaded him from pursuing the fine art gallery career.

"With any industry, once you're on the inside of it, you see everything that comes with it." Simon was unimpressed with the money, excess, and self-indulgence of the art scene. The whole time he was looking for something more.

Simon bought a tattoo machine and taught himself to use it through trial and error on himself and on "a lot of trusting friends." Meanwhile, he was paying the bills freelancing in a fabrication shop, doing carpentry, metalwork, finishing work, and installation for a company that built custom pieces for various occasions.

His first tattoo job happened by serendipity, on a stroll through the neighborhood he had just moved to. "If I hadn't gone an extra block and decided to look in a certain direction, I never would have seen the shop. I just wandered in." As luck would have it, an artist had just left and there was a vacancy. Simon was asked to start the next week. He worked in that apprenticeship for a year and a half before being offered a new spot at a different shop. He was grateful for the opportunity, but ready for something new. "I needed a community who was a little more focused on what the possibilities of tattooing are."

Rather than a walk-in shop, like his first job, Simon's current place is an appointment-only private studio. The shop is handled like a collective, with Simon and other artists paying monthly rent for their station, and making their own schedules. "A lot of freedom, but it's all up to me to make it happen. That's where social media has been really beneficial. Most of my clients find me through Instagram."

A Good Fit

All the aspects of the fine arts world that bothered Simon—the elitism, the inaccessibility—are absent from the world of tattoo. Working with his hands and doing what he loves best, Simon can enter that flow state where his focus is absolutely absorbed with the task at hand. He must be able to attend to the slightest detail and be hyperaware of the person in front of him. This total presence in the moment is something Experiencers such as Simon are better suited to than are most of those with other temperaments.

Simon's work has a lot to do with systems, which shows his Thinking function. "I love the act of tattooing because it's drawing with machines. I like using machines. I think it's cool to be using tools that I'm comfortable doing maintenance on and adjusting, tuning, replacing parts." Simon is cool, competent, and effective. Like many Thinking types, he enjoys reaching mastery over a logical system like a machine, understanding it inside and out.

A Sensor, Simon has a strong aesthetic sensibility and is highly tuned in to details. His work is intricate, and he pulls inspiration from the patterns of aquatic life and birds, the natural world. "I'm always taking pictures of textures of plants and animals for reference." Some tattoos he's done include dragons with hundreds of interlocking scales, an enormous tiger, a delicate bumblebee, a falcon. He also draws inspiration from the Japanese tattoo tradition.

Perhaps the most important part of career satisfaction for an ISTP is autonomy. With his own station in the studio, Simon has total independence and agency. He can travel to meet with clients, say no to tattoos he doesn't want to do, and make his own hours.

Looking Ahead

Simon is already in his dream job. But change is also a huge part of who he is.

"At a certain point of doing something for so long, I will always start to question: I know how to do this, so how can I change? The idea of what a good tattoo is is constantly changing, and it's always in my head."

The tattoo scene has truly exploded in the time Simon has been working. "The accessibility is so much easier now. You can open Instagram and browse through an entire city's worth of portfolios. You can make better choices and find your people. It's no longer as intimidating as it used to be."

Profile 2: Alex, Engineer

"Doing something that doesn't feel like homework."

The Job

Alex believes that a lot of the world's problems can be solved. The trick is to take the pieces apart and put them back together. In his energy systems engineering program, Alex is working toward a master's of engineering, hoping to gain the skills to solve the most pressing issue he feels society is facing today: the problem of renewable energy. Power systems engineering is a subfield of electrical engineering as a whole, and deals with the ways that electric power is generated, transmitted, distributed, and utilized. In a world that is rapidly seeking new ways to use renewable energy and lessen dependence on fossil fuels, Alex's work is more relevant than ever.

Backstory

Alex considered two careers viable when he was seven years old: He could be either a garbageman or a construction worker. In high school, he became interested in

astronomy and telescopes, excelling at AP physics and heading off to an Ivy League college to major in astronomy. Alex realized in his senior year that a degree in astronomy was not as practical as a broader and more foundational degree in physics. He changed programs, planning to get a master's degree in engineering. "It was the most immediately practical way to switch to an engineering field."

Now in a master of engineering in energy systems program at the University of Michigan–Ann Arbor, Alex is learning about power systems in general, with a focus on renewable energy. For his thesis, he and a team of friends are entering the London Business School clean technology competition, a global contest for start-ups or other teams with ideas for green technologies. Alex's idea is to eliminate overnight idling of long-haul tractor-trailer trucks—a huge waste of fuel and major source of pollution—by creating a device in the exhaust smokestack to convert waste heat directly into electricity. The device would run in the smokestack during the day and charge a battery that, at night, would provide enough energy to accommodate the sleeper cab in the truck.

The competition itself acts as a workshop stage for the contestants, who are assigned two mentors who are academic or industry experts in the field. The teams have twenty-four hours to problem-solve what their mentors have deemed the biggest challenge specific to their project. The winners of the competition get a large cash prize with which to begin making their ideas a reality. Ever the pragmatist, Alex doesn't expect to actually win, but sees the contest as a great opportunity to refine his plans as well as network with some important industry professionals and venture capitalists.

A Good Fit

Like many Experiencers, Alex enjoys best the hands-on, physical world. A dominant Thinking type, Alex easily sees and understands mechanical systems. He is competent and quick at solving real-world problems with a pragmatic eye. "I enjoy identifying a problem and building up data for what it would be like under real conditions. You come up with sizing and controls, and then you basically start from scratch and make something."

Alex's auxiliary Sensing function enables him to develop concrete and complex systems that depend on a wide array of quite specific knowledge and skills. Ownership and independence are important to Alex. Most rewarding is "when I get to begin with my own problem, end with my own solution, and focus on my own projects." He is less interested in "sitting in a library producing a graph from lab data" and more interested in getting hands-on and building things from the ground up. "I want to do something fun and real that doesn't feel like homework."

Looking Ahead

If things go well in London and the team receives positive feedback, they hope to find enough funding to develop several prototypes to give to truck fleets to try for free. If that works out, Alex would be interested in starting up a venture. Regardless, he will be developing the prototype this summer to fulfill his thesis requirements. "We're going to go to London and have fun and see what happens." A second-best case scenario for Alex moving forward would be doing project-oriented work in the field of renewable energy, such as wind and solar farms. He'd never want to end up working at a desk job at someplace

like the Department of Energy. "It's more about adapting existing solutions as best as possible—optimizing whatever opportunity presents itself."

Profile 3: Jill, Product Designer

"Other people call them crises—I call them fun."

The Job

When she was in high school, Jill never thought she'd have a job she loved, let alone a career. Today, she is a successful and happy product designer. Jill enjoys the variety, autonomy, individual and creative control, and the opportunity to create interesting and practical products for everyday living.

The company for which Jill works is a small design firm where she is one of two product designers. There are two assistant designers and three mechanical artists who support Jill and the other designer. Each day is different, one of the things Jill enjoys most about the job. She makes sketches of her designs for products, such as packages for new food products, office supplies, and some technical equipment like lighting fixtures. She does much of her design work alone, after receiving the technical specifications from the client. After the designs are made, she creates models of the product for presentation to the client and for testing at the manufacturing plant. Once the design is accepted, Jill stands by to deal with any production problems that arise and to check the actual product while it is on the assembly line.

"The really fun part of my job, after getting to draw and play at my desk, is the troubleshooting. I might get a call that the design needs a size or proportional change in the testing phase or that there's some problem with folding and assembly during the actual production. I run over to the plant and mess around with it right there on the lines."

Backstory

After high school Jill had no interest in attending college, so she spent the next two years working in several different restaurants as a waitress and bartender. She also helped out at a horse stable so she would be able to ride for free. Her parents persuaded her to try returning to school, but instead of college, she enrolled in a professional art and design school because she had always enjoyed drawing. She discovered graphic design and graduated with a degree in graphic and commercial design.

Her first job out of school was at a large advertising agency in the city where she worked as a mechanical artist doing layouts for magazine ads. At first it was challenging, but she began to get bored with the repetition and the fact that the office was so busy she never had time even to leave the studio for lunch. "I wanted to do some of the design work, but the structure of the agency was so rigid that if you were hired as a mech artist, you were never permitted to try anything else. The only way to move up was to move on. So I did."

Her next job was at a printing company, where she learned about production. She worked as a traffic manager, supervising projects through the production process, scheduling printing, ordering paper, and preparing cost estimates. The job required enormous organizational abilities and more follow-through than Jill naturally possessed. Jill was also working sixty hours a week and had no time for any of her friends or hobbies. She lasted less than one year. But, capitalizing on her production experience,

she accepted a position as an assistant product designer and learned firsthand about product design by carrying out the ideas of the designers. They would hand her a rough sketch and she would execute it with accuracy. The job also enabled her to occasionally go with the designer to see the job on the presses. She enjoyed that part best. After four years, one of the designers left and she was promoted to designer. That was two years ago, and Jill thinks this job will last for a long time.

A Good Fit

As a product designer, Jill may work on dozens of different products a year. Since each project has its own unique challenges and problems to solve, Jill's job necessarily involves a great deal of variety. And she gets to work with her hands—drafting and making models. Like most Experiencers, Jill enjoys her relative autonomy and the lack of structure in her day-to-day activities. She also enjoys helping the other designer with his technical challenges. She takes a particularly vexing problem and finds a way to fix it, usually by making a few quick sketches and making a rough model. "It's almost like a magic trick to fool around with some paper and come up with a new container that stacks properly, or to solve whatever the problem was. I get excited about responding to those situations. Other people call them crises. I don't, because I think they're fun."

It is Jill's dominant Thinking function that helps her to think through how something will work best. Hers is largely a technical job requiring close attention to details such as size, proportion, color, and spatial relations. It's imperative to stay objective.

Jill uses her Sensing to get a realistic sense of which materials work best and how the product will be used. The products she designs, such as food packaging and technical equipment, solve mostly practical needs. Jill collects necessary data by talking with production people and, in some cases, clients and end users.

Looking Ahead

Jill doesn't have a lot of career goals. She hopes to combine work and family and occasionally thinks about having her own agency someday. "I would have to be with really great people whose work I respected and who would deal with the clients and the business stuff so I could be free to design and take vacations! Anyway, I have all the elements of career satisfaction now—fun, freedom, good money, challenging projects, and quality people to work with."

Common Threads

Although Simon, Jill, and Alex have different backgrounds, experiences, and careers, there are certain common threads woven through their stories. Their specific interests and abilities may differ, but owing to their similar temperament values and the *same hierarchy* of their psychological functions, there are certain observations we can make about the needs of many ISTPs.

What follows is a list of the most important elements—the formula, if you will—for ISTP satisfaction. Given the uniqueness of all individuals—even those who share a type—this list will not describe each ISTP equally well. The important thing is that these ten elements, with varying degrees of intensity and in different orders of importance, identify what ISTPs need to be satisfied.

After you have reviewed this list, we recommend that you go back and prioritize the elements in order of *their importance to you*. When doing this, think of past work

experiences as well as your present job, and what you found particularly satisfying or unsatisfying. Try to look for *themes* that run through several experiences, not just *events* that might be true for one work situation but not for another.

As an ISTP, I define career satisfaction as doing work that

1. lets me identify and use resources that are available to me in the most efficient manner possible
2. lets me practice, master, and then use skills I have acquired, especially mechanical skills or those requiring the use of tools
3. lets me apply my understanding and technical knowledge of the world around me and see the logical principles underlying my work; lets me engage in troubleshooting and problem solving
4. has clear directions; where I can work expediently and deal with real and practical products
5. is fun and active and lets me work independently with frequent opportunities to get out of my workspace and be outdoors
6. is done in an environment without excessive rules or operating standards imposed by others; where I can enjoy spontaneous adventures and step in to manage any crisis
7. lets me work independently, with a minimum of supervision, and where I am not required to closely supervise others
8. gives me plenty of time to pursue my interests and hobbies
9. gives me a substantial amount of enjoyment and is continually challenging

10. lets me use an economy of motion and energy and does not require needless routine or procedures

Popular Occupations for ISTPs

In listing occupations that are popular among ISTPs, it is important to note that there are successful people of all types in all occupations. However, the following are careers ISTPs may find particularly satisfying, and some of the reasons why. This is by no means a comprehensive listing but is included to suggest possibilities you may not have previously considered. Although all of these occupations offer the potential for career satisfaction, the future demand for some careers is anticipated to be greater than for others.

SERVICE / "ACTION"
- Firefighter
- Police/corrections officer
- Racecar driver
- Ambulance driver and attendant
- Ship and boat captain
- Commercial airplane pilot
- Flight instructor
- Flight engineer
- Commercial helicopter pilot
- Airplane dispatcher and air traffic controller
- Weaponry specialist
- Intelligence agent
- Military officer
- Marshal
- Private investigator/detective
- Child support, missing persons investigator
- High school and college athletic coach
- Criminalist and ballistics expert

The appeal of action careers for ISTPs derives from their desire not to feel confined by a lot of structure and regimentation. They work well on impulse and enjoy situations that are spontaneous and call on their ability to quickly assess their resources and then take appropriate actions. ISTPs work well alone but will pull together as part of a team when necessary. They often enjoy mastery of tools or machinery of a specialized style and enjoy being outdoors and physically active.

TECHNOLOGY
- Electrical/mechanical engineer
- Civil engineer
- Technical trainer (one-to-one setting)
- Information services developer
- Software developer: applications, systems
- Alternative energy systems engineer
- Logistics and supply manager (manufacturing)
- Networking specialist
- Computer programmer
- Marine biologist
- Quality assurance technician
- Reliability engineer
- Systems support operator/installer
- Network systems and data communications analyst
- Home network installer/IT support
- Product tester
- Software engineer
- Geologist
- Product safety engineer

ISTPs often find satisfaction in technical careers because they are interested in how and why things work. They tend to be good in mechanical areas because they possess great observational powers and a capacity to remember and use important facts and details. They usually enjoy working with their hands and like work that provides them with a constant source of sensory information. Their logical analysis is best used when based on solid facts that they themselves gather through their five senses.

HEALTHCARE
- EEG technologist/technician
- Radiological technician
- Emergency medical technician (EMT)
- Exercise physiologist
- Dental assistant/hygienist
- Surgical technician
- Emergency room physician
- Medical evacuation coordinator
- Transportation coordinator

These healthcare fields are particularly satisfying to ISTPs owing to their highly technical nature. Each requires the use of exacting precision, a well-developed practical and mechanical sense, and the patience and concentration necessary to operate and maintain sensitive diagnostic equipment.

BUSINESS / FINANCE
- Securities analyst
- Purchasing agent and buyer
- Banker
- Economist
- Legal secretary
- Management consultant (business operations)
- Paralegal
- Cost estimator
- Insurance adjuster/examiner
- Sports equipment/merchandise salesperson
- Pharmaceutical salesperson

Pragmatic and accurate with numbers, ISTPs can find enjoyment in business and financial careers. The working environment is extremely important, however, and needs to allow for personal freedom and flexibility for ISTPs to be satisfied. Opportunities that allow the ISTP to work autonomously, without excessive meetings or office politics, are best.

ISTPs are often able to bring order to confused data and unrecognizable facts.

They easily see the realities of an economic situation and are ready and able to respond to immediate changes.

TRADES / "HANDS ON"
- Computer repairer
- Airline mechanic
- Robotics and manufacturing engineer
- Coach/trainer
- Carpenter
- Bicycle repair craftsperson
- Photographer
- Tattoo artist
- Mechanic, installer, repairer: electrical and electronic equipment
- Mechanic, installer, repairer: security and fire alarm systems
- Automotive products retailer
- Commercial artist
- Lawn service manager
- Landscape architect
- Forester
- Park naturalist/ranger
- Camera operator
- Insurance appraiser: auto damage
- Criminal investigator
- Locomotive engineer
- Organic farmer
- Studio, stage, and special effects specialist
- Brickmason, blockmason, stonemason, tile and marble setter
- Vehicle and mobile equipment mechanic
- Construction worker
- Heavy and tractor-trailer truck driver
- Silversmith
- Taxidermist
- Gunsmith
- Cabinetmaker and finish carpenter
- Musical instrument artisan
- Sketch artist
- Model and mold maker

The independence and practicality of the trades often appeal to ISTPs, who prefer tasks that are real and concrete and provide the opportunity to use their hands. They work the most diligently on projects that fully absorb their interest, so if theirs is a love of sports, they will enjoy coaching and training much more than another seemingly similar trade career. Making a career out of a hobby is an excellent strategy for the ISTP.

Remember, these are only some of the areas that provide satisfying expression for the unique natural talents of ISTPs.

Customizing Your Job Search

Knowing the particular strengths and blind spots of your type can afford you a tremendous advantage in your job search campaign. In all aspects of the process, from conducting research into available positions, identifying and contacting prospective employers, developing personal marketing tools such as résumés, arranging and conducting job interviews, and negotiating salaries to finally accepting a position, people will act true to their type. Being able to capitalize on your assets and compensate for your liabilities can make the difference between a successful and an unsuccessful job search.

The differences between types are sometimes subtle and other times dramatic. It is the subtle variations in advice we offer that make the real difference between success and failure in a job search. The concept of networking serves as a good example. Extraverts will naturally enjoy networking and are advised to do so on a large scale, while Introverts find more limited and targeted networking, especially with people they already know, easier. Sensors tend to network with people in a defined scope, while Intuitives will go far and wide to find people often seemingly unrelated to their field of interest. Further, Feelers can often take networking personally and enjoy establishing warm rapport, while Thinkers will be more objective and detached in their style. Finally, Judgers tend to ask fewer and more structured questions during their networking, while Perceivers could ask questions of all sorts all day long! One valuable search technique, many ways to implement it.

Pathways to Success: Using Your Strengths

As we will detail in the following pages, your strengths and talents for the job search include your careful attention to detail, logical analysis of current problems, and unpretentious communication style. However, your need for honesty may sometimes prevent you from seeing the importance of establishing rapport with potential employers.

As an ISTP, you will find that your most effective strategies build on your abilities to do the following:

Gather and remember all relevant data.

- Use your tremendous powers of observation to notice the people and surroundings of a potential workplace. Compare your recollections later as you think about whether the setting is right for you.
- Explain your ability to serve as a walking storehouse of information. Provide examples of how that capability has proved useful to past employers.

When Sam interviewed for a new job, she did her homework. She found people who were knowledgeable, people she respected, and sought their advice. She tried to think through the possible interview questions before the interview. Once she was prepared and ready, she felt comfortable winging it on some less important issues.

Adapt and take advantage of available resources.

- Persevere in your job search even when faced with obstacles.
- Demonstrate your skills at developing instant solutions to immediate problems when they pop up during your job search or during an interview.

From her research talking to friends, Marnie knew the attorney who interviewed legal secretaries liked to ask hypothetical questions. Rather than be thrown by it, Marnie decided to act as though the situation were a real one that currently existed, since she knew that she was good at on-the-spot problem solving. So when presented with the scenario, she was able to come up with a good solution to a real problem and impress the attorney in the process.

Demonstrate to potential employers your ability to think things through carefully and logically.

- Take time to apply your ability to figure out how things work to assess the organization and the people in it. Ask yourself how your prospective role will fit within it as it currently exists.
- Be straightforward and honest in your responses to all questions.

During a performance review, Raul was asked what he thought of a newly adopted reporting system. He knew that giving a completely honest answer might hurt his chances of being promoted, because he did not think that the system was an improvement. Rather than speaking with his usual naked honesty and blunt style, Raul took a minute and answered that while the system apparently provided more important information, he didn't think it really affected him because he continued to work according to his own high standards.

Analyze opportunities objectively.

- Use your well-developed logic to see the natural consequences of actions and choices.
- Let prospective employers know you can remain calm, even during unexpected changes in plans or during a real crisis. Include in your listing to prospective employers the ability to keep your head about you when others are upset.

Sol found himself in an interesting spot while interviewing for a position as surveyor for a town building department. About ten minutes into the interview, the town manager got an emergency call from the field. One of the surveyors had been hurt in a fall. Seeing that his interviewer was flustered about what to do, Sol suggested that he call 911 while the town manager drove out to the site. Sol made the call and then followed in his own car, arriving before the emergency team. He pulled a blanket from his car and was able to help comfort the injured man until the professionals arrived. Sol's interview continued over a beer with the rest of the crew once they learned their co-worker was going to be all right.

Take reasonable risks.

- Look for opportunities when it is appropriate to be impulsive and spontaneous. Show your true colors—a person who enjoys working hard and also having a good time. People are more likely to view you as a member of the team if they can imagine having a cup of coffee with you.
- Demonstrate your ability to troubleshoot by researching some of the potential problems a prospective employer is facing and offering your suggestions for ways to solve them.

Penny was beginning to get bored in her job in the corporate finance department of a large insurance company. She had been in many jobs during her long career there and usually got antsy after a couple of years. She was about to put out the word that she was interested in a new assignment when she was asked to serve on a panel to look into a way to restructure the entire company. During her evaluation of the company, she determined that her current position would no longer be needed under the new structure. She reported the findings, with the knowledge that she might be out of a job. She was. But she was offered a new and challenging position once the reorganization was begun. The risk proved to be a win for her.

Possible Pitfalls

Although all people are unique, there are certain *potential* blind spots that many ISTPs share. We specify "potential" because some of the following *may* be true of you, while others may clearly not apply. While considering them, you may notice that these tendencies do not relate just to the job search but rather describe pitfalls that you may have experienced in other aspects of your life as well. It is therefore helpful to consider each one in terms of your past experiences by asking yourself, "Is this true for me?" And if so, "How did this tendency prevent me from getting something that I wanted?" You will probably notice that the key to overcoming your blind spots is the conscious and thoughtful development of your third and fourth functions (Intuition and Feeling). We recognize that many of the suggestions will be difficult to implement, but the more you use these functions, the fewer problems they will cause you in the future.

Try to plan ahead and follow an organized job search.

- Don't move on to a more exciting challenge before waiting to see if your previous efforts have paid off.
- Make a conscious effort to develop your perseverance, remembering that hard work and sticking to your plan of action will give you the results you really want.

Look for possibilities beyond those that exist at the moment.

- Try not to take stopgap jobs. Resist the temptation to prematurely end the process by accepting an adequate but not truly satisfying option.
- Set long-range goals for yourself and your career. Ask yourself what you hope to accomplish five and ten years from now. Assess whether the job you are considering will help you reach those goals.

Beware of the propensity not to exert any more effort than is absolutely necessary.

- Avoid taking tempting shortcuts even though you readily see them. Pay close attention to all phases of your job search and conduct each with the same energy and diligence.
- Remember that employers look for conscientiousness in employees. Demonstrate your willingness to go the extra mile to get the job done right.

Don't postpone a decision too long.

- Make decisions and then move on. Eliminate poor options and keep yourself in the running for job options you really want.
- Don't let yourself appear undependable and lacking direction by procrastinating too long.

The Final Piece: Changing or Keeping Your Job...the Key to Success for ISTPs

Now that you have a solid understanding of your type, you can see how your natural preferences make you better suited for certain kinds of jobs. You can also see how knowledge of your type-related strengths and blind spots can help you conduct a more successful job search. But as an ISTP, you've already realized that you are not equally drawn to *every* career or field listed in the Popular Occupations section. The next and final step is to narrow down the field and find the work you were meant to do.

In addition to Type, several other factors—such as your values, interests, and skills—contribute to your level of satisfaction on the job. The more compatible you are with your job, the happier you'll be. So prepare to use everything you've learned (in this book and in life) to create *your strategic career plan*. The exercises in Chapter 23, "Putting It All Together," are designed to help you do just that.

However, you may have decided it makes more sense (if perhaps only for the moment) to stay in your present job or with your current employer. There may be many valid reasons—financial pressures, family considerations, a tough job market for your specialty, or just bad timing. But take heart! What you've learned in this book can also help you be more content and successful *in your current job*. And should the time come when you're ready to make a major career move, you'll have a much better idea of where you want to go and how to get there.

"So, if you can't have the job you love (yet!)...love the one you've got."

The simple truth is, many jobs allow a good deal of flexibility in the way tasks are performed. Here are some ways you may be able to "massage" your current job into one that better fits your needs:

- Ask supervisors to be clear about their expectations.
- Seek an opportunity to use your negotiation skills.
- Try to get as much independence as you can.
- Find time during the day to get outside and do something physical.
- Think about where you want to be five years from now.
- Make sure you have enough uninterrupted time to concentrate on your work.
- Consider taking a time-management course.
- Seek others with complementary skills to help you evaluate ideas.

One ISTP turns lemons into lemonade:

Theo was a natural with anything tech-related, and frustrated co-workers were constantly asking him for help when they had problems. Although he enjoyed helping out, it took him away from his regular work and left him swamped when deadlines loomed. Recognizing the need for his talent, he suggested to his boss that he be relieved of some of his duties (the ones he really didn't enjoy anyway!) so he could be a part-time IT consultant within his department. This worked well for both Theo and his co-workers, and for the company as a whole. Employees could get their problems fixed more quickly, which made them more productive; Theo gained independence and the opportunity to spend more time solving technical problems—something that he really liked and at which he was naturally adept.

Use what you've got to get what you need.

Simply put, the best advice on how to succeed is to *capitalize on your strengths and compensate for your blind spots.* Learning how to do this can make the difference between succeeding or failing and loving or hating your work. To help you, we include the following inventory of your potential strengths and blind spots. And while every individual is unique, many of the following should apply to you as an ISTP.

Your work-related strengths may include

- ability to work well with defined tasks and tangible products
- keen powers of observation and an excellent memory for factual information
- ability to bring order to confusing data and to recognizable facts
- aptitude for working alone or alongside others you respect
- ability to stay calm and cool in a crisis or under pressure
- adaptability to sudden changes and ability to shift gears quickly
- ability to recognize what needs doing and what is necessary to complete the job
- aptitude for working with your hands and with tools

- practicality and good common sense
- ability to identify and make good use of available resources
- flexibility and willingness to take risks and try new approaches

Your work-related blind spots may include

- difficulty seeing the long-term consequences of actions
- lack of interest in verbal communication, especially superficial conversations
- dislike of advance preparation; you may have trouble organizing your time
- little patience for abstract and complex theories
- tendency to be blunt and insensitive to the feelings of others
- tendency to get bored and restless easily
- difficulty seeing opportunities and options that don't exist at the moment
- impatience with administrative details and procedures
- unwillingness to repeat yourself
- difficulty making some decisions
- strong independent streak and dislike of excessive rules and structured bureaucracy
- resistance to setting long-term goals and difficulty meeting deadlines

---

Using your strengths is easy.
The secret to success for an
ISTP
is learning to

communicate, consider people's feelings, and follow through on your commitments.

21 | ESFP
Extraverted, Sensing, Feeling, Perceiving

"Good Vibes Only"

Profile 1: Sumner, Cycling Instructor

"Getting lost in your body, the room, the energy, and the music."

The Job

Sumner is a bit of a celebrity. She's a senior instructor at a wildly popular indoor cycling company—what she and others in the industry call "boutique fitness." On paper, her job is to teach forty-five-minute, high-intensity cycling classes, including building customized playlists and even designing lights. But Sumner's job is really to create experiences. "We take you on a journey emotionally. It's getting lost in your body, the room, the energy, and music." Because the experience is so intense, Sumner is also managing the emotions of the room. "It's a place where people let go, cry or laugh, release, celebrate whatever they're celebrating. We're kind of holding that space."

What Sumner loves most about her job is the community. "I come back for the people." Her regulars sign up for Sumner's classes specifically, and her classes sell out quickly. Her motto is "Your vibe attracts your tribe." Sumner describes her vibe as "energetic, connected, and motivating." But just as important as having a signature style is reading the room. Sumner must be truly present, flexible, and responsive to the group in front of her—adjusting the physical intensity of the workout or the emotional climate of the room to meet their needs.

Backstory

Since she was three years old, Sumner was a dancer. When she was seven, she began competing. In her junior and senior years of high school, she started traveling on an audition-based competitive dance team. "I got to travel on the weekends with them, and I got to assist famous choreographers, live my best life. It was awesome. It was like a little family." Sumner also designed her team's dance costumes, picking out fabrics and working with the seamstress.

When she graduated high school, she had ambitious plans to go to school for fashion and merchandise design and maintaining dance as well. "It didn't work out that way. School consumed me." Sumner finished school, did internships in fashion, and got several jobs in that world. "I still took dance classes, but nothing serious."

Then her worlds combined and came back together when she got a job as a designer and production manager for a hip-hop clothing brand started by a husband-and-wife team who also happened to be high-level choreographers. "I've looked up to these two famous choreographers my whole life. Now I get to work with them." But the duo traveled constantly, and Sumner was left to work with a second-in-command who made her miserable. When a co-worker mentioned a job opening up in an entertainment company that was recruiting dancers, Sumner took it, and went back to the dance world full-time. "We went on tour to Mexico, Venezuela, performing every night for a week or two, depending on the place. It was great. It was my in."

After that job, Sumner got a dance agent and started auditioning for gigs in music videos, live shows. "I did a tour in Germany with a famous pop star. I lived that out for five years and really committed to it." Eventually, Sumner craved something with more consistency. Her side hustle had been teaching a dance barre class. When the opportunity to become a cycling instructor opened up, her agent reached out. "They wanted to hire performers. Because you're pretty much performing; you've got your lights, motivation, energy, your everything." It was the perfect match.

Five years in, Sumner has worked her way up the levels to senior instructor, which means she gets more control over her schedule, better time slots, benefits. She has stock in the company.

A Good Fit

Sumner's Experiencer temperament is a great match for her work, which is literally to design experiences for her clients. Her work is high intensity, and requires her to be physically and emotionally present. Teaching twelve classes a week, Sumner maintains her physical health as an athlete must.

A dominant Sensing type, Sumner is meticulous about the details of the experience—even the tempo of each song has to be exact so that the music guides the pace of the cycling. She balances curating each class with being able to respond to the vibe of the room and make adjustments as necessary.

As an Extravert and a Feeler, Sumner is all about connecting to her people. "Vulnerability is a huge thing because a lot of people feel vulnerable in class. I talk about my experiences and I try to connect with them and what's happening in their life. I feel like a therapist sometimes. People come to me about the stuff they're going through because I create that environment. Endorphins are up."

Looking Ahead

In the next year, Sumner hopes to become a master instructor—the highest level available. This comes with greater flexibility in her hours, higher pay, and a certain level of status as well. It also enables her to continue working with new instructors that come in, something that she's really been enjoying. "It brings me back to when I was green, and remembering what I needed and what I felt. I help people get through it because it's not easy—you're sort of thrown out there, and good luck."

When looking at the boutique fitness world, Sumner sees sustainability. The company is always designing new types of classes, new technologies that assist people in reaching their goals. And the people keep coming back, even though the classes come at a premium, precisely because of that experience Sumner is working so hard to create. "They come back and realize there's no other workout like this."

Profile 2: Jacob, Pediatrician

"Bedside manner, and the best possible care."

The Job

Jacob is a staff physician at a children's hospital and is assistant professor of pediatrics at a university where he specializes in childhood arthritis. He keeps the thank-you notes and letters he has received from patients and their families. It's one of the ways he knows that he's doing a good job.

He spends about 60 percent of his time seeing children ages one through eighteen from all around the state and the region. Most are referred for evaluation of joint problems by a pediatrician. Jacob reviews previous X-rays, examines the child, talks with the child and parents, and makes a diagnosis. Jacob uses his well-developed skills of establishing rapport and communicating effectively with both the child and parents. Next, he maps out a treatment plan, which usually involves medication, some form of physical therapy, and, occasionally, surgery. "There are some eighty to one hundred disorders but, practically speaking, we see about twenty on a regular basis."

Jacob also teaches. "Most of it is bedside teaching of residents with the patient. We go over a diagnosis and examine the patient together." Jacob also gives formal lectures once or twice a month to the residents and physician's assistants, does community teaching at hospitals, and occasionally teaches nationally. He participates in formal scientific studies on medications and writes reports for publication in medical journals.

It's the patient care that Jacob enjoys the most. "Seeing patients, working with families, helping kids to minimize their pain and improve their functions—just giving the best possible care—that's what I like."

Backstory

Jacob doesn't remember deciding to become a doctor and jokes that when he was a child, perhaps his mother whispered into his ear while he slept each night: "You will become a doctor." He went to a high school geared toward science and math and then took pre-med in college. During his rotations in his third year of medical school, he worked in pediatrics. "I love kids, and I looked forward to going to work each day, so I knew that would be my choice." During his studies, he had a teacher, a rheumatologist, who became a major influence. "I loved his manner and could talk with him for hours. I picked up some real wisdom from him."

Jacob's mentor influenced him to choose a specialization in pediatric rheumatology. In fact, Jacob agreed to take a job at a hospital where his mentor worked before meeting his actual boss. After two years, Jacob relocated and started a clinic at the university and a general pediatric practice. He gradually cut back on the amount of general pediatrics as the rheumatology part of the practice got busier. He was hired as a staff physician at the children's hospital nine years ago, part-time at first, and then full-time three years later. When he was hired, the program served fifty-five children a year, and Jacob increased it to three hundred in the first year. He currently sees about twelve hundred patients a year, three hundred and fifty of whom are new patients.

A Good Fit

Jacob's Experiencer temperament draws him to be an active participant in life, and it is no accident he has chosen work in which he is constantly moving from one challenge to another. His natural curiosity and love for children combine to drive him to discover important facts about their condition that help him treat them. And interacting with children on their level allows him to "play" a lot, another important criterion for Experiencers.

One of the reasons Jacob finds his work so satisfying is that it requires and allows him to use his dominant function, Sensing, continuously. He is constantly gathering data about his patients, using his keenly developed senses to observe, listen, touch, and hear the subtle symptoms and signs that will help him correctly diagnose a patient's illness. Jacob keeps careful track of changes in his patients' progress or changes in their symptoms or condition.

Being a Feeling type, Jacob is naturally empathetic. He is demanding about the quality and consistency of care his patients receive, feels great compassion for their parents, and is upset when the children have been shipped around to several doctors before finding the real cause of their pain or disability.

Looking Ahead

Jacob has, in effect, reached one major career goal of creating and running an excellent program at the hospital. Now his goals are more academic. He is making arrangements to conduct more research,

which will lead to additional publications that will bring him more national recognition. He also hopes to enlarge the program by adding another physician, which will reduce some of the dreaded administrative time.

Career satisfaction for Jacob is as simple as the eagerness to get up in the morning and get to work. But it is also the recognition and thanks he receives from patients and families, and the feedback and support he receives from his peers. "I hope people think of me as a caring and competent physician, and I hope my family and friends think of me as someone who cares, is a good listener, and is available to them when they need me."

Profile 3: Eve, Childcare Center Director

"The work of play."

The Job

Eve describes her job as director of a private, not-for-profit childcare center as "early childhood advocate." She plays that role whenever she can, whether it's directly with the children, with the teachers, or with parents visiting the center who are considering enrolling their children. "I like to give people something they can walk away with. Like the fact that sharing is really an adult concept, although we tend to expect that three-year-olds will grasp it."

Eve spends most of her time "meeting the pressing needs of the day." And each day can be very different. During the course of the day Eve fills in for a teacher on a break, answers requests for information, meets with prospective parents and their child, sits in on planning sessions with her staff, plans staff development programs and parent activities, and prepares to make formal monthly reports to the board of directors. She also serves on the quality committee of a childcare collaborative in the area, working to define the quality of and assess the needs of centers. Her aim is improving and enriching the level of quality in all childcare.

Backstory

Eve has been at the center for twenty-seven years, first as a teacher and now as director. She started her career with a degree in secondary physical education. "I was always a jock and thought I would change the world by helping young people develop a wonderful attitude toward physical education." After her first child was born, Eve was offered a job at a childcare center on the campus of a nearby university. She taught three- and four-year-olds for two years. "I loved it. I realized I had found a better direction for myself."

After a move, the birth of her second child, and a divorce, Eve was looking for a new job. She learned about a position because she was friends with the current director, and was hired as a part-time teacher. For twenty-one years, she taught four-year-olds, obtaining a master's degree in early childhood education during her tenure. Six years ago, she decided that it might be time for a change. "There began to be lots of turnover. I kept spending my time training the new director!" She applied for the directorship and was hired.

A Good Fit

"Seeing the kids respond and develop in creative ways, seeing things I believe in *in action* is the best part of this job. When I hear the children problem solving or see them jump from something high for the first time or express their feelings in words, it's so satisfying!" Eve also is energized by watching the staff handle situations in positive and

creative ways. "Then I know I've reached them."

Eve most enjoys responding spontaneously to all that happens around her. She loves the variety of activities she engages in, as well as the people (students, teachers, and parents) she interacts with. Something is always happening, and most of it is unplanned. Playfulness, a common trait among Experiencers, is a particularly important part of Eve's personality.

A virtual "radar machine," Eve monitors everything with her dominant Sensing. She is constantly scanning all that is going on: using her eyes to watch a kid make it to the top of the climber without falling, her ears to hear them talk out problems with their peers, her arms to hold an unhappy child, even her nose to decide whose diaper needs changing! All the while she is also monitoring her staff to see how she can help them with their jobs.

Eve's strong feelings and convictions about what childcare should be like come from her auxiliary function, Feeling. She develops long-lasting personal one-on-one relationships with students, staff, and parents, and takes great pride that many of the parents of her current students were once students at the school themselves.

Looking Ahead

Eve's most significant work-related accomplishment is "keeping this school going—riding the tide." But she is rewarded by meeting a new parent who has heard about the center from another pleased parent. "And I love reading in the paper or hearing about 'graduates' of this school going on and becoming successful." Her own career goal is being met each day. "I'm scared to retire because I won't be challenged, and I won't have much of a mission anymore."

Common Threads

Although Jacob, Eve, and Sumner have different backgrounds, experiences, and careers, there are certain common threads woven through their stories. Their specific interests, abilities, and values may differ, but owing to their similar temperament values, and the *same hierarchy* of their psychological functions, there are certain observations we can make about the needs of many ESFPs.

What follows is a list of the most important elements—the formula, if you will, for ESFP satisfaction. Given the uniqueness of all individuals—even those who share a type— this list will not describe all ESFPs equally well. The important thing is that these ten elements, with varying degrees of intensity and in different orders of importance, identify what ESFPs need to be satisfied.

After you have reviewed this list, we recommend that you go back and prioritize the elements in order of *their importance to you*. When doing this, think of past work experiences as well as your present job, and what you found particularly satisfying or unsatisfying. Try to look for *themes* that run through several experiences, not just *events* that might be true for one work situation but not for another.

As an ESFP, I define career satisfaction as doing work that

1. lets me learn from hands-on experience, where I look for solutions to problems from gathering all the facts at my disposal and by using common sense
2. lets me get personally involved in the tasks at hand, working directly with clients or customers, out in the field rather than away from the action
3. lets me work with lots of other people in an active and social environment, with variety, fun, and spontaneity
4. requires skillful handling of people and conflicts, the ability to ease tensions to help groups work more cooperatively, and the ability to motivate others
5. lets me juggle multiple projects or activities, especially those that utilize my aesthetic taste and sense of design
6. lets me interact throughout the workday with other easygoing and social people who share my enthusiasm, energy, and realistic point of view
7. lets me work on projects that are of immediate utility and take into account the needs of people around me
8. is done in a friendly and relaxed environment, without hidden political agendas
9. rewards my hard work and good intentions, and where I feel appreciated for my contributions
10. lets me have fun and enjoy everyday surprises, and where there is a minimum of bureaucracy, rules, or restrictions

Popular Occupations for ESFPs

In listing occupations that are popular among ESFPs, it is important to note that there are successful people of all types in all occupations. However, the following are careers ESFPs may find particularly satisfying, and some of the reasons why. This is by no means a comprehensive listing but is included to suggest possibilities you may not have previously considered. Although all of these occupations offer the potential for career satisfaction, the future demand for some careers is anticipated to be greater than for others.

EDUCATION / SOCIAL SERVICE
- Early childhood education teacher
- Elementary school teacher
- Childcare provider
- Teacher: art/drama/music
- Special education teacher
- Athletic coach
- Social worker
- Home health social worker
- Eldercare specialist
- Personal care aide
- Substance abuse counselor
- Child welfare counselor
- Recreational therapist
- Vocational rehabilitation counselor
- Art therapist
- Occupational therapist
- Developer of educational software

ESFPs often find careers in education satisfying, especially when working with young children. Early childhood and elementary ages sometimes are less formal and structured and offer plenty of opportunities for spontaneous learning experiences. ESFPs enjoy teaching foundational skills and helping children get along with one another, a major emphasis in the early grades. They enjoy the activity, energy level, and variety of learning found in elementary school settings. ESFPs, usually active and physically skillful themselves, often enjoy athletics and athletic coaching. Playing sports, learning teamwork, and being active outdoors are enjoyable activities for ESFPs. They are enthusiastic, encouraging, and supportive coaches and teachers. The field of social work allows ESFPs to meet and work with many different people, helping them identify resources available to them. They establish rapport easily and find satisfaction from helping make life easier for someone else.

HEALTHCARE
- Emergency room nurse
- Medical assistant
- Dental assistant/hygienist
- Licensed practical nurse (LPN)
- Physical therapist
- Primary care physician
- Home health aide
- Dietitian/nutritionist
- Optician/optometrist
- Emergency medical technician (EMT)
- Exercise physiologist
- Massage therapist
- Pharmacy technician
- Radiological technician
- Respiratory therapist
- Veterinarian
- Veterinary technologist/technician
- Dog trainer/groomer
- Diagnostic medical sonographer
- Hospice worker
- Emergency room physician
- Podiatrist
- Speech-language pathologist/audiologist
- Pediatrician
- Chiropractor
- Registered nurse
- Nursing instructor
- Cardiology technologist
- Transplant coordinator

Healthcare provides ESFPs with the opportunity to help others. These careers require the acquisition and then repeated use of skills. Most ESFPs enjoy working directly with other people and thrive on a varied and fast-paced workday. Emergency room nursing requires quick thinking and the ability to calm frightened people during a crisis. Many ESFPs love animals and enjoy working with them either in a medical setting or as trainers.

ENTERTAINMENT / "ACTION"
- Travel consultant/tour operator
- Photographer
- Film producer
- Musician
- Dancer

- Comedian
- Promoter
- Special events coordinator
- Painter/illustrator/sculptor
- Costume/wardrobe specialist
- News anchor
- Actor
- Park naturalist/ranger
- Marine mammal trainer
- Personal fitness trainer
- Fitness instructor
- Flight instructor
- Commercial helicopter pilot
- Entertainment and sports agent
- Forester
- Camera operator
- Cartoonist/animator
- Insurance fraud investigator
- Fire investigator
- Police officer
- Wilderness adventure leader
- Rock climbing instructor
- Radio/television announcer
- Sketch artist
- Organic farmer
- Carpenter

ESFPs enjoy entertaining others, in a formal capacity or informally with friends. They often have a strong sense of aesthetics and a good eye for the fresh and beautiful. Some ESFPs enjoy performance of their art; others simply want to be among other artists in the exciting and ever-changing world of entertainment. ESFPs are adept at juggling several projects or elements of a project at once, and often find career satisfaction in special event coordination.

BUSINESS / SALES
- Retail merchandiser/planner
- Public relations specialist
- Fundraiser
- Labor relations mediator
- Receptionist
- Administrative assistant
- Merchandise planner
- Director of diversity, equity, and inclusion
- Team trainer
- Travel salesperson/broker
- Insurance agent/broker: health or life
- Customer service representative
- Insurance and benefits representative
- Real estate agent
- Merchandise displayer
- Sports equipment salesperson/marketer
- Retail salesperson/manager
- Ecotourism specialist
- Home healthcare salesperson
- Manufacturer's service representative

ESFPs do not generally enjoy the world of business, especially the corporate world. But those jobs that involve a high degree of interaction with others, and where there is a less structured schedule, can be enjoyable to ESFPs. They often enjoy real estate sales because they spend much of their time out of the office, working directly with a variety of people, showing all kinds of homes. They often enjoy public relations, fundraising, and mediation, where they are able to use their naturally persuasive nature. These careers let them use their interpersonal skills and their ability to gather information. Many ESFPs are drawn to retail careers, especially when they are able to use their eye for fashion and flair for the dramatic.

SERVICE
- Flight attendant
- Waiter/waitress
- Host/hostess
- Floral designer
- Police/corrections officer (specialty: remedial training, rehabilitation, counseling)
- Landscape architect
- Chef/head cook
- Interior designer
- Gamekeeper

- Landscaper and grounds manager
- Exhibit builder
- Hospitality/Barista

The service industry attracts ESFPs primarily because of the interpersonal contact and the ability to use acquired skills. ESFPs are often warm and friendly and have the ability to make others feel relaxed and at home. They enjoy the atmosphere present in many restaurants and clubs, and are sociable and generous hosts. Their present-moment orientation makes them fun to be around, and it is said that the party often follows the ESFP.

SCIENCE
- Environmental scientist
- Social conservationist
- Zoologist
- Marine biologist
- Geologist

ESFPs are often interested in the sciences and display a natural aptitude for close observation and the gathering of facts and evidence. They are particularly interested in the natural world and can find great satisfaction working with animals in the fields of zoology or marine biology. ESFPs can be wonderful stewards of the natural world and tireless advocates for conservation.

Remember, these are only some of the areas that provide satisfying expression for the unique natural talents of ESFPs.

Customizing Your Job Search

Knowing the particular strengths and blind spots of your type can afford you a tremendous advantage in your job search campaign. In all aspects of the process, from conducting research into available positions, identifying and contacting prospective employers, developing personal marketing tools such as résumés, arranging and conducting job interviews, and negotiating

salaries to finally accepting a position, people will act true to their type. Being able to capitalize on your assets and compensate for your liabilities can make the difference between a successful or an unsuccessful job search.

The differences between types are sometimes subtle and other times dramatic. It is the subtle variations in advice we offer that make the real difference between success and failure in a job search. The concept of networking serves as a good example. Extraverts will naturally enjoy networking and are advised to do so on a large scale, while Introverts find more limited and targeted networking, especially with people they already know, easier. Sensors tend to network with people in a defined scope, while Intuitives will go far and wide to find people often seemingly unrelated to their field of interest. Further, Feelers can often take networking personally and enjoy establishing warm rapport, while Thinkers will be more objective and detached in their style. Finally, Judgers tend to ask fewer and more structured questions during their networking, while Perceivers could ask questions of all sorts all day long! One valuable search technique, many ways to implement it.

Pathways to Success: Using Your Strengths

As we will detail in the following pages, your strengths and talents for the job search lie in your easygoing and friendly nature and your ability to easily establish rapport. Beware, however, of your tendency to put play before work so that your job search suffers from a lack of results. If this happens, you may become discouraged and settle for a less than ideal job rather than sticking with it and holding out for a career that's really right for you.

As an ESFP, you will find that your most effective strategies build on your abilities to do the following:

Establish rapport and sell yourself.

- Present yourself as a member of a work team, eager to take on new challenges and get along well with others.
- Demonstrate your ability to adapt to new situations and remain cool in a crisis.

When Jack arrived for his interview with the school principal to discuss a job as a social studies teacher, the principal met him at the door to explain that they had had an emergency and the interview would have to be postponed. During a routine fire drill, the office sprinkler system had been activated and several offices were flooded. Water was still pouring out of the ceiling, and the fire department had been summoned but hadn't yet arrived. Jack offered to help. He took off his jacket, grabbed a wrench, and climbed onto the desk. In minutes, the water stopped, and Jack helped the principal carry a table and two chairs into a dry classroom, where they conducted the interview. Jack was offered the job then and there, not only for his experience and good references, but because the principal already saw him as a member of the team.

Use your common sense and ability to adapt to turn unexpected problems into opportunities.

- Demonstrate your ability to troubleshoot by recalling for interviewers how you have successfully managed problems in past jobs.
- Look for ways of explaining how your skills can be used in different work situations.

Sumner was ready for a change. She had been working as a dancer but was looking for something with more stability and job security. When she interviewed to become a cycling instructor, she was able to translate her physical stamina, strong work ethic, and natural performer's charisma from the stage to the studio. And the ability to think on her feet and adapt to the moment was an essential talent for both jobs—after all, the show must go on!

Demonstrate a willingness to compromise. Be flexible in negotiations.

- Decide ahead of time what criteria are of critical importance to you in a job and which ones are not. Demonstrate your flexibility by giving in on less important points.

Upon graduation from veterinary school, Rob was interviewing for a staff job at a prestigious emergency animal clinic. While he was similar in standing to many other candidates, Rob got the job because he was willing to accept a rather unusual schedule. For a year, he committed to work three twenty-four-hour weekends a month. The rest of the month was his own, except for being on call for emergencies two other days a month. The other candidates had families or just weren't interested in that kind of schedule. Rob didn't mind, because it gave him the free time he wanted to spend with his friends and also pursue his new interest in hang gliding— a sport that is often very crowded at the times when most people are off from work.

Gather a great deal of information, using your keen powers of observation and your ability to get others to talk.

- Talk directly with people working for the company you are considering to learn about some of the less obvious but very important elements worth considering.

- Notice what people wear, as well as what staff offices and lounge areas are like, to be sure that the position you are considering is in a place that you wish to spend your days.

When Tamra and her husband relocated, she began looking for another job in retail merchandising. She started by going to many of the large department stores to see firsthand what they were like. She talked with several sales representatives about how they liked their jobs, what the management was like, and how flexible working conditions were. After she had narrowed her choices down to four stores, she used her personal references from past jobs to gain interviews. Tamra was able to make selections using realistic information, not just what the store management wanted her to know about them.

Conduct lots of informational interviews, using your large network of friends and associates.

- Most people are happy to help you, so ask them to refer you to others who may know of available jobs. Call on the assistance of past employers who know personally your abilities and skills.
- Ask informational interviewers to look at your list of skills and help you brainstorm other kinds of jobs or careers you might be well suited or qualified for.

Even though Jaden had been out of college for several years, when he was making a career change, he called on his old college career counselor. They got together over lunch one day and generated a list of possible career options based on Jaden's type, skills, and interests, and the experience he had gained from four years in the real world of work. Jaden's career counselor was able to help him see beyond his present career to other, less obvious possibilities.

Possible Pitfalls

Although all people are unique, there are certain *potential* blind spots that many ESFPs share. We underscore "potential" because some of the following *may* be true of you, while others may clearly not apply. While considering them, you may notice that these tendencies do not relate just to the job search but rather describe pitfalls that you may have experienced in other aspects of your life as well. It is therefore helpful to consider each one in terms of your past experiences by asking yourself, "Is this true for me?" And if so, "How did this tendency prevent me from getting something that I wanted?" You will probably notice that the key to overcoming your blind spots is the conscious and thoughtful development of your third and fourth functions (Thinking and Intuition). We recognize that many of the suggestions will be difficult to implement, but the more you use these functions, the fewer problems they will cause you in the future.

Invest the time in preparing a job search plan before jumping in.

- Spend some time reflecting on where you have been and where you wish to see yourself in the near and distant future to add a long-range perspective to your thinking.
- Examine your real needs in a career and your true motivations before rushing into action.

Consider possibilities in addition to those that currently exist.

- Generate a list of possibilities without prejudging any of them during the process. Include even those that seem outlandish or those for which you may not consider yourself qualified.
- Ask a creative friend to help you imagine what you might do outside of your current career area and list how your skills might transfer to another area.

Develop and follow through on your job search plan.

- Even the tedious parts of the job search—following up via email after interviews, staying on top of job availabilities—are important to finding the right job.
- Resist the urge to drop what you've started when a more interesting situation arises or when friends invite you to socialize. It sometimes helps to look at a job search as a job in itself.

Try not to take rejection personally.

- If it happens, remember that you are being turned down for a job only. Many employers make very impersonal decisions, and it is not a personal rejection of you.
- Try not to let yourself get discouraged when things don't happen as quickly as you would like them to. Finding the right job can take several months, but career satisfaction is worth the wait and the hard work.

Don't put off making decisions.

- Waiting to gather enough information before making a decision can be wise.

However, if you wait too long, your opportunities may be eliminated and choices made for you.

- Use some critical thinking to see the cause and effect of options you are considering. Ruling out options can help you focus on the best choices for you.

The Final Piece: Changing or Keeping Your Job...the Key to Success for ESFPs

Now that you have a solid understanding of your type, you can see how your natural preferences make you better suited for certain kinds of jobs. You can also see how knowledge of your type-related strengths and blind spots can help you conduct a more successful job search. But as an ESFP, you've already realized that you are not equally drawn to *every* career or field listed in the Popular Occupations section. The next and final step is to narrow down the field and find the work you were meant to do.

In addition to Type, several other factors—such as your values, interests, and skills—contribute to your level of satisfaction on the job. The more compatible you are with your job, the happier you'll be. So prepare to use everything you've learned (in this book and in life) to create *your strategic career plan.* The exercises in Chapter 23, "Putting It All Together," are designed to help you do just that.

However, you may have decided it makes more sense (if perhaps only for the moment) to stay in your present job or with your current employer. There may be many valid reasons—financial pressures, family considerations, a tough job market for your specialty, or just bad timing. But take heart! What you've learned in this book can also help you be more content and successful *in your current job.* And should the time come when you're ready to make a major career move, you'll have a much better idea of where you want to go and how to get there.

"So, if you can't have the job you love (yet!)...love the one you've got."

The simple truth is, many jobs allow a good deal of flexibility in the way tasks are performed. Here are some ways you may be able to "massage" your current job into one that better fits your needs:

- Make sure you get enough time to interact with co-workers and colleagues.
- Consider taking a time-management course.
- Ask supervisors to be clear about their expectations.
- Find time during the day to get outside and do something physical.
- Try to find people with opposite strengths to consult with.
- Volunteer to help run and/or participate in recreational or socially responsible activities.
- Think about where you want to be five years from now.
- Set some short-term, achievable goals.
- Make sure you have a variety of tasks to perform; try to avoid routine jobs.
- Avoid working alone for extended periods of time.

One ESFP turns lemons into lemonade:

Because of added responsibilities at work, Serena found she could no longer make it to the gym to work out on a regular basis. As a former fitness instructor, exercising was something she really liked and missed. After taking an informal survey of people at her company, Serena discovered several people would be interested in a lunchtime Pilates class—if she ran it. She was able to convince the progressive-minded human resources

manager that employees who worked out regularly were happier and healthier (fewer paid sick days!) and therefore more productive. He provided her with a room, bought twenty mats, and agreed to pilot the program for six months to see how it went.

Use what you've got to get what you need.

Simply put, the best advice on how to succeed is to *capitalize on your strengths and compensate for your blind spots.* Learning how to do this can make the difference between succeeding or failing and loving or hating your work. To help you, we include the following inventory of your potential strengths and blind spots. And while every individual is unique, many of the following should apply to you as an ESFP.

Your work-related strengths may include

- lots of energy and enjoyment of being active on the job
- ability to adapt well to change and shift gears quickly
- sensitivity to people's needs and desire to help them in real ways
- caring nature; you're a cooperative team player
- ability to make work fun and exciting
- practicality and great common sense
- loyalty to the people and organizations you care about
- process-oriented approach; you create a lively and fun atmosphere at work
- flexibility and willingness to take calculated risks and try new approaches
- desire to cooperate, pitch in, and help people in real and concrete ways
- ability to clearly assess current resources and conditions and immediately see what needs to be done

Your work-related blind spots may include

- difficulty working alone, especially for extended periods of time
- tendency to accept things at face value and miss deeper implications
- dislike of advance preparation; you have trouble organizing your time
- difficulty seeing opportunities and options that don't exist at the moment
- tendency to take criticism and negative feedback personally
- trouble making decisions
- impulsiveness and tendency to be easily tempted or distracted
- dislike of excessive rules and structured bureaucracy
- difficulty making objective decisions if they conflict with personal feelings
- resistance to setting long-term goals and difficulty meeting deadlines
- difficulty disciplining self or others

Using your strengths is easy.
The secret to success for an
ESFP
is learning to

**think about the future implications,
not take things too personally, and
follow through on commitments.**

22 | ISFP
Introverted, Sensing, Feeling, Perceiving

"It's the Thought That Counts"

Profile 1: Matt, Record Producer

"Music is really all about people."

The Job

Whether he's recording and producing music or traveling on tour with his band, music is the great love of Matt's life. He spends his days in his studio, working with artists and bands to bring their music into the world. Since Matt is an independent record producer, his relationships with his artists are everything. Often Matt will meet artists and bands on the road while touring. When they're ready to record, they remember Matt. He must make sure both his rates and his manner provide an appealing alternative to the big studios, which are his competitors.

The process begins a couple weeks before an artist actually comes into the studio, when Matt communicates with his clients about their vision for the album and listens to their demos or "scratch tracks." Once he has a band or artist in the studio, Matt is on their timeline. He works to get the best performances he can, encouraging and managing the emotions of the artists while also engineering a rig that includes twenty to thirty pieces of hardware, including microphones, instruments, and cables. Often he helps to write the songs themselves, filling out sections on different instruments; he's something of a musical jack-of-all-trades. Sometimes this process happens remotely with artists across the country or the world. "Entire songs can be built over email." When recording is done, Matt mixes the songs, adding effects and making sure each part is at the right level, and mastering them so they're ready to be heard.

Backstory

Matt has been obsessed with music ever since he picked up a saxophone in the fourth grade. He played saxophone in his high school jazz program, traveling for competitions and gigs, and played guitar in three different bands outside of school. However, there weren't a lot of career musicians around for Matt to emulate: "Nobody ever really suggested that you could write or play music for a living." So Matt went off to college and spent a few years with an undeclared major, finally settling on a double major in music and American maritime studies.

In college, Matt got into a cappella and other vocal arrangements, and began to think he could build a career arranging and recording music. In his senior year, he met with some alumni who worked in the music industry. Choosing to attend an arts and technology school in Florida, Matt matriculated into the recording arts program. There he became familiar with the technical side of recording, studying signal flow and electricity and learning how recording equipment works. "I learned how to take things apart and put them back together, how to use all the gear and about acoustics—all that practical techie stuff." He became proficient in recording software, and after graduation he moved to Los Angeles and started applying for internships at all the major recording studios.

After a few starting gigs interning and working at recording studios, Matt landed a job as an assistant recording engineer at a major studio. Though the work was grueling—fourteen-hour workdays, seven days a week—Matt was happy to be moving up. "I was just stoked to be involved; to get to contribute in any way with these major bands was just a really big deal." He quickly progressed to editing, and when bands found out he could play horns, he started adding his parts to the recordings. "That was amazing—getting not only to edit but to contribute musically to these records." After a year, Matt began handling more of the recording side of things, working with artists and garnering greater experience and independence.

After four years, Matt had learned enough to strike out on his own, and he started working freelance with singer/songwriters, alternately writing, engineering, and recording music in Los Angeles and New York. "I definitely took a big pay cut, and I wasn't working on the prestigious Billboard top-ten stuff I was used to. But I didn't have anybody hovering over me, and I was my own boss, which felt really good." He also joined a popular jam band and now tours six to seven months of the year as a saxophone player and backup vocalist.

A Good Fit

As an ISFP, Matt is a dominant Feeling type. He is soft-spoken, even-keeled, and patient, and his specialty is what he calls "studio manner"—like bedside manner in medicine. "I'm good at making other artists feel comfortable, so I tend to get good performances out of them. People have fun and feel comfortable in the studio, and they like recording with me because I make it easy for them." Matt senses that his work has an impact on people, and seeing people enjoying the product of his labors is very gratifying.

With Sensing as his auxiliary function, Matt is good at staying in the present and has a great capacity to understand the complex and technical aspects of sound engineering and recording. Being an Introvert makes the intimate studio setting ideal, and Matt forms real one-on-one relationships with artists. As an Experiencer, Matt finds freelance much more appealing because he is able to be his own boss, managing his own time and working outside of the constraints of a typical nine-to-five job. "I can't think of any other job in the entire world that I'd want to spend time doing."

Looking Ahead

Matt already feels like he has his dream job. He has several gold albums, and has even been nominated for a Grammy. However, he would make a few adjustments if he could, including touring less with his band. Spending four months of the year on the road and eight months at home making music would be ideal. In five to ten years, he would like to be doing what he is doing now, with more time at home. He can see wanting to stay put and have a family.

Profile 2: Carrie, Medical Assistant

"The office peacemaker."

The Job

Carrie's career satisfaction is newly found, at only three years old. For most of her adult life, she held jobs in the insurance industry, doing work she didn't enjoy or look forward to. "I was biding my time all through my children's early years, when I needed to put them first. And I always hoped I would be able to find work I enjoyed someday." Today, Carrie looks forward to getting to work, where she feels needed, valued, and appreciated. Carrie is a medical assistant in a busy internal medicine physicians group. She spends her day performing medical diagnostic tests on patients as they wait to see one of the five staff doctors.

Carrie's job is about 90 percent patient contact. She performs a variety of medical tests, from blood pressure, weight, and pulse, to more complicated X-rays, EKG tests, and urinalysis. She assists the physicians during examinations and helps the patients before and after the procedures. "I take care of a lot of older patients who need help getting on or off the examination table or getting dressed after the exam. And I see lots of children, too, and enjoy performing the eye tests and other requirements of school physicals." Between patients, Carrie files charts, prepares the schedule of patients for the next day, and handles a minimum of billing and insurance. When the office is particularly busy, Carrie answers phones, calls in prescriptions for patients, and makes appointments.

"I really love this job because of the patient contact. I'm fascinated with the whole field of medicine, and I'm curious about disease and what makes people get better. I get to perform interesting procedures all day long, and I get to keep learning! The inner workings of the human body are amazing to me. I like the fact that I'm always investigating something new. And I ask the doctors a lot of questions and stay involved in a patient's progress long after my duties with them are finished."

Carrie describes herself as easygoing. "I know how to take a deep breath and let the stress pass. I even calm the rest of the staff. And at the end of the day, I leave the work at the office and turn my attention to my family."

Backstory

Carrie's family has always been a focus for her. She began working when she left a liberal arts college after two years to get married. She considered continuing her education toward working in occupational therapy or nursing, but after a divorce went to work in an insurance company. That's where she met and married her husband of eighteen years and continued to work in a variety of claims positions for the next twelve years. Carrie worked at either part-time or temporary positions while her children were young so she could have time off in the summers and during school vacations to be with them. "Every job was pretty much the same—all figure work. I sat at a desk with a calculator, completing forms and figuring out rates and commissions."

About three years ago, Carrie again became a temporary employee at one of the insurance companies so she would have the flexibility to begin looking around for more interesting work. She saw a job posting for a temporary medical assistant position. "They offered on-the-job training, which was perfect for me because I had the interest but not the skills. I loved it right away and quit my other job, even before the doctors offered me a permanent one. Eventually a permanent job opened up, and I've been there ever since."

A Good Fit

Carrie loves the fact that her job keeps her so busy. Her work combines two factors that many Experiencers find gratifying: the opportunity to use specific physical skills they have mastered and the chance to use them with a variety of different people. Like many Experiencers, Carrie is also a very curious person, and she is most curious about how the human body works. Her job involves investigating and constantly learning more about it, which she finds fascinating.

As a dominant Feeler, Carrie is naturally a sympathetic and caring person. Her strengths are dealing with the always varied, often irritable, and sometimes difficult public. "I'm able to soothe demanding patients and tolerate the interpersonal squabbles in the office. I love to have fun and laugh, and so I guess I'm a peacemaker. I just figure if you're nice to others, they'll be nice to you. I use that ability to keep from getting flustered when the office goes crazy so I can help keep things moving smoothly." It's also deeply satisfying for Carrie to help people all day and see her impact on others.

All day, Carrie deals in data. Taking patient histories, performing examinations, recording test results, explaining and conducting procedures on patients, and assisting the doctors with certain procedures and treatments are some of the ways she uses her Sensing.

Looking Ahead

As Carrie has gotten older, she has realized that she always wanted to be a nurse but spent the early years paying attention only to the present moment rather than doing a lot of planning for the future. "I've never been terribly career oriented and kept things on the back burner while my kids and husband came first. I think I'd really like to go ahead and get my degree in nursing at some point. I think I would enjoy a hospital setting, but I'd probably be happy at a lot of jobs within the medical field. It'll happen when I'm ready."

Profile 3: Thomas, Bicycle Craftsman

"No line between work and play."

The Job

Thomas is an elite craftsperson—building something most people will never own. He designs and builds made-to-order lightweight, premium bicycle frames and assembled bicycles. Thomas is a racing cyclist and an uncompromising perfectionist in both the design and construction of flawless frames. He's been in business by himself for nearly twenty years doing something that sometimes gets awfully close to being a hobby for him. "It's my business, but it's also who I am."

Thomas's clients place orders from all over the country for the highest-quality bicycle frames available. The frames are the most crucial part of the bike, especially for a racer, because a less than perfectly aligned bicycle can create problems and injuries for the racer. Although many of his customers never race the bikes he makes, all of them can afford the top-quality product. Thomas compares his bikes to custom-made performance cars or, at the very least, a tailor-made outfit. The frames are made to the size, riding, and handling style of the person who will ride it. After the extensive measurements are made, Thomas cuts the finest-quality tubing to size and then uses complicated and very precise joining processes. He has specially created paints and ornamental finish work done on the frames so they are as handsome as they are functional. Thomas works alone in his studio, producing eighty to one hundred frames a year. "It's an extremely precise operation. It's time-consuming, and there's no faking it here."

Backstory

Thomas's career in bicycle making began quite by accident. Waiting six months for a delayed admission to college, he traveled to Europe to "kill some time and do something interesting." Already an avid cyclist, he took a job learning to make bikes in a family-operated bike-making business, simply for the experience. He returned to the United States, and again, quite by coincidence, got a job with an importer of bicycles made by the same family he had worked with in Europe.

For two and a half years, he helped the company expand their bike line, working at trade shows, doing some repairs, and acting as a technical expert. "I still didn't know very much, and I was really just enjoying myself using someone else's money to make bikes. Eventually the owner began to pressure me to increase my productivity and began

making my work into a chore. I simply didn't have the skill to make bikes any faster. It took me a while, but I finally just left." With a small investment from his family, and no business or long-range plans, he started his own business. "I was only motivated to keep doing what I liked."

A Good Fit

As with many Experiencers, one of the reasons Thomas's work is so satisfying is that it is also fun. He loves everything about bikes—building, riding, and racing them. Therefore, it is both the process, the building—and the product, the bikes themselves—that Thomas enjoys. Another satisfying aspect of his work for Thomas is the freedom that it provides him. He is totally autonomous and free to close his shop—for an hour to go for a ride or a week to go on a tour—whenever the spirit moves him. Thomas also enjoys the physical activity involved in building bikes—a component that is also important to many Experiencers.

For Thomas, building bikes is a labor of love. He puts all of himself into each bike he makes. In fact, he feels as if he is giving away a part of himself when he sells a bike. This depth of feeling, and his belief that a bike must be made by hand to each person's unique specifications and be of absolute top quality, come from his dominant function, Feeling. But Thomas also builds relationships—lasting relationships—with his clients, whom he gets to know and often stays in touch with for many years.

Thomas uses his auxiliary function, Sensing, in many ways. First he finds out all the pertinent facts about the person he is building the bike for, including such detailed information as size, weight, and build, exactly how the person pedals, and what they want the bike to do. Then he takes meticulous measurements. He does all the physical work by hand, including bending metal, filing, finishing. His Sensing also helps him handle the ordering, buying, and billing for his company.

Looking Ahead

These days Thomas is proud of the longevity he has in his business but with characteristic modesty attributes that only to the fact that he just never stopped doing what he's doing. He receives a great deal of publicity in biking magazines and other press and is often described as being uncompromising. "My experience as a racer helps me always remember that I'm making a quality bike that has to work perfectly. But I'm also pleased that I am good at making something real, something that gives people joy." The tangible evidence of his customers' pleasure is the huge box of thank-you letters and notes he keeps in his shop.

"I guess the part that feels like success and satisfaction to me is that I'm not trying to sell anything, I'm just doing what I enjoy, being honest and true to my convictions. But it all turns on whether my customers like what I do. I am most satisfied when I create something that meets my high standards and people try it out and tell me that the bike is as good as they thought it would be. Other people can assign accolades to my work. I just like what I do and love it when other people do too."

Common Threads

Although Carrie, Thomas, and Matt have different backgrounds, experiences, and careers, there are certain common threads woven through their stories. Their specific interests and abilities may differ, but owing to their similar temperament values and the *same hierarchy* of their psychological functions, there are certain observations we can make about the needs of many ISFPs.

What follows is a list of the most important elements—the formula, if you will—for ISFP satisfaction. Given the uniqueness of all individuals—even those who share a type—this list will not describe each ISFP equally well.

The important thing is that these ten elements, with varying degrees of intensity and in different orders of importance, identify what ISFPs need to be satisfied.

After you have reviewed this list, we recommend that you go back and prioritize the elements in order of *their importance to you*. When doing this, think of past work experiences as well as your present job, and what you found particularly satisfying or unsatisfying. Try to look for *themes* that run through several experiences, not just *events* that might be true for one work situation but not for another.

As an ISFP, I define career satisfaction as doing work that

1. is consistent with my strong, inner values, and is something I care deeply about and want to contribute my energy and talents to
2. if done with others, is in a supportive and affirming climate where I am a loyal and cooperative member of a team
3. requires attention to detail, where I work with real things that benefit other people and have practical applications
4. gives me freedom to work independently but nearby other compatible and courteous people, and where I don't feel restricted by excessive rules, structure, or inflexible operating procedures
5. lets me be adaptable yet committed; where I have a sense of purpose and am able to see and experience the actual results of my accomplishments

6. lets me use my sense of taste and aesthetics to enhance my physical work space, personalize it, and make others feel more comfortable

7. is done in a quietly cheerful and cooperative setting and where interpersonal conflicts are kept to a minimum

8. gives me an opportunity to experience inner growth and development within a context of work that I feel is important

9. lets me handle problems promptly and simply, offering practical help

10. does not require me to perform regular public speaking, lead a large group of people I don't know well, or give people negative feedback

Popular Occupations for ISFPs

In listing occupations that are popular among ISFPs, it is important to note that there are successful people of all types in all occupations. However, the following are careers ISFPs may find particularly satisfying, and some of the reasons why. This is by no means a comprehensive listing but is included to suggest possibilities you may not have previously considered. Although all of these occupations offer the potential for career satisfaction, the future demand for some careers is anticipated to be greater than for others.

CRAFTS / ARTISAN
- Fashion designer
- Carpenter
- Jeweler
- Sound designer
- Musician
- Recording engineer
- Gardener
- Potter
- Painter
- Dancer
- Designer: interior/landscape
- Chef
- Artist
- Cartoonist/animator
- Sketch artist
- Tailor
- Musical instrument maker
- Graphic designer

The chief appeal of these careers for ISFPs is the opportunity to work with their hands in the creation of something attractive and, oftentimes, useful. They enjoy using their five senses in a practical way, as well as working with real things in the real world. Many of these careers offer ISFPs the chance to work flexible hours and the freedom to schedule their own work. Most ISFPs prefer to be autonomous, without having to conform to administrative guidelines.

HEALTHCARE / SOCIAL WORK
- Visiting nurse
- Physical therapist
- Massage therapist
- Radiology technologist
- Medical assistant
- Dental assistant/hygienist
- Home health aide
- Primary care physician
- Dietitian/nutritionist
- Optician/optometrist
- Exercise physiologist
- Occupational therapist
- Art therapist
- Respiratory therapist
- Licensed practical nurse (LPN)
- Surgical technologist
- Personal fitness trainer
- Surgeon
- Veterinarian
- Veterinary assistant
- Speech and language pathologist/audiologist
- Pharmacist

- Emergency room physician
- Pediatrician
- Cardiology technologist
- Audiometrist
- Pharmaceutical researcher
- Registered nurse
- Physician's assistant
- Hospice worker/director
- Personal care aide
- Substance abuse counselor
- Apheresis technician
- Recreational therapist
- Home health social worker
- Art therapist
- Child welfare counselor
- Social worker (elderly and child daycare issues)
- Crisis hotline operator

ISFPs often find satisfaction in healthcare and social work careers, especially those where they are able to work directly with clients and patients. They enjoy the hands-on element of many of the therapy occupations, helping others either physically or emotionally, during or after a crisis. They are generally very observant and able to respond well to subtle changes and like short-term problem solving. An essential ingredient in satisfaction within these careers and any other career for ISFPs is to be able to see and experience feedback for their contributions and to believe in the importance of the work they are doing.

SCIENCE / TECHNICAL
- Forester
- Botanist
- Geologist
- Mechanic
- Marine biologist
- Zoologist
- Camera operator
- Soil conservationist
- Archaeologist

- Systems analyst
- Aviation inspector
- Electrical home appliance repairer

ISFPs often enjoy work that deals with facts rather than with theory. They tend to prefer using practical and active skills. The opportunity to be out-of-doors is particularly appealing to ISFPs, and they welcome change and variety in their work.

SALES / SERVICE
- Elementary school teacher: science/art
- Police/corrections officer
- Storekeeper
- Cosmetologist
- Travel salesperson
- Preferred customer sales representative
- Merchandise planner
- Sports equipment salesperson
- Home healthcare salesperson
- Animal groomer/trainer
- Preschool teacher
- Special education teacher
- Teacher's aide, paraprofessional
- Landscape architect
- Childcare worker
- Eldercare specialist
- Fish and game warden
- Bicycle designer/repairer
- Insurance fraud investigator
- Interpreter/translator
- Locomotive engineer
- Airplane dispatcher and air traffic controller
- Commercial airplane and helicopter pilot
- High school and college athletic coach
- Genealogist
- Residence counselor
- Horticultural specialty grower
- Florist
- Organic farmer
- Firefighter
- Wilderness adventure leader

Many ISFPs find fulfilling work in service careers. Careers that let them help meet the needs of people or animals in specific and tangible ways are most rewarding. They tend to prefer work environments that share their values and foster and encourage interpersonal harmony, cooperation, and appreciation for the work of all. Many ISFPs enjoy teaching a specific subject area, usually with young children, where they have the opportunity to include lots of spontaneity and fun.

BUSINESS
- Bookkeeper
- Legal secretary
- Clerical supervisor
- Administrator
- Paralegal
- Insurance appraiser
- Insurance examiner: property and casualty

Clerical careers, if in the right kind of environment, can provide satisfaction for ISFPs. The critical factor is the ability to use their excellent practical skills but in a supportive and affirming climate. ISFPs work best when working as part of a team, in a stable work group that respects the individual need for privacy and growth. They prefer work settings that allow them to create and maintain a pleasant and personalized work environment.

Remember, these are only some of the areas that provide satisfying expression for the unique natural talents of ISFPs.

Customizing Your Job Search

Knowing the particular strengths and blind spots of your type can afford you a tremendous advantage in your job search campaign. In all aspects of the process, from conducting research into available positions, identifying and contacting prospective employers, developing personal marketing tools such as résumés, arranging and conducting job interviews, and negotiating salaries to finally accepting a position, people will act true to their type. Being able to capitalize on your assets and compensate for your liabilities can make the difference between a successful and an unsuccessful job search.

The differences between types are sometimes subtle and other times dramatic. It is the subtle variations in advice we offer that make the real difference between success and failure in a job search. The concept of networking serves as a good example. Extraverts will naturally enjoy networking and are advised to do so on a large scale, while Introverts find more limited and targeted networking, especially with people they already know, easier. Sensors tend to network with people in a defined scope, while Intuitives will go far and wide to find people often seemingly unrelated to their field of interest. Further, Feelers can often take networking personally and enjoy establishing warm rapport, while Thinkers will be more objective and detached in their style. Finally, Judgers tend to ask fewer and more structured questions during their networking, while Perceivers could ask questions of all sorts all day long! One valuable search technique, many ways to implement it.

Pathways to Success: Using Your Strengths

As we will detail in the following pages, your strengths and talents for the job search lie in your personal warmth, desire to please others, and commonsense approach to problems. However, in order to find a satisfying career, you will need to work hard at developing your assertiveness and objectivity so you don't take rejection personally and become discouraged.

As an ISFP, you will find that your most effective strategies build on your abilities to do the following:

Conduct research and collect a lot of data.

- Read as much as you can about the field, position, or organization you are considering. Gather information about a specific company by researching online and talking one-on-one with anyone you can who works there already.
- Go check out the company or business as part of your preparation for interviewing. Look at the way people dress, act, and seem to feel about working where they do. Can you imagine yourself there?

Marc was preparing for an interview for an assistant curator position at a science museum. He decided to get as familiar with the museum and its current exhibits as he could before the interview. He spent hours in the museum getting a feel for the layout and organization. He read as much as possible about the new curator to learn about her career path and her goals for the museum. By the time the interview came, Marc had plenty of questions and was able to offer specific thoughts about what was needed when he was asked what he might contribute to the organization.

Conduct limited, targeted networking.

- Start with your close friends, family, and co-workers (past and present). Ask them to help you generate a list of people who might know of jobs for which you would be qualified.
- Conduct informational interviews with people who actually hold the position you are looking for. Ask them questions to learn what the job, its responsibilities, and limitations really are.

Rohit began his networking at one of many summer backyard cookouts he and his friends had each summer. He began telling his friends of his boredom with his current job and how he wanted to do something different. His friends began brainstorming ideas and then came up with people they knew for Rohit to talk to. It was more of a game than a task, and Rohit was surprised how much help he got from just one evening of talking.

Build and use a support system.

- Remember that searching for a job often takes more time and energy than performing a job. Ask friends for advice and support during this difficult period.
- Take people up on their offers to help. Many of the best contacts are made through purely social connections. Don't rule out anyone as a source of information.

Learn by doing.

- Look for opportunities to be trained on the job, or where employers offer a training program, giving preference to trainees after completing the program.
- Offer your services on a volunteer basis to learn the skills needed to perform the job you seek. You will have both the skills and some real experience to demonstrate to prospective employers.

Remember how Carrie found the job she enjoys? The physicians' office offered on-the-job training, which she took while working temporarily at her previous job. She got the chance to learn on the job and quickly understood what the job would really be like. Luckily for Carrie, she didn't need to try more than one program.

Follow your impulses and natural curiosity.

- Use your short-term problem-solving capabilities by organizing the sometimes long and overwhelming job search into manageable pieces. Reward yourself when you meet each goal.
- If an obstacle arises, meet the challenge with a willingness to adapt. Demonstrate to prospective employers your ability to accept and respond to changing situations.

After careful consideration, Colleen decided that she would enjoy being a dog trainer—it matched her interests, her love of animals, and the opportunity to work hands-on with dogs and with their owners. She researched the best grooming and training center and went on an interview. To her disappointment, she learned that there were no openings for a trainer, but she was offered a job in the grooming department and told there was the possibility that a training position would open up down the road. Her desire to work with animals and the chance to be associated with the high-quality operation she saw during her interview persuaded her to take the job. She decided it was worth the gamble and that it would also give her a chance to demonstrate to the owner her ability to learn quickly and become a valuable member of the staff. After four months, Colleen's patience was rewarded when a trainer position became available and she was offered the job.

Possible Pitfalls

Although all people are unique, there are certain *potential* blind spots that many ISFPs share. We specify "potential" because some of the following *may* be true of you, while others may clearly not apply. While considering them, you may notice that these tendencies do not relate just to the job search but rather describe pitfalls that you may have experienced in other aspects of your life as well. It is therefore helpful to consider each one in terms of your past experiences by asking yourself, "Is this true for me?" And if so, "How did this tendency prevent me from getting something that I wanted?" You will probably notice that the key to overcoming your blind spots is the conscious and thoughtful development of your third and fourth functions (Intuition and Thinking). We recognize that many of the suggestions will be difficult to implement, but the more you use these functions, the fewer problems they will cause you in the future.

Consider all data available to you, even those that may contradict your personal feelings.

- Look at the hard consequences of your actions and decisions. List the pros and cons of a job so you are sure to consider both the positive and the potential negative as well.
- Develop a method of analyzing information before accepting it at face value.

Look for options besides those readily available at the moment.

- Generate a list of possible job options without limiting yourself to what you have done in the past or what you are immediately qualified for.
- Use your ideas of a fantasy job as a springboard to thinking more creatively. Ask a friend who knows you well to help you, and make it a game.

Work hard to prioritize your activities and keep yourself organized.

- Use your skills at short-term planning to get things done and to keep from becoming overwhelmed with the size of the task.

- Develop a complete outline for your career search. Include all the perceivable steps that will be necessary along the way.

Try to make more objective decisions.

- Don't overemphasize the importance of rapport developed with an interviewer. Try to develop some healthy skepticism about others to avoid being too trusting.
- Pay attention to the less tangible but critically important factors, such as the corporate culture and employer's philosophy, which will help keep you from becoming disillusioned after taking the job.

Focus your attention on the future so you will see beyond the present reality and understand choices in their larger context.

- Try imagining a job one, five, and ten years from now. Will this opportunity be one that allows you to grow, or will you be limited in the company or organization?
- Look at the business within the market and decide if the way it is growing or changing will still be acceptable to you in the future. Be sure it isn't just the people you will be working with *now* that make the job appealing.

The Final Piece: Changing or Keeping Your Job . . . the Key to Success for ISFPs

Now that you have a solid understanding of your type, you can see how your natural preferences make you better suited for certain kinds of jobs. You can also see how knowledge of your type-related strengths and blind spots can help you conduct a more successful job search. But as an ISFP, you've

already realized that you are not equally drawn to *every* career or field listed in the Popular Occupations section. The next and final step is to narrow down the field and find the work you were meant to do.

In addition to Type, several other factors—such as your values, interests, and skills—contribute to your level of satisfaction on the job. The more compatible you are with your job, the happier you'll be. So prepare to use everything you've learned (in this book and in life) to create *your strategic career plan*. The exercises in Chapter 23, "Putting It All Together," are designed to help you do just that.

However, you may have decided it makes more sense (if perhaps only for the moment) to stay in your present job or with your current employer. There may be many valid reasons—financial pressures, family considerations, a tough job market for your specialty, or just bad timing. But take heart! What you've learned in this book can also help you be more content and successful *in your current job*. And should the time come when you're ready to make a major career move, you'll have a much better idea of where you want to go and how to get there.

"So, if you can't have the job you love (yet!) . . . love the one you've got."

The simple truth is, many jobs allow a good deal of flexibility in the way tasks are performed. Here are some ways you may be able to "massage" your current job into one that better fits your needs:

- Seek help to resolve any interpersonal conflicts.
- Consider taking an assertiveness-training class.
- Ask supervisors to be clear about their expectations.
- Find time during the day to recharge by yourself.

- Do things that will allow you to help, support, and connect with co-workers.
- Try to make sure there is some variety in your daily activities.
- Participate in recreational activities.
- Seek others with complementary skills to help evaluate your ideas.
- Think about where you want to be five years from now.
- Set short-term, achievable goals.
- Try to find others at work who share similar interests and values.

One ISFP turns lemons into lemonade:

Dana worked for a large pharmaceutical company. When she recently became widowed, she became aware of how many other women in the company were also facing the challenge of working and raising children alone. Although hardly a natural organizer, Dana reached out via email to see if there was any interest in forming a group to help each other with everyday challenges, like carpooling kids to activities, babysitting, and so on. To her surprise and delight, more than a dozen people responded. The group ended up meeting more than her immediate, practical needs. It became a source of emotional support as well, and she developed several close and sustaining friendships.

Use what you've got to get what you need.

Simply put, the best advice on how to succeed is to *capitalize on your strengths and compensate for your blind spots.* Learning how to do this can make the difference between succeeding or failing and loving or hating your work. To help you, we include the following inventory of your potential strengths and blind spots. And while every individual is unique, many of the following should apply to you as an ISFP.

Your work-related strengths may include

- ability to welcome change and adapt well to new situations
- sensitivity to people's needs and desire to help them in real ways
- practicality and realistic perceptions
- good common sense
- warmth and generosity
- loyalty to people and organizations you care deeply about
- attention to important details, especially those that concern people
- thoughtfulness and ability to focus on current needs
- willingness to support the organization's goals
- ability to clearly assess current conditions and see what needs fixing
- flexibility and willingness to take calculated risks and try new approaches

Your work-related blind spots may include

- tendency to accept things at face value and miss deeper implications
- inability to see opportunities and options that don't exist at the moment
- tendency to take criticism and negative feedback personally
- dislike of preparing in advance; you may have trouble organizing your time
- trouble making decisions
- dislike of excessive rules and overly structured bureaucracy
- difficulty making logical decisions if they conflict with personal feelings
- unwillingness to risk disharmony to fight for your idea or position
- tendency to become overwhelmed by large or highly complicated tasks
- resistance to setting long-term goals and difficulty meeting deadlines
- difficulty disciplining direct reports or criticizing others

Using your strengths is easy.
The secret to success for an
ISFP
is learning to

assert yourself, step back and consider
the big picture, and not take
things too personally.

23 PUTTING IT ALL TOGETHER

Creating Your Personal Career Plan

The unique individuals we have met in the previous pages show the infinite variety of satisfying job options available for people of all types. Indeed, there are probably several careers you would find satisfying. But it's not enough to select a job from a list of careers other people of your type have found satisfying. It's not even enough to know your type. Real success lies in taking your awareness of your type-related strengths and blind spots and combining it with an honest appraisal of your personal interests and values. The goal is to find the right match—the career that will let you do what you do best and enjoy most, one that corresponds to your personal interests and is consistent with your basic personality functions and values. And that combination will be unique to you.

To begin to help you visualize the process for yourself, here are examples of how several clients of different types successfully blended their skills and experiences with their individual interests to find the career of their dreams.

Ernie had a career that many ENFPs would have enjoyed. As an organizational development consultant, Ernie worked with teams in businesses to help them understand one another and work more effectively

together. While he enjoyed being self-employed, he was growing bored with teaching virtually the same program year after year and was also thirsty for the intellectual challenge of learning something new. When we asked him to develop a list of interests, Ernie placed the law near the top. His father had been a lawyer, and Ernie had always been fascinated with the legal system and enjoyed watching television shows and seeing movies about lawyers. But he didn't have enough interest in the technical side of law to go through law school and become a lawyer himself. Instead, he decided to use his consulting skills and understanding of psychology to become a trial consultant. Today, Ernie works directly with attorneys, helping them increase their own communication and presentation effectiveness. He also helps attorneys select jurors who are more naturally predisposed to view their side of the case favorably.

Paola, an ENTJ, had been a journalist for nearly twenty years, working her way up to the position of editorial writer at a major daily newspaper. She enjoyed the opportunity to "shine a light on the injustices in society" and spur government to make important changes. She enjoyed the challenge of her job and the daily opportunities to see her articles published.

A child of immigrants, Paola had been an active and vocal member of social justice groups in college, and she continued to participate in trainings and discussions about anti-bias work. In her job as an editorial writer, she began to believe she could do more to further those long-held goals and interests. She decided that she wanted to be a shaper of policy rather than a commentator of change.

So Paola made a list of all the people she knew in her area whose opinions she respected and whose values were similar to her own. She called on these individuals, taking many of them to breakfast or lunch to inquire about potential job opportunities. At one breakfast, she met with a politician she admired. He told her that a position as his executive assistant would become available soon. One of the things he was asking all candidates to do was write a speech on a highly technical financial strategy. Paola researched the information over the next two days and wrote and submitted an excellent speech by the deadline. She was offered the job and is enjoying her newfound opportunity to make a real difference and be a part of important policy-making decisions.

Joy, an ISFJ, got a good job as an administrative assistant for a busy real estate developer. While she made a few friends with the other support personnel, was well paid, and didn't even mind the long hours she put in, she just didn't feel she was making a significant contribution. She was a natural helper and the only person she was helping was her boss—to get richer. Back in high school, Joy had considered becoming a nurse or doctor, but her parents had been unable to afford to send her to either nursing or medical school. While she had managed to save some money, she couldn't afford to quit her job and go to medical school. Finally, Joy decided to follow her original ambition but realized she needed to consider a less expensive alternative to becoming a nurse or doctor. She enrolled in a night program to become a dental hygienist. She kept her job with the developer and gave up her lunch hour a couple of times a week to work for one of the other assistants, who in turn stayed late when necessary on the nights Joy had class. After two years, Joy was able to leave the developer's firm and start working for a small group dental practice that emphasized education with its patients. Joy was able to work using her new skills, helping other people learn about taking care of their teeth and health. Through working closely with her patients and helping them become healthier and happier, Joy found the satisfaction she had been missing.

Matching Your Personality to a Career You Can Love

Evaluating opportunities to determine if they are really right for you is sometimes a difficult task. Guided by the criteria for career satisfaction and the job search strategies in your type chapter, you've most likely been considering specific career options already, perhaps trying on the various possibilities. To develop those options into concrete opportunities, you'll need to examine them closely and measure their suitability for you. A job that's great for one person may not be quite right for another—even if they share a type.

Ten Steps to Creating a Personal Career Plan

While it's helpful and even fun to learn from other people like you as you did in your type chapter, you are a unique individual and need to now take the time to put on paper a true and honest assessment of yourself. The following exercises have been created for you to complete right here in the book, to get the most out of your type chapter. We strongly suggest you take your time with this important process, because answering the questions as thoughtfully and honestly as you can will help you to zero in on satisfying career options and then to design a job search campaign that gets results. Good luck!

Step 1: Your Unique Personality Strengths and Blind Spots

This exercise can help determine whether you have identified your true type and highlight some of your most important personality characteristics. How well does this brief description fit you?

Using your type profiles from Chapter 3 ("Mirror, Mirror"), list the key words or phrases that are MOST true of you and provide examples that demonstrate these qualities.

1. _____

Example:

_____

_____

2. _____

Example:

_____

_____

3. _____

Example:

_____

_____

Which phrases (if any) are NOT true about you?

1. _____

Example:

_____

_____

2. _____

Example:

_____

_____

3. _____

Example:

_____

_____

Again, using your type profile from Chapter 3, "Mirror, Mirror," list the two blind spots that are MOST true for you. Then provide one or two examples showing how that blind spot prevented you from accomplishing or achieving something you wanted.

1. _____

Example:

_____

_____

Example:

_____

_____

2. _____

Example:

_____

_____

Example:

_____

_____

Step 2: Work-Related Strengths and Blind Spots

Our greatest satisfaction comes from doing what we do best. That's why it's so important to identify our work-related strengths so we can make sure our job will be enjoyable.

Using the list of work-related strengths from your type chapter, rank your three greatest strengths and provide one or two examples from your work life that demonstrate how you've used each strength successfully.

STRENGTHS:

1. _____

Example:

_____

_____

2. _____

Example:

_____

_____

3. _____

Example:

_____

_____

Using the list of work-related possible pitfalls from your type chapter, rank your three greatest blind spots and provide one or two examples from your work that illustrate how they prevented you from accomplishing or achieving something you wanted.

BLIND SPOTS:

1. _____

Example:

_____

_____

2. _____

Example:

_____

_____

3. _____

Example:

_____

_____

Step 3: Criteria for Career Satisfaction

Review the list of important criteria for career satisfaction for your type in the Common Threads section of your type chapter. Prioritize the list, determining the most- to least-important elements for you. This will take some serious consideration, since it may be difficult to give more weight to some elements than to others. But your efforts will be rewarded, because the results will be a clearer picture than you ever had before of what it takes to satisfy you.

• Record the top-five criteria below:

1. _____
2. _____
3. _____
4. _____
5. _____

Step 4: Career Satisfiers at Work

Using your current job (if it's satisfying) or a past job that was satisfying, describe one or more situations in which each of the top *three* satisfiers were present.

• Record your observations below:

_____

_____

_____

_____

_____

_____

Step 5: What Interests You?

Think about your strongest interests. They may be specific activities like hiking or writing, or general areas such as music or business. In either case, try to identify those things you enjoy so much you would do them for free (if you could afford to!).

• Record your observations below:

_____

_____

_____

_____

_____

_____

Step 6: Identifying Your Skills

To identify what you do well, review the Skills and Abilities list below. Decide which of these (as well as any others not listed) describe you best. Select your top-five skills and generate an example of how you have used each in the past. (Don't limit your observations only to past work experiences. Consider recreational uses of these skills as well.)

SKILLS AND ABILITIES
Writing
Public speaking
Persuading
Selling
Negotiating
Working on a team
Working with others
Supervising others
Teaching
Coaching
Counseling
Coordinating projects/tasks
Managing
Meeting people easily
Working with numbers

Collecting information
Interpreting data
Solving quantitative problems
Concentration/focus
Research
Attention to detail
Manual dexterity
Understanding how tools/machinery work
Physical stamina
Meeting deadlines
Precision
Aesthetic sensitivity
Imagination
Disciplining others
Making decisions
Seeing possibilities
Mentoring
Facilitating
Resolving conflicts
Developing prototypes
Observing accurately
Establishing procedures/rules
Managing crises
Synthesizing information
Analyzing problems
Strategizing
Maintaining systems
Critiquing
Assessing priorities
Learning new skills
Understanding complicated ideas
Working with theories
Adapting to changing situations
Flexibility

• Record your top-five skills below:

1. _____
2. _____
3. _____
4. _____
5. _____

- Record your examples of how you have used each in the past below:

_____

_____

_____

_____

_____

Step 7: Careers to Consider

Generate a list of possible careers or jobs that are of interest to you at this point. Refer to the Popular Occupations section of your type chapter to help you, and add any other occupations that interest you. Briefly note what appeals to you about each.

- Record your observations below:

_____

_____

_____

_____

_____

Step 8: Evaluating Your Career Options

Analyze each position individually, asking yourself the following:

1. How well does it make use of my best skills and abilities?
2. How well does it make use of my work-related strengths? (Refer back to Step 2 for your work-related strengths.)
3. How well does it meet my top-five criteria for career satisfaction? (Refer back to Step 3 for your top-five selections.)

- Record your observations below:

_____

_____

_____

_____

Step 9: Researching Your Potential Career

To learn as much as you can about the specific fields or occupations you have identified above as a good match for you, you'll need to research them thoroughly. Here are some tips for evaluating good career options:

1. Conduct informational interviews with people already in the job or field to find out what it is really like and how that person found the job. Ask your interviewers how they see your interests, skills, and qualifications fitting with the specific job in question.
2. If additional or specialized training or education is required, research local colleges, universities, or training facilities to learn the cost and length of time such training would require. Consider online training and degrees.
3. Conduct research into areas of interest and specific companies. Explore their websites and read as much as you can online.
4. Research any geographical considerations such as where the jobs are, whether a move will be required, and whether that's a possibility for you.

Step 10: How to Get There from Here

Developing a customized job search plan that capitalizes on your natural strengths and compensates for any possible type-related blind spots is the critical next step.

Consider each Pathway to Success, and think of several instances in the past when you've demonstrated these abilities. (Remember, don't limit your observations to work activities.)

• Record your observations below:

_____

_____

_____

_____

_____

_____

Strength: _____

Example: _____

Strength: _____

Example: _____

Strength: _____

Example: _____

Strength: _____

Example: _____

Now consider each Possible Pitfall and again try to remember instances in the past when NOT paying attention to these blind spots prevented you from achieving something or got you into trouble.

• Record your observations below:

Blind spot: _____

Example: _____

Blind spot: _____

Example: _____

Blind spot: _____

Example: _____

Blind spot: _____

Example: _____

On Your Mark . . . Get Set . . . GO!

Now that you've had a chance to identify at least one—and perhaps several—potentially satisfying jobs, we suggest you keep your type chapter well marked and return to the Customizing Your Job Search section whenever you need to as you begin to implement your plan of action.

One final message of inspiration. Writing this book has taught us many things, most of which we learned directly from the many wonderful, career-satisfied people we interviewed. And perhaps the most important message we have to share is that if your belief in something is strong enough, if it's really right for you, or you feel you were meant to do it, then you will find the inner resources to make it happen. Work can be exciting, fulfilling, rewarding, and fun; it can be what you need and want it to be and you can even be well paid! There is at least one great career out there with your name on it—a career that really rewards you for using your natural gifts and lets you do what you enjoy most and do best. It's possible, you deserve it, and you don't have to settle for anything less.

24 ‖ ENCORE! ENCORE!

*Success Stories of Satisfying
Second Acts*

"Do not go gentle into that good night'!"

When the Welsh poet Dylan Thomas wrote these words, he was referring to not giving in to death without a fight. But we'd like to repurpose his quote to mean "Don't give up on finding satisfying work after retirement." In fact, many people will experience *greater* fulfillment in their "encore careers" than they found in jobs they worked at for most of their lives. This chapter is designed to help you do just that.

The days of retiring at sixty-five are no longer a reality for many people. On one hand, many people do not have the financial resources to retire completely. At the same time, the average life expectancy in the United States has increased to seventy-eight and a half years (seventy-six for men, eighty-one for women). As a result, those who do retire in their sixties have ten to twenty years on average to do...*something*. This chapter will help you discover the "something" that will be intrinsically satisfying, because it makes use of your natural gifts and is in sync

with your values. In other words, you can do what you are well into retirement.

Some Good News...Some Bad News... Some Even Better News!

First the good: You are probably going to live longer that your parents did. However, you may be forced to retire before you want to or feel you can comfortably afford to. But the best news is, you now have an opportunity to find work—either paid or volunteer—that will result in the greatest career satisfaction you've ever had.

A 2012 *Parade* magazine survey asked readers: "If you could do it all over again, would you choose the same career?" It might surprise you to learn that 59 percent said they would *not* select the same career. There are many reasons why this is the case, but here's the shorthand version: Most people make their most important career decisions at a time when they're least prepared to do so. At sixteen or seventeen, students who will soon be graduating high school need to think seriously about their future. Will they go to college (for those lucky enough to have that option), and if they do, what will they study? Most colleges require students to declare a major by the end of their sophomore year—when they're nineteen or twenty years old. Decisions made then start students down a path that will influence their entire life.

Take a moment to think back to how well you knew yourself at that age. If you're like most people, the answer may be "Not very well!" Still, this is when we are all pressured to make some of our most important life-altering decisions.

Consider this pretty common scenario: Brendon is a smart kid without any particular passion in high school. But because he likes to argue, his parents have been telling him from a very early age that he'd make a great lawyer. So Brendon enrolls in a liberal arts college and at nineteen decides to major in policy and government—often recommended for prelaw students. While he likes his courses all right, they neither uncover nor ignite in Brendon a passion for the law.

Brendon's parents invest more than $200,000 in his undergraduate education. And upon graduation, they pressure Brendon to make sure their investment pays off by enrolling in law school. Three years later, after passing the state licensing exam, Brendon becomes an esteemed member of the bar. To pay for law school, Brendon took out a loan, so on graduation day he is $150,000 in debt.

Now the pressure begins in earnest. Fortunately, Brendon manages to land a job pretty quickly as an associate at a midsize firm. Although he is making decent money, he has a grueling schedule, often working fifty to sixty hours per week. Still, he is one of the lucky ones, as a year later many of his classmates are still desperately seeking their first job.

Fast-forward three years. Brendon, now twenty-seven, has a new fiancée and—between his student loans, car and mortgage payments, and condo fees—hefty monthly living expenses. Still working a ridiculous number of hours, Brendon is hoping to grab the brass ring and someday make partner.

The only problem is, Brendon doesn't really like being a lawyer. The other, more exotic and lucrative specialties within his field don't appeal to him either.

Unfortunately, Brendon's story is not terribly unique: Almost half of the lawyers surveyed by the American Bar Association reported dissatisfaction with their careers, and only 40 percent said they would recommend a legal career to others. And Brendon is one of the lucky ones! For seventeen- to eighteen-year-old students who don't have a college option, the challenges of finding satisfying and fulfilling work may be even greater.

As strange as it may sound, most people put more time and energy into researching which new car to buy than which career would bring them the greatest satisfaction and success. The real point of this story is that many—perhaps most—of us end up in careers that are not intrinsically satisfying. And even though we might recognize this pretty early on, we put off making a major career change. Time moves quickly: Days turn into weeks, weeks into months, and months into years. And there comes a point for many of us when we simply feel like we're unable to make the change.

But Now Things Are Different!

You know yourself so much better. With age and experience comes a certain amount of wisdom. You understand your strengths and your blind spots. You know the kinds of activities that energize and drain you. You've learned what kinds of people drive you crazy and, hopefully, how to avoid them.

As you've matured, so has your value system. Time has given you the ability to better see the big picture and know what's truly important in your life. Clearly, many things have changed for, and in, you over the last twenty, thirty, or forty years. But what hasn't changed is your personality type and your temperament—the keys to finding a more satisfying, fulfilling encore career.

Why Temperament Is the Key to Career Satisfaction

In Chapter 4, "What a Character!," we introduced the theory of temperament, which we think of as four different human natures.

For those of you who like more depth, this might be a good time to take a few minutes to reacquaint yourself with Chapter 4. But the majority of you will find the summary we provide here all you need to know to understand the important role your temperament plays in helping you find a satisfying encore career.

You may remember there are four temperaments, which we've labeled Traditionalists, Experiencers, Idealists, and Conceptualizers. And there are four personality types that fall under each temperament.

Traditionalists (SJs): ESTJ ISTJ ESFJ ISFJ
Experiencers (SPs): ESTP ISTP ESFP ISFP
Idealists (NFs): ENFJ INFJ ENFP INFP
Conceptualizers (NTs): ENTJ INTJ ENTP INTP

Why is temperament so critical to career satisfaction and success? Because it reflects our core values and key motivations. Below is a thumbnail sketch of each of the four temperaments:

Traditionalists
Approximately 46 percent of the American population

Traditionalists are driven to be of service. They are super responsible and extremely hardworking. When they say they will do something, they will—their word is their bond. Traditionalists take a tried-and-true approach to life and place great value on the importance of family and institutions. They trust and respect authority, follow rules, and expect others to as well.

Career Satisfiers:

- Being of service
- Having a high level of responsibility and control
- A stable, predictable work environment
- Clear expectations and directions
- Being able to see the results of their efforts

Experiencers
Approximately 27 percent of the American population

Experiencers enjoy living life to its fullest, experiencing as much as they possibly can. Having the freedom to be spontaneous and responsive to opportunities as they arise makes them feel alive. Experiencers tend to take a more laid-back, casual approach to life and often enjoy being physically engaged.

Career Satisfiers:

- Having fun; enjoying their work and co-workers

- Freedom to act; not being micromanaged
- A casual work setting without too many rules
- Being physically engaged
- Using established skills to perform real, concrete tasks

Idealists
Approximately 16 percent of the American population

Idealists seek and thrive on having meaningful personal relationships. Perceptive about people and extremely empathetic, they derive great satisfaction from helping others. To Idealists, authenticity—in themselves and in others— is nonnegotiable. Creative and collaborative, Idealists often feel compelled to take on causes that improve people's lives.

Career Satisfiers:

- Work that is personally meaningful
- Work that helps others
- A tension-free, supportive work environment
- Close personal relationships with colleagues, clients, etc.
- Being able to provide creative input

Conceptualizers
Approximately 10 percent of the American population

Conceptualizers are on a lifelong quest for knowledge. They are quick studies who enjoy intellectual challenges and being able to solve problems creatively. Global and strategic, Conceptualizers set high standards for themselves and others, and place enormous value on competence. Independence is also a hallmark in these

people, who have a strong drive to be successful.

Career Satisfiers:

- Work that continually challenges them
- Applying their creativity to solve problems
- Continuing to learn and develop new competencies
- Having a great deal of independence
- The opportunity for career advancement

How This Chapter Can Help You

In this chapter, you will find two examples of people of each temperament who have found satisfying encore careers. It's most important for you to read the profiles of people who share your temperament, which should resonate strongly with you. Each profile describes the person's first and encore careers. This is followed by our analysis of why this second career choice is a good one for each person profiled.

In our analysis, we discuss the importance of temperament as well as each person's dominant function. As you may remember from Chapter 5, "Who's on First?," each personality type has one aspect that represents that type's greatest natural strengths. We call this the dominant function. Why is it important to know what your dominant is? Because when we are engaging our dominant function, we are more satisfied and successful. Using our dominant actually energizes us. For example, suppose your dominant is Intuition (seeing possibilities and making connections). After a long day at work, you may be bone tired. But if a friend were to ask you to help brainstorm some possible solutions to a problem they are having, you might suddenly come to life and find new energy. This is because you would get the chance to use your dominant Intuition. It's easy to see how much more satisfied people are when their job allows them to use their dominant function a lot. And how dissatisfied people are when their job does not allow them to use theirs very much.

Our analysis also touches on the role that each person's type development plays in making that particular encore career a good choice. Why is this important to know?

Carl Jung, on whose theories Personality Type is based, believed that we are all born with our personality type, which we have for our entire lives. However, as we reach midlife and come to accept that our journey will eventually end, we seek "wholeness." This comes from using the parts of our personality type that do not come naturally to us. Other Type experts have even laid out a timeline by which each of the sixteen types works (unconsciously) to develop various aspects of that type. So although we might say "Once an ISTJ, always an ISTJ" (which is true for all types), a fifty-year-old ISTJ may find herself drawn to use different parts of her personality than a twenty-year-old ISTJ.

An example: If a person who is naturally a Thinking type (logical and objective) is now developing her Feeling function (sensitive and value driven), she might exhibit more interest in others and have greater access to her own emotional life. A job that involves helping people work out their problems—which might not have appealed to her early in her career—might be very appealing now. (For a more in-depth discussion of type development, see Chapter 6, "Aged to Perfection.")

Now it's time to read the two profiles that reflect your temperament.

▌ Traditionalists
Profile 1: Jay

"From running a company to managing a classroom."

Jay was a government major in college, and his first career was as a newspaper reporter, writing four or five articles a week. "It was great being able to go out and talk to people making news in a small town like Albany." Although Jay enjoyed the job, he left after two years to work as the publicity manager for a PR firm. A few years later, he moved back to Connecticut for family reasons. He worked as a financial analyst and got his MBA at the same time. Jay enjoyed accounting and found financial analysis fun, but he left after five years to take an opportunity to work in his family's manufacturing business.

Jay started as a salesperson at the family-owned company, which had been manufacturing industrial sewing machine parts for the garment industry for 160 years. After only two years, Jay became the president. "I loved being able to apply everything I had learned in schooling to a real-life small business. But being a manager in a union shop also presented some real challenges." Because the garment industry had moved to Mexico, Central America, India, and China, competition was fierce. Realizing that if he stayed with the company, he would spend most of his time traveling, Jay decided it was time to leave. As it turned out, the economic writing was on the wall: A year later, the family sold the company's assets.

While he was running the business, Jay had been coaching sports on the side. And with four boys within six years of each other, he got lots of practice. So he decided it was time to follow his heart and became a teacher. He spent the next four years substitute teaching as he earned a second master's degree in curriculum and instruction.

Encore! Encore!

After working for twenty-five years in various businesses, Jay began his encore career at the age of forty-six, teaching history and social studies in a suburban high school in New England. What Jay loves best about teaching is being able to put together plans to reach all kids. He enjoys seeing his plans implemented and watching each student grow. Jay chose to teach high school students because the students are old enough to relate the lessons to their life experiences and make higher-level contributions. But as with any job, Jay experiences frustrations: "It's hard to accept that I can't do everything that I think I should be doing for these kids. There just aren't enough hours in the day."

Another challenge for Jay is that teachers are required to teach new courses each year. "While this makes me more versatile, it's hard to reinvent the wheel. Frankly, I'd prefer to be able to dive deep and really get to know the content—that would make teaching easier for me." Also draining for Jay is the sheer amount of time required: "The first few years were brutal—I learned that if you're not careful, you can easily find yourself working seven days a week."

As for his decision to leave business for teaching, Jay says: "Although it was an economic sacrifice for a few years, I'm really glad I made the change—and wish I'd done it sooner."

Why This Encore Career Works for Jay

After four years teaching, Jay received tenure. While job security is desired by all types, it is particularly valued by

Traditionalists, as is being of service: "My role for the rest of my working career is to help as many people as I can." He appreciates the structure and clear expectations of his public school, like the requirements tied to teaching core competencies. Jay enjoys having a lot of responsibility and control. "I have guidelines for what I have to teach every semester, but I like to create my own lesson plans." Finally, it's important for Jay to be able to see the results of his efforts: "I love to see that light go on for kids who struggle. With hard work and extra help, they're able to really get it."

As an ISTJ (Introverted, Sensing, Thinking, Judging), Jay is a dominant Sensor, so it's not difficult to understand why he would be drawn to teaching history—the chronicling of real events, experienced by real people, over a long time. But evidence is abundant that Jay is in the process of developing his third function, Feeling. In the last few years, "it's become more important than ever to make sure I'm a really good role model to my boys, in everything I do." And as he and his wife have traveled around the world, he has become much more sensitive to the plight of others in less affluent cultures. He describes his "enormous admiration" for his wife, Ashley, who started Asante Sana for Education, a nonprofit organization that builds schools in Tanzania. In addition to supporting her efforts, Jay has developed new empathy for the needs of local people as well, often spending vacation days working in soup kitchens.

Profile 2: Rob

"From insurance claims to adult college advising."

After graduating with a BS in communications, Rob applied to a large insurance company where he hoped to land a job in public relations. Unfortunately, a hiring freeze made it impossible for him to get into the company for two years. When the freeze thawed, Rob found it much easier to get into claims, and planned to move to public relations eventually. But eighteen months later, Rob was promoted to supervisor, and now firmly ensconced in claims, he spent the next twelve years as a supervisor and team leader.

What Rob loved best was coaching employees and helping them do their jobs better. "Many were new college grads, and I enjoyed providing them with their first introduction into business and helping them understand organizational behavior." What Rob liked least was collecting data and having to fill out reports—things that didn't involve the people and relationship side of the business. Although he was technically a field employee, he actively participated in facilitating training at the company's nationally recognized education-focused institute. "My company kept developing me and I kept developing others, which was mutually beneficial. This gave me a chance not just to keep my knowledge to myself, but to share it with others." He also loved meeting people from all over the country who came to the institute, and took pride in his ability to make insurance fun.

After some years, Rob moved to another insurance company and became a supervisor and account manager in charge of commercial accounts. "Although I got to learn about something completely different—commercial insurance and contracts—I still yearned to do more training and coaching." While he continued to work, Rob went back to graduate school for a master's in organizational behavior.

Rob's next job was also in insurance, but this time it was as the director of training

and development. The company was growing very rapidly, and when they lost their major account, they were forced to go out of business. So Rob moved on to another insurer—this one specialized in providing medical malpractice insurance. "I always had great respect for doctors. I took it to heart. I didn't want medical errors to happen, and in this job I got to point out where docs made mistakes and help them to be better."

Rob's tenure at this company lasted ten years. But when the economy turned, Rob was laid off once again. Through luck or providence, he discovered a program run by Leadership Greater Hartford called Encore!-Hartford—a program that helps managers and professionals find work in the nonprofit sector. The program provided him with training, contacts, and confidence that led to his next assignment, as an organizational development consultant at a local hospital, where he was primarily in charge of facilitating groups. While Rob enjoyed the exciting pace, the job as a whole did not turn out to be a great fit.

Encore! Encore!

A couple years ago, Rob secured his dream position at a local university. "Everybody has a path, and my path has taken me in lots of directions, but this is the greatest job I've had yet." It allows him to use many of his best skills in service of a mission he deeply believes in. As assistant director of the Center for Adult Academic Services, Rob recruits and consults with adults who want to secure undergraduate or graduate degrees. And ironically, a fair amount of the job involves public relations—the field that Rob sought to begin his career in so many years earlier.

In addition to recruiting and advising, Rob does a lot of outreach, speaking at community colleges, corporations, and professional associations. There are about 150 adults in the program at various stages of pursuing degrees. "It's especially moving on graduation day when I get to meet their families and celebrate the payoff for the incredible sacrifices they made to get an education. I've been given the privilege of helping these people develop their skills and the confidence to move ahead in their lives."

Why This Encore Career Works for Rob

As an ESFJ (Extraverted, Sensing, Feeling, Judging), Rob is not only a Traditionalist but also a dominant Feeler. An important reason why Rob likes this position so much is that it is in sync with many of his Traditionalist values: Rob believes wholeheartedly in the program's mission, and he gets to help people in real and concrete ways every day. Rob knows exactly what is expected of him and is given the responsibility and resources to do his job well. Traditionalists such as Rob have a very strong work ethic and a desire to see proof that their hard work is paying off. Rob's need for a personal connection with students is also frequently reinforced when he receives feedback that his efforts helped them succeed.

This is the time in his life when people of Rob's type develop their third function—Intuition. A few years ago, Rob found himself starting to ask "why" more, seeking answers to questions that he hadn't thought much about in the past. This manifested itself in more curiosity and an eagerness to learn new things. Not coincidentally, this was about the time he decided to go back and get his master's degree. Rob also reports that he's become more open-minded and "a little more accepting of the changes that life invariably throws at us."

▌ Experiencers

Profile 1: Cindy

"Not your typical banker!"

After graduating from college, Cindy spent the next twelve years holding a variety of positions in banking: retail bank manager, private banking officer, regional sales manager in brokerage services with supervisory responsibility, and ultimately training and development manager. Although she enjoyed certain aspects of banking—especially helping customers and building relationships with co-workers—there was much that rubbed this natural free spirit the wrong way. She found the repetitive nature of several of her day-to-day responsibilities tedious and boring. And there were way too many rules. "I wanted to do the job the way I thought it should be done best, but that just wasn't the way that banks worked. My attitude was 'Tell me what you want me to do, give me a deadline, then leave me alone and let me do it.' But the way you had to do things was so scripted."

Itching for the chance for more real interaction with people, Cindy enrolled in a graduate program that would give her a master's degree in training—and even got the bank to pay for it. Cindy wisely chose a program that fit her well: "Their focus was not theoretical. I don't do theory, it's not real. I'm not conceptual; I'm pragmatic and like to focus on practical applications." Looking for some hands-on experience, Cindy approached her manager and offered to train all of their new reps. And with previous managerial experience already under her belt, she was in a great place to apply—and be hired—when a training manager position became available in the financial services division. Cindy loved working with her team to create all the training programs, but once the programs were in place, it felt repetitive and boring. When her bank was acquired, she transitioned into a senior training manager role, where she worked for another two years.

After that, Cindy got married and moved to New Hampshire, where her husband worked. Her career in banking was about to undergo a big change. While her old bank had 18,000 domestic employees, her new community bank had only 135. Cindy loved the change because she could actually see the application of what she was teaching, observing her students using skills that she had taught them the day before. Although she had started working part-time, Cindy was quickly promoted to VP of employee education and development. She stayed at this job for ten years and "pretty much loved every minute of it. I can count on two hands the number of times they said no to something I wanted to do."

Recently, Cindy and her family moved to Virginia. After twenty-five years of waking up and going to a bank every day, she took a little more than a year off and set up her own consulting practice. Unfortunately, the economy didn't cooperate, and everything fell apart. So in 2010, she went back into banking.

Encore! Encore!

While Cindy's first career was as a banker, her new career is as an educator of bankers. "I found a way to be a free spirit and independent inside a bank." Now the director of training at a community bank in Virginia, Cindy plays a variety of roles, designing, developing, and delivering educational initiatives. "I love the delivery, enjoy the design. The development is doable but drains my energy big time." She also does organizational development work—helping people and teams communicate more successfully, and building leadership curricula, which help people develop trusting relationships. "I help people understand how they learn best, so that they can absorb the knowledge they need to be effective at work. I am a great believer in leveraging people's strengths and helping them truly know their natural capabilities."

Why This Encore Career Works for Cindy

There are many reasons this new career works for Cindy the Experiencer, whose full type is ESTP (Extraverted, Sensing, Thinking, Perceiving). Cindy naturally craves action and loves to work on a variety of tasks, both of which she experiences daily in this position. As the leader of education in the bank, she has a lot of control over what she does and how she does it. Cindy is in her comfort zone, getting to apply her established skills in an industry she already knows well.

Like all Experiencers, Cindy enjoys being in the moment and acting spontaneously. For example, she might be training one module but realize the group needs to go in a totally different direction. "I love having the freedom to turn on a dime." Because she's a dominant Sensor, she "sees things that others just don't see," and her auxiliary Thinking almost compels her to point these things out. However, Cindy's type development plays a role in her success as well. This is the stage in life where ESTPs naturally develop Feeling (their third function). Cindy has become a much more patient and sensitive listener, great at paraphrasing what people are saying and helping them see new perspectives.

Profile 2: Sergio

"From court officer to tax preparer."

Born in Argentina, Sergio was eight when he moved to the United States. When he entered community college, Sergio had no clue what he wanted to do, so he dropped out and explored various options. One job he took was as an assistant teacher of math in a high school equivalency program. "It was great. They let me do whatever I wanted to." What he liked best was using real-life examples that his students related to and could understand.

Eventually, Sergio went back and graduated college with a BS in grant writing. In need of a job, he wrote and received a grant to create a public access television show produced by underserved kids. "They did everything, from writing the scripts and making the props to designing the sets and filming the show." The show ran for twelve episodes and was highly successful. Afterward, Sergio applied for and was offered three different jobs. He chose to work for the state in the judicial department.

Sergio began working as a court officer in child support. His job involved combing through data to find people who were delinquent in payments, trying to make a deal to get them to comply, and then presenting their cases to various judges. What he liked was the flexibility he was afforded managing his own caseload. "I got to set my own priorities and organize my time to make it all work." Sergio was energized when he was put in charge of creating an education program. He traveled around the state teaching workers how to do things like use the computer system and present a case in court, and he got to create a regular newsletter. He was disappointed when the project was turned into a permanent job but given to someone else.

As for his regular duties, there was much that Sergio did not find satisfying. "All the judges were different, so there was practically no consistency. There was a ton

of politics and no team approach. Promotions were heavily influenced by who you knew." His promotion to supervisor made the situation worse: "I lost all freedom. Now I had to supervise a lot of...crazies"— some who would file petty grievances against him for reasons he considered frivolous. "Every day when I walked in the door, I thought: 'Let the games begin!'"

However, the state did provide a large degree of security, which allowed Sergio to meet his family obligations, so he continued to work in this field until he retired at the age of fifty-six.

Encore! Encore!

Unfortunately, Sergio's wife got sick soon after he retired, and their plans to travel were curtailed as her illness progressed. Sergio didn't know anything about taxes but was good at math, and on a whim he took a course with a national tax preparation company. One of the draws for him was the promise of a job if he passed the exam, which he did.

Since then, Sergio has been helping people prepare their taxes. "I really enjoy the variety. One of my clients was an elephant trainer, another teaches etiquette. People come in with all sorts of problems, and I get to help them." Sergio also enjoys the flexibility a seasonal job affords him. He's very busy for about four and a half months, and for the rest of the year gets to take classes that increase both his knowledge and his compensation. "I hate the winter but love the summer, and this job gives me lots of time to do the things I love, like biking, kayaking, and playing tennis." Requiring a solid skill that's in demand, at a company with offices all over the world, this position affords Sergio a lot of options. It's a job he could see himself doing for a while.

Why This Encore Career Works for Sergio

While at first blush, preparing taxes might seem too sedate a job for a normally action-seeking Experiencer, it does provide much that Experiencers thrive on: variety, flexibility, and freedom. One of the most dissatisfying parts of Sergio's first career as a court officer—and especially as a supervisor—was the lack of freedom and autonomy. After so many years, he had basically seen it all—been there, done that. But in his encore career, every person that walks through his door has a different story.

As an ESFP (Extraverted, Sensing, Feeling, Perceiving), Sergio has a dominant function of Sensing, which serves him well in a job that requires very close attention to detail. And he is dealing with real people facing real challenges, something that more literal-minded Sensing types relish. But it is his auxiliary function—Feeling—that compels him to want to help others, and Sergio's Feeling function is nourished by being able to do this every day.

As for Sergio's type development, he now has much greater access to his third function, Thinking. Criticism from a tough supervisor, for example, "just rolls off my back, which wasn't always the case."

‖ Idealists
Profile 1: Guthrie

"From college professor to spiritual life coach."

Guthrie graduated from Princeton and spent the next four years "bouncing around the United States and Europe, traveling and doing a bunch of odd jobs and all kinds of crazy stuff." After moving to New York City,

he got a job working in book publishing as an administrative assistant but quickly rose to director of promotion. His position provided some amazing opportunities for this former English major. One day, he asked an editor colleague if he could read the next book that the editor thought would become a bestseller. That book turned out to be *The World According to Garp* by John Irving. Guthrie remembers, "This was the reason I went into publishing. It was amazing! I couldn't put the book down and spent every spare moment trying to develop a following and get it into bookstores." When he got to meet John Irving, he told him, "I feel like Holden Caulfield [from *The Catcher in the Rye*]! Sometimes you want to call up an author and talk to him, and here you are in my office."

A casualty of massive publishing layoffs at the time, Guthrie freelanced various publishing assignments for a while before moving back to his hometown and trying his hand at journalism. What he liked best about being a reporter was the autonomy and opportunity to write stories he was interested in, but he was frustrated by being, as he says, "restricted to using a sixth-grade vocabulary." He left the paper and became a freelance journalist. One day, he got an assignment that required a historical context that he didn't have. "I started reading and didn't stop until I had a Ph.D."

Upon entering graduate school, Guthrie's goal was to become a college professor. "What I immediately liked about academia was that I could use my entire vocabulary! The whole endeavor seemed to be about exchanging ideas and finding truth—looking for meaning in the past so that people could understand the present more deeply and completely."

While he enjoyed mastering the material, presenting it clearly, and watching students become engaged and make progress, eventually the appeal of the teaching game began to fade. "I lost faith in the whole enterprise of using an academic discipline like history as a way of finding truth. I had proved my competence to myself but needed more meaning."

Encore! Encore!

After seven years of being firmly ensconced in the ivory tower, Guthrie began his second career as a life coach. There are probably as many approaches to life coaching as there are coaches, but Guthrie's is clearly spiritual: "I introduce people to themselves at their deepest level." Guthrie's work is profoundly personal and intensive. "I create enough safety for people to share their deepest pain and vulnerability. Often people think this pain is proof of their weakness and failure. But I help them to understand how precious the pain is, because it helps them appreciate not only their own humanity, but everybody else's." Guthrie has truly found his calling: "It's the thing I do best and it serves other people, and that is deeply, deeply gratifying."

Guthrie is also on the faculty of a coaching school. He leads online classes, runs small groups, and mentors other coaches. "Working one on one is amazing and provides a maximum impact. In a short time, I'm able to understand my mentees on a deep level and make a difference in their journey—especially their belief in themselves as people who can make a difference with their clients."

While being a life coach is clearly fulfilling, there are occasional frustrations. Being a solo practitioner and having to attend to the mundane details of business can be draining. And "after a particularly energizing session, it's hard to go back and do the more routine parts of the business." But Guthrie is very aware of this natural blind spot and uses it to

help himself and his clients grow as a result. "I try to practice what I preach. I'm rigorous about always being fully ready for a session and clear about financial arrangements. Although these can be uncomfortable conversations to have, my clients grow from my modeling this positive practice."

Why This Encore Career Works for Guthrie

Of the four Idealist types, INFPs (Introverted, Intuitive, Feeling, Perceiving), like Guthrie, find it most important to have work that is personally meaningful and that resonates with their deepest values. Not only is it a core value of Guthrie's to be genuine, but one of his missions is "to help others discover and become their authentic selves." Through coaching individuals, mentoring other coaches, and giving workshops, Guthrie has developed many deep and cherished relationships. His extraordinary empathy allows him to experience others' pain and joy, a quality driven by his well-developed, dominant Feeling function.

Over the last five to ten years, Guthrie has become more conscious of the importance of being completely present for others and fully inhabiting his body. He does this by walking in the woods, working out, and practicing yoga—consciously engaging his third function, Sensing. In helping others to become their full, most authentic selves every day, Guthrie finds himself developing his own truest self, and nothing could be more satisfying.

Profile 2: Deb

"From corporate salesperson and manager to therapist and career counselor."

Deb's plan to save the world took an unexpected detour when she went to buy a new phone and ended up spending the next twenty-four years working for the phone company.

Graduating with a BS in child development, with a minor in human sexuality, Deb had originally planned to be a sex therapist. "I fantasized about being the next Masters and Johnson." It was while job hunting that Deb happened to walk into the phone store and discover job openings that were paying almost twice as much as she would have received working for a childcare center, plus tuition reimbursement. Deb figured she'd take the job, get her master's paid for, and then go on to save the world.

Deb began her career at AT&T selling long-distance services to small businesses and went on to sell international services to global companies for most of her career. She loved creating relationships, selling, mentoring, and coaching. "I truly believed that I was helping people by providing a service." As she climbed higher and higher up the corporate ladder, she got to work with very powerful people and travel to exotic places. "I could pretend that I was one of them, and that made me feel important. They accepted my input and respected me, which made me feel affirmed."

What she didn't like was having to pay so much attention to details, or forecasting and delivering bad news to clients or employees. Also, there was little tolerance in her work environment for expressing one's emotions, which made being a Feeling type challenging at times. Deb grew frustrated at the reality that the bottom line—not customers' needs or feelings—drove most business decisions. And although she enjoyed much that came with having such an important job, it could be especially stressful when a customer had a crisis that she had to respond to immediately. "Whenever I had to travel and leave my family, I left with a suitcase full of guilt."

Deb had been at AT&T for twenty-four years when she got sick and landed in the hospital. Feeling compelled to work, even in the midst of an illness, was an awakening. "I realized that I was always taking care of others and not myself." Coincidentally, her job was about to get much more technical, requiring additional education—but not in a field that interested her. Deb decided to take an early retirement package. As part of the deal, she could get a master's degree of her choice. She spent the next two years studying and three in internships before opening a practice as a licensed marriage and family therapist and career counselor.

Encore! Encore!

Deb has an eclectic practice, though she spends the majority of her time working with couples in transition: "What's especially gratifying is that since I know the business world so well, many of the clients from that world are able to relate to me. Particularly with men, because I know their stresses and frustrations and speak their language, they feel safe enough with me to be able to access their emotions." She also helps people changing careers, kids moving from college to the corporate world, and retirees trying to figure out what's next.

Because she was so different from most of her colleagues at the phone company (an Intuitive Feeling type in a very Sensing Thinking culture), Deb often felt like the odd man out. While her career path may seem an unorthodox training for a therapist, Deb says, "If I could have a do-over, I wouldn't change a thing. My long corporate experience separates me from other therapists. I feel like I'm able to bring a different and very useful perspective that few others have." Deb is thrilled with the way her career path played out. "I'm happier than I've ever been. It's taken a while, but I feel like I've finally found my authentic self."

Why This Encore Career Works for Deb

There's a good reason why more therapists are Idealists than any of the other temperaments. Deb's combination of Intuition and Feeling gives her both extraordinary perceptiveness and empathy. Sitting with clients, Deb not only feels how much pain they're in, but also sees a path to how they can heal. "I'm an optimist by nature, and I'm able to reassure people that there is a light at the end of the tunnel: They will feel better." Deb also has superb communication skills, a quality shared by many Idealists.

One of the most fulfilling parts of Deb's first career involved building close relationships with her customers and colleagues, which was driven by her dominant Feeling function. Deb sought every opportunity to be helpful and supportive in that role. But as a therapist and counselor, this ENFJ (Extraverted, Intuitive, Feeling, Judging) has natural gifts that are used and nourished, every single day.

With the development of Deb's third function, Sensing, and fourth function, Thinking, has come a more pragmatic approach to life. In the past, she used to be the enabler, who would help everyone at the expense of herself. "Today, I'm able to put the oxygen mask on first, to take a breath and ask, 'Who am I doing this for, the other person or myself?' I feel great that the answer is me."

‖ Conceptualizers

Profile 1: Adam

"From journalist to international child welfare advocate."

Adam discovered his first passion—journalism—while writing for his college newspaper, an activity that ultimately led to a twenty-two-year career working at the *Boston Globe.* Adam started as a copyeditor, but over the span of his tenure, he had about twenty different jobs, including foreign editor, Washington news editor, diplomatic correspondent, national political correspondent, and family and children's issues reporter.

In addition to the actual writing, what Adam liked best was "chronicling history: the genuinely important mission of journalism to shape people's understanding, leading to change of policies and practices that have real impact on people's lives." He found it exhilarating and exciting to cover the biggest stories of the day, which included wars, major criminal trials, and several presidential elections. "These were vital and important stories about people's lives—some were history changing, others were small and touching."

What Adam liked least were the "bureaucratic aspects and detail stuff—like sitting in on editorial meetings to decide what stories to cover and who would write them," and of course, dealing with internal politics, budgets, and other minutiae.

Encore! Encore!

The seeds of Adam's second career were sown while he was still at the *Globe,* when he and his wife adopted their son. At the first informational meeting he attended, Adam got excited about the adoption process. "I saw a world I didn't know much about and that few people understood, yet affected so many." He pitched a three-part series on adoption to his editors. Although they were initially resistant, Adam persisted, and ultimately the series was not only published, but nominated for a Pulitzer Prize. Adam explains, "Every journalist wants to write a book, and I had found my topic." He took a leave to write *Adoption Nation*—which he wrote with the intent to educate the world and have a lasting impact. *Adoption Nation* changed the conversation and is now considered a seminal book.

As a result of his research, Adam realized that writing his book was more than a mere journalistic exercise. "It was about my kids as well as other people's kids, and about policies that were unfair to so many people." He rewrote the book to make it more personal, which helped him clarify his new mission and ignite his second career as a child welfare advocate.

With a growing reputation as a national expert, Adam decided to strike out as a consultant and was soon offered the position of executive director of a national nonprofit that is the preeminent research, policy, and education organization in its field.

Adam's primary responsibility as executive director is to carry out his agency's mission: to improve the lives of everyone touched by adoption. When he first arrived, the agency was in trouble and quickly running out of funds. Adam takes pride in having turned it around, helping to expand the operation from two to nine employees and secure its financial footing. Adam's daily activities involve a variety of important yet disparate tasks. He develops programs, provides testimony, writes and edits publications, raises money, and manages the board and a staff. Adam also spends a significant amount of time utilizing the media to reach out to the professional and lay communities to further his mission and its impact. Under his leadership, the organization "has become an activist think tank that develops, synthesizes, and disseminates knowledge and works to implement best practices."

Adam's greatest satisfaction comes from "seeing the difference we make in real people's lives." He loves the personal interactions when he gives speeches and conducts training. And he's energized when he's able to change laws "so that gay and lesbian people can have their families" or when he receives a call from an agency to say they use his best practices to train other people. "This is the stuff that really makes me feel like I'm doing something right."

Why This Encore Career Works for Adam

As Conceptualizers, people like Adam are driven by a strong need for competence. And because they set high standards for themselves and others, they often excel at whatever they choose to do. People who share Adam's temperament are often also lifelong learners, continually seeking to increase their knowledge and expertise, as Adam did in becoming an international thought leader in the field of adoption. Conceptualizers are quintessential visionaries who often have the confidence necessary to inspire others to embrace their ideas and causes.

Adam, like most dominant Thinkers, is almost obsessed with fairness. He sees inequities in how people are treated and feels compelled to try to right those wrongs. Logical and objective, Adam is assertive in airing his views. Rather than help people individually, he is energized by creating policy changes that affect the masses.

It's no surprise that people who share Adam's personality type—ENTJ (Extraverted, Intuitive, Thinking, Judging)—are found at the top of most organizations. Their Extraversion draws them into the world, their temperament provides them with a clear vision, and their Judging function compels them to make an impact. But as Adam has grown older and developed his third function, Sensing, he has also become more realistic about just how long it takes to effect real change.

Profile 2: Ronnie

"From inside corporate HR to outside consulting."

"You'd be good in personnel." That observation, offered by a job interviewer for a large retail department store, started Ronnie on a path that led to a thirty-plus-year career in corporate human resources and a second career as a coach, consultant, teacher, and community volunteer.

Although she was not completely sure what the term "personnel" meant, Ronnie was hired as a management trainee and got her first store placement working in personnel. The best part was that "they treated us like we were part of the management team—personnel was strategically integrated into the business." After four years, she got a promotion when she moved to another department store to work in HR. Four years later, and ready for some new challenges, Ronnie was hired as the first HR director at a major bookstore chain, a job that lasted only eighteen months. "Let's just say we didn't see eye to eye. In truth, I went way too far out on a limb and tried to do too much. For example, I tried to change the payroll system—when I didn't know enough about payroll to take on that large a project."

But Ronnie quickly landed on her feet and was hired as the director of HR at a large and prestigious Wall Street law firm. "These were some of the smartest people in the entire world. And they were driven. They drove you—they drove everybody." What did she like best? "Anything I saw as a problem, I got to touch and fix." But time passed, and soon Ronnie was pregnant with her second child, tired of a grueling daily commute, and eager to spend more time with her family. Plus, "I realized that I'd done everything I could do

there." As a result of a job search in North Carolina, nearer to her family, Ronnie was hired at the innovative and highly respected Center for Creative Leadership.

She loved CCL's mission but after a time realized she'd fit better in a more business-driven, less process-oriented organization. "How many retreats can you sit through? I went from Wall Street, where no one ever hugged me in ten years, to CCL, where my first large staff meeting ended with a group hug." So after three years, Ronnie moved back into retailing, but not before getting CCL to train her to be a coach.

Her next assignment was as vice president for HR at Carlyle and Company jewelers. The best aspect of the job was being part of a management team that dealt with business strategy. At Carlyle, she began to understand that "just finding the right answer and implementing it and moving on is not a strategy for success—you have to build relationships, too." And because she had negotiated a four-day workweek, Ronnie was able to continue coaching for CCL. "One of the driving threads through all the changes was that I learned how to use vision to set achievable goals." When the company went bankrupt, Ronnie shepherded it through the liquidation and bankruptcy process, while creating a home office, networking, and building her consulting practice.

Encore! Encore!

Since then, Ronnie has been an executive coach and HR consultant. She also teaches a leadership and career course in the MBA program at the University of North Carolina. Additionally, Ronnie is an active volunteer, working with organizations that support families and children. "People think of me as the consummate networker—I know everyone in town." As if that's not enough, she is the president of the board of an artist's collective.

She considers consulting with nonprofits to be her sweet spot: "I bring in the hard stuff—business strategy and finance—and marry it with organizational development, the softer sciences." For Ronnie, juggling several balls at once is energizing, and each activity satisfies a different need: "With coaching, I get to hear people's stories, connect what's happened in the past, look at all the factors, and help them achieve their goals." And as a volunteer working to help organizations become more effective, she gets to apply all of her business and strategic skills.

Why This Encore Career Works for Ronnie

Conceptualizers like Ronnie need to continue to learn and grow. Never content to rest on past achievements, they continually seek new challenges, a tendency that is evident in Ronnie's career path. They are also gifted problem solvers and strategists; Ronnie gets to draw on these strengths in helping individuals and organizations meet their objectives.

Ronnie is an ENTP (Extraverted, Intuitive, Thinking, Perceiving), and as a dominant Intuitive type, she sees possibilities everywhere, easily makes connections, and thrives on problem solving. Throughout her entire work history, Ronnie has chosen time and again to take on a variety of endeavors simultaneously—a theme consistent with many Conceptualizers, but especially true of ENTPs.

In midlife, people who share Ronnie's type often gain access to their less developed Feeling side. As she prepares to send her youngest child off to college, she's surprised at how much it is affecting her. Further evidence of her emerging Feeling side is Ronnie's more recent desire to create and connect with a community.

25 | FOR CAREER PROFESSIONALS ONLY

If this has been your first introduction to Personality Type, you are no doubt impressed with how powerful a tool it can be for helping clients in every aspect of the career development process. Reading this book is a good start, but it is *only* a start. If you are one of the thousands of career professionals who already use Type in your work, this book has confirmed much of what you know, but it may also have reminded you of how much there is yet to learn.

Since Type provides such a rich model for understanding people and their career-related needs, it is not something that someone can read one, two, even ten books about and become an expert. To use it effectively and ethically takes extensive experiences working with many different types of clients and requires some in-depth professional training.

Using Type Ethically

We often remind workshop participants that Type is a powerful tool—not unlike a hammer. In the hands of a Michelangelo, it can be used to sculpt a wondrous masterpiece such as the *Pietà*. But in the hands of a maniac, it can be used to smash someone's skull.

The difference lies in the skill and motivation of its wielder. The point we wish to drive home is this: People take their type results very seriously, sometimes much more so than we counselors fully appreciate. Therefore, we have an especially strong obligation to make sure we are both skilled and well-intentioned in our use of Type. The ethics concerning the use of Type is a subject of some debate. This is true for many reasons, among them the fact that there are so many applications and people from so many different disciplines and backgrounds using Type.

Access to the Type model is, of course, available to the public through dozens of books published on the subject. But access to the MBTI® and various related materials is restricted to people who meet the publisher of the MBTI®'s qualifications. If you are interested in learning about becoming qualified to purchase, administer, and interpret the Myers-Briggs Type Indicator®, we suggest you contact its publisher, Consulting Psychologists Press, for complete details about their qualification requirements (see the Organizations listing in the Resources section), which may include taking a course on the MBTI® offered by a number of training organizations.

In an effort to promote the ethical use of Type, the Association for Psychological Type (APT) has developed a set of ethical principles. Since not all users of this book are members of APT, and therefore may not see these guidelines, with the permission of APT we have paraphrased them below. We encourage all career professionals to become familiar with them, and use them when working with clients.

---

*Association for Psychological Type, "Ethical Principles"**

1. **People taking the MBTI® should be informed of the purpose and intended use of results before taking the instrument. As with other psychological instruments, taking the MBTI® should be voluntary.**

2. **Individual type results should not be shared with others without the permission of the respondent.**

   In other words, a person's type is confidential information. However, group data which doesn't identify individuals may be shared. For example, if you have administered the MBTI® to a freshman English class, it is permissible to present a type table showing the distribution of types, as long as no individuals are identified by name.

3. **Type information should be used to enhance individual or group satisfaction, not to restrict or limit individual or group functioning in any way.**

   The MBTI® should enhance the workplace. It is unethical to use the MBTI® for screening people out in the hiring process. Also, it is unethical to restrict work assignments based solely on a person's type. Type is helpful in team building and understanding the behavioral preferences of workers.

4. **Adequate information about Type theory and the individual's results should be given in a face-to-face setting.**

   This often presents a dilemma when someone wants to take the MBTI® and receive their results by mail or email. The main reason for offering face-to-face feedback is to increase the chances of helping the person verify his or her type, and to ensure that enough time is provided to assure that the client has an adequate understanding of his or her MBTI® results. Although face-to-face feedback is preferable, email can be used effectively if clients have ample opportunity to ask questions and discuss in depth any concerns they have about their results.

*Excerpted and paraphrased, with permission, from "Ethical Principles," The Association for Psychological Type Directory 1994–1995.

5. **Respondents should always have an opportunity to "verify" their types as accurate for them.**

    In our view, this is probably the single most important guideline, and one which is unfortunately not always adhered to. We believe that any practitioner who uses the MBTI® or Type should have enough skill and time to help all takers of a type instrument verify his or her type, which includes offering to the client a full written description of the type(s) to be explored for verification.

6. **Type characteristics should be described in positive and nonjudgmental terms, using words like "preference," "tendency," and "inclination."**

7. **Respondents should be told that Type reflects an individual's preferences, not abilities or intelligence, nor is it a predictor of success. People should not be counseled toward or away from certain jobs *solely* (our emphasis) on the basis of their type.**

    In reality, type preferences often are related to certain abilities. For example, extraverted Feeling types— ESFJ and ENFJ— often have very good "people skills." However, because this is a tendency rather than an absolute reality, it is dangerous to attribute specific skills to specific types. A danger is that people of a certain type might feel uncomfortable if they don't possess that skill or that people might not believe that someone of another type also possesses that skill.

    As to counseling people toward or away from certain jobs, the key phrase here is "solely on the basis of their type." While type is an important factor in predicting career satisfaction, it is certainly not the only factor that must be considered.

8. **The individual is considered the best judge of whether the type description "fits" or not.**

    This often presents a conflict for experienced users of Type, for it is not uncommon for a client to score as one type, and the counselor to believe quite strongly that the client is really another type.

    It is suggested that you gently explore your tentative hypothesis about the client's type with them, but ultimately it is the client who must decide which type they are most comfortable with, and you must respect that decision.

9. **Counselors should not state or imply that Type explains everything, but rather it is one important component of our very complex human personalities.**

    The "Type explains everything" syndrome is one experienced by many people who become enamored with Type. There are so many applications for this model that it is easy to get carried away. Therefore, counselors are cautioned to be aware of the tendency so as to avoid falling into this trap.

10. **Interpreters should be sensitive to their own type biases and try not to communicate them to clients.**

This is far easier said than done, because all people have biases based on their own types. It is especially important for people who are new to Type to pay close attention to how they present Type concepts and describe preferences to make sure they are doing so in as positive, or at least as neutral, a way as possible.

One way to hone this skill is to practice explaining Type to people with different preferences, and to ask them to critique the objectivity of your presentation.

11. Practitioners should not use Psychological Type indicators with undemonstrated reliability and validity.

Although the MBTI® is the most widely used Type assessment, in recent years other instruments have been developed, some better than others. Counselors should be aware of this and, as with any other testing instrument they use, make sure they have confidence in an instrument's reliability and validity.

12. Practitioners should accurately represent their competence and experience to respondents receiving Type information.

We believe this is true for all counselors, not just those who use Type.

Finally, APT stresses that one of the responsibilities of Type users is to become familiar with the research data available about Type. Inferences about Type or scores on any type indicator should not go beyond the data. The Journal of Psychological Type and the Type Resources Library at the Center for Applications of Psychological Type are excellent resources for Type research.

With Whom Should Type Be Used?

Personality Type is a useful and powerful tool for people of all ages and stages of development. Clearly, the age of the person will affect greatly the level of self-understanding they may gain, but with nonjudgmental and accurate explanations, most clients will be able to harness the new insights to make much better career decisions for themselves. In career counseling, we have found Type to be particularly useful with people from the following groups:

1. High school juniors and seniors
2. College students
3. Graduate students
4. People who have been outplaced
5. Mid-life career changers
6. Retirees, or "encore career" seekers

Some general guidelines for using Type with clients include the following:

1. **Discuss the purpose of learning about one's type and get their reactions to participating in the process:** Prepare them for receiving results by assuring them there are no better or worse, healthier or sicker, smarter or dumber types—that whatever type they come out is fine—and that the information can be very useful in helping them in

the career development process. Explain that they will receive their confidential results during the sessions.

2. **Explain that there are four dimensions to the Type model and describe the most important characteristics of the eight preferences.** There are many different materials available that describe the preference differences in list form, including Chapter 2.

3. **After you have explained each dimension, give clients the opportunity to estimate their preferences on each dimension.** Make a note of their guess.

4. The next step is for the clients to **read the appropriate profiles for their type in Chapter 3 of this book or by using another verifying profile such as the Brief Personality Description section of The Career and Life Planning Profiles** of the type or types they may be, and to see which one fits best. Some clients need to read several profiles until they have found the right fit.

5. Once you have identified the type your clients feel comfortable with, you may **begin to address the issues that brought them to you in the first place:** career choice, help with the job search, etc.

Using the MBTI®

To learn about the qualifications for purchasing and administering and about the materials needed for interpreting and using the MBTI®, we suggest you contact the publisher, Consulting Psychologists Press.

Providing Type Feedback to Clients

Giving Type feedback to clients is an important part of the process, and therefore we have paraphrased, with permission, some essential recommendations from *Guidelines for Explaining the MBTI®* by Gordon Lawrence, respected educator and author of *People Types and Tiger Stripes,* and have added some suggestions based on our experience.

1. Explain that the MBTI® is not a "test," but an "indicator," which has no right or wrong answers, good or bad, sick or well, types. All are equally valuable, with different natural strengths and blind spots.

2. Point out that scores do not indicate the quality of any particular preference, just the relative strength of one element over another.

3. Try to explain the concepts of Type as simply and clearly as possible. Point out that words associated with Type (Thinking and Feeling, for example) often have different connotations from the way we use them in our everyday language.

4. Be aware of your own possible type bias and present the information in as neutral and positive a light as you can.

5. Use words like "tendency" and "patterns" to describe Type preferences. When providing results, you should avoid asserting: "This is the way you are," but rather ask: "Is this true for you?"

6. Expect some confusion, and be prepared to reassure the client that this is a normal reaction. Explaining Type concepts requires skill and patience.

Using Type to Be a More Effective Counselor

In addition to assisting your clients, an understanding of Type can be enormously helpful to you as a counselor. Basically, we are in the business of communicating— understanding others, and trying to convey ideas that will be helpful. But as any enlightened educator knows: "You've got to reach 'em to teach 'em."

Although this is not a workshop on communication, we think it would be helpful to pass along some of what we've learned about Type and communication:

1. People of the same or similar types usually understand each other fairly easily. *(This does not mean they always agree with each other.)*
2. The converse is also true: In general, the more different your type is from your client's, the greater the likelihood of miscommunication. The result is often a mutually frustrating experience.
3. We tend to follow the golden rule when it comes to communicating: We do unto others as we would have done unto us. To communicate effectively, however, the platinum rule is preferable: Do unto others as they would like done unto them. In other words, we need to speak *their* language.
4. Type provides a powerful tool for helping communicate more effectively with clients of all types.

As career counselors, you often work with clients whose types are very different from your own. To help you meet this challenge, we offer a look at what you can expect from people with different preferences, and some specific suggestions for communicating most effectively with them.

It is important to remember that people are not just Es or Is, Ss or Ns, etc., but a combination of different preferences. Therefore this should be taken into account when reviewing the following suggestions, which for simplicity's sake are presented by individual preference.

‖ EXTRAVERTS

- They are likely to give information freely and act quickly, sometimes without enough forethought.
- Their orientation is one of breadth, and they need to be encouraged to explore issues in depth.
- They often need help sticking to exercises or activities that are long and slow, and they should be encouraged to write things down that they want to remember.

A challenge to counselors is to get Extraverts to slow down enough to really think things through before taking action. Some suggestions:

- Let them talk.
- Include a variety of topics.
- Communicate verbally.
- Expect a high energy level.
- Ask them to listen.

‖ INTROVERTS

- Are less likely to let you know what they are thinking and feeling.
- May have a hard time translating ideas into active steps. *When presenting ideas, give them enough time to think about their response (this may range from seconds to days,*

depending on the importance of the issue).

- Introverts, especially introverted sensors, are less comfortable brainstorming and fantasizing about future possibilities and are better at concrete exercises.

A challenge to counselors is to help Introverts move from the thinking stage to the action stage. Some suggestions:

- Ask, then listen.
- Talk about one thing at a time.
- Give them adequate time to reflect and prepare.
- Provide material to read.
- Let them set the pace.

|| SENSORS

- Are less likely to want or be able to see options or brainstorm possibilities.
- Are more likely to be influenced by past experiences and known ways of doing things. *Counselors can capitalize on their ability to focus on the details in helping to get an accurate picture of their strengths, skills, etc.*
- Are better at and get more out of concrete tasks than fantasy exercises.

A challenge to counselors is to help Sensors see possibilities that don't exist at the present and focus on the big picture and long-range implications. Some suggestions:

- Present facts accurately.
- Use real and concrete examples; be explicit.
- Present information step by step.
- Stress practical application.
- Make specific recommendations and suggestions.

|| INTUITIVES

- Are less able and willing to deal with specifics and prefer to focus on the big picture.
- Think in global terms. *Counselors can appeal to their problem-solving abilities (especially NTs) to get them involved in the process. Avoid exercises that are tedious and require patience with details, and watch facts closely.*
- They may have trouble keeping on task or following directions (especially ENPs).

A challenge for counselors is to help Intuitives realistically evaluate career options and plans. Some suggestions:

- Talk about the big picture and implications.
- Talk about possibilities.
- Use analogies and metaphors.
- Engage their imagination.
- Don't overwhelm them with details.

|| THINKERS

- Evaluate ideas and decisions logically and impersonally.
- Need to be convinced that a specific exercise or activity makes sense before they will put energy into it. It may be difficult to find out their true feelings about issues, and they may not think their feelings are particularly relevant to the matter at hand. Because they are naturally critical, they are not likely to show their appreciation for the counselor's abilities or concern. *Knowing this may help counselors (mostly Fs) not to take it personally.*
- Are impressed by competence and the end result.

A challenge for counselors is to remind Thinkers of the human consequences of their decisions, both for themselves and others. Some suggestions:

- Be organized and logical.
- Focus on consequences.
- Emphasize results and outcomes.
- Ask what they think rather than how they feel.
- Don't repeat yourself.

‖ FEELERS

- Make decisions based on their own values, are more people oriented and aware of others' feelings.
- Like to please others and may need to be encouraged to be assertive in getting their own needs met.
- Are happiest in friendly, supportive, cooperative environments, and any potential work situation should be looked at to see if it will meet this important criterion.

A challenge for counselors is to help Feelers evaluate options more objectively and not to take rejection or setbacks personally. Some suggestions:

- Mention points of agreement before any criticism.
- Appreciate efforts and contributions.
- Recognize the legitimacy of their feelings.
- Talk about people-based concerns.
- Respect their values.

‖ JUDGERS

- Like to take in just enough information to make a decision, and prefer to make plans and follow them.
- Are usually well organized, so structured exercises appeal to them

(especially STJs). *They will work toward goals, but may become frustrated when they experience too many delays.*
- May need assistance in reforming plans into more manageable steps.

A challenge for counselors is to help Judgers delay making decisions prematurely, and to stay open to new information. Some suggestions:

- Be organized, on time, and prepared.
- Come to conclusions—try to resolve issues.
- Be decisive and definite.
- Be efficient and don't waste their time.
- Point out the benefits of being flexible.

‖ PERCEIVERS

- Prefer not to decide but to continue collecting information, to keep their options open.
- Enjoy those exercises and activities that allow them to learn something new, and have fun doing it.
- Are flexible, adaptable, and change gears quickly so they may be amenable to many different approaches and techniques. *Their natural curiosity makes them open to explore options.*

A challenge for counselors is to help keep Perceivers on task and to nudge them into making decisions when it is appropriate. Some suggestions:

- Expect many questions.
- Don't force decisions (unless you have to).
- Provide opportunity to discuss options.
- Allow time to process.
- Point out that decisions are not irrevocable.

...That's All, Folks!

Everything we see and hear confirms our belief that our society is moving toward increased self-direction, increased self-management of our careers. The more we know about ourselves, and the more we can help our clients know about *themselves,* the better able we will be to respond to the many changes we will all face and make sounder decisions for our lives. Type is a powerful way to begin and further that discovery process. And you, as the career professional, are poised to ride the wave of this exciting technology.

We encourage you to continue the learning process and invite you to help us continue with ours. If you have ideas or suggestions for future editions of this book, or experiences using Type with clients you'd like to share, we'd love to hear from you. Until then, we wish you great luck and success in your most important mission—helping people find true career satisfaction.

Paul D. Tieger, Barbara Barron,
and Kelly Tieger

Some Final Thoughts and Resources

For those of you eager to learn more about Personality Type, we've compiled a bibliography listing several excellent books written about Type. Although of necessity this is only a partial listing, you can obtain more comprehensive information about available resources from many of the organizations we describe.

Need More Help?

For some of you, this has been your very first look at yourself as it pertains to your career development. For others, you've felt stuck for a while and may now finally see some light at the end of the tunnel. For still others, doing the work in this book has helped you identify some good options and has propelled you along the road to career satisfaction. Whatever your current status, perhaps the time is right to enlist the help of a qualified career professional to help you take the next important steps. In fact, at many points in the process, nothing can replace the one-to-one attention, support, advice, and *real contacts* that a career counselor can provide. Here are three resources that will help you locate professionals near you.

National Career Development Association (NCDA)
   www.ncda.org

Use their online search tool to find career service practitioners in your area.

National Board for Certified Counselors, Inc. (NBCC)
   www.nbcc.org
   Use the Counselor Find tool on their site to locate someone close to you.

The Association for Psychological Type (APT)
   www.aptinternational.org

No matter whom you contact or how you get to them, be sure to ask if they use Personality Type in their practice, or if they are familiar with this book. It's also smart to ask in advance what their rates are and if they see clients on an hourly or project basis.

If you're interested in taking the Myers-Briggs Type Indicator®, find resources at Myersbriggs.org. There you can find online resources and a list of local certified practitioners who can administer and interpret the MBTI® test instrument.

Bibliography

General Introduction to Psychological Type

Berens, Linda V. *Understanding Yourself and Others: An Introduction to Temperament.* Huntington Beach, Calif.: Telos Publications, 2000.

Berens, Linda V., and Dario Nardi. *The 16 Personality Types: Descriptions for Self-Discovery.* Huntington Beach, Calif.: Telos Publications, 1999.

Brownsword, Alan. *It Takes All Types*. Herndon, Va.: Baytree Publication Company, 1987.

Duniho, Terrence. *Wholeness Lies Within*. Gladwyne, Pa.: Type & Temperament, Inc., 1991.

———. *Patterns of Preference*. Gladwyne, Pa.: Type & Temperament, Inc., 1996.

Giovannoni, Louise C., Linda V. Berens, and Sue A. Cooper. *Introduction to Temperament*. Huntington Beach, Calif.: Cooper, Berens, 1986.

Hirsh, Sandra, and Jean Kummerow. *Lifetypes*. New York: Warner Books, 1989.

Keirsey, David, and Marilyn Bates. *Please Understand Me,* 3rd ed. Del Mar, Calif.: Prometheus Nemesis, 1984.

Kroeger, Otto, and Janet M. Thuesen. *Type Talk*. New York: Delacorte Press, 1988.

———. *Type Talk at Work: How the 16 Personality Types Determine Your Success on the Job*. New York: Dell, 2002.

———. *16 Ways to Love Your Lover: Understanding the 16 Personality Types So You Can Create a Love That Lasts Forever*. New York: Delacorte Press, 1994.

Lawrence, Gordon D. *Finding the Zone: A Whole New Way to Maximize Mental Potential*. Amherst, N.Y.: Prometheus Books, 2010.

Myers, Isabel Briggs, with Peter Myers. *Gifts Differing*. Palo Alto, Calif.: Consulting Psychologists Press, 1980.

Myers, Isabel Briggs. *Introduction to Type: A Guide to Understanding Your Results on the Myers-Briggs Type Indicator,* 6th ed. Palo Alto, Calif.: Consulting Psychologists Press, 1998.

Myers, Isabel Briggs, and Mary H. McCaulley. *Manual: A Guide to the Development and Use of the Myers-Briggs Type Indicator*. Palo Alto, Calif.: Consulting Psychologists Press, 1985.

Myers, Isabel B., with revisions by K. Myers & L. Kirby. *Introduction to Type*. Palo Alto, Calif.: Consulting Psychologists Press, 1993.

Myers, Katharine D., and Linda K. Kirby. *Introduction to Type Dynamics and Development*. Palo Alto, Calif.: Consulting Psychologists Press, 1994.

Pearman, Roger R., and Albritton, Sarah C. *I'm Not Crazy, I'm Just Not You: The Real Meaning of the 16 Personality Types*. Palo Alto, Calif.: Davies-Black, 1997.

Quenk, Naomi L. *Beside Ourselves: Our Hidden Personality in Everyday Life*. Palo Alto, Calif.: Consulting Psychologists Press, 1993.

Saunders, Frances W. *Katharine and Isabel: Mother's Light, Daughter's Journey*. Palo Alto, Calif.: Consulting Psychologists Press, 1991.

The Type Reporter. Published five times a year. Contains articles and information on various topics of interest concerning psychological Type. Susan Scanlon, Editor, 11314 Chapel Road, Fairfax Station, VA 22039. (703) 764-5370. Website: www.typereporter.com

Yabroff, William. *The Inner Image: A Resource for Type Development*. Palo Alto, Calif.: Consulting Psychologists Press, 1990.

Careers

Bolles, Richard Nelson. *What Color Is Your Parachute 2006: A Practical Manual for Job Hunters and Career Changers*. Berkeley, Calif.: Ten Speed Press, 2005.

Dunning, Donna. *What's Your Type of Career? Unlock the Secrets of Your Personality to Find Your Perfect Career Path*. Palo Alto, Calif.: Davies-Black, 2001.

Edwards, Paul, and Sarah Edwards. *Finding Your Perfect Work: The New Career Guide to Making a Living, Creating a Life*. New York: J. P. Tarcher, 2003.

Martin, C. R. *Looking at Type and Careers*. Gainesville, Fla.: Center for Applications of Psychological Type, 2009.

Children/Education

Allen, Mollie, Claire Hayman, and Kay Abella. *Discovering Type with Teens: A Comprehensive Leader's Guide with Materials for Presenting Psychological Type to Young People*. Gainesville, Fla.: Center for Applications of Psychological Type, 2009.

Barger, June R., Robert R. Barger, and Jamie M. Cano. *Discovering Learning Preferences and Learning Differences in the Classroom*. Columbus, Ohio: Ohio Agricultural Education Curriculum Materials Service, Ohio State University, 1994.

Fairhurst, Alice M., and Lisa Fairhurst. *Effective Teaching, Effective Learning: Making the Personality Connection in Your Classroom*. Palo Alto, Calif.: Davies-Black, 1995.

Ginn, Charles W. *Families: Using Type to Enhance Mutual Understanding*. Gainesville, Fla.: Center for Applications of Psychological Type, 1995.

Golay, Keith. *Learning Patterns and Temperament Styles*. Newport Beach, Calif.: Manas-Systems, 1982.

Lawrence, Gordon. *People Types and Tiger Stripes: A Practical Guide to Learning Styles,* 3rd ed. 1993. Gainesville, Fla.: Center for Applications of Psychological Type, 1993.

Meisgeier, Charles, and Elizabeth Murphy. *A Teacher's Guide to Type: A New Perspective on Individual*

Differences in the Classroom. Palo Alto, Calif.: Consulting Psychologists Press, 1989.

Murphy, Elizabeth. *The Developing Child.* Palo Alto, Calif.: Consulting Psychologists Press, 1992.

———. *Exploring Personality Type: Discovering My Best and Your Best.* Gainesville, Fla.: Center for Applications of Psychological Type, 2008.

Neff, LaVonne. *One of a Kind: Making the Most of Your Child's Uniqueness.* Gainesville, Fla.: Center for Applications of Psychological Type, 1995.

Payne, Diane, and Sondra VanSant. *Great Minds Don't Think Alike! Success for Students Through the Application of Psychological Type in Schools.* Gainesville, Fla.: Center for Applications of Psychological Type, 2009.

Peters, Martha M., and Don C. Peters. *Juris Types: Learning Law Through Self-Understanding.* Gainesville, Fla.: Center for Applications of Psychological Type, 2007.

Provost, Judith A., and Scott Anchors. *Applications of the Myers-Briggs Type Indicator in Higher Education.* Palo Alto, Calif.: Consulting Psychologists Press, 1987.

Schaubhut, Nancy A., and Richard C. Thompson. *MBTI® Type Tables for College Majors.* Gainesville, Fla.: Center for Applications of Psychological Type, 2009.

Tieger, Paul D., and Barbara Barron-Tieger. *Nurture by Nature.* New York: Little, Brown, 1997.

Wirths, Claudine G., and Mary Bowman-Kruhm. *Are You My Type? Or, Why Aren't You More Like Me?* Palo Alto, Calif.: Consulting Psychologists Press, 1992.

Counseling/Management

Brock, Susan A. *Using Type in Selling: Building Customer Relationships with the Myers-Briggs Type Indicator.* Palo Alto, Calif.: Consulting Psychologists Press, 1994.

Duniho, Terrence. *Personalities at Risk: Addiction, Codependency and Psychological Type.* Gladwyne, Pa.: Type & Temperament, Inc., 1992.

Grant, Richard D., *Symbols of Recovery: The 12 Steps at Work in the Unconscious.* Gladwyne, Pa.: Type & Temperament, Inc., 1990.

Hartzler, Margaret. *Making Type Work for You: A Collection of Exercises and Worksheets.* Gaithersburg, Md.: Type Resources, Inc., 1992.

———. *Management Uses of the Myers-Briggs Type Indicator.* Gaithersburg, Md.: Type Resources, Inc., 1992.

———. *Using Type in Career Counseling.* Gaithersburg, Md.: Type Resources, Inc., 1985.

———. *Using Type with Couples,* 2nd ed. Gaithersburg, Md.: Type Resources, Inc., 1998.

Hirsh, Sandra K. *Using the Myers-Briggs Type Indicator in Organizations: A Resource Book,* 3rd ed. Palo Alto, Calif.: Consulting Psychologists Press, 1998.

Hirsh, Sandra K., and Jane A. G. Kise. *Work It Out: Clues for Solving People Problems at Work.* Palo Alto, Calif.: Davies-Black, 1996.

Hirsh, Sandra K., and Jean M. Kummerow. *Introduction to Type in Organizational Settings: A Resource Book.* Palo Alto, Calif.: Consulting Psychologists Press, 1987.

———. *Introduction to Type in Organizations,* 3rd ed. Palo Alto, Calif.: Consulting Psychologists Press, 1998.

Isachsen, Olaf, and Linda V. Berens. *Working Together: A Personality-Centered Approach to Management,* 3rd ed. San Juan Capistrano, Calif.: Institute for Management Development, 1995.

Jones, Jane Hardy, and Ruth G. Sherman. *Intimacy and Type: Building Enduring Relationships by Embracing Personality Differences.* Gainesville, Fla.: Center for Applications of Psychological Type, 2011.

Kummerow, Jean M. *New Directions for Career Planning and the Workplace: Practical Strategies for Career Management Professionals,* 2nd ed. Palo Alto, Calif.: Davies-Black, 2000.

Kummerow, Jean M., Nancy J.Barger, and Linda K. Kirby. *WorkTypes: Understand Your Work Personality—How It Helps You and Holds You Back, and What You Can Do to Understand It.* New York: Warner Books, 1997.

Pearman, Roger R. *Hardwired Leadership: Unleashing the Power of Personality to Become a New Millennium Leader.* Palo Alto, Calif.: Davies-Black, 1998.

Provost, Judith A. *A Casebook: Applications of the Myers-Briggs Type Indicator in Counseling.* Gainesville, Fla.: Center for Applications of Psychological Type, 1984.

Stein, Murray, and John Hollwitz, eds. *Psyche at Work: Workplace Applications of Jungian Analytical Psychology.* Wilmette, Ill.: Chiron Publications, 1992.

Religion/Spirituality

Grant, Richard D. *The Way of the Cross: Christian Individuation and Psychological Temperament.* Gladwyne, Pa.: Type & Temperament, Inc., 1990.

Grant, W. Harold, Magdala Thompson, and Thomas E. Clarke. *From Image to Likeness: A Jungian Path in the Gospel Journey.* Mahwah, N.J.: Paulist Press, 1983.

Harbaugh, Gary L. *God's Gifted People,* expanded ed. Minneapolis, Minn.: Augsburg Fortress Publishers, 1990.

Hirsh, Sandra K., and Jane A. G. Kise. *Looking at Type and Spirituality.* Gainesville, Fla.: Center for Applications of Psychological Type, 1997.
———. *Soul Types: Finding the Spiritual Path That Is Right for You.* New York: Hyperion, 1998.

Keating, Charles. *Who We Are Is How We Pray: Matching Personality and Spirituality.* Mystic, Conn.: Twenty-Third Publications, 1987.

Kise, Jane A. G., David Stark, and Sandra K. Hirsh. *LifeKeys: Discovering Who You Are, Why You're Here, What You Do Best.* Minneapolis, Minn.: Bethany House, 1998.

Michael, Chester P., and Marie C. Morrissey. *Prayer and Temperament: Different Prayer Forms for Different Personality Types,* rev. ed. Charlottesville, Va.: Open Door Press, 1991.

Moore, Anthony T. *Father, Son, and Healing Ghosts.* Gainesville, Fla.: Center for Applications of Psychological Type, 2000.

Oswold, Roy, and Otto Kroeger. *Personality Type and Religious Leadership.* Washington, D.C.: Alban Institute, 1988.

Richardson, Peter Tufts. *Archetype of the Spirit: Origins of Spirituality— Individual and Collective.* Rockland, Maine: Red Barn Publishing, 2007.

Type and Research

CAPT Bibliography. Gainesville, Fla.: Center for Applications of Psychological Type. Contains nearly 9,000 entries.

Macdaid, Gerald P., Mary H. McCaulley, and Richard Kainz. *Atlas of Type Tables.* Gainesville, Fla.: Center for the Application of Psychological Type, 1986. A compendium of hundreds of tables reflecting the type distribution of people in a variety of occupations.

The Type Reporter. Published five times a year. Contains articles and information on various topics of interest concerning psychological type. Susan Scanlon, editor. 11314 Chapel Road, Fairfax Station, VA 22039. (703) 764-5370.

Zeisset, Ray M. *Statistics and Measurement: An Introduction.* Gainesville, Fla.: Center for Applications of Psychological Type, 2009.

Other Resources/Organizations

SpeedReading People, LLC (SRP)
www.speedreadingpeople.com
SRP is a communication company that specializes in harnessing the power of Personality Type to create innovative yet practical software solutions that help managers, teams, and salespeople communicate most successfully.

The Association for Psychological Type (APT)
www.aptinternational.org
APT is an international membership organization open to all people interested in Personality Type. APT conducts workshops and publishes materials, including the *Bulletin of Psychological Type,* and conducts the APT MBTI® Qualifying workshop. APT sponsors a biannual international conference, and local chapters throughout the country and around the world meet regularly to share information about Type.

Center for Applications of Psychological Type (CAPT)
www.capt.org
CAPT provides training in Type for professionals and the public, offers consulting services for training and research, publishes Type-related materials, compiles research to advance the understanding of Type, does computer scoring of the MBTI®, and maintains the Isabel Briggs Myers Memorial Library.

American Management Association (AMA)
www.amanet.org
AMA offers Myers-Briggs Type Indicator (MBTI®) certification training.

Linda Berens Institute
www.lindaberens.com
Based on the work of Linda Berens, this organization offers training in the Interaction Style Approach as well as consulting in the areas of leadership development, team building, and communication enhancement.

Consulting Psychologists Press (CPP, Inc.) and Davies-Black® Publishing
www.cpp-db.com
The publisher and distributor of the Myers-Briggs Type Indicator instrument and related materials, CPP also provides training and consulting services for organizations. Davies-Black® Publishing, a division of CPP, Inc., publishes business and career management titles.

Type Resources
www.type-resources.com
An organization that specializes in training and consulting with organizations that use the MBTI® and FIRO-B™ for leadership coaching and team development. They also offer MBTI® qualifying workshops and distribute a variety of Type-related books and materials.

Qualifying.org, Inc.
www.qualifying.org
Qualifying.org offers a variety of consulting and training opportunities in the Myers-Briggs Type Indicator (MBTI®) and other instruments, including the Emotional Quotient Inventory (EQ-i®).

Psychometrics Canada Ltd.
www.psychometrics.com
A leading Canadian publisher of tests and assessments relating to personality, abilities, and interests for business, education, and government, Psychometrics Canada Ltd. offers training programs, expert advice, scoring services, and ongoing research, as well as consulting in the areas of test development, personnel selection, and organizational development.

Career/LifeSkills Resources Inc.
www.career-lifeskills.com
Career/LifeSkills Resources Inc. specializes in resources for personal, professional, and organizational development and provides a variety of assessment tools, including the Myers-Briggs Type Indicator, Strong Interest Inventory, and True Colors. They also offer a wide range of career and life skills books and quality certification and professional training programs.

Institute for Type Development (ITD)
www.itd.net.au
ITD provides training and resources for Psychological Type, Personality Type, Myers-Briggs Type Indicator (MBTI®), and Temperament Theory; offers accreditation programs; and runs seminars and training programs. ITD also distributes a wide range of Type-related books, tapes, and workshop materials.

OKA (formerly Otto Kroeger Associates)
www.oka-online.com
OKA provides training and resources for Psychological Type, Personality Type, Myers-Briggs Type Indicator (MBTI®), and Temperament Theory; offers accreditation programs; and runs seminars and training programs. OKA also distributes a wide range of Type-related books, tapes, and workshop materials.

Oxford Psychologists Press Ltd. (OPP®)
www.opp.co.uk
Oxford Psychologists Press Ltd. provides HR professionals and consultants with tools to help them enhance decision making in the areas of selection and assessment, individual and leadership development, team building, organizational change and consulting, and career counseling. They distribute the Myers-Briggs Type Indicator as well as provide training and product-specific workshops.

Career Planning and Adult Development Network
www.careernetwork.org
This organization publishes a bimonthly newsletter and quarterly journal for career practitioners, produces the annual International Career Development Conference, and certifies Job and Career Transition Coaches (JCTC).

Acknowledgments

There are literally thousands of people we could thank for contributing to our understanding of Personality Type. We begin with the hundreds of clients we have worked with over the years and the thousands of career professionals and other workshop participants who, through sharing their stories and experiences, have taught us so much.

We also wish to thank our friends and associates for referring so many of the fascinating and talented people we interviewed. To each of the people profiled in this book and the many others whose input added to each of the six editions of this book, we are indebted for their generous gift of time, experience, and insights. We went to the sources and were taught by the masters—the real experts—about their own career needs and criteria for true satisfaction. It was a pleasure and a privilege to get to know them and to tell their stories.

Although we have studied with and learned from many highly respected teachers, we are particularly grateful to Mary McCaulley and Gordon Lawrence, who first taught us about Type. Their contributions to the world's understanding of psychological type have been enormous, and their passing leaves a huge void. We also wish to express our gratitude to the late Terry Duniho for greatly increasing our understanding.

We thank Nellie Sabin for her immeasurable contribution to the overall quality of this book. Her infusion of creative energy, as well as her many great ideas, thought-provoking questions, and careful organizational assistance have made this a much better, and more helpful, book.

We are grateful for the excellent skills of research assistant Hannah Littler in the updating of this sixth edition. Thanks are due to Chris Littler for his tireless work on the *Do What You Are* brand and digital presence. We thank the many editors we've worked with at Little, Brown, including Marisa Vigilante and Ian Straus, our editors for this edition, and our agent Colleen Mohyde. We are especially indebted to the late Christina Ward, our first editor, later our agent, and always our good friend, for her unfaltering and enthusiastic support since the very beginning of our journey as writers. You are greatly missed, Kit. Thanks also to the hundreds of readers who have taken time to contact us with their stories of how the book has helped them improve the quality of their lives. You cannot imagine the gift that feedback is to us. Thank you.

We owe a special debt of gratitude to our family and friends, who have allowed us to learn what Type is really about by experimenting on them over these many years.

Index

About the Authors

Paul D. Tieger is the founder and CEO of SpeedReading People, LLC. His life's work has involved applying his expertise in Personality Type to help individuals choose satisfying careers, teams collaborate more successfully, and trial attorneys understand and communicate most effectively with jurors. Paul pioneered the application of Personality Type in healthcare, conducting extensive research that has shown strong correlations between Personality Type, medication adherence, and multiple health risk factors. He is the creator of iConnectHealth—a transformative online tool which reduces chronic disease, especially in seniors, by marrying high tech with human touch. He lives in Hartford, Connecticut.

Following her own good advice, **Barbara Barron** made a career shift and now works as an advancement consultant. She coaches independent schools and other nonprofits to help them raise money to meet their strategic goals and create high-functioning development programs. Barbara continues to use her knowledge of Type in her daily interactions, both personal and professional. She lives in Marin County, California.

The daughter of two Personality Type experts and authors, **Kelly Tieger** has been studying and applying Type her entire life. Kelly is a coauthor on the previous edition of *Do What You Are,* and is proud to have taken the helm on this edition and future ones. She lives in Lakeville, Connecticut. You can find her online at KellyTieger.com.

CONNECTHealth

Instant Individual Connections

Do What You Are revolutionized the way career guidance is practiced worldwide by recognizing the critical link between personality type and career satisfaction and success.

Now, we've applied our passion and unparalleled expertise to help people live healthier lives, while dramatically reducing staggering healthcare costs.

We're proud to introduce...

iConnectHealth™

- Enables all medical providers to quickly understand, engage, and motivate each *individual* patient.
- Is based on five robust scientific studies involving over 50,000 subjects.
- Marries high tech with human touch to create trusting provider–patient relationships.
- Employs a validated, online assessment which takes <4 minutes and identifies any individuals' degree of medication adherence and compliance with physicians' recommendations.
- Provides *Individualized Wellness Plans*™—customized strategies to help people of all sixteen types quit smoking, reduce alcohol usage, get more exercise, improve nutrition, and manage stress.

To learn how this game-changing approach to healthcare can benefit you, medical providers, and health plans, please visit iconnecthealth.com

Your personality type affects virtually all aspects of your life. Reading *Do What You Are* is an amazing first step towards finding the perfect career for your type. Here at PersonalityType.com, we offer a number of additional resources you might want to check out:

- Watch our videos and animation to discover your personality type—or confirm that your hypothesis is correct...
- Learn more about how your personality type should communicate with any other type *based on the combination of your two personalities...*
- Learn how your personality type handles:

  - Stress
  - Conflict
  - Innovation
  - Change & Transformation
  - Coaching
  - Sales...

- If you are a coach, learn how to become certified to use personality type in your practice...
- If you are a leader, discover tools that help your team communicate best with one another.

Please visit **personalitytype.com/dwya** to see what special offers we have available!